Trajectories

through Early Christianity

Trajectories

through Early Christianity

JAMES M. ROBINSON

HELMUT KOESTER

FORTRESS PRESS   Philadelphia

To

Anita and Gisela

Contents

Acknowledgments

We wish to express appreciation to the publishing houses that permitted the reprinting in revised form of four of the essays in this volume. "Kerygma and History in the New Testament" was published in 1965 in *The Bible in Modern Scholarship,* edited by J. Philip Hyatt, by Abingdon Press, Nashville, and Lutterworth Press, London; a German translation, "Kerygma und Geschichte im Neuen Testament," appeared at J. C. B. Mohr (Paul Siebeck), Tübingen, in the *Zeitschrift für Theologie und Kirche* 62 (1965): 294–337. "*LOGOI SOPHON:* On the Gattung of Q" appeared in the German original "*LOGOI SOPHON:* Zur Gattung der Spruchquelle Q" in 1964 in *Zeit und Geschichte: Dankesgabe an Rudolf Bultmann zum 80. Geburtstag,* edited by Erich Dinkler, published by Mohr in Tübingen, and will appear in 1971 in the same enlarged English version as appears here, in an English edition of a selection of essays from that volume, *The Future of Our Religious Past,* published by Harper and Row, New York, and SCM Press, London, 1971. "*GNOMAI DIAPHOROI:* The Origin and Nature of Diversification in the History of Early Christianity" appeared in the *Harvard Theological Review* 58 (1965): 279–318; a German translation, "*GNOMAI DIAPHOROI:* Ursprung und Wesen der Mannigfaltigkeit in der Geschichte des frühen Christentums," was published by Mohr, Tübingen, in *ZThK* 65 (1968): 160–203. "One Jesus and Four Primitive Gospels" was published in the *Harvard Theological Review* 61 (1968): 203–247.

The other four essays in this volume have not been previously published, although by special permission most of the introductory chapter was included in the 25th anniversary issue of *Interpretation,* 25 (1971): 63–77.

We are indebted to David L. Doss, research assistant in the Hermeneutical Project of the Institute for Antiquity and Christianity at Claremont Graduate School, for assistance in the editorial process.

ABBREVIATIONS

ADAIK	*Abhandlungen des Deutschen Archäologischen Instituts Kairo*
ATD	*Das Alte Testament Deutsch*
AThANT	*Abhandlungen zur Theologie des Alten und Neuen Testaments*
BG	*Berolinensis gnosticus* 8502
BHTh	Beiträge zur historischen Theologie
Bornkamm, Ges. Aufs.	Günther Bornkamm *Gesammelte Aufsätze:* 1, *Das Ende des Gesetzes,* 3d ed., 1961; 2, *Studien zur Antike und Christentum,* 2d ed., 1963; 3, *Geschichte und Glaube,* 1968 (partial ET of 1 and 2, *Early Christian Experience,* 1970)
CBQ	*The Catholic Biblical Quarterly*
CG	*Cairensis gnosticus* (Nag Hammadi codices)
EKL	*Evangelisches Kirchenlexikon*
ET	English Translation
EVB	Ernst Käsemann, *Exegetische Versuche und Besinnungen,* 1 (1960; partial ET: *Essays on New Testament Themes,* 1964); 2 (1964; almost complete ET: *New Testament Questions of Today,* 1969; since the ET contains the original German pagination, the English pagination is usually omitted from the present volume)
EvTh	*Evangelische Theologie*
ExpT	*The Expository Times*
FRLANT	Forschungen zur Religion und Literatur des Alten und Neuen Testaments
GCS	Die griechischen christlichen Schriftsteller der ersten drei Jahrhunderte
GuV	Rudolf Bultmann, *Glauben und Verstehen,* 1–4 (1933–1965; ET: 1, *Faith and Understanding,* 1969; 2, *Essays Philosophical and Theological,* 1955)
HNT	*Handbuch zum Neuen Testament*
HTR	*The Harvard Theological Review*
HUCA	*Hebrew Union College Annual*
JBL	*Journal of Biblical Literature*

JBR	*The Journal of Bible and Religion*
JTC	*Journal for Theology and the Church*
JTS	*Journal of Theological Studies*
Neotesta-mentica	Eduard Schweizer, Neotestamentica, 1963
n.s.	new series
NTS	*New Testament Studies*
PRE	*Realencyklopädie für protestantische Theologie und Kirche*, 3d ed., ed. by Albert Hauck, 1896 ff.
RB	*Revue Biblique*
RGG	*Die Religion in Geschichte und Gegenwart*
SBT	Studies in Biblical Theology
SHA	Sitzungsberichte der Heidelberger Akademie der Wissenschaften
Strack-Billerbeck	H. L. Strack and P. Billerbeck, *Kommentar zum Neuen Testament aus Talmud und Midrasch*, 1922–1961
ThF	Theologische Forschung
ThLZ	*Theologische Literaturzeitung*
ThR	*Theologische Rundschau*
ThSt	*Theological Studies*
ThWNT	*Theologisches Wörterbuch zum Neuen Testament* (ET: *Theological Dictionary of the New Testament*)
ThZ	*Theologische Zeitschrift*
TU	Texte und Untersuchungen zur Geschichte der altchristlichen Literatur
USQR	*Union Seminary Quarterly Review*
VigChr	*Vigiliae Christianae*
VuF	*Verkündigung und Forschung*
WMANT	Wissenschaftliche Monographien zum Alten und Neuen Testament
WMZNT	Wissenschaftliche Monographien zum Neuen Testament
ZAW	*Zeitschrift für die alttestamentliche Wissenschaft*
ZNW	*Zeitschrift für die neutestamentliche Wissenschaft*
ZThK	*Zeitschrift für Theologie und Kirche*

1. Introduction

The Dismantling and Reassembling of the Categories of New Testament Scholarship

JAMES M. ROBINSON

This volume contains essays that the two authors have written independently; yet they are so intimately interwoven in theme and approach that their arrangement as chapters in a single volume is their appropriate format. They represent, to a considerable extent, stages on a shared path. Both authors studied under Rudolf Bultmann. Both are involved in the current indigenization of the Bultmann tradition on American soil. Both assess in similar ways the direction in which the study of early Christianity should move in the future. Thus the essays reflect an ongoing conversation, expressed and unexpressed, along the shared path. It is the purpose of this introduction and of the concluding chapter to indicate the direction implicit in the essays themselves, by assessing the presuppositions which they bring to the surface and the consequences toward which they programmatically point.

New Testament Scholarship as a Modern Science

New Testament scholarship as an intellectual activity is a modern science, reflecting as well as molding the modern understanding of reality, a reciprocity it shares with the humanities in general, together with the social and natural sciences. Every scholar or scientist who deals with a subject matter from the past does so in terms of his present grasp of reality, and the results of his research in turn flow into the current body of knowledge from which the continual modification of our understanding of reality emerges.

1

The astronomer has to do not with stars as they now are, but with light rays emanating from stars as they were many millions of years ago; yet astronomy is in every sense a very modern science, presupposing the most sophisticated insights into reality, and in turn immensely enlarging our understanding of reality, as the achievements of the space age make abundantly clear.

Similarly, most forms of societal organization and psychological experience antedate recorded history; yet the way such phenomena are grasped scientifically is modern, and the impact of such phenomena as scientifically known has been felt primarily in modern times. The modern technical term *Oedipus complex* is an allusion to the classical dramatic presentation in Sophocles' *Oedipus Rex* two and a half millennia ago. Indeed the psychological reality designated by this term has doubtless existed since time immemorial, certainly prior to classical Greece and quite independently of the historicity of its Theban legend. Yet as a scientific category it is a product of modern psychology and has shaped the understanding of reality primarily in modern times. The term as such is a neologism.

The New Testament too is a classical text of antiquity, based upon legends of varying historicity, yet giving classic expression to certain phenomena—phenomena which scholarship conceptualizes in modern categories and thus releases to play a functional role in the revision of the ongoing understanding of reality. The most familiar instance of this process is found in the phrase *the historical Jesus*. This term obviously refers to a person of the distant past; yet in its technical meaning, namely the historian's reconstruction of knowledge concerning Jesus, the term refers to an innovation of modern science. As such it reflects the understanding of reality distinctive of modern historicism and has a critical cutting edge that has exerted an important influence on Western civilization in modern times, as the impact of Albert Schweitzer's *Quest of the Historical Jesus* makes clear. This impact is inseparable from modern times, and is quite distinct from the role played by Jesus of Nazareth in his own time or by interpretations of Jesus as deity in the intervening period.

What has been said with regard to Jesus is equally true of the

New Testament and of early Christianity as a whole. The inter-action between the modern understanding of reality from which scholarly categories are derived, and the results of scholarly study which in turn modify the understanding of reality, is both in-escapable and legitimate. Progress takes place when the modern categories employed are sufficiently illuminating that they lead to a more adequate understanding of the data, and thus are relatively validated by the successful research itself. But, conversely, the new insights resulting from the application of the facilitating categories tend to put in question these very categories and their presuppositions. This leads ultimately to a basic questioning of the adequacy of former categories in the present stage of research. The outcome is a crisis of categories.

The whole purpose in applying generalizations, in subjecting data to analysis and synthesis, to categorization, is to open both the text and experience to broader and deeper understanding, to a higher degree of intelligibility, to significance beyond particulars. Such generalization is not basically the addition of something extraneous to the data but rather the detection, through rigorous methodical observation, of specific additional data, namely, the interrelatednesses within the data, the ways in which they cohere. Boundaries between categories, the contours and directions they indicate, are assumed to apply in some way to the reality being studied.

A fact separated out of its web of relationships is less intel-ligible than a fact whose context is also known. Yet a generaliza-tion projected back into the data as part of the reality being investigated may become itself outdated. This occurs when a science has not only accumulated more individual facts but also reached a point at which the factuality of the generalization is put in question. Then the retention of the generalization, rather than facilitating research, becomes itself a retarding factor. Caught in the web of its own inadequate generalizations, a science floun-ders. Data may continue to accumulate, but the inadequate cate-gories in which it is amassed reduce its validity and value, and intellectual achievement gives way to busywork.

When a science enters such a period of crisis, the actual state of affairs may go unnoticed for a time, much to the detriment of progress. Shackled by its inadequacies at the conceptual level, a science can hope for a quantum advance only if it achieves sufficient self-awareness to recognize its situation for what it is, and to go about the exacting task of reconceptualization.

The Crisis of Categories

New Testament scholarship has entered a period of crisis with regard to the basic categories with which it assembles its data. Consequently, to reach clarity with regard to this crisis is the most important step that now needs to be taken. The present essay is intended to play a catalytic role by clarifying the crisis. The subsequent chapters are intended to illustrate, as a series of tracers or flares projected over a dark terrain of uncharted contours, some of the experimental efforts called for today when the dismantling and reassembling of the basic categories of the scholarly discipline is the one thing needful. A basic criticism of a discipline is usually not carried on from outside its course, and indeed is most relevant when undertaken from within. For then the dismantling may not only make way for the reassembling, but actually point the way.

Carefully done, the dismantling process brings to light the strong girders which have been preventing total collapse and reveals the points of strain. It locates where the accumulated data has been breaking through the confines of categories, and where apparent stability has only been concealing unstable temporary repairs. It works back down to the foundational points of origin from which whole superstructures began to go out of line, in such a way as to expose structural flaws otherwise discernible only at the final aberrant outcome, long after the source of the problem had been lost from view. Dismantling thus engenders directives, working hypotheses, and new assessments of the present situation, from which the reassembling activity gains its first momentum and initial validity.

The most immediate scientific response to a crash or mechanical failure is an investigation to locate the cause of the accident. This is not done on the assumption that the damage can be undone, or even that the model whose activity may have been suspended due to the accident will necessarily be rectified and put back in service. Rather, the identification of the points at which the mechanical structure was unstable has a permeating influence on the total activity of research and technology in the field. The subtle yet far-reaching implications outweigh in significance the correction of a specific instance of failure, for specific instances of inadequacy, systematically investigated, point to inadequate directions in the total process and thus cumulatively provide the contours for redirecting the discipline.

Thus, in the study of the synoptic gospels, various source theories were proposed in the 1920s to clear up problems remaining after the triumph of the two-document hypothesis. All proved to be inadequate. But their failure pointed less to the inconclusiveness of specific proposals than to the limitations of literary criticism itself as an instrument for approaching the data. The next advance was made possible only by the redirection of the discipline as a whole into the study of oral traditions.

New Testament scholarship took its original point of departure from the traditional picture of the New Testament that had grown up during the centuries between the point in the early church when the historical facts had been forgotten and the time when modern critical historiography emerged to attempt to reconstruct them. Criticism was not at first directed to the New Testament as it was when it was written, since that had ceased to be available once the historical facts of its composition had been lost from memory. Rather, the only available subject of investigation was the New Testament as known in the precritical centuries.

The first task of textual criticism was to remove precritical distortions that had crept in and conjecturally to reconstruct a text more nearly approaching the original. The same process had to take place just as really, though often less visibly, in each area of New Testament studies. Just as textual criticism began not with the original but with the uncritically received Byzantine text, so other New Testament studies emerged in criticism of the various layers of tradition, legend, and interpretation superimposed upon the text, more than in criticism of the actual original layer itself.

This dismantling of the precritical tradition was not necessarily a negative or destructive activity, any more than is the dismantling of the modern scholarly tradition here being proposed. What critical scholarship did was to distinguish secondary or tertiary layers from more nearly original layers of meanings associated with the text. Just as the patina, the richness of tone resultant upon aging, on an antique bronze or ivory or stone work of art may be as beautiful, or even more so, than was the original artifact when new, just so a medieval layer of significance that grew up around a text may be greater than the original import of the text. Critical research need not reject the medieval significance; it merely distinguishes: one meaning is the significance associated with the text at a given stage late in the text's history, another meaning is that associated with the text nearer the time of the author and original recipients.

When modern art restorers detect that a Renaissance painting or fresco has been painted directly on top of the work of an earlier master, they may undertake the painstaking task of removing bit by bit the superimposed layer and then carefully reassembling it with an absolute minimum of damage. They maintain due respect for the irreplaceable value of the later masterpiece—but also full respect for the Cimabue, Giotto, or previously unknown master of the Trecento that the restorative work first makes accessible. So too in biblical scholarship: the value of the underlying text is, to be sure, the incentive for the critical operation directed at the superimposed layers. And, as the result of the critical operation, the layers of patina are of course identified no longer with the original layer (whence the frequent offense), but with the subsequent period to which they actually belong. Yet as objects of Christian veneration, as cult symbols, they are worthy of the respect shown an icon, whose resemblance to the historical appearance of the saint portrayed is not a factor in assessing its worth.

To be sure, many an individual scholar was not interested in the top layer upon which he initially struck, and did not direct his energies to reassembling it once he had peeled it off. Though his interest originated in the precritical identification of the overlay as the original text, his interest may well have shifted to the original text, even when the top layer was seen not to be identical with it. Once having distinguished the assumption of the apostolic authorship of the Fourth Gospel from the facts concerning the earliest stratum, he may well have shifted his interest from interpreting the assumption of apostolic authorship (as to where it emerged and how it developed and what it meant) to— he assumes—the original layer itself: Who *did* write the Fourth Gospel?

Yet it is all too little recognized that this critical question, though addressed *to* the original layer, is not a question arising *from* the original layer; rather, it arises from the secondary overlay, namely from the ascription of apostolic authorship to the document. The interest, the categorization, the focus of investigation inherent in the critical assertion that John did *not* write the Fourth Gospel, is, as approach, surprisingly akin to the precritical view. For the focus upon the authorship issue was derived from the tradition, not from the original layer of the Fourth Gospel itself (which lacked John 21:24–25), for which the authorship issue is not acute, and whose own concerns and categories may well have been overlooked in the critical engrossment with refuting the secondary level.

The absence of an unmediated encounter with the original text was the initial source of distortion in the categories adopted by modern critical scholarship. The emphasis by critical scholarship upon objectivity in distinction from ecclesiastical subjective involvement, its removal of later accretions from the critically reconstructed New Testament, and its intention to narrate the past as it actually happened and interpret the text as it was originally intended, were all such an improvement over traditionalism as to obscure the fact that critical access was through the patina, and that the critical historical method was oriented to the problem of penetrating the patina. The contours of the surface level at which it set to work were those of the patina; thus the slants, the directions, the problems with which it initially came to grips, tended to be determined primarily by the patina. The fact that critical scholarship was, point by point, disagreeing with the patina—removing it, reversing it (with regard to assertions made about the original text)—obscured the fact that this critical operation received its orientation from the only data originally accessible: the patina itself.

One reason the subdivision known as "Introduction to the New Testament" has lost its focal role so markedly over the past generation is that it "introduced" primarily in the sense of grappling successfully with the patina. It succeeded in penetrating through the patina to touch the surface of the text itself; nonetheless its soundings were largely at those points which the patina called to attention. Once the patina has been removed, the direction and intensity of those soundings, now seen as moving through empty space, seem arbitrary or overdone. Students so distant from their cultural tradition that the patina is not present, or whose point of departure is the critical reassessment, now itself become traditional, are not "led into" a text itself by the answering of questions that they never raised or that they regard as long since settled, questions that in any case are not significantly raised by the text itself. The negative overtones often associated with "Introduction to the New Testament" have their deepest basis not in its frequently valid negations of the tradition or in the inconclusiveness of many a well-worn debate, but rather in the gnawing realization that the issue, irrespective of how it is or is not solved, really has little to do with the text itself, whose claims to generate structures for the discipline go unheard.

From "Background" to "Trajectories"

The current crisis at the basis of New Testament scholarship moves through the whole spectrum of its presuppositions and categories, from such empirical items as the correlated categories "Palestinian" and "Hellenistic" (presupposing a nonexistent correspondence between geographical and cultural boundaries) to the most abstract presuppositions of scholarship, its metaphysical (or antimetaphysical) assumptions. One of the basic instances of the latter has to do with the very concept of the "background" of the New Testament itself; indeed the title of the present volume, *Trajectories through Early Christianity*, suggests a dismantling and reassembling of perhaps the most embracing and foundational category of all: the traditional static, substantival, essence/accidence–oriented metaphysics which gave our inherited categories their most basic form. It suggests the need to replace that metaphysics with a dynamic, historic, existence/process–oriented new metaphysics, in terms of which a whole table of restructured categories may be envisaged. The prevalent rejection of metaphysics today is due not only to epistemological considerations, to the effect that such speculation about ultimate categories can never be scientifically controlled and verified as knowledge, but also to some awareness that traditional metaphysics has loaded our concept of reality in a way prejudicial to our own being as historic persons.

It is precisely the historic consciousness of modern times that has drawn attention to the inadequacy of the essentialist categorization of science. This historic consciousness has of course also led to modern historiography, whose results have been a catalyst in accelerating the prevalence of historic thinking. Yet these results have been impeded by the burden of conceptualizations inherited from an ahistoric metaphysics. The increasing incommensurability between the direction in which the accumulating data itself points and the direction provided by the categories under which that data is assembled is a problem at the most basic level of modern historiography, namely, its emergence on the basis of traditional metaphysics at the dawn of the modern historic consciousness. It is this incongruity which is at the root of the dual fact that historiography has been the most obvious instance of the modern historic consciousness and yet has been a deficient mode of its expression.

This sweepingly general assertion can be brought into focus by investigating an instance central to the objective of the present volume. As a result of the dawn of historic consciousness, New Testament studies shifted away from providing authoritative documentation for revealed eternal truth—truth that was only peripherally historic, encased in earthen vessels or husks, an accidental condition readily justifiable in terms of divine condescension and removable by coordination of the text with dogma and/or reason to identify the eternal treasure or kernel of truth. Gradually the historic in the text became of interest in its own right, and the changelessly monolithic divine eternal truth gave way to a history of dogma, a process in the history of ideas. To be sure, such a historicizing of theology was not carried through consistently, and the divine continued to be shrouded in changelessnesses, perhaps as the outline of a dialectic movement through history, or the progressive evolution of ethical ideals and institutions, or the predetermined will of the Lord of history acted out in *Heilsgeschichte,* or a constant understanding of existence beneath the flux of mythological and other extraneous language patterns.

We now have, as a result of two centuries of critical historiography, its limitations notwithstanding, a history of early Christianity which makes indisputable the theological change from Jesus to Paul, from Paul to Mark or Ignatius, from Ignatius to Irenaeus or Origen, and then to Augustine or Athanasius. This is not simply a case of random variety, of pluralism. A more penetrating analysis reveals individual items to be exponents of intelligible movements. Thus one can trace a course from the subphilosophical cultural level of primitive Christianity, via the philosophical pretenses of the apologetes, to the philosophical ability of the Alexandrian theologians; or from Paul's theology to that of the gradually bifurcating Pauline school, with one stream moving via Ephesians to 1 Peter, Luke-Acts, the Pastorals, and on to orthodoxy, the other via Colossians to Valentinus, Basilides, Marcion, and on to heresy; or from an "unworldly" antiinstitutionalism rooted in the apocalyptic ideology of imminent expectation, toward a bifurcation into a relatively "worldly" Christian establishment whose eschatological hope has lost its imminence or at least its existential urgency, and an "otherworldly" disestablished Christianity, whose ideology has become gnostic rather than apocalyptic.

Such sequences of development have come to the surface in the course of the critical historical research of the past generations. Yet the implications of their discovery have been obscured by the context in which they arose and continue to be used. These stages were generally found in the process of seeking a fixed date for a document, or at least enough chronological accuracy to rule out apostolic authorship; or as part of an argument to establish that one document attests to the existence and circulation of another. These and similar inquiries, many of uncontested validity, in effect distracted attention from the historic reality, the movement itself, to pose a question extraneous to the movement as such. The fixed point was taken for the historical fact, whose degree of reality was hardly equaled by the penumbral areas of influences that led up to it and consequences that grew out of it. In such an orientation the movement itself would tend to be a deficient mode of reality, the space between discrete atoms of factual reality.

The Hegelian dialectic and the evolutionary theory of inevitable progress in their day provided an ontological basis for directing attention to the movement. But once they had come to be recognized as speculative abstractions not verified by the data but superimposed upon it, positivistic historiography seemed justified in confining itself methodologically to the discrete factual entity. In any case such a concentration was more readily coordinated to the accelerated specialization of the day.

The focus upon individual literary documents and their authors could even narrow from the history of ideas to a primary concern for the psychological state in the author's experience at the time he composed the text. Yet this "psychologism" was in fact transcended. The interpretation of the text in terms of the author shifted from his psychological state or stream of consciousness to his understanding of existence objectified in the text. In many instances the focus upon individual authorship gave way to a concern for the community and the *Sitz im Leben* there: the group would be the actual entity coming to expression in the text. Yet in all these alternatives the shared presuppositions were to the effect that the text gave expression to the individual or group, and that the individual or collective author was static, as a set "setting" rather than a moving process.

11

Such an author or editor thus "located" in a communal "setting" was in turn cast upon a history-of-religions "background." Whereas some movement had been identified within early Christian history, as one moved from fixed point to fixed point, the "background" tended to remain largely a static backdrop or stage setting. Such a double standard can hardly be explained solely in terms of traditional metaphysics petrified in language; one must look also for specific conditions in the area of research itself. New Testament scholarship's recognition of discrete stages in the development of early Christian theology stood in contrast to the status of history-of-religions research in the "environment," where a monolithic unity seemed to prevail.

This contrast was due to a variety of factors. Some of the religious movements contemporary with early Christianity tended to be more confined to oral transmission. Such was the case with rabbinic Judaism, where the posture of noncompetition with the written word placed a priority upon oral tradition, and with mystery religions, where arcane discipline succeeded in preventing wide public knowledge and in limiting written documentation to veiled allusions. Also, the proclivity to overcome error by burning books created an imbalance in favor of the religion enforced since Constantine. In part the victory of the languages of the West, Greek and Latin, favored the survival of texts from (Western) Christianity over those from Eastern religions with more exclusively oriental literatures. And the heavy concentration of scholarly manpower upon the texts of the establishment's religion, together with the advantages from the past already cited, catapulted biblical and Christian studies ahead of the study of their original religious competitors.

The result is that the religious world through which early Christianity moved has been conceptualized as strangely immobile. Rabbinic Judaism, Gnosticism, an oriental cult, a given mystery religion—each was presented as a single position. Research had not advanced to the point where layers of tradition could be distinguished. The fragmentary state of the documentation did not permit tracing step by step a series of developments but required the amalgamation of references scattered over half a millennium into one coherent and harmonized picture. Whereas Origen's theology would not be attributed to Jesus, or even to Paul or Ignatius, his contemporaries in Gnosticism or Judaism could be fused with their predecessors when one presented a construct of those religions; that construct might have some relative value as a standardization or typology, but it never actually existed as such in history.

Augmentations in scholarly manpower and available source materials (Qumran, Nag Hammadi) have tended to expose inadequacies of such mocked-up "backgrounds." The resultant shaking of the foundations, the uncertainty as to the validity of the categories, has tended to foster a disintegrated positivistic caution: rather than risk a generalization, such as describing a view as "Jewish" or "gnostic" or "Hellenistic," one limits oneself to recording that it is present in a particular document at a given place. Yet a list of unrelated instances of a given term, exact and free from all error though the list may be, is hardly a historical assertion, any more than a chronicle is history.

The vacuum created by the experienced inadequacy of the given table of categories is not merely the liberation of scholarship from prejudice but its end as an intellectual enterprise. A crisis in the basic categories of scholarship is a crisis at its foundation, a basic crisis for scholarship as such. Such a categorical crisis in a science can be met effectively only at the presuppositional level, in terms of recategorization. The Jewish, Greek, or gnostic "background" or "environment" cannot be mastered by reducing it to a mass of disorganized parallels to the New Testament; it must be reconceptualized in terms of movements, "trajectories" through the Hellenistic world.

The static categories "background" or "environment" or "context" are all-embracing as well as specific. Their recategorization as "trajectories" applies both to the most embracing movement in which a whole culture is caught up, even to the history of its ontological presuppositions (such as the trajectory of Western civilization from essentialist to historic metaphysics), and to more specific streams, such as the course of its religious understanding or the trajectory of one specific religious tradition within the wider streams of movement. Just as a fixed datum was "located" on a spectrum or grid of static positions, so a trajectory of limited extent moves along as a variant or eddy within a broader religious or cultural current. Indeed only if the more pervasive flow is charted can the course of the specific trajectory be relevantly distinguished in its variance from that of the broader movement.

To be sure, the term *trajectory* may suggest too much determinative control at the point of departure, the angle at which the movement was launched, the torque of the initial thrust. The time is past when predestination, an eternal plan or apocalyptic scheme, a Hegelian outline, a prophecy-fulfillment structure, an unalterable will of a changeless deity, can be presupposed in one's understanding of history and human existence. The future is open, though not because we exist in an unhistoric vacuum, like empty space lacking atmosphere; rather we move among a plurality of spinning worlds, with conflicting gravitational fields pulling upon us. In this sense one is free to redefine one's trajectory, to go against the stream, to add one's own twist, to pull for modification of course, much as auxiliary guidance systems or retrorockets rectify a trajectory misdirected at the initial launching or misled by climatic conditions or gravitational fields of force. Although one is not free to stop the rocket (or world) and simply get off, one's freedom does consist in knowing the direction of the trajectory along which one is being borne, assessing alternate movements, and then taking relevant steps to redirect one's course toward a better outcome.

The extent to which a future is opened up by the clarification of a cultural past that gives direction to the present is nowhere better illustrated than in the Black Power movement, where the demand on campus after campus has been for a Black studies center in which Black cultural history will be taught. Man's being is historic, and therefore his freedom takes place in terms of modifications of his given course.

If, as Hans Jonas suggests in *The Gnostic Religion,* there was at the beginning of the Christian Era a general trend toward ascetic private religiosity, toward religious loss of world, then the emergence of an unworldly apocalyptic sect we call primitive Christianity cannot be regarded as a purely inner-Jewish phenomenon, nor can its unworldliness be regarded as its specific differentiation from the world; indeed it was perhaps its unworldliness which was most in step with at least one major trend of the times. Nor can the emergence of Gnosticism be explained simply in inner-Jewish or inner-Christian terms, e.g., as the effect of the collapse of Jewish apocalypticism's imminent hope in a final military deliverance, or as the radical Hellenizing or orientalizing of Christianity. It had to do with the "spirit of late antiquity," as Hans Jonas put it. When related to the wider stream, Gnosticism is seen to stand in a more fundamental relation to apocalypticism and other religious movements of the day than would seem to be indicated by reference merely to the failure of apocalypticism in the Jewish revolts or to generally progressing syncretism.

If, as the reorganization of Judaism at Jamnia toward the end of the first century A.D. and neoclassical trends in pagan culture suggest, there was a widespread move from the first century to the second century A.D. toward stabilizing, normalizing, rigidifying, standardizing, then the rise of a Christian establishment cannot be regarded as a purely inner-Christian phenomenon. It can no longer be interpreted simply in terms of the delay of the parousia or the passing of the first generation and its replacement by persons born Christian, nor defended simply in terms of the validity of standing immovably on the truth. Rather, the emergence of a normative Christianity becomes an instance of conforming to a trend of the times.

What was distinctive of Christianity was not the general cultural trends in which it shared but its modification of such trends in ways distinctive to itself. The course of early Christianity thus should not be evaluated on the basis of its degree of departure from a unique and pristine unworldly eschatological existence toward a gnostic escapism or an established organizationalism. Any religious movement is inextricably caught up in the course of its culture. Such a question as whether it maintained a critical, creative tension to and in its world can be investigated only with reference to its own particular variant upon the cultural trajectories, not in terms of whether it did or did not share the trajectories along which the whole culture was moving.

Not only are specific trajectories to be understood and evaluated with reference to their interplay with overarching trajectories; also specific events, individuals, documents, and positions become intelligible only in terms of the trajectories in which they are caught up. At one stage of a movement a document may function in a specific way, have a certain meaning or influence on the movement; at a subsequent stage on the trajectory that document, unaltered, may function or cut in a different way, may mean in effect something different, may influence the movement differently.

Walter Bauer's epochal work *Orthodoxy and Heresy in Earliest Christianity* drew attention to a bifurcating trajectory: out of a fluid, amorphous primitive Christianity there gradually emerged a polarized antithesis between secondary developments, known to us as orthodoxy and heresy, as the initial plurality gave way to the dominance of the Roman view. Dialectic theology engendered within quite different value structures a somewhat analogous trajectory pattern: the decline of eschatological orientation, related to the delay of the parousia and the movement out of Jewish culture, gradually led to an orientation to the cultural values of antiquity that was sufficiently positive to allow Constantinian Christendom to emerge. More conservative theological orientations have defended the traditional trajectory pattern of a consistent straight-line development, thus producing an apology for the history of the church, freed of the implications of defection implicit in the critical reconstructions. Indeed much of what previous scholarship has discovered can be reassembled within the patterns of trajectories, even though the Procrustean categorical beds into which such research was often forced, thereby separating what belongs together, have obscured the quantity of scholarly material already at our disposal for a recategorization enterprise.

The essays here brought together exemplify, each in a somewhat different way, exploratory efforts to plot the course of specific trajectories, moving from one document to another, from one generation to another, seeking to trace the connections where one fixed point leaves off and another begins. These connections are not only of the usual cause-and-effect kind, where one author necessarily depended upon the preceding one. Rather, the connections are explored to show how the overarching movement of the trajectory itself comes successively to expression as one moves downstream from the point of departure.

Chapter two, "Kerygma and History in the New Testament," investigates the correlative categories "kerygma" and "historical Jesus," and finds them to be, not univocal, fixed concepts juxtaposed to each other in one set relationship (however that may be defined), but rather terms referring to movements within early Christianity whose trajectories can be charted. For functionally they came to mean successively different things, and interacted with each other in successively differing ways, as the overarching trajectory of early Christianity modulated their interaction in successively different situations.

Chapter three, *"LOGOI SOPHON:* On the Gattung of Q," directs itself narrowly to one specific category, the collection of sayings, such as Q has been assumed to be and the *Gospel of Thomas* has turned out to be. This essay seeks to trace the trajectory of this genre of literature, from Jewish wisdom literature to Gnosticism. In the process the very curve of the trajectory that bears this genre along can be seen to give a twist to the sayings of Jesus transmitted within this genre. The result is that the original collections of Jesus' sayings, at an earlier stage in that trajectory, fitted appropriately within the accepted viewpoints of primitive Christianity, but successive collections, indeed even so early a collection as Q, when read at a later point on the curve, received unacceptable gnosticizing overtones. This might well be the ultimate cause for Q's becoming "lost" and the best surviving exemplar of the gattung turning up not in the orthodox canon, but rather in the gnostic library of Nag Hammadi.

Chapter four, *"GNOMAI DIAPHOROI:* The Origin and Nature of Diversification in the History of Early Christianity," traces the course of early Christianity through the first century of its existence, in those regions of the eastern half of the Roman Empire in which Christianity for the first time took visible shape.

The monolithic concept of one church history gives way to a series of trajectories, each determined in part by the course of history in the differing regions and in part by interactions of an inner-Christian nature. The various ways in which "Jesus" as the ultimate force behind such diversified theological developments reappeared in different cultural contexts draws attention to the dialectic structure of the Christian's appropriation of both his tradition and his environment. The writings now bound together in the New Testament "canon" emerge as conflicting witnesses to this process, in which they often contradict each other, or appear as theological compromises of only passing historical significance.

Chapter five, "One Jesus and Four Primitive Gospels," traces the trajectories through which traditions about Jesus moved, seeking to identify directionalities in the original forms of independent sayings of Jesus and narratives concerning him. These directionalities influenced the way such traditions were collected, and predetermined the orbit in which they would finally be codified. The plurality of gospel forms is recognized as the outcome of trajectories that go back to early oral forms inherent in the original independent units of tradition themselves.

Chapter six, "The Structure and Criteria of Early Christian Beliefs," suggests a corollary hypothesis for the analysis of various forms of early Christian creeds and symbols. It sees a number of cultural and religious presuppositions at work in the formation of early Christologies, which are epitomized in such basic expressions of faith as symbols and creeds. The essay seeks on the one hand to relate these formulations of faith to certain aspects of the history, work, and life of Jesus, and on the other to relate them to the ecclesiological consequences in the formation of varying Christian communities.

Chapter seven, "The Johannine Trajectory," seeks to reorganize Johannine research by drawing attention to the layers of tradition imbedded within the Fourth Gospel. One can trace the Johannine trajectory from oral units (and in one place perhaps an oral cycle) to a written miracles source, where the theological implications of the miracle story become uncritically explicit, and then to the evangelist, who builds upon this source, which he accepts both as factual and as relatively true. Yet he uses it in such a way as to bring to the surface, in criticism of the source, the higher or deeper level of meaning to which he himself has advanced, perhaps with the help of a gnosticizing trend in his cultural trajectory. Finally there is an orthodox redactor, whose achievement is to have introduced sufficient middle-of-the-road material missing from the evangelist's product to blunt the direction toward gnosticism that the gospel had come to have, as advancing Gnosticism provided an interpretive trajectory and thereby appropriated the gospel for its own use. Thus the redactor, though no longer quite able, in view of his altered situation, fully to approve of the evangelist, yet rescued the gospel for the canon and for posterity.

To be sure, these individual essays were not composed as illustrations of an already-laid-out program. Indeed the basic reflection suggested in the present essay took place along the course of the research itself, and was formulated explicitly in retrospect rather than in prospect. Observation and reflection, practice and theory, research and method, data and generalizations, memory and imagination, accuracy and intellectuality, are interacting foci in a total movement of scholarship. In progressing along a scarcely discernible jungle trail, one can determine the far-distant contours of its course only by setting on the way, trusting that at each successive advance the next segment of the trail will come into view. The concluding essay attempts to assess, as does this retrospective introduction, the prospect toward which the essays seem to point as the next step along the path.

2. Kerygma and History in the New Testament

JAMES M. ROBINSON

The Dismantling and Reassembling of the Title

In addressing ourselves to the assigned topic, "Kerygma and History in the New Testament," our first task is to seek in the language of this topic the subject matter intended. Hence I begin by dismantling the topic in order to derive the structures of the subject matter in terms of which the more detailed investigation will be ordered.

This preliminary analysis is intended as an exemplification of the *Grundlagenkrise*—the crisis with regard to our basic categories—in which biblical scholarship finds itself today. The general categories with which we of necessity have been operating, such as normative Judaism, Hellenistic Judaism, apocalyptic, gnostic, cultic, existential, history, kerygma—such categories *are* the capsules in which the heritage of scholarly achievement is transmitted from generation to generation. But they are also the blinds that block out fresh light and help perpetuate the preconceptions and limitations of the past. The synthetic achievements of the past *do* provide the working hypotheses out of which our research grows. Yet the advancement of research calls for a critical analysis of inherited categories, and for their dismantling and reassembling in new synthetic efforts that grow out of the *present* reading of the subject matter.

What is implicit in the fact that the assigned title pairs the two terms *kerygma* and *history?* In the literature in the field there

This paper was one of the invitational addresses presented at the hundredth meeting of the Society of Biblical Literature in New York, December 28, 1964. It was published in *The Bible in Modern Scholarship*, edited by J. Philip Hyatt, 1965, pp. 114–50. An abridgment, especially of the notes, was necessary in that publication; the full text, only slightly edited, is here reproduced. The essay, with somewhat less abridged notes, was published in German as "Kerygma und Geschichte im Neuen Testament," *ZThK* 62 (1965): 294–337.

is one important issue often designated with a phrase juxtaposing just these terms. In 1960 a lengthy collection of essays debating the new quest of the historical Jesus appeared in German under the title "The Historical Jesus and the Kerygmatic Christ," [1] and in 1964 an English collection of essays on the same topic appeared with the same title.[2] Indeed, a standard international bibliographical tool in the New Testament field introduced for the years 1961/62 and 1962/63 [3] a new subdivision with much the same title. Rudolf Bultmann's Heidelberg address criticizing the new quest bore in German a somewhat similar title, "The Relation of the Primitive Christian Message about Christ to the Historical Jesus," which became more explicit in the translated version: "The Primitive Christian Kerygma and the Historical Jesus." [4] Gerhard Ebeling answered Bultmann's criticism with an extended essay entitled "Kerygma and the Historical Jesus." [5] My own book, *A New Quest of the Historial Jesus,* appeared in German in 1960 with the title "Kerygma and Historical Jesus." [6]

If the phrase *kerygma and history* thus has its primary focus

---

1. Helmut Ristow and Karl Matthiae, eds., *Der historische Jesus und der kerygmatische Christus: Beiträge zum Christusverständnis in Forschung und Verkündigung,* 1960.
2. Carl E. Braaten and Roy A. Harrisville, trans. and eds., *The Historical Jesus and the Kerygmatic Christ: Essays on the New Quest of the Historical Jesus,* 1964.
3. *Internationale Zeitschriftenschau für Bibelwissenschaft und Grenzgebiete,* 8 (1961/62): 14–15, "Kerygma und historischer Jesus"; and 9 (1962/63): 18–22, "Historischer Jesus und kerygmatischer Christus."
4. Rudolf Bultmann, *Das Verhältnis der urchristlichen Christusbotschaft zum historischen Jesus,* SHA, Philos.-hist. Klasse, Jg. 1960, 3. Abh., 1960. ET: "The Primitive Christian Kerygma and the Historical Jesus," in *The Historical Jesus and the Kerygmatic Christ,* ed. Carl Braaten and Roy Harrisville, pp. 15–42.
5. Gerhard Ebeling, "Kerygma und historischer Jesus," pt. 3 of *Theologie und Verkündigung,* Hermeneutische Untersuchungen zur Theologie, 1, 1962. ET: "Kerygma and the Historical Jesus," in *Theology and Proclamation,* 1966, pp. 32–81.
6. James M. Robinson, *Kerygma und historischer Jesus,* 1960. This is a reversion to the original title of my address at the congress on "The Four Gospels in 1957" at Christ Church, Oxford, August 1957: "The Kerygma and the Quest of the Historical Jesus." This address was published in *Theology Today* 15 (1958): 183–98, under a title assimilated to the journal's title, "The Quest of the Historical Jesus Today." The enlargement requested by the publisher of the series Studies in Biblical Theology was initially planned to bear the original title, but at the publisher's request another title was sought; after discussing several alternatives the title *A New Quest of the Historical Jesus* was accepted (SBT, 25, 1959). Already in 1956 I had published a class lecture in *Religion in Life,* 26: 40–49, entitled "The Historical Jesus and the Church's Kerygma."

for New Testament scholarship in "Christ Jesus," then it is rather apparent that the innocent-sounding connective *and* is a euphemism, covering up a problem, to put it mildly. For "Christ Jesus" was a primitive Christian confession not only implying the copula "is," "Jesus is Christ," but also calling forth the variant: "Jesus be damned" (1 Cor. 12:3). And one may also note that in our century the positive correlation currently being sought between kerygma and historical Jesus has in its background other alternatives expressing themselves in antithetic connectives. The emphasis of dialectic theology between the two world wars can be summarized in such formulae as: *"Not* the historical Jesus *but* the Easter kerygma is the foundation of Christianity." The form-critical variant ran: "The gospels are kerygma, *not* history." Such antithetic formulations stand polemically over against alternatives current at the turn of the century, where the signals were reversed and the terminology somewhat different, though the same issue was involved: "Jesus preached the kingdom *but* Paul preached Christ." *"Either* Jesus *or* Paul." *"Back* (from Paul) *to* Jesus." Put in more recent Bultmannian terms, it is the issue of how and with what degree of legitimacy the proclaimer became the proclaimed.

One can in this way work back terminologically from the current pair "kerygma and history" to the terminological pair current in the systematic theology of half a century ago: "faith and history." There were reasons why the seemingly more subjective term *faith* was replaced by *kerygma,* a synonym for "the word of God"; there are also reasons why the terminology current today is itself less than final!

Both *kerygma* and *history* are, first of all, quite ambiguous terms. *Kerygma* refers both to the content of preaching, in which sense C. H. Dodd primarily used it, and to the act of proclamation, in which sense Rudolf Bultmann primarily used it. The difference in implication can be indicated by pointing out that in Dodd's sense the resurrection of Jesus is in the kerygma, and hence a necessary Christian belief; but in Bultmann's sense Jesus rose into the kerygma, lives as what happens in preaching, and keeps the church's witness alive. *History* is equally ambivalent.

It means both *Historie* and *Geschichte,* loan words that can hardly be translated "history" and "story," since the latter term is too weak. Perhaps the adjectival forms "historical" and "historic" come nearer to some of the distinctions intended by the German terminology. Yet even the simple English term *history* has the complexity of referring both to research and to the subject matter of research. Since each of the members in the correlation "history and kerygma" has at least two clearly distinct foci of meaning, the seemingly simple correlation is on reflection seen to involve at least four distinct correlations, plus various combinations of these four, and any of these alternatives can be implied by the supposedly simple phrase in the title.

In the second place, the terms *kerygma* and *history* do not actually fit the intended distinction between Jesus and the Easter faith. For the term *kerygma* emerges only at two points in the primitive Christian literature, in 1 Cor. 1:21; 2:4 to designate Paul's word of the cross (which is, as itself a kind of Easter faith, a corrective of another kind of resurrection faith); and in Q (Luke 11:32; Matt. 12:41), to designate Jonah's preaching to the Ninevites and hence by implication Jesus' message.[7] Furthermore, Jesus and the Easter faith certainly cannot be distinguished in terms of one's being historical, i.e., the result of reconstruction on the part of the critical historian, and the other's not being historical. Anything we know about the primitive Christian kerygma is known by means of critical historical reconstruction, whether by disengaging kerygmatic hymns and confessions imbedded in the New Testament literature or by analyzing the explication of the kerygma in a given New Testament writing or by tracing the progressive kerygmatizing of Jesus traditions prior to and within the gospels, by means of form criticism and *Redaktionsgeschichte,* the history of the editing of the material by the evangelists. Thus both Jesus' message and the apostolic preaching were called kerygma, and both are known to scholarship only in terms of historical research, as the historical Jesus and as the historical reconstruction of the primitive church's

7. Cf. Gerhard Ebeling, *Theologie und Verkündigung,* p. 37 (ET: p. 41); Ernst Käsemann, *EVB,* 2:46–47, 49.

kerygma. The current modern categories "kerygma" and "history" have foisted upon us a distinction which is neither in the language of the sources nor in our relation to the sources.

Our inherited categories, ambiguous at best, thus superimpose on our work a polarity which a transcendental reflection upon the categories themselves shows not to exist. Obviously the urgent task is not to collect more data under these categories but to revise the categories themselves. This is what is meant by the statement that we are in a *Grundlagenkrise,* a crisis consisting in the recognition that our categories themselves are the problem. They are less our heritage than our fate. *Fate* means literally "what is spoken"—not what we speak but what is spoken "upon" us, so as to predetermine our future by blocking our free access to the reality with which we have to do. A distinction has been built into our language—in this case into the categories "kerygma" and "history"—a distinction which continues to speak out audibly as we use the categories but which on reflection we can no longer affirm to be real. Precisely because of our unawareness of this structuring of the problem, the prevalent categorization has not been subject to our critical control but has rather been a power over us, a word spoken upon us through our language, which all the more predetermines the lines along which our research will run and hence controls our results. Thus our categories have indeed become our fate. As an avenue of escape from such fate, a crisis of categories can have a liberating effect on our work and effect a measurable quantum advance in our knowledge.

In view of this subliminal role inherited categories usually play in our research, it is important to note in the title what seems to be a not insignificant, indeed perhaps an intended, modification. Rather than its being the phrase *historical Jesus* that is correlated with the term *kerygma,* it is merely the word *history,* as if the problem usually focused in terms of Jesus were symptomatic of a broader problem. Furthermore the title goes on to specify: in the New Testament. To be sure, this could be taken to refer us simply to the historical Jesus and the primitive Easter kerygma, in that both of these, though antedating the New Testament by a generation or more, are to be reconstructed from New Testament material, and hence are an important aspect of New Testament scholarship. Yet the title seems to be calling for a confrontation with the problem in the New Testament texts themselves, and I propose to take seriously this hint heard in the assigned title. This does not imply that one should turn one's back on the debate going on within contemporary theology about the kerygma and the historical Jesus. Indeed one reason why that debate is becoming repetitious may be that it is spinning vacuously, without adequately getting geared to reality. Therefore an analysis of what "kerygma" and "historical Jesus" actually were, and how they were actually related to each other in a segment of past history, could serve to implement a restructuring of categories in terms of which the contemporary debate could profitably be refocused. The contemporary debate is simply the current stage of the same hermeneutical movement that is to be analyzed here in terms of its beginnings in early Christianity.

There seems to be no problem in regarding *kerygma* as a term applicable to what we find "in the New Testament," for kerygmatic theology has taught us that the New Testament itself is to be understood as an explication of the kerygma, a hermeneutic for the kerygma. But what then is the history with which this New Testament explication of the kerygma has to do? Not simply the historical Jesus! The historical Jesus had been undergoing kerygmatization for a generation before the New Testament writings began. The history with which the New Testament as kerygma had directly to do was not the historical Jesus but rather "the history of the transmission of the traditions" [8] about Jesus.[9]

8. It takes this whole phrase to produce a hermeneutically responsible translation of *Traditionsgeschichte*. Cf. the discussion of this point in the preface to *Theology as History*, New Frontiers in Theology, 3, 1967.
9. Ernst Käsemann makes a somewhat similar distinction in his polemic against Joachim Jeremias: "Further, no one is proposing to deny that Jesus was the origin of Christian existence and no one can seriously envisage his being absorbed into an anonymous original community, just because he is, and remains, the irreplaceable 'origin'. But the historicizing language used by Jeremias at this point puts the question-mark in the wrong place. It is not a matter of what role we do or do not ascribe to Jesus, but of what weight we give within the framework of New Testament proclamation to the 'historical' reports about Jesus. If exegetes who employ critical methods are to avoid the charge of making illegitimate encroachments on others' territory, these two issues may neither be simply identified nor confused with each other. Yet it cannot well be denied that the New Testament letters provide us with surprisingly little material about the historical Jesus. Still more important, Jeremias himself admits, and indeed

And our access to that history is via the method itself called *Traditionsgeschichte,* the tracing of the traditions with their changing use, shape, and meaning.

Now, in such an investigation it becomes clear that a lot more was happening to the traditions about Jesus than simply a straight-line development such as the term *kerygmatizing* might seem to suggest. This is not only because other influences than the kerygma were at work upon the tradition. It is also because the kerygma pointed the tradition in various directions. That is to say, the kerygma itself was subject to a plurality of understandings.[10]

This variation of the kerygma itself was due to the fact that the kerygma had still another relation to history than its relation to the history of the transmission of traditions about Jesus. For the kerygma was related to the series of historical situations in which it was proclaimed and heard. The very language in which the kerygma happened was historically determined—and not simply because the kerygma was talking about historical events. It was talking about them in historically conditioned categories; such terms as *preexistence, incarnation, resurrection, exaltation, ascension* do not simply refer to historical occurrence, but are also themselves historically conditioned language. Rather than the saving event's simply being described as it happened, to some extent it happened as it was described; for whatever happened, happened among people living within language. Man's being is not logically prior to his language, but is constituted in terms of his linguistic world. Hence whatever happened, to whatever extent it was an event in the lives of man, happened as a linguistic event. The event itself included a process of understanding in terms of given categories. To this extent the saving event, as an event in human experience, cannot be distinguished as a brute fact lurking behind the language witnessing to it. As human history, it has no being apart from language; the possibility of

---

demonstrates in *The Parables of Jesus,* that narrative material about Jesus is found embedded in the community witness and nowhere else. Why is this?" (*New Testament Questions of Today,* 1969, p. 26 [ET of *EVB,* 2, 1964, pp. 33–34.]).
10. Cf. Käsemann: "Yet this kerygma, of which Bultmann never wearies of speaking, exists not in some autonomous 'objective' form, but under the form of very diverse 'kerygmata', as comes out most clearly in the case of eschatology." (*New Testament Questions,* pp. 47–48; *ET of EVB,* 2:53.)

discussing it in any other way than by the mere repetition of the language in which it originally took place lies only in the universal possibility of discussing language's subject matter in ever new language. Language is not simply verbalizing. It conveys a point that can be heard by careful listening. And then that point can be scored in other language—and indeed must be scored in a different language if it is to be scored in a different historical situation where the original language is hardly intelligible or has begun to shift its meaning.

Even though the kerygma takes place in different language in different situations for the sake of scoring the equivalent point, still such hermeneutical translation will to some extent involve alteration of meaning. This is not simply because there is the constant possibility of mistranslation. Were that the only problem, it could be eliminated by simply not translating. Yet in a new situation the old language itself means something different. The nonidentity of meaning even within the continuity of scoring the equivalent point is due to the fact that the live options in the new situation were not the options in the prior situation, either in terms of courses of action that are open or in terms of nuances, overtones, and implications of meaning.

Thus the rapid changes in the kerygma's historical setting— from Palestine to the Diaspora, from Jew to Gentile, from the context of imminent expectation to that of the delay of the parousia, from an apocalyptic to a gnostic environment, from the social and political role of a Jewish sect to that of a world religion— all these contextual alterations necessitated a rapid series of translations of the kerygma. And thus we are confronted with a still further relation to history that inheres in the kerygma as kerygma. For the kerygma not only by its very nature kerygmatized Jesus or Jesus traditions, and was itself conditioned by historical situations or language worlds in which it happened; it also by definition kerygmatized the situation in which it spoke by pronouncing upon it the lordship of Christ. Proclaiming Jesus as Lord meant laying his claim on the concrete situation; the proclamation in word and deed was itself the carrying out of the saving event, the event's own future. Thus the saving event goes on as a language event that names God in our world; it identifies him in performatory language in which reality is cast in the mode of creation. This ongoing linguistic transaction in which the kerygmatic point is successively scored in ever changing historical contexts is a central dimension in which "kerygma" and "history" are related "in the New Testament."

We have analyzed the topic "Kerygma and History in the New Testament" into hermeneutic, the translation of the point of the "kerygma" in such a way that it strikes home in each new situation, and into *Traditionsgeschichte,* the "history" of the transmission of traditions. We have argued that the category "kerygma" really refers "in the New Testament" to a series of understandings, translations, reformulations, language events; and that the category "history" really refers "in the New Testament" to the transmission of traditions about Jesus into varying historical situations that influenced them and were influenced by them.

We have carried through a transmutation of Bultmann's kerygmatic categories with which we began into the current categories of hermeneutic and *Traditionsgeschichte,* categories being used for alternate structurings in the theologies of Gerhard Ebeling and Wolfhart Pannenberg and, nearer home, in theology directed to the secular meaning of the gospel for a culture in which the consciousness of God is dead, and in process theology. Hence I would suggest that the restructuring of basic categories, set out here in a preliminary way, could point the way to a real relevance of biblical research for contemporary theology. Such a relevance was real in the early years of the Society of Biblical Literature, when the spread of critical historical method played a major role in liberalism's dismantling of the dogmatic systems; and it has been real in German biblical scholarship in more recent times, in the theological orientations provided, for example, by Bultmann and von Rad. But such a real relevance has to a large measure been lacking in American biblical research of late. This is in considerable measure the cause for the apparent lack of vigor with which creative New Testament research has been carried on in America since the retirement of Edgar Goodspeed and Henry Cadbury.

A crisis in the basic categories of a discipline is a crisis at its very foundations. Such a crisis can unleash new creative powers and introduce an epoch of vigorous research, if it leads to new structures more commensurate with the subject matter and with the categories in which our age understands reality to be actually ordered. It is to be hoped that the analysis of the categories of dialectic or kerygmatic theology into those of hermeneutic and *Traditionsgeschichte* may serve such a purpose.

The following exegetical analyses are hardly more than a pair of rough sketches, two trial runs into an uncharted future. They are intended to investigate in turn "kerygma" and "historical Jesus" in the New Testament in terms of the reformulation of those categories along the lines of hermeneutic and *Traditionsgeschichte.*

The investigation of the "kerygma" will be primarily in terms of hermeneutical translation in varying situations, even though one may sense that this is simply a focus in terms of hermeneutic for what could also be cast primarily in terms of a history of the transmission of traditions. Not only was there such a thing as the transmission of the Easter kerygma as a tradition; the history of the transmission of traditions about Jesus could also be included in an investigation of "kerygma," in that varying understandings of the kerygma variously affected traditions about Jesus, and in that Jesus traditions themselves had something to say, and therefore were "kerygma." Our sample of the "kerygma" will be largely confined to the interpretation of the resurrection in the kerygma, with only incidental observation of its bearing upon the kerygmatic transmission of sayings of Jesus.

The investigation of the "historical Jesus" will be primarily in terms of the history of the transmission of traditions about Jesus, even though one may sense that this is simply a focus in terms of *Traditionsgeschichte* for what could also be cast primarily in terms of a process of hermeneutical translation. Not only does the varying way the stories about Jesus were told reveal an ongoing process of hermeneutical translation; the hermeneutic of the Easter kerygma could also be included in an investigation of the traditions about Jesus, in that varying understandings of these traditions variously affected the interpretation of the kerygma of

Jesus' death and resurrection, and in that the kerygma had its own tradition. Our sample of "history" will be largely confined to the history of the transmission of the miracle stories, with only incidental observation of their bearing upon the history of the understanding of the Easter kerygma.

Kerygma as Hermeneutical Language Event in the New Testament

First, the "kerygma." What more obvious place to begin than 1 Cor. 15:3–5? Paul says it is the gospel, the word he preached to the Corinthian Christians. Furthermore the succinct and strictly paralleled affirmations about Jesus' death and resurrection betray the hand of careful codification, so that the passage stands out as an ancient crystal imbedded in a later composition. And Paul not only puts the formula in quotation marks (ὅτι *recitativum*), but even introduces it with the concession that it is something for which he is dependent on the tradition. For our purposes it is important also to note that Paul describes it as what the Corinthians had received from him, and hence as common ground—or at least a common point of departure. For Paul's Corinthian opponents seem to have accepted Paul's kerygma but promptly departed from Paul's understanding of it.

The Corinthians' misunderstanding of the Pauline kerygma could derive from the very baptismal instruction Paul gave them, if we may judge by such a Pauline locus classicus on baptism as Romans 6; there baptism is described kerygmatically as dying and rising with Christ. Or is it? We have usually assumed so, namely, that in baptism our experiencing of Jesus' resurrection is quite parallel to our experiencing of his death, just as in 1 Cor. 15:3–5 Jesus' death and resurrection are themselves so rigorously paralleled. But when one looks more carefully, one notes that although Paul speaks in the perfect tense of our having experienced baptismally Jesus' death, he speaks in the future tense of our *going to* experience his resurrection (Rom. 6:5, 8), with eternal life only the *goal* (Rom. 6:22). Indeed, according to v. 12 we are still in *mortal* bodies, so that we have hardly completed our dying and already entered into resurrection, unless it be that the body is just a mortal coil that does not participate in the resurrection but is simply to be shuffled off. Thus Paul can speak in the indicative of our having died with Christ as a basis for the imperative to put to death sin in our lives, but he does not speak in the indicative of our having risen with Christ as a basis for the imperative to walk in newness of life.

This omission was largely overlooked, or regarded as purely accidental, until Ernst Käsemann drew our attention to it to exemplify the "eschatological reservation" in Pauline theology, the theologically relevant role that futuristic eschatology plays for Paul. The following paragraph, which illustrates the modern oversight, represents a viewpoint that may be somewhat analogous to the Corinthian misunderstanding. Overlooking the eschatological reservation in Rom. 6 that Käsemann was subsequently to emphasize, Erich Dinkler in an article in 1952 summarized the Pauline position on eschatology as follows:

> Hence one may say that for Paul mythological eschatology is not the basis but [only] a form of expression for the eschatological consciousness of existence, not a [constitutive] motif but [only] a [nonessential] inference. But this means simply that it is an existentialist eschatology that is expressing itself in cosmological eschatology, and that the real intention of Paul is preserved when we interpret as follows: The eschatological promise pointing into the future has already [!] created the eschatological existence of the Christian here and now. With regard to the world the Christian already [!] *has* "freedom" (Gal. 5:13; 1 Cor. 10:29; 2 Cor. 3:17), among the "unrighteous" the Christian *is* already [!] "new creation" (2 Cor. 5:17).[11]

11. Erich Dinkler, "Zum Problem der Ethik bei Paulus: Rechtsnahme und Rechtsverzicht bei Paulus (1. Kor. 6, 1–11)," *ZThK* 49 (1952): 167–200, esp. pp. 187–88. Reprinted in his *Signum Crucis*, 1967, pp. 204–40, esp. pp. 225–26. My translation; italics by Dinkler. Elsewhere (p. 194; *Signum Crucis*, p. 232) Dinkler recognizes the "tension" between statements in Romans 6 about being in Christ on the one hand and a "not yet," the "emphatic futurity of real participation in the resurrection of Christ." But then he goes on to add: "Here to be sure the paradoxicality of Christian existence becomes clear in that what is future is at the same time already [!] present: 'thus you, too, consider yourselves to be . . . alive' (v. 11)." But since Dinkler himself correlates the tension between present and future with that between indicative and imperative, it is inconsistent to appeal to a present imperative to document the present (which in this structure would have to be documented by a present indicative). Without sensing this anomaly Dinkler refers a few lines later to "Romans 6, where the imperative arises on the basis of the indicative [*sic!*]." Here the Bultmannian system seems to have replaced exegetical care.

Here we have an illustration of the way one can begin with Paul's kerygmatic interpretation of baptism, overlook the eschatological reservation, and end up with a triumphant emphasis upon salvation as already achieved. The eschatological reservation hardly survives even in demythologized form, since the "already" is about as undialectical as we conjecture it to have been in Corinth. If it can happen today on the part of an outstanding Pauline interpreter, it could probably happen then. Indeed 2 Tim. 2:18 indicates that a generation or so after Paul's time it did happen: Hymenaeus and Philetus "have gone astray with regard to the truth, by affirming: 'The resurrection has taken place already [!],' and they are upsetting the faith of some." To this the Deutero-Paulinist author counters with the "safe formula": "If we have died with him, we shall [!] also live with him; if we endure, we shall [!] also reign with him" (2 Tim. 2:11–12). Thus two sides of a debate as to whether the Christian has or has not achieved resurrection already begin to emerge.

Recent research has indicated that the fanatical or mystical form of belief in the resurrection combatted in the pastorals was emerging in Corinth in Paul's own time. The form of expression used in the names of the factions in Corinth, to "belong to" someone (1 Cor. 1:12), was the form of expression normally used to designate people as Christians when they were baptized (see Gal. 3:27–29). And Paul's way of disassociating himself from the Pauline party was to play down his role as a baptizer. He disassociated himself from the role of mystagogue or mediator of salvation, in such a way as to indicate that baptism itself is not the saving act for the Corinthians (1 Cor. 1:13–17).[12] All this

---

12. Helmut Koester, in his review of Ulrich Wilckens, *Weisheit und Torheit: Eine exegetisch-religionsgeschichtliche Untersuchung zu 1. Kor. 1,18—2,16,* 1959, in *Gnomon* 33 (1961): 590–95, has shown (p. 591) that the names of the parties cannot refer to baptizers in Corinth. But the use in the party names of the idiom derived from baptism suggests a special kind of baptism, if not actually in the name of Paul, Apollos, or Cephas, then by one who stands in their succession and hence mediates through such a baptism an especially efficacious salvation associated with their names. Cf. my article, "The Sacraments in Corinth," *Journal of the Interseminary Movement of the Southwest,* 1962, pp. 19–32, esp. p. 23 and n. 4 on pp. 31–32. The added efficacy of baptism in the right succession is clearly taught in Acts, where the decisive question as to whether in baptism one receives the Spirit is analogous to the Corinthian question as to whether in baptism one has risen. The role of the founding fathers as coredemptors is intimated in Col. 1:24. The extent to which the apostle could replace Christ,

would suggest that the Corinthians saw in baptism not simply their union with Christ, whose resurrection was the breaking of the grip of evil over all men so that *his* resurrection is the indicative on the basis of which the Christian imperative is built, but also, for all practical purposes, their attainment already now of the final consummation itself. Their own dying had been gotten over quickly and painlessly by means of a symbolic act, and they were now already [!] in the rest of the blessed—what we would call at ease in Zion.[13]

This can be inferred also from Paul's corrective in 1 Cor. 15:23, which is in substance saying: Hold on! Not so fast! "Each in his own order: Christ the firstfruits, then those who belong to [!] Christ at his parousia [and only then!]."[14] Death is the last enemy to be destroyed (15:26). Hence when Paul criticizes "some of you" for asserting that "there is no resurrection of the dead" (15:12), one now[15] assumes he is alluding to a position that is not to be taken as the enlightened rationalism of the Greek philosophic mind but rather as the turgid fanaticism of those who have already risen and are living it up in glory. For although

given the concept of the believer reenacting the redeemer's ascent, is indicated by the *Apocalypse of Paul* from Nag Hammadi, where the kerygmatic passage in terms of the redeemer's descent and ascent to redeem the captives in Eph. 4:8-10 is transferred to Paul himself, who during his ascension at his conversion says (23:13-17): "I will descend into the world of the dead to capture the captivity captured in the Babylonian captivity." (In Alexander Böhlig and Pahor Labib, eds., *Koptisch-Gnostische Apokalypsen aus Codex V von Nag Hammadi im Koptischen Museum zu Alt-Kairo.* Wissenschaftliche Zeitschrift der Martin-Luther-Universität Halle-Wittenberg, Sonderband, 1963.)

13. The climate of ideas conjectured for Corinth would have been like that of the Therapeutae in Philo *De vita contemplativa* 13: "Because of their longing for the immortal and blessed life, thinking their mortal life to be over already, they turn over their property to their . . . kin." I am indebted to my colleague Hans Dieter Betz for calling my attention to this parallel.

14. For this interpretation of the verse see Werner Georg Kümmel in the supplement to Lietzmann's commentary (*HNT,* vol. 9, 4th ed., 1949), pp. 192–93. *First Clement* 24:1 interprets Paul's concept "first fruit" as confirming "the resurrection to come." In the case of *1 Clement* the Corinthian problem seems to be the delay of the parousia (see 23:3-5). Hence Clement emphasizes that the resurrection takes place "in due time." But the delay does not become explicit in 1 Corinthians, and hence it is unclear whether baptismal resurrection arose in Paul's congregation to some extent as an answer to the delay; in any case in the time between Paul and Clement baptismal resurrection either was replaced by or merged with the problem of the delay. Walter Bauer's simple identification of the two situations (*Rechtgläubigkeit und Ketzerei im ältesten Christentum,* BHTh, 10, 2d. ed., 1964, p. 104) is thus in need of some modification.

15. Since Julius Schniewind's essay "Die Leugner der Auferstehung in Korinth," in *Nachgelassene Reden und Aufsätze,* 1952. pp. 110–39.

the word *already* is lacking in 15:12, it is present with all its presumptuous and potentially heretical overtones in Paul's description of his opponents in 1 Cor. 4:8. "Already you have feasted to the full; already you have reached wealth; without us you have taken over the reign."

It would seem to be this heretical interpretation of the kerygma in terms of an already consummated eschaton for the initiated that is behind the various Corinthian excesses to which Paul addresses himself in 1 Corinthians. They are literally above concern for such mundane matters as what their bodies do or how their secular affairs are carried on or whether at the holy sacrament every body gets a square meal; they are in mystic sweet communion with realms above, and indeed speak with the voice of angels, as 13:1 seems to interpret speaking in tongues. They "know all mysteries and all knowledge" (13:2), so that at the gnosis level Paul also has to emphasize the eschatological reservation: *"Now* we know [only] in part; *then* [and only then] will we have the full knowledge on a level with heavenly knowledge" (13:12). The opponents' attitude toward their weaker brothers in the matter of meat offered to idols, expressed in their doctrinaire, unsympathetic slogan "We all have knowledge," is met with the Pauline rejoinder: *"Gnosis* puffs up; love builds up" (1 Cor. 8:1). Yet these hardhearted protognostic fanatics actually believed the primitive Christian kerygma Paul had proclaimed in Corinth, as Paul himself conceded (1 Cor. 15:1–11). Their heresy must hence be acknowledged to be an interpretation of the kerygma.[16]

One can to some extent trace the missing links in such a development (missing largely because writings from the opposing side have not survived) by noting how such views gradually worked their way into the part of the Pauline school that gained

16. Similarly Hans Conzelmann, "Zur Analyse der Bekenntnisformel 1. Kor. 15:3–5," *EvTh* 25 (1965): 1–11, esp. pp. 10–11. (ET in *Interpretation* 20 [1966]: 15–25, esp. pp. 24–25.) To be sure, he prefers to regard the heretics as "spirit-enthusiasts," doubtless because for him the term *gnostic* would involve a "gnostic Christology," which he in distinction from Wilckens denies to be involved in the heretical position. How little current research is equipped with reliable categories requisite to investigating the New Testament from this point of view is made clear by Käsemann's critical answer, "Konsequente Traditionsgeschichte?" *ZThK* 62 (1965): 137–52.

admission into the canon. The interpretation of baptism in Col. 2:12–13 has already brought the believer's rising into line with his dying by omitting the eschatological reservation: ". . . having been buried with him in baptism, in which you were also raised with [him] through faith in the working of God who raised him from the dead. . . . He made you alive with him." That this is a growing edge in the Pauline school is indicated by Eph. 2:5–6, where even our enthronement in heaven is already accomplished: "He made us alive with Christ—by grace you have been saved— and he raised us with [him] and seated us with [him] in the heavenly places in Christ Jesus." In view of this direction of Pauline interpretation in the Deutero-Pauline period it is not too surprising when the same Paul who had opposed baptismal resurrection in Corinth came to be claimed as theirs by precisely those gnostic movements that held to this heresy, such as the Valentinians; indeed Paul was hailed by them as "apostle of resurrection." [17] The Coptic gnostic library from near Nag Hammadi has filled in one missing link, by turning up a gnostic document "On the Resurrection" that affirms explicitly (49:15–16), "Already you have the resurrection," [18] and quotes Paul (45:24–28) in support of precisely the same left-wing Deutero-Pauline development once opposed by Paul himself that was moving toward that heresy: "But then the apostle said: We suffered with him and we arose with him and we went to heaven with him." [19] Thus

---

17. Tertullian *De praescriptione haereticorum* 33. 7; *Excerpta ex Theodoto* 23. 2. Both are cited by the editors of *De resurrectione* (see n. 18 below), pp. xi and 27.
18. *De resurrectione (Epistula ad Rheginum)*, from the Jung Codex, ed. M. Malinine, H.-C. Puech, G. Quispel, and W. Till, 1963. See also Malcolm Lee Peel, *The Epistle to Rheginos: A Valentinian Letter on the Resurrection,* 1969.
19. The quotation apparently presupposes the passages cited above. The commentary provided in 45:28–35 is also relevant for the relation to Colossians and Ephesians. It seems to reflect the same symbolism of the sun that is present in the little fragment of a baptismal [!] hymn of resurrection [!] quoted in Eph. 5:14:

> Awake, O sleeper,
> And arise from the dead,
> And Christ will shine on you.

The commentary says: "But if we are made manifest in this world wearing him, we are his beams and we are encompassed by him until our setting, which is our death in this life." Having put on Christ in baptismal resurrection, gnostics manifest the heavenly life as rays shining from the heavenly sun upon the earth. This view has clearly moved further from Paul than was the case in

we have fairly early in the second century a clean split in the understanding of Paul: gnostics appeal to him for support of baptismal resurrection, while the pastorals reject that view as heresy (2 Tim. 2:18). Of course even orthodoxy could not avoid the trajectory through which the Christian understanding of baptism was moving,[20] and hence expressed a not dissimilar understanding of baptism in the safer language of regeneration (Titus 3:5)—safer in that it does not seem to jeopardize the future resurrection.

Colossians. Colossians has indeed taken the first step in affirming that we have risen with Christ, as an indicative upon which the imperative can be based: "If then you have been raised with Christ, seek the things that are above, where Christ is. . . ." (3:1). Yet our relation to our resurrected selves is in Colossians still understood as paradoxical or indirect: "Our life has been hidden with Christ in God. When Christ is revealed [and it is he who is] our life, then [and only then] will we also be revealed with him in glory" (3:3-4). Cf. Günther Bornkamm, "Die Hoffnung im Kolosserbrief: Zugleich ein Beitrag zur Frage der Echtheit des Briefes," in *Studien zum Neuen Testament und zur Patristik,* Klostermann festschrift, TU, 77, 1961, pp. 56-64, esp. p. 63, n. 1. The position represented in *De resurrectione* of being manifest as rays of the sun is well illustrated in Seneca *Ad Lucitium epistulae morales* 41. 4-5 (Loeb edition, 1:274-75): "If you see a man who is unterrified in the midst of dangers, untouched by desires, happy in adversity, peaceful amid the storm, who looks down upon men from a higher plane, and views the gods on a footing of equality, will not a feeling of reverence for him steal over you? Will you not say: 'This quality is too great and lofty to be regarded as resembling this petty body in which it dwells. A divine power has descended upon that man.' When a soul rises superior to other souls, when it is under control, when it passes through every experience as if it were of small account, when it smiles at our fears and at our prayers, it is stirred by a force from heaven. A thing like this cannot stand upright unless it is propped by the divine. Therefore, a greater part of it abides in that place from whence it came down to earth. Just as the rays of the sun do indeed touch the earth, but still abide at the source from which they are sent; even so the great and hallowed soul, which has come down in order that we may have a nearer knowledge of divinity, does indeed associate with us, but still cleaves to its origin; on that source it depends, thither it turns its gaze and strives to go, and it concerns itself with our doings only as a being superior to ourselves." *De resurrectione* 45. 36-46. 2 gives one instance of the kind of spiritual resurrection at death this heresy could envisage. For after referring to "our setting, which is our death in this life," it goes on: "We are drawn upward by him like the beams of the sun, without being held back by anything. This is the spiritual resurrection which swallows up the psychic alike with the fleshly." It is unclear whether it was a conceptualization like this that Paul describes as affirming that there is no resurrection, or whether by the second century gnostics had introduced the word *resurrection* to their presentation of the ascent of the soul, so as to commend the orthodoxy of their view. Polycarp (see n. 21 below) describes the heresy as flatly as does Paul in terms of not accepting the doctrine of resurrection, although by this time the term resurrection may well have been in use by heretics. Hence in Paul's case too it may be merely a matter of refusing to consider the view of the soul's ascent at death as worthy of the name resurrection.

20. Cf. my article on "Regeneration" in *The Interpreter's Dictionary of the Bible,* vol. 4, 1962, pp. 24-29.

When Bishop Polycarp of Smyrna attacks the same heresy of baptismal resurrection at the opening of the second century,[21] we catch sight of an ingredient in the heresy that has not been mentioned thus far. Polycarp (7. 1) asserts: "Whoever distorts the sayings of the Lord to his own lusts and says there is neither resurrection nor judgment, he is the firstborn of Satan." [22] The pastorals, so akin in various ways to *Polycarp,* and in 2 Tim. 2:18 our basic source for the heresy of baptismal resurrection, seem also to combat this second ingredient in the heresy, namely, the distorting influence of the kerygma (understood in terms of baptismal resurrection) upon the transmission of sayings of the Lord. First Tim. 6:3 condemns someone who "teaches heterodoxly and

---

21. It is significant that Polycarp was writing to a congregation that Paul had reproached for much the same heresy. In Phil. 3:12 Paul contrasts himself with the Philippians by saying: "Not that I have already [!] received or were already [!] perfected." "Those already perfect" is a synonym for the baptized in the Pseudo-Clementine *Homilies,* 3. 29. 3. Cf. Walter Schmithals, "Die Irrlehrer des Philipperbriefes," *ZThK* 54 (1957): 326, reprinted in *Paulus und die Gnostiker,* ThF, 35, 1965, p. 73. Polycarp is himself writing from the west coast of Asia Minor, where baptismal resurrection may have been represented in the heresy of the Nicolaitans attacked in Rev. 2. For Hippolytus (Fragment 1 of his *De resurrectione,* in Syriac, p. 251, 10–17, Achelis edition, quoted by the editors of the *De resurrectione* of Nag Hammadi, p. xi.) cites 2 Tim. 2:18 and traces the heresy back to Nicolaus the proselyte of Antioch, one of the seven Hellenist deacons mentioned in Acts 6:5. If the Nicolaitans of Rev. 2 were also named after this person, as G. Kretschmar (*RGG,* 3d ed., vol. 4, 1960, p. 1486) maintains, then they may have been the same heretical movement Hippolytus accused of baptismal resurrection. For even if Hippolytus is inaccurate with regard to the historical Nicolaus, he is doubtless reflecting what the name stood for in the second century.

22. For the meaning of this epithet for the heretics, especially in its relevance in relating them with the opponents attacked in the Johannine literature, cf. Nils Alstrup Dahl, "Der Erstgeborene Satans und der Vater des Teufels (Polyk. 7, 1 und Joh. 8, 44)," in *Apophoreta,* Haenchen festschrift, suppl. 30 to *ZNW,* 1964, pp. 70–84. How sayings of the Lord could be used in such a debate on the west coast of Asia Minor in the second century is illustrated on the one hand by the letters to the seven churches in Rev. 2–3, which are presented as speeches of the Lord addressed to the congregations infested with Nicolaitans, and on the other hand by the sayings of the Lord that comprise the peroration to Melito of Sardis's *Paschal Homily,* secs. 101–3, e.g.:

> It is I who released the condemned,
> It is I who made the dead alive,
> It is I who raised up the buried. [Sec. 101.]

Here the Lord is spokesman more for the baptismal resurrection side of the argument. See Michel Testuz, ed., *Papyrus Bodmer XIII. Meliton de Sardes, Homélie sur la Pâque,* 1960. Cf. Sherman E. Johnson ("Christianity in Sardis," in *Early Christian Origins,* Willoughby festschrift, 1961, p. 84), who cites Ignatius *Phld.* 7:1: "When I was among you, I spoke with a great voice, with the voice of God." Cf. also Ignatius *Eph.* 15:2: "He who truly possesses the word of Jesus is also able to hear his silence."

does not agree with the sound words of our Lord Jesus Christ." [23] Indeed it would not be too surprising for gnostics considering themselves already resurrected to claim a higher grasp of the hidden meaning of the Lord's sayings than the common Christian understanding, a viewpoint rather like the gnostic claim to be in possession of new ("hidden") sayings of the resurrected Lord that are of higher authority than the sayings of the earthly Jesus claimed by orthodoxy. Thus the debate about the meaning of the Easter kerygma in the lives of the believers may have run parallel to a debate in the history of the transmission of the traditions about Jesus, specifically with regard to the sayings of Jesus.

Such a view would seem to be confirmed when one examines sayings of the Lord in a gnosticizing environment. Although the *Gospel of Thomas* does not refer to the resurrection as such, it certainly reflects the gnostic concept of having attained the goal of the higher life; and it associates with this achievement a higher understanding of the sayings of Jesus.[24] Saying 51 reads: "His disciples said to him: 'On what day will the rest for the dead occur, and on what day does the new world come?' He said to them: 'That [rest] for which you are waiting has come, but you, you do not recognize it.' " [25] Here the reader is clearly urged

23. Martin Dibelius-Hans Conzelmann, *HNT*, 3d. ed., 1955, pp. 21–22 and 64, take the phrase to refer to the church's message, as is the case with "sound doctrine" (1 Tim. 1:10; 2 Tim. 4:3; Tit. 1:9; 2:1) and "sound words" (2 Tim. 1:13; cf. also Tit. 1:13; 2:2, 8). But then one would have to do with a tautology in 1 Tim. 6:3, which puts in parallel position to the phrase in question the phrase "doctrine in accordance with piety"—a problem obscured by the typographical error in *HNT*, 3d. ed., of omitting in the German translation the first of the two phrases! Of course the Pastorals would not assume any difference in content between sayings of the Lord and the teaching of the church, and may be here referring to the two forms in which the same message is conveyed or distorted. In *Polycarp* 7:1 one also has a combination of the two, for in quite parallel fashion the heretics are described on the one hand as distorting both the church's message (in not confessing "Jesus Christ to have come in the flesh") and "the testimony of the cross," and on the other hand as "distorting the sayings of the Lord." In view of the other affinities of the Pastorals to *Polycarp*, this parallel should have been considered in interpreting 1 Tim. 6:3, as well as parallels within the pastorals.
24. Cf. Philipp Vielhauer, "ANAPAUSIS: Zum gnostischen Hintergrund des Thomas-Evangeliums," in *Apophoreta*. Haenchen festschrift, suppl. 30 to *ZNW*, 1964, pp. 281–99. On p. 283 he points out that the Ethiopic version of the *Epistula apostolorum* can replace *rest*, found in the Coptic, with *resurrection*, which illustrates the material identity of the two concepts within Gnosticism. *Did.* 4. 2 speaks of finding "rest" in the *logoi* of the saints.
25. *Barn.* 4. 10 also opposes a heresy that asserts one is "already made righteous," by asserting this to be still future, "when we enjoy true rest" (15. 7). Thus here

to discover the eschaton to be already actualized, and the opening saying of the *Gospel of Thomas* relates this discovery to the gnostic interpretation of Jesus' sayings: "He who finds the interpretation of these words will not taste death." The *Gospel of Philip,* Saying 90, is quite explicit in advocating baptismal resurrection: [26] "Those who say: 'One will first die and [then] rise,' are in error. If one does not first receive the resurrection while one is still alive, one will receive nothing upon dying. This is the way they also speak of baptism, saying: 'Great is baptism, for in receiving it one will live.' " To be sure, this formulation is protected from the accusation of heresy to the extent that it leaves room for a future resurrection as well as a present sacramental resurrection, upon which the emphasis nonetheless lies. (Such a sacramental resurrection also is analyzed in the *Exegesis on the Soul* from Nag Hammadi.) The *Gospel of Philip,* Saying 21, shows how the kerygma itself can be brought into line with this interpretation of the gnostic experience of the kerygma: "Those who say: 'The Lord died first and [then] rose,' are in error. For he first rose and [then] died."

The Gospel of John also suggests that after Jesus' earthly life there will be a higher understanding of his sayings through the Spirit. And it is precisely this one of the four canonical gospels that speaks of resurrection in this life: "Truly, truly, I say to you, the hour is coming, and now is, when the dead will hear the voice of the Son of God, and those who hear will live" (5:25). To this verse Ernst Haenchen says: "From the viewpoint of the earthly Jesus the hour is still to come, for the Spirit has not yet been poured out. But from the viewpoint of the church this hour is now." [27] Hence one higher understanding following Jesus' exaltation would seem to be the understanding that one is already resurrected. "Whoever lives and believes in me shall never die"

---

too the opponents would seem to have claimed already to have entered into the rest.

26. Cf. R. McL. Wilson, "The New Testament in the Nag Hammadi Gospel of Philip," *NTS* 9 (1962/63): 292. Philipp Vielhauer, *Apophoreta,* pp. 290–91 n. 52, points out that the resurrection takes place at baptism, the entrance into rest at death.

27. Ernst Haenchen, " 'Der Vater, der mich gesandt hat,' " *NTS* 9 (1962/63): 214; reprinted in the first volume of his collected essays, *Gott und Mensch,* 1965, p. 75.

(11:26). To be sure, it may not be without significance that John seems to avoid the category of baptismal resurrection, as if it were suspect, and introduces a different category, (baptismal) regeneration: "Unless a person is born anew from above, he cannot see the kingdom of God" (3:3; cf. 3:5). When the new life is described as regeneration, it seems to jeopardize less the role of future resurrection. Still, the emphasis upon present life in 5:25 may have needed some protection from the suspicion of heresy, and the emphasis on futuristic eschatology in 5:28–29 may be the work of an ecclesiastical redactor, designed to achieve this safeguard. To be sure, John stands in some tension to his protognostic environment; yet, even if in a broken way, he provides information about that environment, both in terms of views he shares with it and in terms of views attributable to it on the basis of his correctives. For John tends to confirm the picture derived from gnostic sources, to the effect that the trajectory moving toward baptismal resurrection caught up into its wake a deeper or higher interpretation of sayings of the Lord.[28]

We have suggested that the gnosticizing interpretation of the primitive Christian kerygma of the resurrection probably carried with it a gnosticizing interpretation of the sayings of the Lord, and hence that the debate about the translation of the kerygma involved also a debate in the history of the transmission of these traditions about Jesus. Now if this heretical interpretation of the kerygma was already the subject of debate in 1 Corinthians, one may well wonder whether at this early a time the corresponding debate about sayings of the Lord was not also under way. This possibility cannot, in view of the paucity of source material, be conclusively affirmed; but there are a few factors that point in that direction. Rather than pursue them here, it may be sufficient merely to note the possibility, and to suggest that it would not be as surprising as we have assumed, over the past generation, should it prove to be the case. For 1 Corinthians stands in contrast to the general Pauline pattern of making practically no use of sayings

28. Cf. the recent debate on the Gnosticism of the Fourth Gospel: Ernst Käsemann, *Jesu letzter Wille nach Johannes 17*, 1966 (ET: *The Testament of Jesus: A Study of the Gospel of John*, 1968); Günther Bornkamm, "Zur Interpretation des Johannes-Evangeliums," in *Geschichte und Glaube*, Ges. Aufs. 3, 1968, pp. 104–21. Cf. chap. 7 below, "The Johannine Trajectory."

of the Lord. Of the four instances in which Paul explicitly cites sayings of the Lord, three occur in 1 Corinthians: on divorce (7:10–11), on paying the preacher (9:14), and on the institution of the Lord's Supper (11:23–25). It is significant that apart from the last instance, derived from the eucharistic liturgy, Paul does not actually quote the saying in question, but only scores its point in his own language. One may compare Q: "For the worker is worthy of his food (or: pay)" (Matt. 10:10; Luke 10:7); with Paul: "Thus the Lord gave orders for those who proclaim the gospel to live from the gospel." Paul even uses a different term for divorce than Mark and Q. It is equally difficult to find in the only other Pauline citation of a saying of the Lord (1 Thess. 4:15–16) any specific terms shared with the synoptic gospels.

If simply scoring the point of a saying was Paul's way of using it, it would be difficult, in cases where a quotation formula is lacking, to say whether Paul intended to allude to a saying of the Lord or not. Such an allusion may be intended in the reference to faith that removes mountains (1 Cor. 13:2), for which there are parallels in Q and Mark.[29] In that case Paul's allusion to the saying would be remarkable, in that the word of the Lord is not used as final authority settling the issue. Rather, Paul criticizes it; or, more exactly, he criticizes the use made of it, much as in the case of speaking in tongues, where Paul recognizes a religious experience as a divine gift and still criticizes its misuse. First Cor. 13:2 might then tend indirectly to suggest that the Corinthians were misusing sayings of the Lord.[30]

---

29. Matt. 17:20; Luke 17:6; Mark 11:22–23; Matt. 21:21. Cf. Bultmann, *RGG*, 2d ed., vol. 4 (1930), p. 1028: "It is also possible that, in Paul's parenesis, sayings of the Lord are echoed (e.g., Rom. 12:4; 13:9–10; 16:19; 1 Cor. 13:2). But it is precisely such parenesis as originates, for Jesus and for Paul alike, from Jewish tradition or Jewish spirit." Strack-Billerbeck, *Kommentar zum Neuen Testament aus Talmud und Midrasch* vol. 1 (1922), p. 759, gives parallels for "uprooting mountains" as an idiom for doing the impossible; but the association of this power with faith is not there attested. Similarly, Lucian *Navigium* 45; cf. Hans Dieter Betz, *Lukian von Samosata und das Neue Testament*, TU, 76, 1961, p. 169, n. 6.

30. That this saying was capable of gnostic interpretation is evident from its use in the *Gospel of Thomas*, Sayings 48 and 106. In *Thomas* "faith" has been replaced by the more gnostic category of overcoming duality and returning to primordial unity. On the gnostic meaning of the saying see Bertil Gärtner, *The Theology of the Gospel of Thomas*, 1961, pp. 246–48. It is also possible that this

An area in the debate between Paul and his Corinthian opponents in which sayings of the Lord may have played a role is Paul's defense of his "kerygma" against the "wisdom" of which the Corinthians were so proud. The so-called Johannine pericope of Q (Matt. 11:25; Luke 10:21), in spite of its roots in wisdom literature, is critical of that wisdom context: "Thou hast hidden these things from the wise and understanding and revealed them to babes." Paul begins his criticism of the Corinthian wisdom in much the same vein, by asserting the gospel to be "foolishness," i.e., hidden, to those who perish (1 Cor. 1:18), who are identified as the "wise" and "understanding" (1:19), but to be God's power to the "saved," the "babes in Christ" (3:1). Ulrich Wilckens has shown that most of the material in 1 Cor. 1:18 ff. can be explained on the basis of wisdom literature.[31] Yet one item finds no adequate explanation there: Why does Paul widen his attack to brand a two-pronged opposition, "Jews demand signs and Greeks seek wisdom" (1:22), if his interest here is only in combatting the Corinthian wisdom? Perhaps simply because the initial listing of a series of factional slogans in 1:12 is still in mind. Yet it is rather striking that this association of "signs," "kerygma," and "wisdom" occurs in only one other place in primitive Christianity, namely in Q (Matt. 12:38–42; Luke 11:29–32). Here the demand of the Jewish leaders for a *sign* is connected with Jonah's *kerygma* and Solomon's *wisdom*. Indeed these are the only two places in first century Christianity where the term *kerygma* occurs at all. And for it to occur in these two cases in precisely the same associations does tend to suggest some common tradition.

If it is true that Paul's criticism of the wisdom of the Corinthians has parallels in Q, the Corinthians themselves could have

---

saying was used by the Corinthian dissidents upon whom the wandering missionaries of 2 Corinthians built, since miracle-working faith was focal to that heresy. Although their primary appeal would have been to miracle stories about Jesus, they could have made use of just such sayings. On the basis of 2 Cor. 13:3 Gerhard Friedrich assumes the heretics of 2 Corinthians thought Christ was speaking in their ecstatic language: "Die Gegner des Paulus im 2. Korintherbrief," *Abraham unser Vater: Juden und Christen im Gespräch über die Bibel*, Michel festschrift, 1963, pp. 182–83.

31. Ulrich Wilckens, *Weisheit und Torheit: Eine exegetisch-religionsgeschichtliche Untersuchung zu 1. Kor. 1 und 2*, BHTh, 26, 1959.

found other parts of Q quite congenial to their position. Indeed the very gattung of "Sayings of the Sages" of which Q is an instance seems to have been moving through a trajectory that led from wisdom literature to Gnosticism.[32] It is also Q that presents Jesus as Wisdom's spokesman: Luke 11:49 introduces a saying of the Lord as spoken by Wisdom, and another Q saying (Matt. 11:19; Luke 7:35) refers to John and Jesus in terms of wisdom: "Wisdom is vindicated by its works [or: children]." Thus we have in Q one of the connecting links between the hypostasizing of Sophia in Jewish wisdom literature and the gnostic redeemer myth attested in the second century systems. First Corinthians and Q have in common the issue of Jesus and wisdom. It is possible that the Q material may in part have had a *Sitz im Leben* similar to the conflict in Corinth; that is to say, the prevalent Bultmannian assumption that the sayings of the Lord are not likely to have played a role in Pauline Christianity might not be as obvious as it has seemed.

There is one collection of sayings that occurs in free variation frequently enough in the early church [33] to suggest it must have been some common catechetical cluster. It is at the core of the Sermon on the Mount (or Plain) in Q, recurs in *1 Clement* 13:2 and Polycarp *Phil.* 2. 2–3, and was introduced into the Two Ways in *Didache* 1. 3–5.[34] Hence when one finds in 1 Cor. 4:5–13 similar material in somewhat the same context,[35] though without quotation formula or verbal quotation, one may at least wonder whether a debate over such a cluster of sayings is in the background. Paul's critical description of his opponents in 1 Cor. 4:8 suggests the woes of the Sermon on the Plain (Luke 6:24–25). This could well be Paul's response to a distorting use of the

---

32. See the next essay in this collection, "LOGOI SOPHON: On the Gattung of Q."

33. See the page of parallels cited by Kurt Aland, *Synopsis Quattuor Evangeliorum*, p. 106.

34. On the complex problem of the *Didache* material see Helmut Koester, *Synoptische Überlieferung bei den Apostolischen Vätern*, TU, 65, 1957, pp. 217–41; Bentley Layton, "The Sources, Date, and Transmission of Didache 1. 3b—2. 1," HTR 61 (1968): 343–83.

35. In *1 Clement* there is an attack upon the wise who boasts in his wisdom, comparable to the attack in 1 Cor. 1–4; in Polycarp the passage is related to the future resurrection that his—and Paul's—heretical opponents deny.

beatitudes. Although the concept of reigning or being king is not the goal of the beatitudes in the canonical gospels, which speak instead predominantly of the kingdom of God, still to reign is a gnostic equivalent to that goal (see *Gospel of Thomas*, Saying 2); indeed the beatitudes at the conclusion of *Thomas the Contender* from Nag Hammadi do climax in one's finally reigning with the king. The gnostic need only eliminate the eschatological reservation and declare the initiate already at the goal of life, as one finds in the *Gospel of Thomas*, Saying 58:

> Blessed is the man who has suffered; he has found life.

Saying 69 internalizes [36] this suffering, while retaining the "realized eschatology" emphasis:

> Blessed are those who have been persecuted in their hearts;
> these are they who have known the Father in truth.

Thus a gnostic could well develop beatitudes, which in themselves emphasize in their first member the present, into an anticipation of the eschaton in the form of a present spiritual reigning over the tormenting "world." Paul would then in his corrective reassert the earthly literalness of suffering, as in the beatitudes of Q, with the eschatological reservation as the inevitable concomitant of that earthiness (1 Cor. 4:11–13).

Not only do we have in these verses something rather like the beatitudes of the Sermon on the Plain; imbedded in the middle occur three parallel lines,

> When reviled, we bless,
> When persecuted, we endure,
> When slandered, we conciliate,

that are very much like what immediately follows the beatitudes and woes in the Sermon on the Plain (Luke 6:27; cf. v. 35):

36. See Ernst Haenchen, *Die Botschaft des Thomas-Evangeliums*, 1961, pp. 41–42 on these sayings, esp. p. 42: "The persons under discussion were not suffering from the anger of the masses or governmental persecution. Rather they felt pressured internally; it was the world itself that was after them."

> Love your enemies,
> Do good to those who hate you,
> Bless those who curse you,
> Pray for those who abuse you.

Perhaps in analogy to the following section in the Sermon on the Plain against judging (Luke 6:37 ff.), Paul in 4:5 expresses his eschatological reservation against judging "before the time, until the Lord comes."

None of these parallels is compelling; even a cluster of imprecise parallels is far from convincing. As Bultmann says of similar cases: "All at most possibilities!" [37] If this remains only a striking coincidence, then in any case by Polycarp's time, if not in Paul's, one can see the way in which the debate about the kerygma carried with it a debate about sayings of the Lord.[38]

The first trial run in relating (the hermeneutical translation of

37. Rudolf Bultmann, *GuV*, 1:191 (ET: *Faith and Understanding,* vol. 1, 1969, p. 223.

38. See *Polycarp* 2. 2:
> Do not return evil for evil
> Or blow for blow
> Or curse for curse.

As in the case of Paul, this is not introduced by a quotation formula (though it *is* preceded by an allusion to "his commandments"); yet it apparently suggested sayings of the Lord to Polycarp, for he immediately continues, 2. 3: "But remember what the Lord said, teaching:
> Judge not that you be not judged.
> Forgive and you will be forgiven.
> Be merciful that you may receive mercy.
> The measure you give will be the measure you get back.

That is to say, Polycarp appends to an unspecified use of material like Luke 6:27–28 a more explicit quotation of material like Luke 6:37–38, with which 1 Cor. 4:5 has been compared. Cf. also 1 Cor. 6:7–9:
> So it is already a complete loss of the case for you that
>   you have judgings against one another.
> Why not rather be wronged?
> Why not rather be defrauded?
> But you yourselves wrong and defraud, and that even your own brethren.
> Do you not know the unrighteous will not inherit the kingdom of God?

Similarly Polycarp concludes with a summary of the beatitudes:
> Blessed are the poor,
> And they who are persecuted for righteousness' sake,
> For theirs is the kingdom of God.

The immediately following *Laskerkatalog* in 1 Cor. 6:9–10 and the reference to baptism in 6:11 suggest that catechetical material may also be in the background here.

the) "kerygma" and (the) "history" (of the transmission of traditions about Jesus) "in the New Testament" has sought to trace the trajectory of debate about the meaning of the resurrection in the life of the Christian, and to see it pulling into its orbit a segment of the history of the transmission of the sayings of the Lord. Both underwent parallel distortions and corrections as they were caught up into an increasingly gnosticizing cultural development. The simple factors kerygma and historical Jesus have thus been seen to be quite complex factors, as the translation of the kerygma, necessitated by changing historical situations, swept with it, whichever way it went, the history of the transmission of the sayings of the Lord. Yet the flow is not simple or unilateral. Both "kerygma" and "historical Jesus" were under the influence of the same historical situations. And a development within the history of the transmission of the traditions about Jesus could just as well influence the translation of the kerygma as the reverse. One may therefore turn to a second trajectory moving through primitive Christianity, where indeed it seems that factors in the history of the transmission of traditions about Jesus are the primary moving force in an emergent debate.

History as the Transmission of Traditions in the New Testament

The second trial run begins, not with the kerygma, but with the historical Jesus. What had seemed such a simple and unambiguous thing as "the kerygma" in 1 Cor. 15:3–5 came to seem complex and ambiguous as soon as one considered how it was understood and translated. One must recognize that "the historical Jesus" too was less "common ground" than a common point of departure, when one thinks in terms of the history of the transmission of traditions about Jesus.

In his criticism of the new quest of the historical Jesus, Bultmann said: "If one inquires as to the material continuity between Jesus and the kerygma, then surely one does not inquire as to Jesus' personal faith, but at most as to whether the understanding of existence encountered in Jesus' activity as a possibility and claim (for decision) involves believing in him." [39] Yet how ambiguous such a historical fact as Jesus arousing faith in himself would be, even if it could be established, is evident from the presentation by those pupils of Bultmann who favor a positive answer. Günther Bornkamm asserts: "With all due attention to the critical examination of tradition, we saw no reason to contest that Jesus actually awakened messianic expectations by his coming and by his ministry, and that he encountered the faith which believed him to be the promised Savior. The faith which is expressed by the two disciples at Emmaus: 'But we hoped that he was the one to redeem Israel' (Luke 24:21), seems to express quite accurately the conviction of the followers of Jesus before his death." [40] Erich Dinkler has recently argued even that Peter's confession to Jesus as Christ is a historical fact that took place during the public ministry.[41] Yet even if this were a certain conclusion, it would hardly be an unambiguous common ground. Indeed Dinkler goes on to argue that Jesus' rebuke to Peter: "Get behind me, Satan," did not originally follow the first prediction of the passion, but rather followed directly upon Peter's confession. That is to say, Dinkler's view is that the historical Jesus flatly rejected the title *Messiah*. Bornkamm himself in the context cited above goes on to speak "of a movement of broken messianic hopes, and of one who was hoped to be the Messiah, but who, not only at the moment of failure, but in his entire message and ministry, disappointed the hopes which were placed in him." Of course Bornkamm means this quite positively, in that he is appealing to the historical Jesus over against falsely understood messianic hopes. He also speaks of "a faith which first had to break down at the cross of Jesus, only to be rebuilt upon his cross and resurrection." In other words, Bornkamm appeals finally to the kerygma to establish the normative interpretation of Jesus. This is also that to which Bultmann appeals, in order to

39. Bultmann, *Das Verhältnis der urchristlichen Christusbotschaft zum historischen Jesus,* p. 19 (ET, p. 33).
40. Günther Bornkamm, *Jesus of Nazareth,* 1960, p. 172.
41. Erich Dinkler, "Petrusbekenntnis und Satanswort: Das Problem der Messianität Jesu," in *Zeit und Geschichte,* Bultmann festschrift, 1964, pp. 127–53; reprinted in *Signum Crucis,* pp. 283–312.

clarify the ambiguity of a possible pre-Easter faith in Jesus. Bultmann immediately adds to his original statement: "Hence one can ask: Is, or to what extent is, the disciples' understanding, even before Easter, to be designated as believing in Jesus Christ, the crucified and resurrected?"

This sketch of alternatives within the Bultmannian school should serve to indicate that primitive Christianity had a common, but not an unequivocal, point of departure for its Christology in the pre-Easter period. For either there was a Christology at best implicit in Jesus' self-understanding prior to Easter, which could then be made explicit in the believer's self-understanding in various ways, or there was a quite ambiguous or even wrongheaded messianic view about Jesus in the disciples' faith, which stood in potential tension to the kerygma.

In the present context one is to face this problem, not in terms of modern reconstructions of the historical Jesus, but in terms of the New Testament church, that is to say, in terms of the early history of the transmission of traditions about Jesus. If the first trial run beginning with the kerygma pulled into its wake the transmission of the sayings of the Lord, this second trial run beginning with the stories about Jesus, primarily the miracle stories, will tend to indicate that these traditions about Jesus affected the ongoing understanding of the kerygma.

The emergence of the gospel as a literary form has been defined kerygmatically by Martin Kähler as the prefixing of a long introduction to the kerygmatic passion narrative. We wish here to focus upon that long introduction, which in the case of Mark consists primarily in a collection of miracle stories, whose importance is accentuated in the Marcan summaries, and by the emphasis upon miracle working in the narration of the mission of the Twelve.[42] This cycle of miracle stories presents Jesus sufficiently in the role of a glorious divine man that it can culminate in what would otherwise be comprehensible as a resurrection story,[43] but which is here simply the culmination of the cycle

---

42. Cf. Dieter Georgi, *Die Gegner des Paulus im 2. Korintherbrief: Studien zur religiösen Propaganda in der Spätantike*, WMANT, 11, 1964, p. 210 ff.
43. Cf. Charles Edwin Carlston, "Transfiguration and Resurrection," *JBL* 80 (1961): 233–40, for the argument that the transfiguration story was originally a

of miracle stories: the transfiguration. Mark has bound this cycle to the passion narrative in a rather jarring manner, by overlapping the first prediction of the passion with Peter's confession, and thus with a messianology that could point in the direction of making Jesus king [44] (John 6:15); as a result the "confession" becomes in Mark "Jesus' temptation by Peter, Satan's tool," [45] and the glorification of Jesus at the transfiguration which follows upon the confession becomes paradoxical in its Marcan setting in view of its proximity to the passion motif. The evangelist has then given a veneer of overall unity to the gospel by means of the messianic secret, which undercuts the direct demonstration of Jesus' messiahship originally intended by the miracle stories. Thus one can to some extent sense in Mark a tension between traditions about Jesus, in this case primarily the miracle stories of the first half of the gospel, and the kerygma, in this case represented by the passion narrative around which the last half of the gospel is organized.

---

resurrection story. Frank W. Beare, *The Earliest Records of Jesus*, 1962, p. 142, maintains that "it would seem that the time has come to relegate this theory to the museum of antiquities." C. H. Dodd, "The Appearances of the Risen Christ: An Essay in Form-Criticism of the Gospels," in *Studies in the Gospels*, R. H. Lightfoot festschrift, 1955, pp. 9–35, has proved that the transfiguration does not follow the outline of the resurrection stories accepted as such in the circles in which our gospels were written. Yet he has not shown convincingly that the transfiguration is different in form from earlier views of resurrection appearances, such as the appearances to Stephen and Paul in Acts. The very fact that these are not included by Luke within the forty days of official appearances suggests one reason for the disparity between the old list in 1 Cor. 15:3 ff. and the later appearance stories at the end of our gospels (to which E. L. Allen calls attention in "The Lost Kerygma," *NTS* 3 [1957]: 349–53): the older stories of appearances in glory did not qualify in terms of the later apologetic in defense of a physical resurrection. Dodd presents (p. 25) a polemic against "critics of a certain school" for regarding the identification of the transfiguration with a resurrection appearance as a "dogma"; but he neglects to refute their arguments. Rather he somewhat easily concludes: "I cannot find a single point of resemblance"—a conclusion rendered at least suspect for its absoluteness, by Carlston's essay. The most recent "museum of antiquities" into which the view of the transfiguration story as a resurrection appearance has gained admittance is the third edition of *RGG*, Ernst Käsemann's article "Wunder IV, Im NT," in vol. 6, 1962, p. 1835.

44. Oscar Cullmann, "L'Apôtre Pierre, instrument du Diable et instrument de Dieu: La place de Matt. 16, 16–19 dans la tradition primitive," in *New Testament Essays*, T. W. Manson festschrift, 1959, p. 96; reprinted in German in Cullmann's *Vorträge und Aufsätze, 1925–1962*, ed. Karlfried Fröhlich, 1966, p. 205: "For at the same moment when Peter made the declaration, 'You are the Messiah,' he must already have had, according to the narrative of Mark, the diabolical conception of the political role of the Messiah, the view which the majority of the Jews shared with the disciples and which excluded his suffering."

45. Ibid.

This state of affairs has led Harald Riesenfeld to detect the redactional hand of Mark in the last half, but, in view of the absence of the church's kerygma in the first half, to sense here more nearly a direct report about the historical Jesus.[46] Yet Dibelius posited that preaching, taken in a broad sense to include the various kinds of Christian witnessing, was the *Sitz im Leben* even of the miracle stories; indeed the role of exorcisms and healings in the narration of the mission of the Twelve would suggest that miracle stories were a prominent part of early Christian missionary propaganda. One should investigate the history of the transmission of the traditions about Jesus as itself a kind of kerygma, to see what that kerygma had to say, and how it stood in relation to the kerygma of cross and resurrection. Julius Wellhausen seemed to be right about Mark when, on the one hand, he affirmed that "the gospel is imbedded in the nest between Peter's confession and the passion," [47] but, on the other hand, goes on to say of the first half of Mark: "The miracles and exorcisms, the recognizing of Jesus by the demons, fitted popular

---

46. Harald Riesenfeld, "Tradition und Redaktion im Markusevangelium," in *Neutestamentliche Studien für Rudolf Bultmann,* suppl. 21 to *ZNW,* 1954, p. 162, affirms that the redactor "attempts to carry through a division into two parts, somewhat in the sense of 'call and discipleship.' But the odd thing is that the latter has apparently colored the way Mark presents Jesus' instruction of the disciples, while miracles and Jesus' preaching in parables on the one hand and the kerygmatic proclamation of the primitive church on the other correspond in this case only in a schematic way." Hans Conzelmann, in a lecture on "Das Selbstbewusstsein Jesu" in Uppsala on Sept. 24, 1963, agreed with Riesenfeld to the extent "that we can recognize within the Gospel of Mark a certain shift, in style and content, of what is reported. Through Mark 8:26, Jesus is portrayed as a teacher in Galilee. But no specific content of this teaching is given. From Mark 8:27 on, the content of the teaching is described: messiahship and suffering. Here the structuring reflection of the evangelist is at work. Hence a tension between tradition and redaction becomes visible." However, Conzelmann does not agree with Riesenfeld's inference that the first part of Mark goes back directly to Jesus: "Yet doubts are to be registered against his inferences. The philological analysis of the text shows that not only *two* layers are to be distinguished (tradition and the evangelist's reflection), but rather that there is a layer between Jesus and the evangelist that already contains important elements of reflection. Precisely the comments about Jesus as teacher belong not to the oldest layer, but rather are often literarily wooden, and hence clearly secondary, interpolated into the oldest layer." Conzelmann had already called attention to the fact that the messianic secret is imposed not on historical premessianic material, but on material that was already all too messianic: "Gegenwart und Zukunft in der synoptischen Tradition," *ZThK* 54 (1957): 293–94 (ET: "Present and Future in the Synoptic Tradition," in *God and Christ: Existence and Providence,* JTC, 5, 1968, pp. 42–43).
47. Julius Wellhausen, *Einleitung in die drei ersten Evangelien,* 1905, p. 82.

taste; perhaps, as 'signs' of messiahship, they even possessed the most force as publicity in the missionary preaching of the gospel, in those circles in which Christianity did most of its recruiting." [48]

Paul himself seems to concede much the same thing, though he states it somewhat sarcastically: "Tongues are a sign not for believers but for unbelievers" (1 Cor. 14:22). Indeed miracle working was listed prominently by Paul among the spiritual gifts in 1 Cor. 12:8–10, where there is a significant cluster of "gifts of healing," "working of powers" (i.e., miracles), and, in first place in this cluster, the odd gift of "faith"—odd because normally for Paul "faith" is the response of every Christian to God, and not a special gift of God reserved for a select few. In this case one seems to have to do with a technical term of miracle workers, namely the faith that moves mountains (13:2). The miracle workers were faith healers, and in the two synoptic gospels most dependent on them, Mark and Luke, these faith healers have left their characteristic slogan imbedded in the miracle stories of Jesus they transmitted: "Your faith has healed you" (Mark 5:34 parr.; 10:52// Luke 18:42; Luke 7:50; 17:19.[49]

Unfortunately recent research on Mark has not, in a way comparable to that on Matthew and Luke, produced a basic advance in insight into what Mark intended to do. Hence, rather than pursue the question of the history of the transmission of traditions about Jesus in terms of the miracle stories in the first half of Mark, one may shift to what seems to be a rather striking parallel, which will serve the present purpose and perhaps indirectly be of relevance for the study of Mark: the miracles source used by the Fourth Gospel.[50] This source was first detected by

48. Ibid., p. 53.
49. Ernst Käsemann, in *RGG,* 3d. ed., vol. 2 (1958), p. 995. Matt. 20:34 omits the slogan, but in an analogous story (9:29) says: "According to your faith be it done unto you." Matt. 15:28 has the statement: "Great is your faith! Be it done for you as you desire." Günther Bornkamm in his essay "The Stilling of the Storm in Matthew," and Heinz Joachim Held in "Matthew as Interpreter of tne Miracle Stories," both in *Tradition and Interpretation in Matthew,* 1963, pp. 52–57 and 165–299, show that for Matthew the miraculosity as the point of the miracle story had given way to the edifying use of the story for the teaching of discipleship within the church. Similarly the problem of faith tended for Matthew to become the inner-Christian problem of augmenting "little faith." Cf. Matt. 6:30; 8:26; 14:31; 16:8; 17:20.
50. Helmut Koester, "Häretiker im Urchristentum," in *RGG,* 3d ed., vol. 3 (1959), p. 19, has already associated the heresy opposed in 2 Cor. with the

Alexander Faure,[51] was accepted by Bultmann,[52] and has become the one of his sources for John that has withstood best the recent trend toward discounting Johannine sources in the light of the pervasive unity of style in the Gospel of John. Both Käsemann[53] and Haenchen,[54] while quite skeptical about the dis-

miracles source, as well as with Mark and parts of Acts. Koester also formulates well the issue: "The question was whether the church would succeed in appropriating theologically this narrative tradition and in working out in terms of the tradition about this history the question of the historicity of the revelation and of the divineness of its manifestation." See further the section "Literary Source Theory" in chap. 7 below.

51. Alexander Faure, "Die alttestamentlichen Zitate im 4. Evangelium und die Quellenscheidungshypothese," *ZNW* 21 (1922): 99–121, esp. 107–12.

52. Rudolf Bultmann, *Das Evangelium des Johannes (Meyer-Kommentar)*, 10th (1941) and subsequent editions, esp. p. 78.

53. Ernst Käsemann, review of Bultmann's commentary, *VuF: Theologischer Jahresbericht, 1942–46* (1947): 186–89; *RGG*, 3d ed., vol. 6, 1962, p. 1836. Käsemann rejects the discourses source in *ZThK* 54 (1957): 16, i.e., *EVB*, 2:25.

54. Ernst Haenchen, "Aus der Literatur zum Johannesevangelium 1929–1956," *ThR* 23 (1955): 303; idem, "Johanneische Probleme," *ZThK* 56 (1959): 19–54; idem, " 'Der Vater, der mich gesandt hat,' " pp. 208–9, the latter two articles repr. in his *Gott und Mensch*, 1965, pp. 78–113, 68–77. The criticism of Haenchen's work on the miracles source by Wilhelm Wilkens, "Evangelist und Redaktion im Johannes-Evangelium," *ThZ* 16 (1960): 81–90, is valid only on the assumption of the validity of his own theory about the origin of John set forth in his dissertation *Die Entstehungsgeschichte des vierten Evangeliums*, 1958; but that theory is hardly tenable. For, apart from the implausibility of his reconstructions (cf. my review article, "Recent Research in the Fourth Gospel," *JBL* 78 (1959), 242–46), his attributing of an original Book of Seven Signs to the same (apostolic) author who composed the succeeding stages overlooks the theological tension between the miracles source and the Fourth Gospel. D. Moody Smith, Jr., *The Composition and Order of the Fourth Gospel: Bultmann's Literary Theory*, 1965, p. 110 n. 181, asserts "Haenchen rejects Bultmann's *semeia*-source hypothesis," but adds: "[Haenchen's] own understanding of the way in which the evangelist employs narrative material is, after all, not so different from Bultmann's." It is the latter statement that is the focus of Haenchen's work, who envisages a written source used in the Fourth Evangelist's home congregation and hence cited freely, a source containing more of the synoptic-type materials than just the miracle stories. It gives a reversed impression of Haenchen's assessment of Bultmann's analysis to refer to. this as a "rejection." Somewhat similarly Käsemann's view is presented as making Bultmann's source theory "superfluous" (p. 63), to which is appended the remark that Käsemann does in fact hold that the evangelist used such a document as the miracles source. Similarly Smith seems to cast the course of the discussion in a way less favorable to a miracles source than is the case when he cites as a first ground for skepticism about the miracles source the fact that Bultmann does not accept "the clue which Faure thought decisive, namely, that the Old Testament is cited differently in the first twelve chapters from the remainder of the gospel" (p. 111 n. 183). This is a misleading statement. For Faure (*ZNW* 21, 1922, 112 n. 3) recognizes that Old Testament quotations are absent from the miracles source. Thus at most the miracles source could be an argument for Faure's separation of the gospel into two parts, in that only the first part (with the exception of 20:30–31) used the miracles source as he conceived of it; but the distinctive use of the Old Testament in the first half of John is not conversely for Faure an argument for the miracles source, much less "decisive." Finally, factors which "only suggest that he [the Fourth Evangelist] used a 'Book of Signs' in the composition

courses source, do assume the evangelist used, though freely, the miracles source, and Kümmel concedes that the places where typically Johannine stylistic traits are most lacking fit rather well the places where the miracles source seems to be most faithfully followed.[55] Hence the most recent survey of the literature on the problem of Johannine sources by D. Moody Smith, Jr. concludes: "The *prima facie* possibility of something approximating Bultmann's *semeia*-source is to be granted, although the characterization and delineation of that source remain doubtful." [56]

What makes this miracles source stand out in the Fourth Gospel

---

of his gospel without helping to define its extent" do not belong in a footnote listing "reasons for being somewhat skeptical about the *semeia*-source" (p. 111 n. 183), since the question of the source's existence should be clearly distinguished from that of our ability to reconstruct it. Kurt Aland, "Glosse, Interpolation, Redaktion, und Komposition in der Sicht der neutestamentlichen Textkritik," *Apophoreta,* Haenchen festschrift, suppl. 30 to *ZNW,* 1965, p. 7, has rightly drawn attention to this frequent non sequitur in Johannine research, as has Smith (pp. 71–72). Thus his "skepticism" does not logically question the existence of the source, but only its extent and nature.

55. Werner Georg Kümmel, *Einleitung in das Neue Testament,* 14th ed. of Feine-Behm, 1965, pp. 146–47: (ET: *Introduction to the New Testament,* 1966, p. 152): "On the other hand it has also become apparent that in individual pericopes the characteristics distinctive of John are so clearly lacking that one must assume that here traditions have been incorporated (. . . esp. 2. 1–10, 13–19; 4. 46–53; 12. 1–8, 12–15)." Eduard Schweizer, "Die Heilung des Königlichen: Joh. 4, 46–54," *EvTh* 11 (1951): 64–71, esp. p. 65 n. 5 (reprinted in *Neotestamentica,* 1963, pp. 407–15, esp. pp. 407–8 n. 5), gives the details with regard to 4:46–54. To be sure, Kümmel does not himself draw the positive inference, but rather continues: "But this does not at all lead to a written 'Signs Source' used by the evangelist."

56. D. Moody Smith, Jr., *The Composition and Order of the Fourth Gospel,* p. 113. See also "The Sources of the Gospel of John: An Assessment of the Present State of the Problem," *NTS* 10 (1964): 336–51, esp. 345. Thus it would seem that Peter Riga, "Signs of Glory: The Use of 'Semeion' in Saint John's Gospel," *Interpretation* 17 (1963): 402–24, is a bit over-hasty in dismissing in a note Bultmann's miracles source as having "been abundantly proven to be a figment of the author's literary imagination" (p. 402 n. 4). Sources are usually rejected as unnecessary by those who accept apostolic authorship for gospels (p. 416; Riga also assumes Saint Peter wrote 2 Peter, p. 414). Some recognition of the problem on Riga's part is provided when he follows H. van den Bussche, "La structure de Jean I–XII," in *L'Evangile de Jean,* Recherches Bibliques, 3, 1958, pp. 61–109, in regarding chaps. 2–4, (i.e., de facto, the "first" and "second" signs, 2:1–11 and 4:46–54) as "the section of signs proper," where "they are not expanded," and chaps. 5–12 as the section in which "there is a deep analysis of the significance of the signs as works, and of their relation to the works of the Father" (p. 417). But these "two levels of revelation" do not quite fit the chapter divisions as simply stages in a homogeneous document. John 4:48 contains the evangelist's criticism of the more superficial level of the miracles source; and chaps. 5–12 contain the superficial view of faith as credulity in the miracle worker characteristic of the miracles source (e.g., 12:37), as well as the deeper view of the evangelist. Thus the dismissing of the miracles source is accompanied by a schematizing that obscures problems in the text.

is precisely those traits that characterize it as a collection of miracle stories by a faith healer designed for missionary purposes. At least in the early chapters of John the miracles source also stands out because of literary seams, the wooden redactional style one would rather expect in the synoptics. The second miracle, the healing of the centurion's son (4:46–54), occurs in the same setting of coming from Judea to Galilee (4:43, 45, 54) as does the first miracle, the wedding in Cana (2:1–11). The evangelist even takes Jesus back to Cana for the second miracle (4:46a), without really having anything further for him to do there, except leave for Capernaum. This is best explained, not historically, but editorially, reflecting the evangelist's effort to restore a broken connection with the wedding in Cana (just as 2:12, which takes Jesus to Capernaum without action there, reflects the original connection to the Capernaum story beginning in 4:46b).[57]

It is also striking, not only from the point of view of literary criticism, but now also from the point of view of a critical distinction of subject matter, that the first two miracles are numbered: In 2:11 the wedding in Cana is called the "beginning of the miracles," and in 4:54 the centurion's son is called the "second miracle." Not only is this counting of miracles not continued in the Fourth Gospel, and indeed seems without point in its presentation; it is even somewhat contradicted by the intervening Johannine material, which speaks in 2:23 and 3:2 (see also 4:45) of a plurality of signs having been done, a clash between source and redaction only faintly covered over by the fact that it is indeed only the second miracle performed explicitly in the context of coming from Judea to Galilee (4:54).[58]

57. Eduard Schweizer, "Die Heilung des Königlichen," p. 65 (*Neotestamentica,* p. 407) n. 7, argues that the nonfunctional allusions to Jesus' brothers and to Capernaum in 2:12 are best intelligible on the assumption that they were in the source as a transition to 4:46 ff., and that 4:46a is here recalling the original context of the first sign.

58. Ibid., p. 65 (*Neotestamentica,* p. 407) n. 4, shows how this numbering makes sense only on the assumption that the two miracles belong together following upon one same trip from Judea to Galilee. If the trip to Galilee referred to in 4:54 is that of 4:43, then the one intervening miracle could not in 4:54 be numbered the second; hence the trip of 4:54 must be that presupposed at 2:1. This indicates that the two numbered miracles (2:1–11; 4:46–54) originally stood together.

Yet from the point of view of the source itself, the numbering of the miracles fits well its apologetic emphasis on the quantity of miracles. "When the Christ appears, will he do *more miracles* than this man has done?" (7:31).[59] "What are we to do? For this man performs *many miracles!* (11:47). *"So many miracles* he had done before them, and yet they did not believe in him" (12:37). Apparently in Faure's and Bultmann's view this verse led directly to the conclusion of the miracle source, whose ending was shifted from the end of the miracles source and put at the end of the Fourth Gospel (20:30–31): "Now Jesus did *many other miracles* before his disciples, which are not written in this book." And now comes the apologetic, missionary scope or *Sitz im Leben* of the miracles source: "But these were written down that you may believe that Jesus is the Christ, the Son of God." It is the very quantity of such miracle stories that produces faith, and the narrator had assured the reader he could continue indefinitely recounting such miracle stories of Jesus.

Thus there is a direct, unambiguous, nonparadoxical, causal relation between the miracles that demonstrate Jesus to be a divine man, and the resultant faith (or credulity) in him as just such a miracle worker. It is the same reasoning attributed to Nicodemus: "Rabbi, we know that you are a teacher come from God; for no one can do these miracles that you do, unless God is with him" (3:2). It is also the reasoning of some primitive Christian missionaries: Luke conceives of Peter's commending Jesus to the Jews as "a man attested to you by God with mighty works and wonders and miracles which God did through him in your midst" (Acts 2:22).[60]

The Fourth Evangelist himself maintains that the true form of faith is faith in Jesus' word.[61] "He who hears my word and be-

59. Faure, *ZNW* 21 (1922): 109 n. 1, seems to include this verse in the miracles source; Bultmann, *Das Evangelium des Johannes* p. 231, regards it as a transition between 7:37–44 and 7:31–36 (*sic*!) that reflects a view the evangelist looks down on. Haenchen, *NTS* 9 (1963): 208 (*Gott und Mensch*, p. 68) attributes it to the source. There seems general agreement among the advocates of the miracles source that the passages cited next are to be included in the source. Fortna first departs from this position (see Chapter 7 below).
60. Haenchen, *NTS* 9 (1963): 208–9 (*Gott und Mensch*, pp. 68–69), draws the parallel to make this point.
61. Already Faure, *ZNW* 21 (1922): 111–12, makes this contrast.

lieves him who sent me, has eternal life; he does not come into judgment, but has passed from death to life" (5:24)—which happens to be precisely the context cited earlier as the nearest Johannine approach to the heresy of baptismal resurrection! It is as if, in backing away from the inadequate interpretation of the earthly Jesus represented by the miracles source, the evangelist backs into a position suspiciously near the converse error. Thus the position of orthodoxy tends to be a mathematical point, or at best a dialectical position, or hardly a position at all, but rather a direction: "Orthodox" were not the traditions or conceptualizations one used, but the direction one went with them, the point one was scoring. Traditions and conceptualizations tend to be swept along the course of a culture's trajectory, for better or worse, and the right or orthodox thing to do is to be critically aware of this fact and, when necessary, to seek to modify the directionality they have thus been given, for the sake of retaining the flow distinctive of Christian faith.

By focusing attention upon the general orientation of the miracles source we have come to hear the point being scored as it transmits traditions about Jesus, specifically miracle stories; and we have conjectured that such a point may have been commonly heard in such stories in their oral transmission. Yet the very fact that such a point is subjected to some criticism by the Fourth Evangelist, who also transmits these stories, would tend to indicate that the missionary purpose, the point, intended by such transmission of traditions could vary, just as the understanding of faith varies between the Fourth Evangelist and the traditions transmitted to him. If in the case of the kerygma we conceptualized this process in terms of hermeneutical translation, we propose in this case to analyze the debate in terms of the history of the transmission of traditions about Jesus. That is to say, listening to the way the tradition is shaped and altered, hearkening to the way the stories are told, should betray the point they were intended to convey, the trajectory of faith to which they witness and for which they call.

This can be illustrated by the story of the healing of the centurion's son, a story that occurs both in Q (Matt. 8:5–13; Luke

7:1–10) and in the miracles source (John 4:46–54). In Q this miracle story has seemed to be a problem, since Q is not supposed to contain narrative materials, and this story is the main exception to that rule. As a matter of fact it does not really contradict the general understanding of Q as a source focused on Jesus' word. To begin with, very little of the narrative material in the story is common to Matthew and Luke. Hence the part clearly attributable to Q is mostly dialogue. There is really no more narrative in the part clearly attributable to Q than is absolutely necessary to make sense of the dialogue. The same phenomenon is to be found in a few places in other sayings collections such as the *Gospel of Thomas* (e.g., Sayings 22, 60, 99, 100). But even more relevant with regard to Q's orientation to Jesus' word is the fact that this is precisely the one story about Jesus in which the very point is faith in his word. The centurion says Jesus does not even need to come home with him. "Just say the word and my servant will be healed" (Matt. 8:8 par.). The centurion goes on to state that as an officer he is quite familiar with the authority of commands that effect what they say. And it is this faith in Jesus' word that is elevated to the point of the whole story. "With no one in Israel have I found such faith" (Matt. 8:10 par.). What more perfect story to follow upon the contrast between the stability of those who "hear my words and do them" (Matt. 7:24 par.), and the shaky status of those who do not! It is not even clear that Q went to the trouble to tell whether the miracle actually happened; indeed such a continuation of the narration would seem anticlimactic, once the effective word had been spoken.

Quite the reverse is the case in the miracles source! For at the point where the story ends in Q, it has hardly begun in the miracles source. We follow the father on the way home, where his servants come to meet him, and tell of the miraculous cure, which is shown to have happened at exactly the same hour that Jesus had spoken. Then the father and all his house believe—now that they see the evidence, the miracle itself. Where does this leave the faith the father had when Jesus gave his word? It seems forgotten, as is Jesus' word itself. Rather we are told that the story is the second *miracle* Jesus worked (4:54). That is to say, the story that in Q was oriented to faith in Jesus' word, is oriented in the miracles source to faith in Jesus as a miracle worker. This is apparently too much for the Fourth Evangelist, who interpolates the remark (4:48): "Unless you see miracles and wonders, you will not believe." [62] And Q also criticizes by implication the directionality taken in the miracles source, in rejecting the miracle worker interpretation of Jesus' divine sonship by means of the three temptations, significantly absent from the miracles source and Mark, but prominent near the opening of Q.

The Fourth Evangelist's backing away from a kind of primitive Christian faith, imbedded in traditions about Jesus as a miracle worker, on behalf of a more profound and spiritual Christianity, almost pushed him into the camp of the spiritualists. Something not dissimilar seems to have been the outcome for Paul, when similar traditions arrived in Corinth. One may assume that the arrival of 1 Corinthians in Corinth brought into line the radical, gnosticizing left wing of the congregation. This Pauline victory not only pulled the congregation together, but to some extent strengthened the other wing of the congregation, the weaker brethren with Jewish leanings. They agreed heartily that one was not already completely in the eschaton, for they were so convinced of their unbroken continuity with the past that they could not free themselves from their former taboos. This side of the congregation had been relatively spared in the attacks of 1 Corinthians (though critical allusions to them are possibly implied in the general listing of party slogans at the opening, 1:12, 22, and the

---

62. For this comparison of the varying forms of this story see especially Haenchen, *ZThK* 56 (1959): 23–31 (*Gott und Mensch*, pp. 82–90). For this criticism of miracles as typically Johannine see also Eduard Schweizer, "Die Heilung des Königlichen," p. 68 (*Neotestamentica*, p. 411) n. 15. However, Schweizer attributes the alteration and extension of the story beyond the Q form to the Fourth Evangelist rather than his source (with the exception of 4:48). But this leads to a relation of believing to seeing that undoes the Johannine corrective in 20:29. Faith based on seeing the miracle, "put above that initial faith without sight" by 4:53, is a view attributed to the evangelist (*Neotestamentica*, p. 413). Similarly "the story contains for the evangelist the presentation of faith growing from step to step" (*Neotestamentica*, pp. 411–12). It would be more consistent to attribute this view of faith in 4:50, 53, and thus the last part of the story, to the source; or to interpret 4:48 as uncritical of the demand for miracles. But Schweizer states of 4:48: "Jesus chastises a desire for miracle that demands the miracle to legitimize Jesus as a prerequisite of faith" (*Neotestamentica*, p. 409). Hence Haenchen's attribution of the Johannine prolongation to the miracles source is more consistent.

general listing of spiritual gifts at the conclusion, 12:9–10; 13:2),
whereas in the central section on meat offered to idols (1 Cor.
8—10) Paul had come to their defense.

Thus it happened that the congregation was ripe for wandering
missionaries, who had meanwhile arrived in town (2 Cor. 11:4),
and who emphasized their continuity with Israel's glorious past
(2 Cor. 11:22). Apparently they saw this past in terms of the
potency of divine men transmitted in the divine tradition, reach-
ing from Moses' miracles in the court of Pharaoh to Jesus' equally
numerous miracles, and embracing the no less impressive faith
healings of the missionaries themselves, who like Moses and Jesus
are "transfigured from glory to glory" (2 Cor. 3:18). These
wandering missionaries came equipped with letters of recommendation (2 Cor. 3:1) that must have listed their glorious deeds,
as did the many lurid "Acts" of various apostles later; and they
also boasted of having to their credit the "miraculous signs of an
apostle," namely the ability to work "miraculous signs and wonders and miracles" (2 Cor. 12:12). It is no wonder the Corinthians now "demand proof that Christ is speaking" in Paul (2
Cor. 13:3). The word of Christ—whether in terms of sayings of
the Lord or whatever—is not itself convincing revelation, but
needs to be supplemented by the confirming miracle. Such a re-
quirement recalls the shift in directionality in the story of the
centurion's son from the Q version, with its orientation to faith
in the authority of Jesus' word, to the miracles source, where real
faith takes place when one sees the miracle has been performed.

Paul satirizes the self-esteem of these wandering miracle workers, by referring to them as "superapostles" (2 Cor. 11:5; 12:11).
He presents a parody of their self-commendations in the way he
presents his own autobiography (11:23–33). For Anton Fridrichsen has recognized here the stylistic traits of what he calls a "Peri-
stasis Catalogue," the listing of a potentate's glorious triumphs
over all kinds of hardships, "such as one finds in the inscriptions
of oriental kings, in the *res gestae* of Roman Caesars, and in
Greek novels. From this stylistic tradition are to be explained the
asyndeta, the numbering, the occurrence of πολλάκις, the alter-
nation of lists and narratives, the chronicle-like addition in

11:32–33, and the like. To be sure, the fact that the praise of the apostle consists only in suffering turns the use of this stylistic form into a clearly intended paradox." [63]

This debate between Paul and the "superapostles" concerning which way of life legitimizes [64] the apostle, the life of ignominious suffering or the life of glorious triumph over every impediment, is also carried on in terms of traditions about Jesus. It may be no coincidence that the name Jesus occurs so frequently in 2 Corinthians unadorned with an accompanying title *Lord* or *Christ*.[65] Paul accuses his opponents of preaching "another Jesus" (2 Cor. 11:4), and the evidence seems to indicate that this other Jesus is a power-laden glorious miracle worker, much as in the miracles source, whose earthly ministry could well be epitomized by comparing his glory with that of Moses, as in 2 Cor. 3 [66]—and in the cycle of miracle stories dominating the first half of Mark and culminating in the transfiguration alongside of Moses and Elijah, where again the concept of "glory" emerges (Luke 9:31–32; 2 Pet. 1:17; cf. Mark 8:38). Hence Dieter Georgi can assert:

So it is not true that Paul developed his Christology in complete ignorance of the contents and tendencies of the developing tradition about Jesus. Rather he knew about them and hence clearly rejected a motivation that at least at times clearly asserts itself, namely the objective of using a certain form of presentation to make of the life of Jesus an unambiguous manifestation of the divine, to cover over the offense of the cross and the humanness of Jesus in general

63. So Werner Georg Kümmel, *HNT*, vol. 9, 4th ed., 1949, p. 211, in his summary of Fridrichsen's work, first presented in "Zum Stil des paulinischen Peristasen-Katalogs 2. Kor. 11, 23 ff.," *Symbolae Osloenses* 7 (1928): 26–29. Cf. also Hans Dieter Betz, "Eine Christus-Aretalogie bei Paulus (2. Kor. 12, 7–10)," *ZThK* 66 (1969) 288–305, where Paul's autobiographical use of the form of a miracle story is made to perform the same function.
64. It is this aspect that is rightly brought to the center of the discussion by Ernst Käsemann, "Die Legitimität des Apostels: Eine Untersuchung zu II. Korinther 10–13," *ZNW* 41 (1942): 33–71; reprinted in *Das Paulusbild in der neueren deutschen Forschung*, Wege der Forschung 24, ed. K. H. Rengstorf, 1964, pp. 475–521, as well as separately, 1956.
65. Georgi, *Die Gegner des Paulus im 2. Korintherbrief*, pp. 282 ff. But cf. the very critical review by Erhardt Güttgemanns, *Zeitschrift für Kirchengeschichte* 77 (1966): 126–31, esp. p. 131.
66. Georgi, *Die Gegner des Paulus im 2. Korintherbrief*, pp. 265–82. In John 2:11 Jesus' miracles "manifest his glory."

and to replace the eschatological revelation of God with historically ascertainable "proofs of God." [67]

Perhaps the most dramatic confirmation of the fact that the historical Jesus—in the form of a certain segment in the history of the transmission of traditions about Jesus—is claimed by the opponents in 2 Corinthians, is 2 Cor. 5:16, where Paul emphasizes the irrelevance of knowing Christ according to the flesh. This is strikingly reminiscent of the cry of the gnosticizing party in 1 Corinthians, "Jesus be anathema," which Paul condemned in 1 Cor. 12:3, but which could have been directed against much the same portrayal of Jesus as Paul himself now rejects. That is to say, we again find Paul, in opposing one potential heresy, making use of formulations that are so hard to distinguish from the other potential heresy that Walter Schmithals could with some plausibility (though no doubt wrongly) argue that 2 Cor. 5:16 was a gnostic gloss.[68] And what is equally striking is that, in opposing the emphasis on continuity with the past, Paul so emphasizes realized eschatology (2 Cor. 5:16–17; 6:2) as to sound remi-

67. Ibid., p. 289 n. 3. This stands in contrast to Bultmann, e.g., *RGG*, 2d ed., vol. 4, 1930, p. 1028: "No matter whether Paul knew much or little of that tradition [sc., about Jesus]! For his message of salvation, the content of Jesus' life, as that of the teacher, the prophet, the miracle worker, the one crowned with thorns, plays absolutely no role."

68. Walter Schmithals, "Zwei gnostische Glossen im 2. Korintherbrief," *EvTh* 18 (1958): 552–73, esp. 552–64. Some such position becomes necessary when one regards, as does Schmithals, the heresy of 2 Corinthians as the same as that opposed in 1 Corinthians. For then 2 Corinthians 5:16 is so near the gnosticizing view of the assumed opponents that one can hardly make sense of Paul's using it as an argument against them. Hence Dinkler, who assumes the same heresy to be combatted in both 1 and 2 Corinthians (cf. *RGG*, 3d ed., vol. 4, 1960, p. 18), consistently with this view, has maintained (orally) that 2 Cor. 5:16 is not directed against the heresy. Bultmann, who also maintained the unity of the heresy of 1 and 2 Corinthians (*Exegetische Probleme des Zweiten Korintherbriefes: Zu 2. Kor. 5, 1–5; 5, 11–6, 10; 10–13; 12, 21*, Symbolae Biblicae Upsalienses, 9, 1947; reprinted separately in 1963, and in the collection of his essays ed. by Erich Dinkler, *Exegetica*, 1967, pp. 298–322) held that "Christ according to the flesh" would refer to him as the miracle worker, a view of Jesus liked by gnostics. But the term *gnostic* is then used so broadly as to become imprecise, since such a Christology is far from distinctive or typical of Gnosticism, even if it, like other religions of antiquity, conceived of miraculous power as belonging to divinity. Thus the position opposed by 2 Cor. 5:16 would not include many who in the narrower sense are called gnostics, and perhaps not even the gnosticizing heresy of 1 Corinthians. Cf. Georgi, *Die Gegner des Paulus im 2. Korintherbrief*, pp. 293–94 n. 3. Thus Georgi is methodologically correct in seeking to clarify the difference in nuance between the center of opposition in 1 Corinthians ("spiritualists") and that in 2 Corinthians ("apologists"), without denying the many elements of continuity between the two.

niscent of the heresy of baptismal resurrection he himself combatted in 1 Corinthians.[69]

Again we see that primitive Christian statements cannot be understood, much less evaluated, as doctrinal assertions in and of themselves, in isolation from the situation into which they spoke, and hence apart from the way they cut. Not only have orthodoxy and heresy not yet separated into different ecclesiastical organizations; they have not even yet separated their theological conceptualizations. Rather, from a common body of traditions, ambiguous in their concrete meaning, each side transmits interpretively, in terms of understandings that only gradually came to objectify themselves into fixed positions that could be branded as right or wrong in and of themselves. By that time the tagged theological vocabulary was already dead or dying, and the real issues, out of which the heresy and orthodoxy of the next period would emerge, were already being debated in not yet dogmatically defined areas, where freedom and ambiguity still prevailed.

In 1 Corinthians, Paul was primarily confronted by a mistranslation of the kerygma in terms of baptismal resurrection, and he replied with a corrective interpretation of the kerygma, emphasizing: the eschatological reservation; love and the upbuilding of the congregation, as the point of the action to which the Christian is empowered; the power of the resurrection as the power to endure; and hence the limiting of the kerygma to the focus of Christ crucified. This debate about the valid translation of the kerygma colored the transmission of the sayings of Jesus whenever that debate came in contact with this tradition. In 2 Corinthians, Paul was primarily confronted by a distorting transmission of traditions about Jesus as a glorious miracle worker, and he replied with an ironic presentation of himself within that succession, to document the invalidity of such a scope for the traditions; and by repudiating such knowledge of Jesus. However, we might expect him to argue his case in 2 Corinthians, not only

69. Contrast Dinkler's appeal to 2 Cor. 5:17, *ZThK* 49 (1952): 188, cited above, in attributing to Paul in 1 Corinthians what would be more in analogy to than a corrective of the position of his opponents there. His appeal to Galatians is also hardly valid, in that here (as in 2 Corinthians) Paul is facing a front converse to that in 1 Corinthians. Hence neither 2 Corinthians nor Galatians can be used as the hermeneutical principle for interpreting Paul's stance in 1 Corinthians.

in terms of such traditions, but also in terms of the kerygma of cross and resurrection. And one might indeed wonder whether that kerygma, which for Paul clearly was primary to Jesus traditions, would not color his view of the traditions about Jesus. There are some indications that point in this direction.

The pattern of the kerygma to which Paul appeals is provided by 2 Cor. 13:4: "For he was crucified in weakness, but lives from the power of God." Here divine power is precisely attributed, not to the earthly Jesus, but to the resurrected. That is to say, we have here a parallel to early kerygmatic texts such as Rom. 1:3–4 and Phil. 2:6–11, which first at the exaltation accord honorific titles to Jesus, in the sense of enthroning him in an office he had not previously held, investing him with "all authority in heaven and earth" (Matt. 28:18).[70] Hence the relation of the apostle's ministry to Jesus is not that of continuing a power Jesus had on earth, but rather that of submitting in service to the rule Jesus received as Lord in heaven. "For we preach not ourselves but Christ Jesus as Lord, but ourselves as your servants because of Jesus" (2 Cor. 4:5). The apostle's relation to the Lord is that of earth to heaven, servant to Lord, and such service takes the form of serving his body the church.

Paul's addition, that this service is not only subjection to the Lord reigning in heaven, but also takes place because of Jesus, suggests to Georgi[71] that the apostle's earthly service is the true parallel to the earthly Jesus, whom Paul would interpret by seeing the public ministry in a scope provided by the phrase "crucified in weakness."[72] That is to say, Paul would conceive of the earthly Jesus as a long introduction to and of a piece with

70. Cf. Günther Bornkamm, "Der Auferstandene und der Irdische: Mt. 28, 16–20," in *Zeit und Geschichte,* Bultmann festschrift, 1964, pp. 171–91. One may compare "receiving from God the Father honor and glory" at the transfiguration (2 Pet. 1:17), which transaction would for Paul, and probably for his generation (and still in 2 Peter?), be located at the resurrection, from which it was secondarily transferred back into the public ministry.
71. On this passage see Georgi, *Die Gegner des Paulus im 2. Korintherbrief,* pp. 285–86. In general cf. Hans Dieter Betz, *Nachfolge und Nachahmung Jesu Christi im Neuen Testament,* BHTh, 37, 1967.
72. Käsemann, *New Testament Questions of Today,* p. 48 (ET of *EVB,* 2:53) interprets Paul's "word of the cross" in the same way: "But in so doing he calls men into the shadow of the earthly Jesus. Certainly the Cross is for him a saving event and, to this extent, mythologically decked out, transfigured and overpainted. Yet his eyes do not see the 'cross of light' of the gnostics, but the folly and shame in which the historical Jesus suffered."

the passion narrative. This scope given both to Jesus' life and to the believer's life by the cross is made explicit in 2 Cor. 4:10–11: "We always carry in the body the killing of Jesus. . . . For in this life we are always being given up to death because of Jesus." Here Christian existence defined by (i.e., "because of") Jesus means living in acceptance of death, or, as the kerygma puts it of Jesus, "obedient unto death" (Phil. 2:8). That is to say, the Christian life is not understood as a resurrected life that has finished its dying and needs merely at the end of life to return to the sun from which it came, nor as standing in the glorious tradition of a miracle-working earthly Jesus whose power one continues to exercise, but as life freed from the demonic way of the fear of death, so that the apostle may persist in obedience, in service.

It is this freedom from the grip of evil, the power of death, to a life of suffering and service, that is the paradoxical presence of the resurrection in this life. For Paul takes the phrase "life of Jesus" (which Georgi suspects is derived from Paul's opponents, who would have used it to refer to the miracle-working earthly Jesus), and casts it in the role played in the kerygma by Jesus' resurrected life.[73] Thus *life,* in the sense of higher or divine life, is, like the terms *power* and *glory,* shifted from the earthly Jesus to the resurrected, and hence is only paradoxically related to this life for the believer.

This analysis of Paul's position in 2 Corinthians began with the argument that the situation he confronted in Corinth had to a large extent reversed itself between 1 Corinthians and 2 Corinthians, and that Paul accordingly shifted the categories in which he argued, and to this extent shifted his position. For not only was

---

73. Georgi (*Die Gegner des Paulus im 2. Korintherbrief,* p. 287) concedes that in Rom. 5:10 and generally *life* refers to the resurrected. And he concedes (p. 294) that this is the meaning in 2 Cor. 13:4. But he seems to regard 2 Cor. 4:10 ff. as an exception (p. 287–88): (1) The name *Jesus* would seem to suggest the earthly Jesus. Yet apart from the general question as to the extent that one can assume a rigid consistency on Paul's part in his use (or nonuse) of christological titles in this regard, 2 Cor. 4:14 would seem to use *Jesus* without titles within the context in question to refer to the resurrected. (2) "Jesus' life" is to be manifested in the *present* life of the Christian. Although Georgi is correct here in opposing the contrary assumption of some exegetes, his tacit inference that "life of Jesus" must then refer to Jesus' earthly life is unwarranted, in view of its position after the reference to Jesus' death.

the one argument primarily about the right translation of the kerygma, and at most only secondarily a debate about the right transmission of traditions about Jesus, whereas in the other case the primary focus was the Jesus tradition. Furthermore the position Paul had assumed in the first debate to some extent prepared the ground for the potential heresy that blossomed between 1 Corinthians and 2 Corinthians; and the position he assumed in 2 Corinthians was to some extent parallel to that of his opponents in 1 Corinthians. Thus a great fluidity in the use of concepts and traditions has been observed, and Pauline theologizing has turned out to be not simply the citation of relevant materials from an abstractly conceived generalized system or static position, but rather the development of materials to fit one situation, and a different development to fit another. Yet one can sense, in where Paul comes out in the two structures of thought related to the two situations, an analogous point being scored. Rather than being a relativist or opportunist, Paul was a responsible theologian moving through a trajectory of theologizing which was relevantly related to his trajectory of historic experience.

Paul's opponents in the two cases could emerge in a Pauline congregation with the claim to be rightly translating the kerygma and transmitting the traditions, in part by appealing to Pauline structures of thought to implement a divergent point. To the extent such structures were themselves taken as Pauline theology, it would be easy to shift a Pauline congregation from one point to the other, as long as the modification of structure remained minimal. And Pauline pupils could readily emerge to complete one or the other instance of a Pauline "system," with widely fluctuating points; perhaps their expansions were also at times more nearly dull and pointless, too weak to withstand unintended points latent in the language itself, so that the deutero-Pauline trajectory was at times simply an uncritical following of the trajectory of a given cultural stream.

From such an analysis one should infer that any meaningful discussion of Pauline theology on our part would have to move beyond the common body of concepts and traditions he shared with other Christians of his day, beyond the particular structurings of such materials he developed in concrete situations he confronted, to a listening for the points scored, and in their continuity with each other—and not without the language in which they were scored—to a catching sight of the direction of movement, i.e., of the Pauline trajectory. In this way one could attempt to attain a more nuanced and comprehensive understanding of the historical phenomenon "Pauline theology" than that which characterized the deutero-Pauline period and which characterizes much Pauline study even today.

Inferences from the Two Trial Runs

Two "trial runs" have traced trajectories through primitive Christianity that are significant in and of themselves. Yet they were intended to be illustrative of certain broader matters, which may now be summarized.

1. The use of current categories in the assigned topic provided an occasion for pointing up the crisis in the basic categories of our discipline which exists today. This crisis has emerged partly because of the careful detailed research that has, in spite of inadequate categories, established facts calling for a revision of these inherited categories. Yet the inadequate categories persist, and in many cases continue to provide guidelines that mislead research, so that results of even carefully detailed research may be less relevant than would have been the case had the approach, the alternatives, the issues been more accurately focused.

This could have been exemplified in various areas. For example, at a time when the study of early Gnosticism is calling attention to the important role that the interpretation of the Old Testament within heterodox Judaism played in that development, the older pattern of argument persists, insofar as one still finds that a text can be disassociated from the gnostic problem by showing its Old Testament or Jewish rootage. The inherited conceptualization in terms of mutual exclusivity, built upon the antithesis between normative Judaism and advanced Gnosticism in past generations of scholarship, has been carried over into a period where the development from heterodox Judaism to early Gnosticism, from Qumran to Nag Hammadi, calls for a new conceptualization, more like a continuous progression, through a period of contiguous centuries and cultures. The emergence at Nag Hammadi of apparently non-Christian Jewish Gnosticism whose mythology is dependent on Genesis (i.e., *The Apocalypse of Adam, The Paraphrase of Shem*), not to speak of the detailed paraphrase of Genesis 3 in Codex IX, *3,* should indicate the emergence of missing links that demonstrate the inadequacy of conceptualizations based upon a mutual exclusivity of Judaism and the Old Testament on the one hand and Gnosticism on the other.[74]

The present paper has intended to carry through such a restructuring of categories in the case of the inherited pair "kerygma" and "history," from which emerged more adequate conceptualizations in terms of the hermeneutically understood process of translating the point of kerygmatic language and in terms of the history of the transmission of traditions. Such illustrations of a crisis of categories are designed to sharpen our critical awareness of the fact that we confront our sources through the mediation of the inherited language of scholarship. This should not be taken as an invitation to a kind of primitivism, according to which outsiders free of the ballast of scholarship could see what the scholars had not. It is from those who have worked their way through the history of scholarship to its growing edge that further advances are to be expected. It was to them that this paper was originally addressed, in the hope that they would be encouraged to be more explicit as to the basic inferences for the structuring of research that can be drawn from their present insight into the state of things in the sources.

2. Both "the kerygma" and "the historical Jesus" turned out to be abstractions, when confronted with the realities of the church of New Testament times. One found, instead, a process of understanding and translating the kerygma; no instance of the kerygma, however carefully codified, was anything but another instance of that hermeneutical linguistic process. And one found, instead of instances in which the historical Jesus was directly a factor in the time of the church, as memorized sayings or un-

---

74. Cf. my essay "The Coptic Gnostic Library Today," *NTS* 14 (1968): 356–401, esp. sec. 3, "The Question of Non-Christian Gnosticism," pp. 372–80.

altered memories, rather a process of the growth, deletion, and shifting involved in the meaningful transmission of traditions. The "kerygmatizing" of "the historical Jesus" turned out on examination to be a series of conflicting influences on the transmission of traditions about Jesus, in terms of varying understandings of the kerygmatic meaning of Jesus. On the other hand, these traditions were seen to have "kerygmatic" implications of their own, so that it became increasingly difficult for the Pauline development to ignore them or to leave them unrevised in terms of understandings of the kerygma. In some instances the kerygmatic overtones involved in such traditions could have imposed themselves on the kerygma of Jesus' death and resurrection, so that the process of influences between "kerygma" and "historical Jesus" could have been mutual, a process of interaction. Indeed such an interaction seems to go back to the beginning, in that Jesus' word had kerygmatic relevance, and the Easter kerygma translated the Christology implicit in that word into the new situation created by Jesus' death. Thus the clear distinction, not to say antithetical relationship, characteristic of the traditional scholarly terms *kerygma* and *history,* can be recognized as actually derived from the pendulum swings in the last century of scholarship, as the historical Jesus replaced dogmatic Christology and then the kerygma replaced the historical Jesus, rather than being derived from the situation in the sources themselves, where a much more nuanced and complicated series of relationships calls for recognition.

3. The relation of heresy and orthodoxy in the primitive church becomes a topic in need of further investigation. The situation would seem to be neither that of a pristine purity, the tensions in which one can either dismiss as purely personal or remove from historical investigation by attributing them to Satan leading the faithful astray, nor that of a later day in which an unambiguous separation, at least in doctrine and eventually in organization, could be assumed. For the reading back of such clear distinctions into the beginnings on the part of subsequent orthodoxy is as unreal a procedure as Hollywood's or the Cold War's neat separation between "good guys" and "bad guys." We have seen Paul,

in facing one front, make use of conceptualizations analogous to those of the other front, and, on turning against the second front, using such as are reminiscent of the first front. There seems not yet to be a central body of orthodox doctrine distinguished from heretical doctrine to the right and to the left, but rather a common body of beliefs variously understood and translated or transmitted. In such a fluid situation one must ask not simply what was said, but rather which way what was said cut, what happened when the language was used, what was the directionality or flow. To this extent the terms *heresy* and *orthodoxy* are anachronistic. To be sure, such a recognition does not lead to the complete relativism suggested by the emphasis upon the variety of theolog*ies* in the New Testament. This common emphasis may simply be replacing the historical reality of recognizable continuity within primitive Christianity in order to mirror a modern pluralistic society with a denominationally organized Christianity, much as the prior assumption of one standard system of doctrine in the New Testament was an unhistorical reflection of a monolithic understanding of Christianity in the preecumenical age. One has been able to sense convergences in Paul's points, in spite of the different positions he assumed in differing situations; and one may suspect some underlying continuities between the differing "heresies" of 1 and 2 Corinthians, facilitating the efforts of the wandering "superapostles" opposed in 2 Corinthians to gain control not only of the party most congenial to them, but also of the "opposite" party that Paul had temporarily brought back into line by writing 1 Corinthians. And at the level of directionality, connections with other bodies of primitive Christian literature have been sensed, so that something like ongoing streams of orientation have been detected. These trajectories are the reality of historical process, and should not be overlooked in favor of a wooden lining up of occurrences of given conceptualizations or traditions, where indeed conflicting directionalities have been observed within the same conceptualization or tradition.

4. The dismantling and reassembling of the categories "kerygma" and "history" in terms of a hermeneutic of the kerygma and a history of the transmission of Jesus traditions involved by

implication both a restructuring of the subdivisions within New Testament scholarship, such as New Testament theology and early Christian history, and also a reassessment of the relations among the various theological disciplines, as biblical studies leads from its history-of-religions matrix, via the history of doctrine and church history, to contemporary theology, ethics, phenomenology of religion, various forms of practical theology, and ecumenical and intercultural objectives.

It has been difficult of late for some to find a theologically relevant place for historical research, e.g., the matters handled in New Testament introduction, now that the basic critical revision of the traditional picture has been carried through with such a high degree of success as to present much less of a challenge than was the case a generation or so ago. This is no doubt responsible for the quick generalization, the skimming of the cream, the harmonized unity of the Bible, that has made of "biblical theology" a discipline hardly more respectable academically than its predecessor, "English Bible."

The present paper has advocated the thesis that only the most penetrating analysis of the specific historical situation in which the source was written is able to make possible a penetration *within* the conceptualizations and traditions used *into* the point being scored, which is really what should be referred to as the theology of the text. Indeed von Dobschütz's call for "an individual hermeneutic for every New Testament writing," left unheeded over forty years ago,[75] may be the way in which the discipline of New Testament introduction could, in relation to the history of religions and a philosophical reconceptualization of its categories, be more relevantly integrated into the ongoing enterprise, thus restoring to responsible historical research the importance it deserves and attaining for critical New Testament theology the scholarly respectability it deserves.

75. Ernst von Dobschütz, *Vom Auslegen des Neuen Testaments,* 1927, p. 16.

3. *LOGOI SOPHON*
On the Gattung of Q

JAMES M. ROBINSON

This essay makes use of early suggestions by Rudolf Bultmann, in whose honor it was originally published, in order to initiate a systematic investigation of the literary genre to which "Q" belongs. The trajectory of this genre of "sayings of the sages" is traced from Jewish wisdom literature through Gnosticism, where the esoteric nature of such collections can lead to the supplementary designation of them as "secret sayings." The essay illustrates the extent to which the Coptic gnostic library from near Nag Hammadi facilitates the tracing of such trajectories, by filling in previously inaccessible stages in the development.

In his *History of the Synoptic Tradition* Rudolf Bultmann drew attention to the affinity between sayings of the Lord and wisdom literature. The *"logia* in the narrower sense" were designated "wisdom sayings." [1] A presentation of the basic forms found in wisdom literature, moving beyond Walter Baumgartner's investigation of the forms of wisdom sayings in *Sirach,* [2] introduced the analysis of this group of sayings of the Lord. Thus Jesus' *logia* were understood in analogy to Jewish *meshalim.*

Form criticism was concerned to move beyond the preceding generation's focus on literary units, and hence shifted attention to the smaller, oral units of tradition. This meant that the genre

An English draft of this paper was read at the meeting of the Western Section of the Society of Biblical Literature in Berkeley, California, February 15, 1964. The published form was composed in German and appeared in *Zeit und Geschichte: Dankesgabe an Rudolf Bultmann zum 80. Geburtstag,* edited by Erich Dinkler (Tübingen: J. C. B. Mohr [Paul Siebeck], 1964), pp. 77–96. The English translation presented here represents a considerable enlargement.
1. Rudolf Bultmann, *Die Geschichte der synoptischen Tradition,* 6th ed., 1964, p. 73 (ET: *The History of the Synoptic Tradition,* 1963, p. 69).
2. Walter Baumgartner, *ZAW* 34 (1914): 165–69.

or gattung[3] of the sayings collection was not as such investigated, although to be sure Bultmann did note in passing "that the book of *Sirach* is in a sense analogous to the collection and redaction of the discourse material in the synoptics."[4]

Bultmann used his recognition of a connection between sayings of the Lord and wisdom sayings to move in another direction. His original designation *"logia* in the narrower sense, wisdom sayings,"* corresponds in form rather well to the designations he uses for the other groups of sayings of the Lord ("prophetic and apocalyptic sayings"; "legal sayings and congregational rules"). Yet his actual title of the section treating the "wisdom sayings" reads *"Logia* (Jesus as Wisdom Teacher)."[5] This personal, rather than material, formulation was not itself discussed. Yet, in Matt. 23:34–39, among the "prophetic and apocalyptic sayings," one finds a significant analogy. For, as the parallel Luke 11:49 still attests, Q here quotes a Jewish saying spoken by personified Wisdom, Sophia. "For the subject of this reflection about history must be a transhistorical subject, namely Wisdom."[6] Bultmann concludes that this passage is documentation for the

---

3. Presupposed is the terminological distinction proposed by Hans Conzelmann (*EKL*, vol. 1, 1956, p. 1310) between *Formgeschichte*, dealing with the smallest (normally oral) units of tradition, and *Gattungsgeschichte*, devoted to the study of the subsequent stage of collection into larger (normally literary) compositions. Although this terminological distinction was not current at the time the classical form-critical works appeared, its use is not intended to imply a material divergence from those works. It is merely an attempt to render terminology more precise.

4. Bultmann, *Geschichte*, p. 104 (ET, p. 99). Not only the form-critical works of Bultmann and Dibelius, but especially Karl Ludwig Schmidt's essay "Die Stellung der Evangelien in der allgemeinen Literaturgeschichte," *EUCHARISTERION*, Gunkel festschrift, FRLANT, n.s. 19, 1923, 2:50–134, provide the beginnings of such a *Gattungsgeschichte*, although with only passing allusions to Q. On the gattung of *POxy* 1 (*Gospel of Thomas*) cf. already Johannes Weiss, *ThR* 1 (1898): 228.

5. Bultmann, *Geschichte*, p. 73 (ET, p. 69).

6. Ibid., p. 120 (ET, p. 114). Weiss, *ThR* 1:230–31, made a similar suggestion with regard to the "new *logia*": "The sayings are suitable only on the tongue of the Resurrected, who looks back in melancholic lament to his earthly pilgrimage and his entry into the world. . . . Perhaps the saying is taken from a source in which the identification of Jesus with *Sophia* had already taken place. Cf. Luke 7:35; 11:49; Matt. 23:34 ff." In view of the fact that the saying in question is *POxy* 1. 3 (*Gospel of Thomas*, Saying 28), one should not only note in terms of the history of research the point of departure provided to Bultmann by his teacher; one should also acknowledge the task posed by the discovery of the *Gospel of Thomas* to carry through the clarification of the relation between Q and the "new *logia*."

"myth of the divine Wisdom," which he considers to be parallel to the "myth of the Primal Man." [7]

This suggestion was followed up two years later in an essay on "The History-of-Religions Background of the Prologue to the Gospel of John." [8] Here an investigation of what has subsequently become familiar under the designation "gnostic redeemer myth" takes its point of departure precisely by drawing a connection between the saying in Q attributed to Wisdom and the book of *Sirach*. Hence it was the Gospel of John, rather than the synoptics, or Q with its close correlation to the sayings tradition, that provided Bultmann with what one might call a christological explication of the connection between sayings of the Lord and wisdom literature. Just as the further application of form criticism moved from the synoptics to kerygmatic confessions and hymns embedded in the letters, and as Bultmann moved from his *Jesus and the Word* to his *Theology of the New Testament*, just so in this case what was first seen in Q and came to expression in the concept "wisdom teacher" was not further pursued in the context of sayings of the Lord.

Such passing insights, which Bultmann has not himself followed up, are left for our generation to pick up and work through. Only when we honor such hints by treating them as topics for further research are we able to honor a scholar so much more absorbed in the issues than in himself as is Bultmann. Hence the question of the gattung of the gospels as whole literary units must, like the question of the historical Jesus, be posed anew. This essay, then, seeks to confirm, clarify, and carry further Bultmann's association of *logia* with *meshalim* under the concept of "wisdom teacher," by working out a name for the gattung of Q, "λόγοι σοφῶν," "sayings of the sages," or "words of the wise," [9] as a

---

7. Bultmann, *Geschichte*, 120–21 (ET: 114–15).
8. Rudolf Bultmann, "Der religionsgeschichtliche Hintergrund des Prologs zum Johannes-Evangelium," *EUCHARISTERION*, 2:3–26, esp. p. 6 (reprinted in the collection of his essays, *Exegetica*, 1967, pp. 10–35, esp. pp. 11–12). This first step in the history-of-religions investigation of the Gospel of John by Bultmann was carried further in the essay "Die Bedeutung der neuerschlossenen mandäischen und manichäischen Quellen für das Verständnis des Johannesevangeliums," *ZNW* 24 (1925): 100–46 (reprinted in *Exegetica*, pp. 55–104).
9. It is difficult to find a single suitable translation for λόγος and its plural λόγοι, for the term covers a wide spectrum of meanings. The English term

reflection in the sources themselves of the tendency constitutive of the gattung to which Q belongs. It does not carry through the further task of tracing structures of the genre through the Jewish, Christian, and gnostic literature cited; a more thorough investigation of Greek literature with regard to this gattung is a still further need.

Logia, Logoi, and Gospel in the Coptic Gnostic Library

The designation of sayings of the Lord as *logia* derives from the Papias fragments. The term occurs not only in the name of his treatise, "Interpretation of the Lord's *Logia*" (Eusebius *Hist. eccl.* 3. 39. 1). With regard to the Gospel of Mark, he speaks of Peter's "not making, as it were, a collection of the Lord's *logia*" (3. 39. 15). There is also his statement about Matthew that has been repeatedly, though never conclusively, related to Q: "So Matthew collected in the Hebrew language the *logia*, but each person interpreted them as he was able" (3. 39. 16).[10] The

---

word should come nearest in providing a comparable breadth. It not only designates an individual vocable, whose plural then designates a word-by-word sequence of vocables (cf. German *Wörter*); it can also designate a whole statement, in such expressions as "a word for today," or "a word to the wise is sufficient." This usage corresponds to the use of the term *word* to designate the self in responsible commitment, in such expressions as "to give one's word"; "to be as good as one's word"; "one's word is as good as one's bond." (Cf. the French *parôle* in distinction from *mot*, and the German plural *Worte*.) It is an aspect of the superficiality with which the role of language is often grasped today that this usage is recessive, expressing itself primarily in such traditional expressions. Hence it is sometimes preferable to translate the plural as "sayings," to prevent an unconscious literalistic identification with a plurality of vocables, even though the term *sayings* tends to lack the deeper, more authentic overtones present in λόγοι; sometimes it is preferable for a further reason to translate the singular as "saying," namely to make it clear that "word" is not a disembodied idea, but rather in its basic form is a linguistic reality. Since consistency in translation would in some instances produce an unnatural or inaccurate rendering, the reader's attention should be oriented to the one term in the original language (λόγοι, *logoi*, except where otherwise noted), translated "words" or "sayings."

10. An illustration of such translational variants with regard to the term here under consideration is provided by the Greek translation of the Syrian *Acts of Thomas*, a translation which is not very precise, especially with regard to Semitic formulae. Cf. my study "Die Hodajot-Formel in Gebet und Hymnus des Frühchristentums," *Apophoreta*, Haenchen festschrift, suppl. 30 of *ZNW*, 1964, pp. 194–235, esp. pp. 199–200, 233–34. Chap. 39 (Lipsius-Bonnet, 2. 2. 156. 12–15) speaks of "Christ's twin, the apostle of the Most High, and fellow-witness of the hidden *logos* of Christ, who received his hidden *logia*." This is probably an allusion to the incipit or opening words of the *Gospel of Thomas* (*POxy* 654), which uses *logoi*, of which *logia* in the *Acts of Thomas* is apparently a translational variant. Perhaps the presence of the term *logos* as a christological title in the same sentence led as a stylistic variant to the term *logia* to refer to Jesus' sayings. Cf. also the same variants in *Test. Ben.* 9. 1 and Justin *1 Apol.* 14. 5; *Dial.* 18. 1.

result has been that a less accentuated term in Papias, *logoi,* whose precise meaning is even more obscure, has not been adequately noted. This term is involved in such phrases as the following: "the preface of his [sc., Papias's] *logoi* [sayings?—Lake: treatises]" (Irenaeus, in Eusebius 3. 39. 2); "I investigated the *logoi* of the presbyters" (Papias, in Eusebius 3. 39. 4); "Papias affirms that he had received the *logoi* of the apostles from their followers" (Eusebius 3. 39. 7); "interpretations of the Lord's *logoi*" (by Aristion, mentioned by Papias according to Eusebius 3. 39. 14).

If it is difficult to clarify in terms of gattung the *logia* mentioned by Papias, it is even more difficult to relate to the history of a gattung these passing allusions to the *logoi* of Papias, the presbyters, the apostles, and the Lord.[11] Hence it is not too surprising that the first fragment of a sayings source discovered at Oxyrhynchus was published under the title *Jesus' Logia,*[12] and that the scholarly discussion was carried on in terms of the loan word *logia.*[13]

This usage was so firmly established that the publication in 1904 of *POxy, 654* (the opening of the *Gospel of Thomas*), whose first line spoke of *logoi,* had no influence at all on the terminology.[14] But now that the *Gospel of Thomas* has rendered

11. On the imprecision of the term *logia* in Papias in matters relevant to gattung, see, e.g., Karl L. Leimbach, *PRE,* vol. 14 (1904), p. 644; further, E. Bammel, *RGG,* 3d ed., vol. 5 (1961), p. 48: "[Papias's] book contained annotated reports about sayings and deeds of Jesus." Ernst Haenchen, *Der Weg Jesu,* 1966, p. 8, translates Papias's reference to Matthew as "stories of Jesus." The word *logos* is very common, has many meanings, and is often very imprecise. Quite apart from its christological meaning in the incipit of the Gospel of John and as a designation for a "volume" (Acts 1:1) or "treatise" (e.g., the title at the end of *De resurrectione* from the Jung Codex, "The Logos concerning Resurrection"), it can refer to deeds as well as sayings. Cf. Henry J. Cadbury, *The Beginnings of Christianity,* vol. 2 (1922), p. 509 on Luke 1:4: "Perhaps here περὶ λόγων is used for variety much as περὶ πραγμάτων in verse 1, but of course λόγοι are events reported rather than events fulfilled." Hence one cannot, e.g., distinguish clearly between Aristion's "narrations of the Lord's *logoi,*" and Luke 1:1: "Narration concerning the deeds fulfilled in our midst." The term ῥήματα can serve as a synonym for λόγοι in some cases, as in Jude 17 of the apostles' sayings. On the comparable Hebrew term in the titles of historical works in the Old Testament see below.

12. *LOGIA IESOU: Sayings of Our Lord from an Early Greek Papyrus,* ed. Bernard P. Grenfell and Arthur S. Hunt, 1897. The document is *POxy* 1.

13. See the bibliography by Joseph A. Fitzmyer, S.J., *ThSt* 20 (1959): 556–60.

14. *New Sayings of Jesus and Fragment of a Lost Gospel from Oxyrhynchus,* ed. Bernard P. Grenfell and Arthur S. Hunt, 1904. Although they conjectured

impossible the identification of the Oxyrhynchus fragments with the collection of *logia* referred to by Papias, one can note in the new wave of publications called forth by the discovery of the Coptic *Gospel of Thomas* a gradual adoption of the term *logoi* to designate the Oxyrhynchus fragments.[15]

This usage seems on first glance hardly applicable to the Coptic version of the Oxyrhynchus sayings, since the Coptic text bears at its end the title *"Peuaggelion pkata Thomas."* The Greek grammar reflected in this title suggests that the Greek work from which the Coptic is generally agreed to have been translated already bore this title.[16] Thus one has, so to speak, two titles for this work, one the free use of the designation *logoi* in the opening clause of the text (the "incipit"), and another at the end, written apart as a more formal title after the body of the text has ended, "The Gospel according to Thomas."

To be sure, one can conjecture that the title "gospel" was popular in a polemical or apologetic context as a flag under which various kinds of writings circulated at the time when the canonical gospels and hence the title "gospel" had gained wide acceptance in the orthodox church. Thus the incipit of a Nag Hammadi tractate that is not a gospel in terms of its gattung, *CG* I, 2,[17]

(p. 10) quite correctly "that the present text [sc., *POxy* 654] represents the beginning of a collection which later on included the original *'Logia,'* " they did not draw the terminological inference that one should refer to *POxy* 1 as *logoi* rather than *logia*.

15. Joseph A. Fitzmyer, S.J., "The Oxyrhynchus *Logoi* of Jesus and the Coptic Gospel according to Thomas," *ThSt* 20 (1959): 505–60; Gérard Garitte, "Les *'Logoi'* d'Oxyrhynque et l'apocryphe copte dit 'Evangile de Thomas,' " *Le Muséon* 73 (1960): 151–72. Fitzmyer points out (p. 513) that *logion* normally refers to a saying of a deity, and that "in A. Resch's collection of Agrapha [TU, 30, 1906] we find the word used only twice, and in each case it refers to the Old Testament."

16. See Hippolytus *Ref.* 5. 7. 20 (GCS, 26, ed. Paul Wendland, 1916, p. 83): "in the Gospel entitled 'according to Thomas.' " On the relation of this document to the *Gospel of Thomas* from Nag Hammadi see Puech in Hennecke-Schneemelcher, *Neutestamentliche Apokryphen,* vol. 1 (3d ed., 1959), pp. 203–4 (ET: *New Testament Apocrypha,* trans. R. McL. Wilson, vol. 1, 1963, pp. 283–84).

17. The numeration of the codices proposed by Martin Krause and Pahor Labib (*Die drei Versionen des Apokryphon des Johannes im koptischen Museum zu AltKairo,* Abhandlungen des Deutschen Archäologischen Instituts Kairo, Koptische Reihe, 1, 1962), is that of both the Coptic Museum and UNESCO, and has now prevailed over those used by Doresse and Puech. For a catalog of the Nag Hammadi codices including a conversion table for the divergent numerations see my article "The Coptic Gnostic Library Today," *NTS* 12 (1968): 356–

reads: "The gospel of truth is joy for those who have received grace from the father of truth," and Irenaeus (3. 11. 9) may have understood this as a polemical title: [18] "For indeed they go on to such great audacity as to entitle what they themselves only recently wrote as 'The Gospel of Truth,' although it agrees at no point with the gospels by the apostles, so that not even the gospel can be among them without blasphemy. For if what they publish as of truth is the gospel, but is dissimilar to those handed down to us by the apostles, persons who so wish can learn (as is shown from the writings themselves), that what was handed down from the apostles is not the gospel of truth."

One may also compare *CG, IV, 2,* commonly called the *Gospel of the Egyptians*.[19] After the text ends with "Amen" at 69. 5, and decorative marks confirm this break, the rest of the page is filled with two different titles, the scribe's spiritual and fleshly names, the Christian fish cryptogram, and again titles. Line 6 reads: "The Egyptian Gospel." Lines 7–8 give a further title: "The Holy Hidden Book Written by God. . . ." Lines 15–17 give a variation of this title: "The Holy God-Written Book of the Great Invisible Spirit." Again there occurs "Amen," and again lines to mark the end of the text. Then, in lines 18–20, occurs a final title: "The Holy Book of the Great Invisible Spirit. Amen." This source, which has "absolutely nothing to do with a gospel," [20] still received as one of the titles appended at the con-

---

401; "The Institute for Antiquity and Christianity," *NTS* 16 (1970): 188–90; and *Novum Testamentum* 12 (1970): 83–85. The designation of the Nag Hammadi material as *CG* (*Cairensis gnosticus*) is derived from Walter Till, *Die gnostischen Schriften des koptischen Papyrus Berolinensis 8502,* TU, 60, 1955, and is adopted by W. C. van Unnik, *Evangelien aus dem Nilsand,* 1960, p. 23.
18. Hans-Martin Schenke, *Die Herkunft des sogenannten Evangelium Veritatis,* 1959, questions whether the incipit is a title, since the work is a homily. Yet gnostics would have no reason to limit the designation "good news" to works conforming to a gattung defined by orthodox sensitivities. Johannes Munck, *"Evangelium Veritatis* and Greek Usage as to Book Titles," *ThSt* 17 (1963): 133–38, calls attention in this connection to Ernst Nachmanson, "Der griechische Buchtitel: Einige Beobachtungen," *Göteborgs Högskolas Årsskrift* 47, no. 19 (1941). Martin Krause, *Apokryphon des Johannes,* pp. 28–29 regards the incipit here (and elsewhere) as the title, and indeed as the original title, to which subsequently (though prior to the copying of the Nag Hammadi codices) briefer titles, set apart (and decorated) as subscriptions or superscriptions, were added.
19. Jean Doresse, " 'Le livre sacré du grand esprit invisible' ou 'L'Evangile des Egyptiens,' " *Journal asiatique* 254 (1966): 317–435.
20. Puech in Hennecke-Schneemelcher, *NT Apokryphen,* 1:270–71 (ET, 1:362).

clusion of the text the designation "The Egyptian Gospel." Though the incipit is fragmentary, it clearly begins, "The holy *book*. . . ." One may further note the possibility that the title of the *Gospel of Philip* was not originally present in Codex II, since it is not set off in the usual manner.[21]

In general, one may sense that the titles appended as subscriptions at the end of tractates may be logically secondary to the titles implicit in an incipit, even in cases when both were already present when the Nag Hammadi codices were written. Martin Krause concludes his investigation of the titles of codices I–VI with the following generalization: "In terms of literary historical method we must assume some such procedure as the following. After a period in which the tractates were transmitted without title, there came one in which the writings received a title that we refer to as the 'original' one and that is sometimes designated the 'introduction.' Still later this long title was shortened and was given the 'decorated' form present in the codices." [22] Puech, to whom Krause refers, assumes that the introduction to the *Gospel of Thomas* (including Saying 1) was secondarily added.[23] Since it is present in both the Coptic and the Greek texts available to us, it is a mere conjecture to assume that this particular collection of sayings existed in writing without its present introduction.

---

21. Johannes Leipoldt and Hans-Martin Schenke, *Koptisch-gnostische Schriften aus den Papyrus-Codices von Nag-Hamadi*, ThF, 20, 1960, p. 82: Leipoldt argues that when the Nag Hammadi copy was made the tractate had no title. In distinction from the style of Codex II elsewhere, the empty part of the last line of text is not filled out with decorations, but with the beginning of the title ("Gospel"). The rest of the title ("according to Philip") stands somewhat off-center on the next line, whereas usually the title is centered on two independent lines. In the case of this tractate, less space than usual separates it from the following tractate, which would suggest that the space originally left blank between tractates had been partially filled by adding the last part of the title. Yet Schenke remarks that the hand of the title seems to be the same as that of the rest of the tractate. To be sure, the hand of Codex II is so similar to that of Codex VIII that Krause ascribed both to the same scribe (*Apokryphon des Johannes*, p. 297), and then later ascribed each to a different scribe ("Zum koptischen Handschriftenfund bei Nag Hammadi," in *Mitteilungen des Deutschen Archäologischen Instituts*, Abteilung Kairo, 19 (1963), p. 111 n. 2.
22. Krause, *Apokryphon des Johannes*, p. 29 n. 6. Whether the tractates ever existed without their incipit may be questioned in specific instances; it would be more cautious to speak of sources of the present tractates having been enlarged by various supplements, at times including an incipit, where such redactional activity seems to have taken place.
23. Puech in Hennecke-Schneemelcher, *NT Apokryphen*, 1:205 (ET, 1:285).

One could more readily assume that generally such collections may have circulated without such an extensive introduction, even though they tend to be designated as "sayings" collections in quotation formulae and other allusions to them. In any case, the trend of Krause's analysis is to suggest that the introduction to the *Gospel of Thomas,* defining the work as a collection of sayings, is more primitive than the subscription, which designates it as a gospel.

In the *Gospel of Thomas* the term *gospel,* apart from the title appended at the end, is completely lacking (as it is also from Q). But the designation *logoi* is at home in the sayings tradition it uses, and was taken over from that tradition into the introduction.[24] Hence one may seek in the term *logoi* the original designation for the gattung. Not only does Saying 38, discussed below, speak of the desire "to hear these sayings which I say to you"; Saying 19 also speaks of Jesus' sayings: "Blessed is he who was, before he came into being. *If you* become my disciples and *hear my sayings,* these stones will minister to you. For you have five trees in Paradise which are unmoved in summer (or) in winter and their leaves do not fall. Whoever knows them *will not taste death.*" Here the idea that knowledge of the sayings brings salvation is secondarily expanded by use of independent conceptuali-

24. Cf. esp. Saying 13, which refers to "sayings" of Jesus that only Thomas knows and that the other disciples ask him to divulge, which he fears to do. The fourth line of *POxy* 654 reads: ἃν τῶν λόγων τούτ [. This documents the term *logoi* in the Greek *Vorlage* of Saying 1 of the *Gospel of Thomas:* "Whoever finds the explanation of these *sayings* will not taste death." The content of this saying suggests it belongs to the introduction of the collection. This is also suggested by the fact that it is introduced with the aorist tense, "he said." For in the Greek text Jesus' name and the present tense, used as a historical present, are so predominantly (though not exclusively) used in the quotation formula for Jesus' sayings that one may even wonder whether the subject of Saying 1 is not found in the nearer antecedent, Thomas. To be sure, in the *Testaments of the Twelve Patriarchs,* their discourses begin with the aorist, and the subject is not the immediately preceding sons or parents of the patriarch in question, but obviously the patriarch himself, who had been mentioned at the beginning. Yet this aorist does not stand out as an exception to a fairly fixed formula, as is the case with the *Gospel of Thomas.* Nonetheless the fact that elsewhere (e.g., John 8:52) variants upon this saying are attributed to Jesus, together with the overriding impression that we have to do with a collection of Jesus' sayings (cf. the incipit: ". . . Jesus spoke . . . Thomas wrote"), should indicate caution in ascribing the first saying in the author's intention to Thomas. It is inadvisable to infer from such a fragile possibility that a divergence from the standard numeration of sayings is called for, as does Johannes Leipoldt, *Das Evangelium nach Thomas,* TU, 101, 1967, p. 21.

zations.[25] The original concept, which is suggested at various points in the Gospel of John, is especially clear in John 8:52: "If any one keeps my *logos,* he will never taste death." It is this original concept which is apparently presupposed in Saying 1, which serves as the conclusion to the introduction of the *Gospel of Thomas:* "Whoever finds the explanation of these sayings will not taste death." [26]

If the term *logoi* is at home in the sayings tradition, and a saying referring to Jesus' *logoi* was taken up into the introduction of the *Gospel of Thomas,* it would seem to be the logical outcome of this development that the term would be taken up into the incipit itself: "These are the secret sayings. . . ."

This is not intended to suggest that the designation was taken up into an incipit first by the *Gospel of Thomas,* and only then elevated to the designation for a gattung.[27] The connection between individual sayings referring to themselves as *logoi* and the use of this term to designate collections of sayings no doubt has a longer history. Hence we turn further afield to trace the broader context of this development.

CG, II, 7, usually referred to by the title at the end (145. 17–19), "The Book of Thomas the Contender, which he writes

25. Paul E. Kahle, *Bald'izah: Coptic Texts from Deir el Bald'izah in Upper Egypt,* 1954, 1:476. Cf. Walter Ewing Crum, *JTS* 44 (1943): 176–79, "Lo, I have explained . . . unto thee, O Johannes, concerning Adam and Paradise . . . and the Five Trees, in an intelligible allegory." Cf. also Carl Schmidt and Walter Till, *Koptisch-gnostische Schriften,* vol. 1, CGS, 3d ed., 1959, "Bäume" in the index.
26. The Gospel of John shows that the matter of the right relation to Jesus' *logoi,* which the first half of Saying 1 puts hermeneutically, can be formulated in various ways. In addition to "believing," the Fourth Gospel speaks of "hearing" the *logos* (5:24; 8:43; 14:24) or *logoi* (7:40; cf. 8:47), as well as of "becoming disciples" (8:32). The last half of Saying 1 uses a formula that occurs elsewhere, e.g., at the end of Saying 18 just before the allusion to Jesus' sayings in Saying 19. A variant to John 8:52 is found in John 8:51: "If any one keeps my *logos,* he will never see death."
27. To be sure, some particular affinity of *Thomas* to sayings of the Lord may be suggested in the scene in Saying 13, which modifies in Thomas's favor the scene we know as "Peter's confession." "And he [sc., Jesus] took him [sc., Thomas], withdrew, and spoke three sayings to him." Hippolytus takes this to refer to three vocables rather than to three sayings (*Ref.* 5. 8. 4, ed. Wendland, p. 89, cited in Walther Völker, *Quellen zur Geschichte der christlichen Gnosis,* Sammlung ausgewählter Kirchen- und dogmengeschichtlichen Quellenschriften, n.s. 5, 1932, p. 17; ET: Robert M. Grant, *Gnosticism,* 1961, p. 107): "These are the three supremely important *logoi,* Kaulakau, Saulasau, Zeesar: Kaulakau is of Adam above; Saulasau, of the mortal below; Zeesar, of the Jordan which flows upward."

to the perfect ones," has as its incipit: "These are the secret sayings that the Savior spoke to Judas Thomas, which I wrote, I myself, Mathaias, as I walked, listening to them speaking with each other." [28] This provides a further attestation for the designation "secret sayings," for the Coptic of this term is identical with the Coptic text of the *Gospel of Thomas*.[29] One would have an instance of this incipit's functioning as a title, if *Thomas the Contender* could be identified with the Basilidean source ascribed to Matthias by Hippolytus *Ref.* 7. 20. 1: [30] "So Basilides and

28. The word order of the incipit varies slightly, in that *Thomas the Contender* begins, "The secret sayings are these," whereas the *Gospel of Thomas* begins, "These are the secret sayings." *POxy* 654 (Fitzmyer) provides the Greek *Vorlage* for the incipit of the *Gospel of Thomas:* οὗτοι οἱ λόγοι οἱ [ἀπόκρυφοι οὓς ἐλά]λησεν Ἰη(σοῦ)ς ὁ ζῶν κ[αὶ ἔγραψεν Ἰούδας ὁ] καὶ θωμᾶ⟨ς⟩ καὶ εἶπεν. The closest parallel is Luke 24:44, "These are the words that I spoke to you, while I was still with you." Other parallels are less oriented to collections of sayings. Fitzmyer ("The Oxyrhynchus *Logoi* of Jesus," p. 513) also compares *Bar.* 1:1, "These are the words of the book that Baruch wrote." Much the same incipit is used in a martyrdom of James, in which is imbedded a discourse of the resurrected Christ, *CG*, V, *4*, the *(Second) Apocalypse of James*. The incipit reads: "This is the word that James the Just spoke in Jerusalem, that Marim one of the priests wrote down. He told it to Theuda, the father of this just man, since he was a relative of his, saying:. . . ." The reconstructed end of the text reads: "[His] word[s were written?] then [in a] *logos*." (*Koptisch-gnostische Apokalypsen aus Codex V von Nag Hammadi im Koptischen Museum zu Alt-Kairo*, ed. Alexander Böhlig and Pahor Labib, a special volume of the Wissenschaftliche Zeitschrift der Martin-Luther-Universität Halle-Wittenberg, 1963, pp. 56–85.) One may compare Deut. 1:1: "These are the words that Moses spoke to all Israel beyond the Jordan." The incipit of Deuteronomy does not seem to have been sufficiently noticed to account for the frequency of this incipit; for it is not used in a Qumran document so dependent on Deuteronomy that J. T. Milik suggested one might call it "Little Deuteronomy" (*Discoveries in the Judean Desert*, vol. 1, 1955, p. 92). According to Milik's reconstruction (pp. 91–97), it refers several times to "words": "the words of the law" (1. 4); "these words from his mouth" (2. 6); "all the words of the law" (2. 9); "all these words of the covenant" (3. 3). Yet the incipit reads: "And God [addressed] Moses . . . saying:. . . ." The modern title finally given the document, "Words of Moses" ("Dires de Moise," abbreviated *1QDM*), does not occur in the document itself.
29. Cf. Puech in Hennecke-Schneemelcher, *NT Apokryphen*, 1:223 (ET, 1:307).
30. This identification advocated by Jean Doresse, *Les livres secrets des gnostiques d'Egypte: Introduction aux écrits gnostiques coptes découverts à Khénoboskion*, 1958, p. 244 (ET: *The Secret Books of the Egyptian Gnostics: An Introduction to the Gnostic Coptic Manuscripts Discovered at Chenoboskion*, trans. Philip Mairet, 1966, p. 226) is given up by Puech in Hennecke-Schneemelcher, *NT Apokryphen*, 1:227 (ET, 1:313), since, contrary to Doresse, he reads "Matthew" rather than "Matthias" in the incipit of *CG*, II, 7. The identification is held to be "very probable" by Siegfried Schulz, *ThR* n.s. 26 (1960): 247–48. The Coptic itself is, in spite of Puech's statement, indecisive, since it reads *Mathaias*, i.e., neither exactly Matthew (*Maththaios*) nor Matthias (*Maththias*), Puech, "Les nouveaux écrits gnostiques découverts en Haute-Egypte," in *Coptic Studies in Honor of Walter Ewing Crum*, 1950, p. 120, and in Hennecke-Schneemelcher, *NT Apokryphen*, 1:224–28 (ET, 1:308–13), discusses the relation to the "gospel" and "traditions" of Matthias mentioned in patristic sources.

Isidore, the actual son and disciple of Basilides, say Matthias told them secret *logoi* that he heard from the Savior as he was privately taught" (see also 7. 20. 5: "one of Matthias' secret *logoi*"). In any case the title at the end, naming Thomas the Contender as the scribe, is put in question by the incipit, ". . . which I have written, I, Mathaias." For this reason the title at the end is to be regarded as secondary, and hence hardly an expression of the gattung under whose influence the document was originally composed.

The fact that the incipit of *Thomas the Contender* is almost identical in form with that of the *Gospel of Thomas* does not mean that *Thomas the Contender* is necessarily a further instance of the same gattung. Rather, it is more nearly in transition to the gattung of dialogues of the resurrected Christ with his disciples. This gattung of course makes use of sayings ascribed to Jesus, and can refer to "sayings," although such a reference would be less constitutive of this revelation gattung [31] than it is of a sayings

31. The *Apocryphon of John, CG,* II, *1;* III, *1;* IV, *1; BG,* 8501. *2,* begins in its longer recension (II, 1. 1–4) with the following reconstructed text: "The teaching [and the words of the Savior. And he revealed these mysteries] that are hidden in a silence, [namely, Jesus Christ did, and] he taught them to John [who] hearkened." After a brief narrative framework there follows a dialogue that rapidly turns into a discourse, which concludes (31. 28–31): "But I have told you all things, in order that you record them and given them to your fellow spirits in secret. For this is the mystery of the race that is not shaken." The concluding framework states (31. 32–34; 32. 4–5): "And the Savior gave him these [mysteries], that he write them and safely leave them behind. . . . And he went to his fellow disciples and he proclaimed to them the [words] that the Savior had said to him." The title following the end of the text is "Apocryphon of John." Thus it is not certain that to describe itself this text uses the term *words,* which has been conjectured or added by the editors. But the conclusion of the shorter recension (III, 40. 6–9) does use the term: "[He] went to his fellow disciples [and] began to speak with them [of the] words that the Savior had said to [him]." Cf. *BG,* 76. 18—77. 5: "And he came to his fellow disciples and began to say to them what had been said to him by the Savior." In any case the term *secret sayings* from the *Gospel of Thomas* has been replaced in the *Apocryphon of John* to a large extent by revelation terminology such as *mystery* and *what is secret (apocryphon).* For this text see Martin Krause and Pahor Labib, *Die drei Versionen des Apokryphon des Johannes im Koptischen Museum zu Alt-Kairo,* ADAIK, Koptische Reihe, 1, 1962; and Walter C. Till, *Die gnostischen Schriften des koptischen Papyrus Berolinensis 8502,* TU, 60, 1955, of which there is a revised reprint in W. C. van Unnik, *Evangelien aus dem Nilsand,* 1960, pp. 185–213. Another gnostic "apocalypse" also entitled "words" can readily escape notice, due to an oversight on the part of Jean Doresse. He successfully deciphered the cryptogram at the end of *CG,* VIII, *1* (132. 7–9), and identified it with the allusion in Porphyry to documents used by Plotinus's opponents, who cite "apocalypses of Zoroaster, of Zostrianos, of Nicotheos, of Allogenes, of Messos, and of other such ones." " 'Les Apocalypses de Zoroastre, de Zostrien, de Nicothée, . . .' (Porphrye, Vie de Plotin, 16)," in *Coptic Studies*

collection. The allusion to "words" in the incipit of *Thomas the Contender,* if not simply coincidental or indicative of dependence on the *Gospel of Thomas,* may be due to the long section at the end of the document, where the dialogue with Thomas gives way to something more like a sayings collection, consisting of a chain of woes (cf. Matt. 23) and beatitudes, and other material similar in form and content to the Sermon on the Mount. It is perhaps indicative of some such original relation between the incipit and this concluding section of the document that the latter is introduced by a final question of Thomas concerning "these words" that Jesus speaks. Since *Thomas the Contender* seems to be a secondary compilation of traditions or sources, such a conjecture is possible; but clarity must await a thorough investigation of this unpublished document.[32]

---

in Honor of Walter Ewing Crum, 1950, pp. 255–63. He argues on the basis of the cryptogram that this usual translation of Porphyry is inaccurate, in that the first apocalypse was entitled "Apocalypse of Zoroaster and Zostrianos." For he deciphers the cryptogram to read: "Discourse of Truth of Zostrianos, God of Truth; Discourse of Zoroaster." Puech pointed out that since Porphyry and Amelius divided the task of criticizing the gnostic writings, the one addressing himself to the work of Zostrianos, the other to that of Zoroaster, there must be two distinct works, not one, as Doresse had argued. "Les Nouveaux écrits gnostiques découverts en Haute-Egypte (Premier inventaire et essai d'identification)," in the same Crum festschrift, pp. 91–154, esp. pp. 107–8, 131 ff. However, even Puech failed to note that Doresse inaccurately deciphered the cryptogram; indeed, he himself repeats Doresse's oversight. For the term *logos,* which Doresse translates "discourse," is both times in the plural. The title is then *"Logoi* of Truth of Zostrianos; God of Truth; *Logoi* of Zoroastros." Martin Krause, "Der koptische Handschriftenfund bei Nag Hammadi: Umfang und Inhalt," in *Mitteilungen des Deutschen Archäologischen Instituts,* Abteilung Kairo, 18 (1962), pp. 121–32, esp. 128, holds that this tractate begins at VIII, 1. 1, rather than somewhere later (as Doresse and Puech assume). In that case the fragmentary incipit provides some confirmation of this title. For 1. 1 includes the expression "these words," 1. 2 the personal pronoun in the first person singular, and 1. 3 the name "Zos[trianos]." This would suggest an incipit in which Zostrianos refers to himself as related to the *logoi,* much as in the case of *Thomas the Contender* discussed above. Whether Zoroaster is also mentioned in the incipit is unclear because of its fragmentary nature; and the role of "God of truth," which is not as obviously in apposition to "Zostrianos" in the cryptogram as Doresse would lead one to assume, remains unclear. The document seems primarily related to Zostrianos, since in the line just prior to the cryptogram (132. 6), his name appears alone, centered on the line and ornamented, i.e., treated as a title.

32. Martin Krause, "Der Stand der Veröffentlichung der Nag Hammadi Texte," in *Le origini dello Gnosticismo,* Studies in the History of Religions, 12, suppls. to *Numen,* 1967, p. 76, lists *Thomas the Contender* among those tractates that have been secondarily reworked to make them Christian. He does so on the basis of contradictions within the text, for which he refers to his forthcoming publication of the document, *Gnostische und hermetische Schriften aus Codex II und VI,* ADAIK, Koptische Reihe, 2.

In its present form *Thomas the Contender* attests the triumph within Gnosticism of the gattung of dialogues of the resurrected Christ with his disciples over the gattung of sayings collections. This victory was inevitable, as the oral tradition died out and Gnosticism advanced in its speculation increasingly beyond the range of interests that a traditional sayings collection could readily serve.

Pistis Sophia represents in various ways the end point of the development. Here we find the final definition of who the scribes of the words of the Lord were: Philip, Thomas, and Matthew. This is less a reflection of the situation in *Pistis Sophia,* where only Philip functions as scribe, than a retrospective résumé of the whole literature, for which *CG,* II has provided partial documentation.[33] Furthermore, *Pistis Sophia* does not hesitate to put side by side traditional sayings and their interpretive expansion, so that one can see the dissolution process taking place. The dialogue consists basically in a discourse by the Lord, followed periodically by its "resolution" or "analysis" by a disciple (or one of the women). Just at this point, between the discourse and its resolution, a characteristic formula occurs—"But it came to pass as Jesus stopped speaking these words to his disciples"—whereupon a disciple volunteers a "resolution of the words." Thus we are carried step by step through the final stage in the procedure that one can only sense to have been proposed by the introduction

33. *CG,* II provides among the "apostolic" works (in addition to the *Apocryphon of John*) sayings of the Lord written by Thomas, Philip, and Mathaias: *CG,* II, 2, "These are the secret sayings that Jesus the living spoke and Didymus Judas Thomas wrote," i.e., "The Gospel according to Thomas"; *CG,* II, 3, "The Gospel according to Philip," a gnostic tractate partially presented as a dialogue (cf. R. McL. Wilson, *The Gospel of Philip,* 1962, pp. 7–11); *CG* II, 7: "These are the secret sayings that the Savior spoke to Judas Thomas which I wrote, I myself, Mathaias," i.e., "The Book of Thomas the Contender." Puech, in the Crum festschrift, pp. 117–18 refers to Deut. 19:15 and Matt. 18:16. Cf. also Doresse, *Livres secrets,* p. 239 (ET, p. 221). Helmut Koester, *"GNOMAI DIAPHOROI,"* chap. 4 in this volume, points out that the double ascription of *CG,* II, 7 to Matthew (?) and Judas Thomas may reflect the association of these two with parallel strands of the sayings tradition, in western and eastern Syria respectively. It is perhaps significant that when the *Letter of Eugnostos the Blessed* (*CG,* III, 3; V, 1) is Christianized as the *Sophia of Jesus Christ* (*BG,* 8502. 3; *CG,* III, 4), the dialogue form superimposed on the original work names only three disciples who (in addition to Mary) pose questions: Matthew (*BG,* 82, 17–83. 4, 93. 12–15), Thomas (87. 8–11, 106. 10–13), and Philip (86. 13–16). Cf. Martin Krause, "Das literarische Verhältnis des Eugnostosbriefes zur Sophia Jesu Christi: Zur Auseinandersetzung der Gnosis mit dem Christentum," in *Mullus,* Klauser festschrift, Jahrbuch für Antike und Christentum, suppl. 1, 1964, p. 218 n. 36.

to the *Gospel of Thomas.* In the *Gospel of Thomas* the "secret sayings" of Jesus that the gnostic is to "interpret" have in some instances already received a gnosticizing interpretive reformulation, which is then carried a step further when the gnosticized saying is again interpreted for a still deeper meaning. Yet the saying and its interpretation are not kept distinct, side by side, as in *Pistis Sophia,* but rather are presented in fusion with each other, as a single statement. In *Pistis Sophia,* the speech of Jesus that the disciple proceeds to resolve is already gnosticized; yet the side-by-side presentation in *Pistis Sophia* of two advanced stages in the process illustrates what was less visibly happening in the earlier stages as well. Thus the introduction to the *Gospel of Thomas* points to the outcome in *Pistis Sophia,* which, in the formula it uses and in the elaboration it presents, is only bringing to unmistakable clarity what one can already sense in the *Gospel of Thomas.*

We thus arrive in *Pistis Sophia* at the point in the trajectory of the sayings collection where it is absorbed into and finally replaced by the gattung which had no doubt all along been most typical of Christian Gnosticism, namely the dialogue of the resurrected Christ with his disciples, a gattung whose trajectory has most recently been traced by Kurt Rudolph.[34]

Primitive Christian Collections of Jesus' Sayings

This development ending in Gnosticism also had its prehistory going back into the primitive church. The expansion of the "Two Ways" in the *Didache* over and above the form attested in the *Epistle of Barnabas* is partially under this influence. In distinction to *Barn.* 19. 1a, the introduction to the "way of life" in *Did.* 1. 2

34. Kurt Rudolph, "Der gnostische 'Dialog' als literarisches Genus," in *Probleme der koptischen Literatur,* Wissenschaftliche Beiträge 1968/1 (K 2), Martin-Luther-Universität Halle-Wittenberg. Cf. Hennecke-Schneemelcher, *NTApokryphen,* vol. 1, esp. sec. 6, "Conversations between Jesus and his Disciples after the Resurrection," pp. 125–57 (ET, pp. 188–230). Cf. for the conflation of these gattungen with that of the testament the title of a Syriac work of apocalyptic contents, retranslated into Greek by de Lagarde: "First Book of Clement called Testament of our Lord Jesus Christ. The sayings that, after he rose from the dead, he spoke to his holy apostles." Adolf Harnack, *ThLZ* 9 (1884): 340, refers to it, citing de Lagarde, *Reliquiae iuris ecclesiastici antiquissimae,* 1856, pp. 80–89. Cf. William Wrede, *Das Messiasgeheimnis in den Evangelien* (1901), 3d ed. 1963, pp. 246–51.

consists of the saying of the Lord concerning the greatest commandment (Matt. 22:37–39). Then, in distinction to *Barn.* 19. 1b, the further expansion in *Did.* 1. 3 is introduced with the phrase, "Now these sayings' teaching is as follows," [35] followed by a series of sayings of the Lord that are absent from *Barn.* 19. Thus the given form of the "Two Ways" is led in the direction that has already become visible in the gnostic dialogues, where such a formula connected sayings of the Lord with their exposition in the form of expanded material.[36] To be sure, such a comparison also draws attention to the *Didache's* more conservative relation to the tradition in presenting the interpreting sayings, which may have been taken over from the Gospel of Matthew.[37] The other section of the "Two Ways" that has no parallel in *Barnabas* is characterized by a form of address absent from *Barn.* 18–20, "my son" (*Did.* 3. 1, 3, 4, 5, 6; 4. 1; the plural in 5. 2), which however is common in wisdom literature.[38] There emerges in this context a piety that is reminiscent of Papias, in its exhortation to be "always revering the *logoi* you have heard" (3. 8; cf. *Barn.* 19. 4) and its desire to be with "the saints, to find rest in their *logoi*" (4. 2).

From here one can move to the New Testament book most akin to the *Didache,* the Gospel of Matthew. It is especially in

35. On Qumran's similar hermeneutical formula "the interpretation of the saying is that [or: about]", from which the *"pesharim"* receive their name (e.g., 1QpHab, familiarly known as the Habakkuk Commentary; 4QpIsa, *JBL* 77 (1958): 215–19) cf. already Jean Paul Audet, *La Didaché: Instructions des Apôtres,* Etudes bibliques, 1958, pp. 261 f.

36. Cf. also Mark 10:24: "And the disciples were amazed at his sayings," whereupon the preceding saying is repeated, but enlarged by means of a comparison, in such a way as to serve as an interpretation of the original formulation. This repetition of the preceding saying is absent from Matthew and Luke. Cf. also Luke 9:44–50, discussed below.

37. See Bentley Layton, "The Sources, Date, and Transmission of *Didache* 1. 3b—2. 1," *HTR* 61 (1968): 343–83.

38. Bultmann, *EUCHARISTERION,* 2:11 n. 3 (*Exegetica,* p. 19 n. 17), appeals to Prov. 8:32 ("son") and *Sir.* 4. 11 ("wisdom exalted her sons"), to speak of a "form of address current in catechetical terminology." As roughly synonymous forms of address one finds, in addition to υἱέ, also παιδίον (e.g., *Tob.* 4. 12) and τέκνον (Prov. 31:2; *Sir.* 2. 1; 3. 12, 17; 4. 1; 6. 18, 23, 32; 10. 28; 11. 10; 14. 11; 16. 24; 18. 15; 21. 1; 31. 22; 37. 27; 38. 9, 16; 40. 28) or the plural τέκνα (*Sir.* 3. 1; 23. 7; 41. 14). Esp. significant is *Sir.* 31. 22, "listen to me, [my] son, and do not scorn me, and in the end you will [approve] my *logoi*."

Matthew among the gospels that the term *logoi* seems related to collections of sayings and thus to point toward *logoi* as a designation for the gattung of such collections.[39] A peculiarity of Matthew is his composition of five discourses, which are actually collections of sayings, and each of which ends with almost the same formula. This formula designates these collections as *logoi*. Even though in one case the commissioning of the twelve introduces into the formula the variant "commissioning" (11:1), and in the collection of parables the variant "parables" is used (13:53), we still find in the other instances (7:28; 19:1; 26:1), representing the basic form of the formula, the term *logoi:* "and it came to pass when Jesus completed [26:1: all] these *logoi*."

This trend, though clearest in Matthew, leaves some traces in the other gospels as well. One may compare Luke 9:28: "And it came to pass after these *logoi*," a clause added at the conclusion of a small Marcan collection which itself contained an allusion to Jesus' *logoi* (Luke 9:26; Mark 8:38). This sensitivity on Luke's part toward recognizing small collections of *logoi* in his gospel is to be seen in the broader context of his (and Matthew's) policy of locating the gattung of the sayings collection within the public ministry, by imbedding Q in the Marcan framework.

A rather similar trend can perhaps be sensed in the way Luke uses quotation formulae referring to Jesus' *logoi*. Such formulae occur only after the resurrection. Yet the passages in question betray a desire on Luke's part to refer sayings of Jesus current after Easter back to the public ministry as their original location. To be sure, in Acts 20:35 it is unclear whether a saying of the earthly Jesus or a saying of the resurrected Lord is intended; the saying is absent from Luke's Gospel. But the reference in Acts 11:16, which points back to Acts 1:5, does not go back only to the

---

39. Indicative of Matthew's interest in *logoi* is also 10:14, where the term *logoi* has been introduced redactionally into Mark 6:11, ". . . nor hear you," to produce "nor hear your sayings." To be sure, Matthew reveals traces of a trend to designate such sayings collections as "gospel," the same conflation of terminology characteristic of the title of the *Gospel of Thomas.* For in Matt. 4:23 and 9:35 Matthew inserts into summaries derived largely from Mark, but used by Matthew to introduce the Sermon on the Mount and the Mission of the Twelve, the term *gospel*. Cf. Willi Marxsen, *Der Evangelist Markus: Studien zur Redaktionsgeschichte des Evangeliums* (1956), 2d ed. 1959, p. 81 (ET: *Mark the Evangelist,* 1969, p. 123). This terminology is analogous to his compositional procedure of imbedding the sayings collection Q in the Marcan Gospel outline.

Resurrected, for Acts 1:4 refers it further back, to the public ministry. Luke 24:44 not only uses a quotation formula like the incipit of the *Gospel of Thomas,* suggesting that he was aware of collections of the resurrected Lord's sayings; for by means of its careful formulation Luke 24:44 makes it clear that these are not new sayings but rather reminiscences of sayings from the public ministry: "These are my *logoi* that I spoke to you while I was still with you." Gnostic texts, such as the *Letter of Peter to Philip* (*CG,* VIII, *2*), make similar references to the effect that Jesus' (gnostic) teaching is the same as what he had previously taught. In both cases there is an apologetic concern to protect the teaching from the suspicion that it is not based on the authority of Jesus. If for the gnostics the effect was a defense of their gattung of resurrection discourses, the effect in Luke's case was to replace it with the biography of the earthly Jesus.

The empty tomb story with which Luke 24 begins does not have the Resurrected appear at all. Yet he is represented by "two men" (*angeli interpretes*), whose function is to announce the resurrection and to quote from the public ministry the standard prediction of the passion. The quotation formula (24:6) is almost identical with 24:44: "Remember how he spoke to you while he was still in Galilee." Following the quotation is the affirmation (24:8): "And they remembered his words" (with *rhemata* as a stylistic variant for *logoi*). Thus the resurrection message becomes the same as that of the public ministry. At 9:44 Luke begins the second prediction of the passion with the clause: "Let these *logoi* sink into your ears," a clause which seems to function as a superscription for a small sayings collection he composes out of originally disparate dialogues. He frees the subsequent Marcan material from its changes in scene (Mark 9:33–35) and thus molds it into a continuous dialogue as an interpretation of the prediction. Thus the prediction becomes a "secret saying" to be interpreted. This is suggested both by the exhortation to harken (see below), and by the fact that Luke adds "secret . . . saying" to the Marcan *Vorlage.* The resolution of the secret saying is a discussion, which is in effect the Lucan preparation for the way of the cross that begins at 9:51. Wrede argued [40] that Luke 24:24–25, 44 ff.

40. Wrede, *Messiasgeheimnis,* pp. 164 ff.

reflects the pattern of the Marcan messianic secret, to the effect that the secrecy of the so-called public ministry would be replaced by public or open or decoded proclamation after Easter. But if this pattern meant for Gnosticism a way to attain higher authority for their teachings as revelations of the resurrected Christ, it meant for Luke only an occasion to validate the teachings of the earthly ministry of Jesus.

Although Luke is at this point going beyond Mark, the latter seems himself to have proceeded to a similar composition leading up to the third prediction of the passion. The pericope 10:17–22 concludes with the note that the rich man was quite upset by Jesus' *logos* on giving his wealth to the poor. Mark adds another saying about how hard entrance into the kingdom is. Thereupon the disciples are dumbfounded at his *logoi* (10:24). This observation is followed by a repetition of much the same saying, which is then amplified, each time stimulated by further wonder on the part of the disciples. Mark 7:14 ff. provides a further instance of such a saying (called in 7:17 a "parable," i.e., "riddle") that mystifies and hence has to be repeated with accompanying commentary.

The collection of parables and sayings in Mark 4:1–34 also reflects the hermeneutical problem of how the material in such a collection is to be understood correctly. The first parable is followed by the thematic statement of its mystifying nature, which is expressed in the language of Isa. 6:9 about looking but not seeing and listening but not understanding. This Old Testament text, quoted in Mark 4:12, is in substance integrated into the whole collection of Mark 4, both as the burden of what the parable of the sower means (note the contrast between inadequate hearing, 4:15, 16, 18, and "hearing and receiving," 4:20), and in connection with other exhortations to hearken. Indeed, the collection begins, in a way reminiscent of the first saying of the *Gospel of Thomas,* with Jesus' exhortation, "Hearken!" Mark 4:24 exhorts to "see to what you hear." This apparently echoes the Old Testament language about seeing and understanding.

There are other instances of Marcan conflation of Isa. 6:9 with exhortations to hearken. One instance is especially similar to Mark 4. Mark 7:14 introduces a difficult saying with the exhortation:

"Hear me, all of you, and understand." In 7:17 this saying is called a "parable" or "riddle," which the following sayings are intended to clarify. Thus the structure is the same as in chap. 4, and as in other instances of a secret saying to be interpreted through further sayings, such as in the *Didache, Pistis Sophia, pesharim,* Luke 9:44 ff., etc.

Mark 8:18 makes use of the same Old Testament passage, but varies the Old Testament language: ". . . and having ears do you not hear?" (Cf. Luke 9:44, "let these *logoi* sink into your ears.") This variation of Isa. 6:9 in Mark 8:18 suggests that the Old Testament passage has been associated with the saying: "He who has ears to hear, let him hear." This latter saying follows immediately upon the parable of the sower in 4:9 as a transition to the hermeneutical discussion in which Isa. 6:9 is quoted at 4:12; and it immediately precedes (in 4:23) the exhortation to "see to what you hear" (4:24). There it follows upon the statement that what is hidden will be revealed (4:22), which in this context may be meant hermeneutically, in analogy to 4:11, 33–34.

This same saying about having ears to hear is appended, with only minor variations, to difficult sayings in Matt. 11:15 and Luke 14:35, and to an interpretation of a parable in Matt. 13:43. It is a floating saying that attaches itself readily to other sayings as a hermeneutical warning. In the manuscript tradition it is attached frequently, especially to parables, e.g., to Matt. 25:29–30; Mark 7:16; Luke 12:21; 13:9; 21:4. And it is used regularly toward the conclusion of each message from the Lord in the seven letters of Revelation (2.7, 11, 17, 29; 3:6, 13, 22), and at random in the *Gospel of Thomas* (Sayings 8, 21, 24, 63, 65, 96). When the *Letter of the Blessed Eugnostos* (*CG,* III, *3;* V, *1*) was Christianized into the form of a dialogue between Jesus and his disciples under the title *Sophia of Jesus Christ* (*CG,* III, 4; *BG,* 8502. 3; *POxy,* 1081), one of the Christianizing insertions is this saying (*BG,* 89. 4–6; 90. 13–15; 100. 10–12; 107. 13—108. 1; *POxy,* 1081. 6–8, 35–36).[41] In Mark 4 the saying's connec-

---

41. Martin Krause, "Das literarische Verhältnis des Eugnostosbriefes zur Sophia Jesu Christi: Zur Auseinandersetzung der Gnosis mit dem Christentum," in *Mullus,* Klauser festschrift, Jahrbuch für Antike und Christentum, suppl. 1, 1914, p. 219. Cf. *The Oxyrhynchus Papyri Part VIII,* ed. Arthur S. Hunt, 1911, pp. 16–19.

tion with the other material about hearkening reveals its herme-neutical relevance in a collection of obscure sayings, and its presence in other such collections tends to confirm the definition of Mark 4:1–34 as such a collection.

In other respects Mark 4:1–34 betrays the traits of a sayings collection. It uses a rather set quotation formula (reminiscent of the regular use in the *Gospel of Thomas* of the historical present, "Jesus said"), with only minor irregularities. The basic form is in the imperfect tense, "and he said" (4. 9, 26, 30), to which can be added "to them" (4. 2, 11, 21, 24; cf. 4. 34), or in the historical present "he said to them" (4. 13).[42] One may com-pare Rev. 2–3, "thus says" (2. 1, 8, 12, 18; 3. 1, 7, 14); *Pirke Aboth,* "[Shammai] says," or "he used to say," (cf. 6. 7–8 "and it says" in a sequence of scriptural passages); Lucian, Demonax, "he said," [43] placed postpositively within the quotation itself. And the concept, already encountered in *Pistis Sophia* (see also Deut. 1:5), of "resolving" sayings, occurs in Mark 4:34, a term used elsewhere of the allegorical interpretation of parables, e.g. in the *Similitudes* of Hermas, 5. 3. 1–2, 5. 4. 2–3, 5. 5. 1, 9. 10. 5, 9. 11. 9; cf. the noun *resolution* in 5. 5. 1, 5. 6. 8, 5. 7. 1, 8. 11. 1, 9. 13. 9, 9. 16. 7. In Mark 4 the interpretation makes use of a formula for identifying the persons intended by the allegory, "these are the ones who. . . ," or the like (4:15, 16, 18, 20). This formula is used in Jude 19 to interpret an apostolic saying, and in Jude 12, 16 and 2 Pet. 2:17 to interpret Scripture. A somewhat similar style is used by Matthew in the interpretation of the parable of the tares (Matt. 13:37–39).

The collection of Mark 4 refers to itself as "parables," (4:2, 10, 11, 13, 30, 33, 34; cf. 3:23). Of course it is, strictly speaking,

---

42. Joachim Jeremias, *The Parables of Jesus,* rev. ed., 1963, p. 14, esp. n. 11, uses these variants as a basis for reconstructing the stages in the growth of the collection. For "and he said [imperfect] to them" is typically Marcan (2:27; 6:10; 7:9; 8:21; 9:1, whereas "and he said" [imperfect] is not, and hence may be "pre-Marcan." He does not comment on the historical present "and he said to them" in 4:13, which he attributes to the pre-Marcan stage (pp. 13–14, 18 n. 31). Yet the use of the historical present tense is as distinctly Marcan as is the addition of "to them." This can be seen by the frequency of its occurrence in Mark and by the tendency of both Matthew and Luke to change to a past tense. Of course, Mark could also have edited his source into conformity to his own preferred usage.

43. ἔφη, rather than λέγει, ἔλεγεν, and εἶπεν in the Christian usage cited above.

not quite correct to translate παραβολαί here as "parables."
Jülicher has taught us that the term *parable* should be restricted
to stories that score simply and clearly a point, i.e., what we today
would call sermon illustrations.[44] This distinction was lost on the
evangelists, who had no hesitation in calling an allegory such as
the wicked husbandman a "parable" (Mark 12:1, 12). This is
not only due to their lack of form-critical concern and the fluidity
of the Greek term and its Hebrew equivalent,[45] but also to the
fact that the evangelists had lost sight of the parable in its own
right, and misunderstood it as allegory. In Mark 4 παραβολαί
are allegorical "riddles" intended to obscure the point for the outsiders (4:11–12, 33–34). In Mark 7:17 the term occurs in connection with the disciples' question requesting clarification; i.e.,
it tends to mean "riddle," as does παροιμία in John 10:6; 16:25, 29.
In Mark 3:23 a riddle, resolved by interpretive allegorized similes
and a parable, is called speaking "in parables."

Thus "parables" for Mark approach what the *Gospel of Thomas*
calls "secret sayings," i.e., statements whose true meaning is not
evident but is to be established by means of special interpretation.
(In Mark 13:28 "parable" seems to refer to this deeper, interpreted meaning.) In such a context, the allegorical interpretation
given to the parable of the sower, 4:13–20, is quite appropriate
(cf. Matthew's *pendant,* the interpretation of the parable of the
tares, 13:36–43). From Mark's point of view Mark 4 is then a
collection, not of parables, but rather of riddles, allegories, secret
sayings. Between the parable of the sower and the two concluding

---

44. For the discussion of the understanding of the nature of parables since
Jülicher see my essay "Jesus' Parables as God Happening," in *Jesus and the
Historian: Written in Honor of Ernest Cadman Colwell,* ed. F. Thomas Trotter,
1968, pp. 134–50.

45. Joachim Jeremias, *Parables,* p. 20, presents the wide spectrum of meanings
for the Hebrew *mashal* (Greek παραβολή, "parable"). On p. 16, n. 22, he
presents the material for the meaning "riddle, dark saying," which seems to
have been near the original meaning of "magical saying" or "riddle" (so
Eissfeldt, *Einleitung in das Alte Testament,* 2d ed., 1956, p. 94, 98 [ET of the
3d ed. of 1964 by P. R. Ackroyd: *The Old Testament: An Introduction,* 1965,
pp. 82, 86]). Jeremias, *Parables,* pp. 97–98, correlates the Marcan pattern of
presenting the deeper meaning to the inner circle with the contemporary rabbinic
practice to which David Daube called attention: "Public Pronouncement and
Private Explanation in the Gospels," in *The New Testament and Rabbinic
Judaism,* 1956, pp. 141–50. The locus classicus on this topic is Wrede, *Messiasgeheimnis,* pp. 51–65, esp. 51–54, 65 on private vs. public, and 54–65 on the
Marcan theory of "parables."

parables of the seed growing secretly and of the mustard seed (4:26–29, 30–32), Mark inserts a series of sayings (4:21–25). It may well be the case, in view of the framework material at 4:21a, 23–24a, that Mark grouped the sayings into what he would consider a further pair of "parables" (4:21–22, 24–25), but this should not be taken to imply the corollary "and not as a collection of sayings." [46] For to Mark a collection of "secret sayings" and a collection of "parables" in the sense of "riddles, dark sayings," would belong together rather than being mutually exclusive. The *Gospel of Thomas* would concur in this view. Not only does it contain parables (*less* allegorized than in Mark), but it also contains precisely the sayings found in Mark 4:21–25, as Sayings 33, 5, 41. Thus Mark 4 is not simply a collection of parables in our sense, but rather a collection of obscure sayings in need of interpretations—i.e., "parables" in Mark's sense, quite comparable to a collection of "secret sayings" such as the *Gospel of Thomas.*

Yet Mark 4 avoids the term *logoi.* This avoidance may be due not simply to his use of the term *parables* to convey the concept of "riddles," which after all could have been expressed with the term *secret sayings,* but also to the fact that he uses the singular *logos* as a synonym for *gospel* (Mark 1:1, 14–15; 8:35; 10:29; 13:10; 14:9). It is in this sense that *logos* is used in 4:14, 15 bis, 16, 17, 18, 19, 20, to designate what the parable of the sower is talking about. The parable becomes itself a hermeneutical discussion about right and wrong ways of "hearing" the "word." This hermeneutical problem is then met in exemplary fashion by the Marcan method of "resolving" riddles, from which process the "word" emerges into clarity: "And with many such riddles he spoke to them the word, . . . but privately to his own disciples he resolved everything" (4:33–34). Thus the same kerygmatic trend that led Mark to the (Pauline) term *gospel* led him to the term *word* as its synonym. It was then more appropriate for him

46. Jeremias, *Parables,* p. 41 n. 69, says these *"logia"* were included by Mark here because he regarded them as a pair of parables, but adds, "and not as a collection of sayings" (p. 91). When Jeremias appeals to the frequent exhortations in Mark 4 to hearken, as evidence that Mark 4 is not a collection of sayings, he has overlooked the evidence presented above that such exhortations are characteristic of such collections of secret sayings as the *Gospel of Thomas.*

to refer to sayings that were in his view still coded as "riddles" rather than as *"logoi"*; for Jesus "spoke the word openly" (8:32) —as when he preached the kerygma of cross and resurrection.

Nonetheless Mark may not have been unaware of the tendency to refer to such collections as *logoi*. This may be suggested by the saying, put significantly near the end (v. 31) of the collection of apocalyptic sayings and parables in Mark 13: "Heaven and earth will pass away, but my *logoi* will not pass away."

If one may discern in Mark 4 traces of a pre-Marcan collection, it is possible that what we know in expanded form as the Sermon on the Mount (or Plain) is the outgrowth of another such early cluster of sayings and parables.[47] It uses as its conclusion a double

47. The cohesion of the collection suggests that the Sermon on the Mount (or Plain) is derived from an oral or written collection of its own, and did not first come into being in the context of Q. Cf. W. D. Davies, *The Setting of the Sermon on the Mount*, 1964. The end seems to be the conclusion of a collection, and this not simply because of the occurrence there of the term *logoi*. Rather the eschatological climax is the same concluding motif that one can sense in the *Didache* (chap. 16), the gospels (Mark 13 parr.), and even in Q (Luke 17:20–37). This develops into what Günther Bornkamm (*Die Vorgeschichte des sogenannten Zweiten Korintherbriefes*, SHA, Philos-hist. Klasse, 2. Abh., 1961, pp. 23 ff.) has called the "form-critical law" to the effect that one sign of the end, the emergence of heretics, can become a trait characteristic of the end of a document. In this regard, as in others, the Sermon on the Mount goes beyond the Sermon on the Plain. Matthew seems to have recognized the unity of this collection over against the rest of Q. For he did not compose the Sermon on the Mount simply by scanning the whole of Q for suitable material, as Vincent Taylor has shown to be the regular Matthean practice in composing his other sayings collections: "The Order of Q," *JTS* n.s. 4 (1953): 27–31; and "The Original Order of Q," in the T. W. Manson festschrift, 1959, pp. 246–69. Rather, as the Lucan Sermon on the Plain shows, Matthew has acknowledged the framework of the collection as the framework of the Sermon on the Mount, merely filling out the given outline with further material gleaned partly from Q (see Taylor's tables in "The Order of Q," pp. 29–30, and in the Manson festschrift, p. 249). Of course one could argue that Matt. 3–12 tends to follow the original (Lucan) order of Q (see esp. Matt. 3, 4, 5, 7, 8, 11, 12), and that it is for this reason that Matt. 5 and 7 do not follow the "gleaning" method of the four later Matthean discourses, but prefer the method of the "rest of Matthew" in retaining the Q order. Yet each of the two small collections from the same period found in *1 Clem.* 13. 2 and *Did.* 1. 3–6 (see below) seem to reflect a similar unity. Helmut Koester's research (*Synoptische Überlieferung bei den apostolischen Vätern*, TU, 65, 1957, pp. 12 ff., 217 ff.) leads to the conclusion that in both cases we have to do with small collections antedating their use in the documents we know, collections very similar in content to the Sermon on the Mount (Plain). In the case of the *Didache*, this may in part be due to dependence on Matt. and Luke, as Bentley Layton, "The Sources, Date, and Transmission of *Didache* 1. 3b—2. 1," suggests. Yet even in this case the removal of this block of material from Matt. and Luke to insert it into the "Two Ways" and thus into the *Didache* may be due to a surviving awareness of the traditional unity of the cluster. See also Justin *Apologia* 14. 5; Athenagoras *Supplicatio* 11. 1, 3.

parable exalting Jesus' *logoi* in much the same way as does Mark 13:31. For the double parable Luke 6:47 // Matt. 7:24 (cf. v. 26) begins: "Every one who comes to me and hears my *logoi* and does them." Hence the term *logoi* may have functioned as a designation for this early collection. In that case it would be the trend toward alluding, near its end, to such a collection as *logoi,* which would have provided Q with the catchword for connecting this collection to the rest of the Q sayings by means of what is the most prominent exception to its policy of including only sayings material. For here Q presents the story of the healing of the centurion's servant, oriented to the centurion's trust in the authority of Jesus' word (Luke 7:7 // Matt. 8:8).[48] It would be this same trend at work in Matthew that leads to the fixed formula with which he concludes his five sayings collections, the first occurrence of which follows directly upon the double parable (Matt. 7:28). Thus we seem to be able to trace the beginnings of a designation for the gattung of collections of sayings back into the earliest such collections of the primitive church.[49] Somewhat as in the case of the *Gospel of Thomas,* the term would seem to be initially imbedded in the sayings themselves, and to move towards a title first by means of the significant placement of such sayings, from which it is taken into redactional subscriptions.

From the Quotation Formula to the Collection of Sayings

An analysis of the way in which the individual saying is introduced in the early church will reveal a similar terminological sensitivity. For quotation formulae can be used both with individual sayings and with sayings collections.

A saying that has just been quoted can be referred to with the term *logos* (Mark 9:10; Mark 10:22 // Matt. 19:22; Mark 14:39 // Matt. 24:44; Matt. 15:12; 19:11; John 2:22; 4:50; 6:60). Even a saying quoted much earlier can be recalled and repeated with a quotation formula using that term: "And Peter

---

48. See Ernst Haenchen, "Johanneische Probleme," *ZThK* 56 (1959): 23-31, repr. in *Gott und Mensch,* 1965, pp. 82-90; and my discussion in chaps. 2 and 7 of the present volume.
49. See Helmut Koester, *"GNOMAI DIAPHOROI,"* chap. 4 below, for further comments on such primitive collections.

remembered the *logos* (*rhema?*) of the Lord, how he had said to him" (Luke 22:61); [50] "Remember the *logos* that I said to you" (John 15:20); or, replacing "remembrance" with "fulfillment," "This was to fulfill the *logos* that he had spoken" (John 18:9).[51] One may also compare Paul's quotation formula in 1 Thess. 4:15: "But this we declare to you by the *logos* of the Lord." It is apparently from this quotation formula that Bultmann derived his favorite designation *Herrenwort*, "dominical saying," "word of the Lord."

In tracing the sensitivity of the sources for the name appropriate to collections of sayings, an odd trait is of particular significance: the plural form *logoi* is so standard in one quotation formula that the plural is even used when introducing a single saying rather than a plurality of sayings. One of the last dissertations under Bultmann, that of Helmut Koester,[52] called attention to this formula. It combines the verb *remember*, already encountered in Luke 22:61 and John 15:20, with the plural *logoi*. The passages where this formula occurs are the following: "To remember the *logoi* of the Lord Jesus, that he said" (Acts 20:35); "Remember the *logoi* of the Lord Jesus, for he said" (*1 Clem.* 46. 7–8); "Especially remembering the *logoi* of the Lord Jesus that he spoke when he was teaching gentleness and long-suffering, for he spoke thus" (*1 Clem.* 13. 1–2).[53] These passages tend to indicate that sayings collections as well as individual sayings were referred to as "*logoi* of the Lord Jesus." In fact, this

---

50. The variant reading with *rhema* has been usually rejected as derived from the parallel in Matt. 26:75 (Mark 14:72); yet the support for the reading provided by P. 69 and P. 75 may prove decisive (as in *The Greek New Testament* of the Bible Societies). Luke uses the same term in Luke 24:8, "and they remembered his words," and Acts 11:16, "and I remembered the word of the Lord, how he said. . . ."

51. The same variant occurs in John 18:32, "to fulfill the *logos* that Jesus had spoken." The reference is apparently to 12:32, to which 12:33 is seen also to refer with the simple expression "he said this."

52. Koester, *Synoptische Überlieferung bei den apostolischen Vätern*, pp. 4–6.

53. A variant of this formula, again used with an individual saying, occurs in Jude 17: "Remember the sayings [*rhemata*] foretold by the apostles of our Lord Jesus Christ, that they said to you. . . ." The parallel in 2 Pet. 3:2 adds a reference to the prophets and roots the apostles' authority in the Lord's commandment, although in this secondary setting the saying is less clearly marked as such. For the identification of "Jude" and "Thomas" see Koester, *"GNOMAI DIAPHOROI,"* chap. 4 below. The affinities between the books of Jude and *Thomas the Contender* call for special investigation.

quotation formula provides a path for tracing sayings collections down to their final discontinuation in the orthodox church as the canonical gospels took their place.

In Acts 20:35 the quotation formula is followed by a single saying: "It is more blessed to give than to receive." This rule, ascribed in Greek tradition to the Persian court,[54] is also found in *1 Clem.* 2. 1: "giving more gladly than receiving." Probably in *1 Clem.* 2. 1 this rule is also understood as a saying of Jesus, in view of the remark in the same sentence, "paying attention to his *logoi* you stored them up carefully in your hearts," even though an explicit quotation formula is here lacking.[55] The exhortation to "give" is already found in the collection of sayings of Jesus in *1 Clem.* 13. 2.[56] Since both Acts and *1 Clem.* are aware of sayings collections such as Q, one can infer that this quotation formula, making use of the plural *logoi* rather than the singular *logos,* is derived from a formula alluding to such a collection.[57]

In *1 Clem.* 46. 7–8 the quotation formula is followed by a woe and two threats. Comparison with a double tradition in the synoptics leads Koester to the conclusion: "There remains only the assumption that *1 Clem.* 46. 8 is related to a stage behind the synoptics, and one doubtless thinks of Q. Indeed all the sayings in *1 Clem.* 46. 8 that are related to the synoptics could have stood in Q." [58] Thus one may assume that such collections were familiar to Clement, and also that excerpts from such collections were introduced with the quotation formula cited above making use of the plural form *logoi.*

54. Ernst Haenchen, *Die Apostelgeschichte,* Meyer commentary, 3, 13th ed., 1961, pp. 526–27.
55. Contrary to Haenchen, *Apostelgeschichte,* p. 2.
56. Koester, *Synoptische Überlieferung,* p. 13.
57. This transition from the singular to the plural could have a parallel in 1 Thess. 4:15–18, which begins in the quotation formula with the singular, "*logos* of the Lord," and closes with the exhortation: "Therefore comfort one another with these *logoi.*" For Paul normally speaks in the singular of *logos* in the sense of the "gospel," and uses the plural only in connection with the wisdom teaching of the Corinthian heretics, 1 Cor. 2:13, "in *logoi* not taught by human wisdom but taught by the spirit." In 1 Cor. 2:4, there occurs the variant reading "in plausible *logoi* of wisdom," comparable to *Corpus Hermeticum* 1. 29, "I sowed in them the *logoi* of wisdom." In 1 Cor. 12:8 one finds in the singular, "*logos* of wisdom."
58. Koester, *Synoptische Überlieferung,* p. 18.

In *1 Clem*. 13. 2 the quotation formula is followed by a chain of seven sayings. They are partly attested in the gospels (mostly in the Sermon on the Mount), partly elsewhere; yet they can be derived from no surviving source. Hence Koester concludes: "Perhaps the author is making use of some written collection of sayings of the Lord no longer known to us, but perhaps earlier than our gospels (cf. Saying 3). Perhaps it is the reproduction of an oral, though firmly formulated, local catechism." [59]

There is a quite similar collection in Polycarp *Phil*. 2. 3, though varied in details and enlarged by the first saying of the Sermon on the Mount. Here too the collection is introduced with a quite similar quotation formula, though the term *logoi* is lacking: "but remembering what things the Lord said as he taught." (Another instance of the quotation formula without the term *logoi* is *2 Clem*. 17. 3: "Let us remember the commandments of the Lord.") Even if Polycarp is here dependent on *1 Clement* and the gospels,[60] the freedom with which he adapts his collection still attests his connection with the free development of such sayings collections; to be sure, his tendency to bring *1 Clem*. 13. 2 into line with the gospels points to the beginning of the end of this freedom in the orthodox church.

In the case of Polycarp one can detect what was no doubt generally a major factor in the restriction of that freedom: the misuse of the sayings tradition by gnosticizing heretics. The other instance of his appeal to sayings of the Lord stands in just that context. In 7. 1 he warns against "whoever perverts the *logia* of the Lord for his own lusts, and says that there is neither resurrection nor judgment." Over against this heresy Polycarp presents an exhortation exemplifying the right use of such sayings. This is followed by the language of Matt. 26:41a // Mark 14:38a, brought into conformity to that of the Lord's Prayer. Then a quotation formula introduces a verbatim quotation of Matt. 26:41b // Mark 14:38b: "Wherefore, leaving the foolishness of the crowd, and their false teaching, let us turn back to the *logos* that was

59. Ibid., p. 16.
60. Ibid., pp. 115–18.

delivered to us in the beginning, watching in prayer and persevering in fasting, beseeching the all-seeing God in our supplications to 'lead us not into temptation,' as the Lord said, 'The spirit is willing, but the flesh is weak.' " [61]

A somewhat later but quite clear instance of the gnostics' use of Jesus' *logoi* in their appeal to orthodoxy is found in Ptolemaeus's *Letter to Flora.* Here a Valentinian tripartite division of the Old Testament law is proven "from the *logoi* of our Savior" (Epiphanius *Panarion haer.* 33. 3. 7), by means of citing (in 33. 4. 4 and 33. 4. 11) Matt. 19:8, 6; 15:4–9.[62]

Justin attests the continuing shadowy existence of collections of sayings at a time when the gospels have replaced them and the gattung as such is hardly alive any longer in the orthodox church. The term *logoi* usually means something quite different for him, namely Scripture (understood prophetically and hence also called "prophetic sayings"), or an individual proof text. Hence a frequent quotation formula for introducing an Old Testament quotation is: "And these are the *logoi*" (*Dial.* 31. 2, 39. 4, 62. 3, 79. 3), or the like. Of course, the transfer of such a Scripture formula to sayings of Jesus would not be difficult. For Christ already spoke in the Old Testament (*1 Apol.* 49. 1; 63. 14; *Dial.* 113–14). Hence revelation is transmitted both "through the prophetic spirit and through Christ himself" (*1 Apol.* 63. 14), just as truth is "in his *logoi* and those of his prophets" (*Dial.* 139. 5). The common phrase used to mark a transition in a chain of scriptural passages, "in other *logoi*" (*1 Apol.* 35. 5, *Dial.* 12. 1, 56. 14, 58. 6, 97. 3, 126. 6, [133. 4]), is also used in a sequence of sayings of Jesus, *Dial.* 76. 5 (cf. 76. 6). Furthermore, in *Dial.* 17. 3–4 (see also 18. 3) sayings of Jesus are quoted in a chain of scriptural passages with the following comment: "recalling short *logia* of his together with the prophetic (*logia*)" (18. 1), in which case Jesus' sayings, though termed *logia* rather than *logoi,* are described with a term commonly used of scriptural

---

61. For a further investigation of this heresy combatted by Polycarp in its relation to the sayings tradition and to the heresy combatted by Paul in 1 Cor., cf. chap. 2 above.
62. Cf. Völker, *Quellen zur Geschichte der christlichen Gnosis,* pp. 87–93; Robert M. Grant, *Gnosticism,* 1961, pp. 184–90.

passages.[63] Thus we find ourselves at the stage in the trajectory of Jesus' sayings in which they are not only derived from the gospels but are even treated as one would treat passages of Scripture.

Yet Justin also refers to his "Second Apology" (i.e., the appendix to his *Apology*) as *logoi* (12. 6). He even refers to the *Dialogue* [*dialogos*] *with Trypho* as *logoi* (11. 5, 39. 8, 45. 1, 47. 1). One may compare especially *Dial*. 80. 3, "I shall make a composition of all the *logoi* that have gone on between us," with *2 Apol*. 1. 1, "to make the composition of these *logoi*," and 15. 2, "because of this only have I composed these *logoi*." Trypho also understands his speeches as *logoi* (38. 1). What the two are doing is "sharing *logoi*" (38. 1, 64. 2, 112. 4; cf. *2 Apol*. 3. 5). That is to say, they understand themselves as philosophers, such as those whose *logoi* are mentioned in *Dial*. 2. 2.

Of course it was also the *Logos,* i.e., Christ, who spoke through Socrates (*1 Apol*. 5. 3–4, 46. 3; *2 Apol*. 10. 8). Yet when an individual Socratic saying is quoted (*2 Apol*. 3. 6), it is introduced simply with "the Socratic (thing)," rather than with a quotation formula making use of the term *logoi*. This may be a negative indication that in Justin's usage it would have been inaccurate to refer here to *logoi*. A "Socratic *logos*" [64] was precisely such a discourse or dialogue as the philosopher Justin himself carried on, and as he conceives of Plato composing; the term would hence not fit an individual saying.[65] Yet he does use the

63. In *Dial*. 65. 3; 109. 1 Justin designates scriptural passages of a few verses as "short *logoi*." The designation seems to be almost identical with the term *section* or *pericope*, 65. 3; 110. 1.
64. First attested in Aristotle; see *Poetica* 1447[b]. 11. From Karl Joel's investigation, "Der *LOGOS SOKRATIKOS*," *Archiv für Geschichte der Philosophie* 8 (1895): 467 ff., one finds "that the 'Socratic dialogue' in Aristotle's time was a long-since established literary genre, and that these *logoi* were regarded by Aristotle, in agreement with the current view, as 'artistic reproductions,'" (so Heinrich Maier, *Sokrates: Sein Werk und seine geschichtliche Stellung*, 1913, p. 27).
65. Diognetus 8. 2, "*Logoi* . . . of philosophers," perhaps means "*sayings* . . . of philosophers," since the context is a discussion of conflicting doctrines of God each succinctly put, e.g., "some say fire to be God, others water." In the *Gospel of Thomas*, Saying 13, Matthew compares Jesus to a "philosopher," which occurs as a loan word in the Coptic text. Thus a connection of "sayings" with the "philosopher" is not excluded; indeed the term *philosopher,* like the term *sophist,* is etymologically related to the term *sage*. On the Platonic "*Logoi* on the Good" see Hans Joachim Krämer, *Arete bei Platon und Aristoteles*, 1959, p. 408

term *logoi* with regard to Jesus: *Dial.* 8. 2 = 35. 8 = 100. 3;
113. 7 = 113. 5. And in one instance he is still able to present a
collection of loosely connected sayings of Jesus, *1 Apol.* 15–17
(see also 14. 3–4). But when he refers to this collection as *logoi,*
he does so with the apologetic clarification (14. 5): "But short
and concise *logoi* came from him. For he was not a sophist;
rather his *logos* was the power of God." This is a good characterization of the gattung of sayings collections in its distinction
from discourses, dialogues, and tractates. Yet the very fact that it
was necessary to make the distinction indicates that the traits constitutive of the gattung had become noticeable as defects; [66] it
could be defended only by means of a contrast to the scorned
"*logoi* of the sophists." [67]

n. 53; on the sayings of the Greek sages see Ulrich Wilckens, "σοφία," *ThWNT*
7 (1964): 469. On the relation of Greek gnomic sayings to traditions about Jesus
see Arnold Ehrhardt, "Greek Proverbs in the Gospel," *The Framework of the
New Testament Stories*, 1964, pp. 44–63; Hildebrecht Hommel, "Herrenworte
im Licht sokratischer Überlieferung," *ZNW* 57 (1966): 1–23. This has been
examined in detail in terms of a single saying by Albrecht Dihle, *Die Goldene
Regel: Eine Einführung in die Geschichte der antiken und frühchristlichen Vul-
gärethik*, Studienhefte zur Altertumswissenschaft, 7, 1962; cf. my review in the
Journal of the History of Philosophy 4 (1966): 84–87. The tradition of Greek
collections of sayings is Christianized in the *Sentences of Sextus* (the Coptic
version of which has turned up at Nag Hammadi: *CG*, XII, *1*). In connection
with editions of the *Sentences of Sextus* further literature is to be found: Josef
Kroll in Hennecke, *NT Apokryphen*, 2d ed., 1924, pp. 625 ff.; Henry Chadwick,
The Sentences of Sextus, Texts and Studies, 5, 1959; Gerhard Delling, "Zur
Hellenisierung des Christentums in den 'Sprüchen des Sextus,'" in *Studien zum
Neuen Testament und zur Patristik*, Klostermann festschrift, TU, 77, 1961, pp.
218–41. On Aesop's fables see *Babrius and Phaedrus*, ed. and trans. Ben Edwin
Perry, Loeb Classical Library, 1965. Johannes Leipoldt, *Das Evangelium nach
Thomas*, TU, 101, 1967, pp. 4–5, has listed further Greek literature that should
be brought into consideration.
66. A somewhat similar sensitivity is reflected in the covering letter Arrian wrote
to accompany Epictetus's *Discourses*. The letter nowhere refers to them by this
accepted title (lit., "diatribes"); rather they are introduced as his *logoi*. And
Arrian's first concern is to make clear that it is a collection, not a literary composition "as one might be said to 'compose' books of this kind." They were not
written for publication. "But whatever I heard him say I used to write down,
word for word, as best I could, endeavoring to preserve it as a memoir, for my
own future use, of his way of thinking and his effective speech. They are, accordingly, as you might expect, such remarks as one man might make offhand to
another, not such as he would compose for posterity." Thus, though they are
more nearly a random collection of informal brief discourses than a collection of
sayings, Epictetus's *logoi* are clearly distinguished by Arrian from the formal
philosophical discourse. Yet Arrian is concerned to claim for them that they
achieve the purpose of "the *logoi* of the philosophers," namely, "to incite the
minds of his hearers to the best things."
67. Aristotle *Sophistici Elenchi* 165ᵃ. 34. Cf. Justin *Dial.* 129. 2: "The sophists
[are] able neither to say nor to think the truth." For a comparison between the
logoi of the prophets and those of the philosophers see *Dial.* 7. 2.

The *Gospel of Thomas* falls within much the same situation of transition as do Clement,[68] Polycarp, and Justin, when the sayings collections derived from the oral tradition were becoming dependent on the written gospels, but had not yet been entirely replaced by gospels, discourses, dialogues, and treatises. Even if it were the case that the *Gospel of Thomas* derived its sayings in large part from the canonical gospels, which is far from obvious,[69] in any case it retained the gattung of sayings collections.[70] With the final discontinuation of the oral transmission

68. Koester, *Synoptische Überlieferung*, pp. 12–16, 220–37, as well as "*GNO-MAI DIAPHOROI*," below, p. 135 n. 56, suggests that the transition takes place between Clement and *Didache*.

69. Ernst Haenchen, *Die Botschaft des Thomas-Evangeliums*, 1961, p. 11, presents a theory making dependence on the gospels seem conceivable, in spite of the omitted narrative ingredient of the gospels: "Gnosticism was . . . only concerned with the redeeming message, not with any miracles of the redeemer or his death for our salvation. Gnosticism, at least in its pure form, was a piety that saw all salvation contained in the *word* that assured the elect of his union with the divine and thus of his eternal salvation. If such a gnostic read the gospels, then this gnostic presupposition functioned like a sieve. The miracle stories that take up considerable room in Mark, Matthew, and Luke, and also are important in John, disappeared on their own accord, so to speak. Just like the passion narrative, they were unimportant. Hence one need not presuppose any kind of sayings collection as source of the *Gospel of Thomas*, in order to explain its nature as a pure collection of sayings of Jesus." Yet other Nag Hammadi tractates indicate that Gnosticism tended not to carry elimination through consistently but rather to proceed by means of interpretation of given traditions. The retention, in gnostic reinterpretation, of the passion narrative in the *Second Treatise of the Great Seth* (*CG*, VII, 2) is a case in point. Johannes Leipoldt in his review of Haenchen's book (*ThLZ* 87 [1962]: 755), and in his own edition (*Das Evangelium nach Thomas*, TU, 101, 1967, p. 16), assumes dependence on the synoptics, and yet locates the *Gospel of Thomas* correctly within the history of the gattung of sayings collections. Wolfhart Schrage, *Das Verhältnis des Thomas-Evangeliums zur synoptischen Tradition und zu den koptischen Evangelienübersetzungen,* (suppl. 29 to *ZNW*, 1964) is the first to present a detailed argument to show dependence of the *Gospel of Thomas* upon the canonical gospels. However, as John Sieber, "A Redactional Analysis of the Synoptic Gospels with Regard to the Question of the Sources of the *Gospel of Thomas*" (Diss., Claremont Graduate School, 1965), has indicated, his argument is not fully convincing. For he considers a demonstration of the Coptic translator's dependence on the Coptic New Testament (if this is chronologically likely) as an argument for an analogous dependence of the Greek original on the Greek New Testament. Another alternative, to the effect that the source of those close parallels to the New Testament that do occur is the Coptic translator's dependence on the Coptic New Testament, rather than the original Greek author's use of the Greek New Testament, has not been adequately considered. Schrage's own investigation of the Greek fragments, "Evangelienzitate in Oxyrhynchus-Logien und im koptischen Thomas-Evangelium," *Apophoreta*, Haenchen festschrift, suppl. 30 to *ZNW*, 1964, pp. 251–68, somewhat contrary to his own purpose, indicates the Greek to be further from the New Testament than the Coptic. See also the criticism by Koester, "*GNOMAI DIAPHOROI*," chap. 4 below, p. 131 n. 45.

70. It is precisely at this point that the position, most recently advocated by Werner Georg Kümmel, seems to be misleading: "The document [sc., the *Gospel*

102

of Jesus' sayings, the *Sitz im Leben* of the gattung was gone; hence orthodoxy contented itself with the canonical gospels, while Gnosticism devoted itself all the more to imaginary dialogues of the Resurrected with his disciples.

The gattung of sayings collections has become comprehensible under the designation *logoi* in light of quotation formulae referring to *"logoi* of the Lord Jesus" or the like. This designation was then taken up into the conclusion or incipit of written collections, thus serving to designate the gattung. Thus the incipit of the *Gospel of Thomas* was not to be explained simply in terms of the one document, but required for its explanation a context of usage in early Christianity as part of the history of a gattung. Just so this whole early Christian development is to be seen in a more encompassing trajectory, if the course of this gattung and its cultural *Sitz im Leben,* and thus its history, are to be understood.

Jewish Wisdom Literature and the Gattung LOGOI SOPHON

The history of the early Christian designation for the "sayings" gattung came first into view in its gnostic variant, as "hidden sayings." This poses the question as to what there may have been in the tendency of the gattung itself that contributed to this outcome. Bultmann provided a useful suggestion, when he sensed in Matt. 23:34–39 (// Luke 11:49–51; 13:34–35) a speech by Sophia cited from some lost wisdom document, whose conclusion "you will not see me again until . . ." was explained in terms of "the myth of the divine Wisdom. . . , who, after tarrying in vain on earth and calling men to herself, takes departure from earth, so that one now seeks her in vain." [71] For this myth

---

of *Thomas*] is as such certainly no late form of the same literary gattung as Q, but rather a late stage, different in kind, of the development in the tradition of Jesus' sayings." *Einleitung in das Neue Testament,* 12th ed. of the standard work by Paul Feine and Johannes Behm, 1963, p. 41 (ET: *Introduction to the New Testament,* trans. A. J. Mattill, Jr., 1966, p. 58). See further literature there. Koester, "*GNOMAI DIAPHOROI,*" chap. 4 below, pp. 135 f., accepts the view presented above and suggests that *Thomas* "represents the eastern branch of the gattung '*Logoi,*' the western branch being represented by the sypnoptic *Logoi* of Q."

71. Bultmann, *Geschichte,* pp. 120–21 (ET, p. 115).

does seem to be presupposed in the *Gospel of Thomas,* to judge by Saying 38: "many times have you desired to hear these sayings that I say to you, and you have no other from whom to hear them. There will be days when you will seek me (and) you will not find me" (cf. Q: Luke 10:24; 13:34–35 par.). Thus Bultmann's suggestions of an early Christian association of Jewish wisdom literature's personified Sophia with Jesus and of the absorption of part of a collection of wisdom sayings into a collection of Jesus' sayings may in their way point to the prehistory of a gattung that, though apparently not gnostic in origin, was open to a development in that direction, once a general drift toward Gnosticism had set in.

If the *Gospel of Thomas* shows the way in which the Sophia tradition used in Q ends in Gnosticism, an early Catholic theologian attests equally clearly its origin in Jewish wisdom literature. "The All-virtuous Wisdom said thus: 'Behold I will bring forth to you the expression of my spirit, and I will teach you my *logos,* since I called and you did not obey, and I put forth *logoi* and you did not attend. . . . For it shall come to pass when you call upon me, I will not hear you. The evil shall seek me and they shall not find me. For they hated wisdom . . .'" (*1 Clem.* 57. 3 ff.). Here one has much the same content as in the *Gospel of Thomas,* Saying 38, and in Q (Matt. 23:34–39 // Luke 11:49–51; 13:34–35), with a quotation formula reminiscent of that in Q (Luke 11:49), "Therefore the Wisdom of God said." Yet in fact what we have is a verbal quotation from the LXX of Prov. 1:23–33, and the quotation formula is simply making use of the primitive Christian name for the book Proverbs. Yet the Old Testament origin of the passage neither separates it from Jesus, "who is also called Sophia . . . in the *logoi* of the prophets" (Justin *Dial.* 100. 4), nor from the gnostic *Gospel of Thomas.* When Bultmann first worked out the gnostic redeemer myth, he appealed to Prov. 1:23–33 as "the most important passage. . . , in which the whole myth is reflected." [72] The personified Wis-

---

72. Bultmann, *EUCHARISTERION,* 2:9. The unwillingness of Ralph Marcus, "On Biblical Hypostases of Wisdom," *HUCA* 23, 1 (1950/51): 157–71, to assume a move beyond "poetic personification" to "hypostatization" for Sophia in Judaism, in criticism of Helmer Ringgren, *Word and Wisdom: Studies in the Hypostatization of Divine Qualities and Functions in the Ancient Near East,* 1957, seems based on an idealized view of early Judaism (see pp. 169–71).

dom of Old Testament wisdom literature developed into the gnostic redeemer myth, especially as it identified Jesus with that redeemer, and thus understood Jesus as bringer of the secret redemptive *gnosis* or *logoi*.

The fact that such a development comes into view especially in the sayings tradition is more comprehensible when one has noted the close connection between sayings collections and the sages, the *sophoi*. It is partly because the gattung was itself associated with the "wise" that it could easily be swept into the christological development moving from personified Wisdom to the gnostic redeemer. It is this relation with the "wise" that becomes clear from the antecedent history of the gattung within Judaism, as *logoi sophon*, "words of the wise" or "sayings of the sages."

Already in *Pirke Aboth* one has to do with a collection of sayings that (especially in its first parts) corresponds formally to this gattung. One finds here a chain of loosely connected sayings. In distinction from most of the material studied thus far, the sayings are attributed to different rabbis, rather than to a single sage. Nonetheless the common designation *Pirke Aboth* ("Chapters of the Fathers") is misleading. For these six *perakim* or "chapters" from the Mishnah, when they contain references to themselves, use only the term *devarim*, "sayings." The critical edition by Taylor [73] begins with the title "Sayings of the Ancient Fathers" and ends with the subscription of the title to chap. 6 as "Sayings of Meir," rather than the frequently-heard title *Pirke R. Meir.* Also, the oldest [74] rabbinic reference to *Pirke Aboth,* found in the Gemara, B. Kam 30[a], cites Rabbi Jehudah (d. A.D. 299) as referring to "the *sayings* of 'Nezekin'" and Raba (d. A.D. 352) as referring to "the *sayings* of the fathers." Here the Aramaic term translated "sayings" refers to the Hebrew equivalent that is found in the source itself. For *Pirke Aboth* speaks not only of "the words of the law" (2. 5, 8; 3. 3–4; 4. 7), but also of the "sayings" of a given rabbi, i.e., "the sayings of Eleazar ben Arach" (2. 13–14; see also 5. 10; 6. 6).

Furthermore the quotation formulae do not refer to the rabbis

73. Charles Taylor, *Sayings of the Jewish Fathers,* 2d ed., 1897.
74. R. Travers Herford, *Pirke Aboth: The Ethics of the Talmud: Sayings of the Fathers,* 4th ed., 1962, p. 4.

as "fathers," and the title *rabban* does not occur there until Gamaliel I (1. 16; middle of first century A.D.); not until Jehudah (2. 1; ca. A.D. 200) does the title *rabbi* enter a quotation formula. In the sayings themselves the title *rab* is mentioned in passing in 1. 6, 16; 6. 3; and "fathers" are mentioned in 2. 2. But the sayings refer to the bearers of the sayings tradition predominantly as "sages": "May your house be a meeting place for the sages, and cover yourself with the dust of their feet and drink thirstily their sayings" (1. 4). The "wise" are exhorted to watch their "words" (1. 11). When a person challenges this way of life, he does so with the comment that he has lived his whole life among the "wise" and has learned to prefer silence to the many "words" that only give rise to sin (1. 17). Hence the bearers of this tradition are called "sages" in a quotation formula (1. 5), and at the opening of the subsequently added sixth chapter. The inference seems unavoidable that the sayings tradition recorded in *Pirke Aboth* would have considered itself "words of the wise," "sayings of the sages," even though this formulation does not occur as such in *Pirke Aboth*.

One also finds elsewhere in the Judaism of this period such an association of "sayings" with the "sages." The *Testaments of the Twelve Patriarchs* are of course regarded as testaments, as the incipit "Copy of the testament of Naphthali that he gave at the time of his departure" and the like attest. But in seven of the twelve cases the incipit is varied to refer to *logoi,* e.g.: "Copy of the *logoi* of Dan which he spoke to his sons in his last days." Then follows the exhortation to hearken to the *logoi* (*Dan* 1. 2; *Naph.* 1. 5; *Gad* 3. 1 v.l.; *Rub.* 3. 9; *Jud.* 13. 1); when *logoi* has already been used in the incipit, the synonym *rhemata* is used in the exhortation (*Iss.* 1. 1b; *Zeb.* 1. 2; *Jos.* 1. 2). Then the patriarch's experiential wisdom is given in analogy to wisdom literature. One may compare the common form of address "my sons," the speech in praise of "the wisdom of the wise" (*Levi* 13. 7), the exhortation "became then sages in God, my sons" (*Naph.* 8. 10), and the parallels to Ahikar.[75] Thus there seems

75. R. H. Charles, *The Apocrypha and Pseudepigrapha of the Old Testament,* vol. 2 (1913), p. 291. The form of address "my son(s)" fits of course the imagined situation of a testament, where a father addresses his son(s). Yet this

to be some overlapping between the gattung of the "testament" and that of "sayings of the sages." Just as the gattung "sayings collections" can gain profile by more thorough correlation with the trajectory of the gattung of revelatory discourses of the resurrected with his disciples, both would gain in profile if the course of the gattung of testament in this period were to be fully plotted.

Much the same situation is found in the *Apocalypse of Adam*. To be sure, this document is from Nag Hammadi's gnostic library (*CG*, V, 5), and hence could have been treated above in the section dealing with the Coptic gnostic library. Yet it is regarded by the editor Alexander Böhlig [76] and by Kurt Rudolph [77] as an outgrowth of Syrian-Palestinian baptismal sects, documentation for pre- or non-Christian Jewish gnosticism.[78] Although the work is designated "The Apocalypse of Adam" in the title found both before (64. 1) and after (85. 32) the text, and has an incipit (64. 2–4) using the loan word *apocalypse* ("The revelation that Adam taught his son Seth in the 700th year"), it is in form much like the *Testaments of the Twelve Patriarchs*. The text continues immediately (64. 4–5): "And he said, 'Hear my words, my son Seth.'" Adam says (64. 12–13) that Eve taught him "a word of knowledge of God," and that he heard "words" from the three great men (66. 9–10), namely, the revelation he gives Seth (67. 14–21). When Adam's narration of the future arrives at Noah, the latter's testament is similarly introduced (72. 18–19): "He [Noah] will say to them, 'My sons, hear my words.'" And at the end of the work Adam's speech closes (85. 3–18): "The words of the God of the aeons that they (those with gnosis) have preserved did not (of themselves) come into the book nor are they written (at all). Rather angelic ones will bring them, whom all generations of men will not recognize.

---

situation itself is characteristic of wisdom literature (Ahikar; Prov. 31); and the sonship is readily spiritualized and thus made generally applicable (*Corpus Hermeticum* 13). To be sure, the testaments are less collections of transmitted sayings than invented discourses. Hence these *logoi* are in form more comparable to the gnostic and apologetic *logoi*, where the collector has been replaced by the author and the sayings collection by the dialogue, discourse, or tractate.
76. Böhlig and Labib, *Apokalypsen*, p. 95.
77. Kurt Rudolph, in his book review in *ThLZ* 90 (1965), 361–62.
78. See my report in "The Coptic Gnostic Library Today," *NTS* 12 (1968): 377–78.

For they will come on a high mountain on a rock of truth. Hence they will be called 'the words of incorruption and of truth,' of those who know the eternal God with wisdom, gnosis, and doctrine from angels for eternity. For he knows everything." In the concluding framework the concept "apocalypse" recurs (85. 19–29): "These are the revelations that Adam revealed to Seth his son and that his son taught his seed. This is the hidden *gnosis* of Adam that he gave to Seth, the holy baptism of those who know the eternal *gnosis* through those born of *logos*, [and] the imperishable luminaries who came forth from the holy seed." Here those "with wisdom," called "luminaries," [79] could well be a gnosticized and mythologized development of the concept of the sages as the bearers of the saving "words."

The situation is similar with another "apocalypse," the Ethiopic Enoch, which according to the oldest documentation was called the "Words of Enoch the Righteous" (*Test. Ben.* 9. 1; cf. *Jub.* 21. 10, "in the words of Enoch and the words of Noah"). The incipit reads: "Words of the blessing of Enoch," and a superscription in 14. 1 reads: "The Book of the Words of Righteousness" (cf. 14. 3: "words of wisdom"), just as at the end of the parenetic book in chaps. 91–105 the terms *words* and *wisdom* recur. This relationship of words to wisdom is especially clear in the *Similitudes*, chaps. 37–71, whose origin as an independent work is recognizable by means of the superscription in 37. 1–2.[80] Here the work is introduced as "Words of Wisdom," as well as with the exhortation to listen to the "words of the holy one" (v.l., "holy words"), since the Lord of spirits has never before granted such "wisdom." Hence it is not surprising to find in

79. The gnostic redeemer is named "luminary" (*phoster*), (76. 9–10, 28; 77. 15; 82. 28); so are his parents (82. 7), who, according to Böhlig, *Apokalypsen*, p. 93, are the sun and moon (cf. Gen. 1:16 and Rev. 12:1), and the gnostics themselves (75. 14–15; 85. 28). Cf. also the four "luminaries" of the *Apocryphon of John*, CG, II, 7. 33 ff. (Krause and Labib, *Apokryphon*, pp. 129 ff.). This term *luminaries* (Gen. 1:14–16 LXX) occurs in the title, preserved on a fragment, of a Qumran document, "Words of the Luminaries" (4QDibHam). Both the meaning of the title and its relation to the liturgical contents are unclear. Maurice Baillet, "Un Recueil Liturgique de Qumrân, Grotte 4: 'Les Parôles des Luminaires,'" *RB* 68 (1961): 195–250, esp. p. 249, conjectures that the title does not refer to the contents, but rather to the occasion when the material was used. On this assumption he arrives at the translation "liturgie d'après les luminaires," i.e., "office selon les jours de la semaine." Such a translation seems, however, to be quite strained.
80. Eissfeldt, *Einleitung*, p. 764 (ET, p. 618).

chap. 42 the locus classicus for the Sophia myth, attesting the otherwise only "conjectured view that the hiddenness of wisdom [alluded to in wisdom literature] is the consequence of her rejection by men." [81] Thus we are directed a step further back, into the wisdom literature in the narrower sense.

The term *wisdom literature* is itself a reflection of an early Christian title for the book of Proverbs. For Eusebius (4. 22. 9), in discussing Hegesippus, says: "And not only he but also Irenaeus and the whole company of the ancients called the Proverbs of Solomon All-Virtuous Wisdom." The use of this title in *1 Clem.* 57. 3 has already been noted.

The book of Proverbs "bears on its forehead more clearly than do other books the traces of its origin. For its individual parts have special superscriptions, and these show that the section following each one comprised at some time an independent collection.[82] Since the first collection, 1:1—9:18 (like the second, 10:1—22:16, and fifth, chaps. 25–29) bears the superscription "Proverbs of Solomon," the whole book was subsequently given this name. Hence the term *proverb* has been the basic term used in discussing the sayings in wisdom literature. Less noticed is the term used in other collections in the book of Proverbs. Chapter 30 bears the superscription "The Sayings of Agur Son of Jakeh of Massa," and chap. 31, the superscription "The Sayings of Lemuel, King of Massah, which his mother taught him." Both superscriptions are less clearly set apart as superscriptions in the LXX than in the Hebrew, which may account for their having been less noted than the term *proverb*.

Already in the Hebrew text the superscription of the collection in Prov. 22:17—24:22 "was taken up into the first verse of the collection it introduces (22:17); but, as the LXX shows, it belongs before this verse." [83] This superscription reads "The Sayings of the Sages" [84] (cf. the incipit in the LXX: "To the *logoi*

81. Bultmann, *EUCHARISTERION*, 2:9.
82. Eissfeldt, *Einleitung*, p. 579 (ET, p. 471).
83. Ibid., p. 580 (ET, p. 471).
84. It is unclear whether in the superscription to 24:23–34, "also these are of the wise," the term *proverbs* is to be understood, or, as the preceding superscription, 22:17 (LXX, 30:1) would suggest, the term *sayings*. Cf. RSV: "These also are sayings of the wise."

of the sages lend your ear and hear my *logos*"). Here the super-scription "Sayings of [a given Sage]" used for Prov. 30 and 31 is generalized into "Sayings of the Sages" (LXX: *logoi sophon*), and so presents itself as the fitting designation for the gattung that the sources here investigated have tended to put in profile.

The designation "sayings" occurs in a superscription again in Eccles. 1:1, "The Words of the Preacher, the Son of David, King of Jerusalem," although to be sure the LXX here uses the trans-lational variant *rhemata* in place of *logoi*. Toward the conclu-sion (12:10) the book speaks again of the preacher's "sayings of delight" and "sayings of truth." Then in 12:11 one finds praise of the "sayings of the sages," the same expression as at Prov. 22:17. Even though Eccles. 12:11 is not readily tranlat-able [85] (RSV: "The sayings of the sages are like goads, and like nails firmly fixed are the collected sayings which are given by one Shepherd"), we seem to have to do with the designation for a gattung that is recognizable as such.

When one inquires behind Jewish wisdom literature, one finds similar collections in Egypt and in Mesopotamia. In Egypt the common incipit of such collections of sayings is "Beginning of the instruction." Hence the expression "Sayings of the Sages" at the opening of the sayings collection in Prov. 22:17—24:22, a source that has been shown to go back to the book of wisdom of Amen-em-Opet, cannot itself be attributed to the Egyptian *Vor-lage*.[86] Perhaps an antecedent for the title can more clearly be found in Mesopotamia. For the Ahikar collection, from which Prov. 23:13–14 seems to have been borrowed,[87] may have been designated as "sayings." To be sure, the Ethiopian fragments,

---

85. The obscure words could mean "collected sayings" (RSV), "(Spruch)samm-lung" (Zimmerli, *Altes Testament Deutsch, ad loc.*), and thus could be under-stood as a description of the gattung. Yet the LXX has here a different reading, and commentators have emended the text in various ways. Further, it is unclear whether the one shepherd to whom the sayings of the sages are attributed is God (RSV) or Solomon (so Eissfeldt, *Einleitung,* p. 608 [ET, p. 493], who takes the phrase to allude to the book of Proverbs). In the latter case the use of the plural ("sages") to designate the sayings of an individual sage would be in-telligible best on the assumption that a current designation for a gattung is simply taken over without adaptation.
86. See the section "Egyptian Instructions" in *Ancient Near Eastern Texts Re-lated to the Old Testament,* ed. James B. Pritchard, 2d ed., 1955, pp. 412–25, esp. "The Instruction of Amen-em-Opet," pp. 421–24.
87. Cf. Eissfeldt, *Einleitung,* p. 584 (ET, p. 475).

preserved in the "Book of the Wise Philosophers," reflect Egyptian usage in the superscription "Instruction of Ahikar the Sage." [88] But Ahikar's collection of sayings in the Syrian version A begins by calling upon his son Nadan to regard Ahikar's "sayings" as he would God's words.[89] And the Aramaic version (fifth cent. B.C.) speaks occasionally of Ahikar's "counsel and sayings." [90] The Ahikar collection is also relevant in terms of its contents, in that parallels with various other collections, including Q, occur (Matt. 24:48–51 // Luke 12:45–46); the Syrian version also shows affinities of style with the "Sayings of Agur" (Prov. 30).[91]

It should be well known that designations for gattungen are less precisely and consistently used as technical terms in the sources themselves than in modern scholarship. Furthermore, we are not obliged to derive our designations for gattungen from the sources. It is enough that the gattungen themselves have been shown to exist there. However, the tendency or direction of a gattung comes more readily to our attention if a movement of language can be found in the sources that names what is constitutive of the gattung and thus brings its tendency to expression. The fact that the sayings collection as a gattung tended to associate the speaker of the sayings with the sage has become audible in noting the connection between "sayings," *logoi,* and "sages," *sophoi,* which in substance leads to *logoi sophon,* "sayings of the sages" or "words of the wise," as a designation for the gattung.[92]

---

88. See *The Story of Ahikar,* ed. F. C. Conybeare, J. Rendel Harris, and Agnes Smith Lewis, 2d ed., 1913, pp. xxiv–xxv, 128–29.
89. Ibid., p. 103.
90. To be sure, Karl Ludwig Schmidt, *EUCHARISTERION,* 2:63, seems to go too far in claiming that the Aramaic title read: "Sayings of a wise and instructed scribe named Ahikar, which he taught his son." The decisive first word is lacking in the fragmentary text and is not presupposed in the English translation (*The Story of Ahikar,* p. 168).
91. E.g., Prov. 30:21: "three things . . . and four"; 30:24: "four things are . . ."; cf. *The Story of Ahikar,* p. lvii; Eissfeldt, *Einleitung,* p. 98 (ET, pp. 85–86).
92. To be sure, the term *words* seems to occur in the incipit of various kinds of Hebrew works, such as Deut. 1:1; 28:69; Amos 1:1; Neh. 1:1; Bar. 1. 1. It figures in the superscription of the Ten Commandments (Exod. 20:1; 34:28; cf. 24:3, 4, 8). In the titles of the historical sources of the books of Kings the term *devarim of days* occurs, with quite a different meaning from *words,* i.e., the whole phrase means "history," or (RSV) "chronicles". In the case of Solomon, 1 Kings 11:41, "The Book of the History [or Chronicles] of Solomon" is a

The movement of the sayings of Jesus into collections of sayings has already been discussed. There remains only the question as to what effect there would be upon such collections in view of the wisdom implications they bore. It can be presupposed that some wisdom sayings were among Jesus' sayings from the beginning, which could of course have facilitated the collection of his sayings into this gattung. The addition of further wisdom sayings would be facilitated within the gattung, whose proclivities were to be more concerned with the validity or "truth" of the sayings incorporated than with their human authorship or "authenticity." Ulrich Luck [93] has sketched the development from the apocalyptic context that may have predominated in Jesus' sayings to a wisdom context predominating in the sayings in Matthew, who of all the canonical evangelists retains closest affinities with the gattung of sayings collections, in spite of his having imbedded Q in the gospel gattung of Mark. This movement is made all the more comprehensible in view of the emerging scholarly awareness that apocalypticism and wisdom, rather than being at almost mutually exclusive extremes within the spectrum of Jewish alternatives, share certain affinities and congruencies that encourage a transition from one to the other.

There are in the synoptic gospels peripheral indications of an association of Jesus with personified Wisdom. In Q (Matt. 11:19 // Luke 7:35) Jesus and John the Baptist seem to function as bearers of or spokesmen for Wisdom; in Luke 11:49 a Q saying is introduced as spoken by Wisdom, which in Matt. 23:34 is spoken by Jesus himself. M. Jack Suggs [94] has worked out this christological development from Q, which regarded Jesus

---

title to which the content, as established by Martin Noth, (*Überlieferungs-geschichtliche Studien*, 2d ed., 1957, pp. 66–67) would be well suited. Yet in this one instance "of days" has been omitted, either in deference to the usage of *devarim* at the opening of the verse to embrace both action and wisdom, or as a scribal error. Hence not only could the dangling "*devarim* of . . ." be taken to mean "The Book of the *Acts* of Solomon" (RSV), in analogy to other such historical works, but it could also be mistaken as analogous to the other Solomon literature, i.e. wisdom literature. Hence the shortened title could be taken to mean "Book of the *Sayings* of Solomon." Such a misunderstanding would be a further reflection of the association of *words* and *sages*.

93. Ulrich Luck, *Die Vollkommenheitsforderung der Bergpredigt*, Theologische Existenz heute, 150, 1968.
94. M. Jack Suggs, *Wisdom, Christology, and Law in Matthew's Gospel*, 1970. Cf. Koester, chap. 6 below, pp. 137 ff.

merely as Wisdom's envoy, to Matthew, which identified Jesus directly as Wisdom. Thus, prior to the elimination of the gattung of sayings collections completely from emergent orthodoxy, one can sense a development whose more radical correlative and ultimate outcome can be seen only in Gnosticism.[95]

Q's association of Jesus with Wisdom, together with its criticism of the sages (Matt. 11:25 // Luke 10:21), provides a foretaste of the debate to come. The *Gospel of Thomas* indicates the gnosticizing distortion of sayings that took place readily within this gattung. Hence the ongoing orthodox criticism of this distortion provides something of a context for understanding the process in which Q [96] is imbedded in the Marcan outline by Matthew and Luke and continues to be acceptable in the orthodox church only in the context of this other gattung, that of "gospel."

The tendency at work in the gattung *logoi sophon* was coordinated to the trajectory from the hypostasized Sophia to the gnostic redeemer. As "hidden sayings," the gattung found a place in Gnosticism. But with the dying out of the oral tradition of Jesus' sayings, it fell into disuse even here, for the gattung of dialogues of the Resurrected with his disciples provided a freer context for the imaginary gnostic speculations attributed to Jesus.

95. It is hoped that the rev. publication has here overcome the ambiguity of the 1964 German text responsible for the critical question of Wilhelm Wuellner, *JBL* 84 (1965): 302: "I question the view that the *Gattung* 'as such' provoked subsequent association of Jesus with the *sophos/hakam* tradition, and wonder whether it was not the other way around." The article does not presuppose the absence of such an association prior to the time Jesus' sayings were brought into collections. Wisdom sayings may well have been transmitted as individual sayings of Jesus prior to their incorporation in a collection (just as Matt. 11:19 par. may be older than Q); and there were early christological developments related to wisdom outside the sayings tradition (see my remarks in "A Formal Analysis of Col. 1,15–20," *JBL* 76 [1957]: 270–87, esp. 277–80). The purpose of the present essay is to draw attention to the gattung and the tendency at work in it, and thus to gain some awareness of the influence that would be at work upon the sayings tradition by being transmitted in this gattung. This is intended to help to make intelligible the development from Q to the *Gospel of Thomas*, as an aspect of the general development from Jewish wisdom to Hellenistic Gnosticism, from God's Sophia to the gnostic redeemer. This scope is well sensed by Koester, *"GNOMAI DIAPHOROI,"* chap. 5 below, pp. 166–87.
96. See with regard to Q my papers "Basic Shifts in German Theology," *Interpretation* 16 (1962): 76–97, esp. 82–86; and "A Critical Inquiry into the Scriptural Bases of Confessional Hermeneutics," *Journal of Ecumenical Studies* 3 (1966): 48–49; the latter, repr. in *Encounter* 28 (1967): 28–29.

4. GNOMAI DIAPHOROI

The Origin and Nature of
Diversification in the History
of Early Christianity

HELMUT KOESTER

The Crisis of the Historical and Theological Criteria

Walter Bauer, well known as a lexicographer but unfortunately little known as a historian of the ancient church, demonstrated convincingly in a brilliant monograph of 1934 [1] that Christian groups later labeled heretical actually predominated in the first two or three centuries, both geographically and theologically. Recent discoveries, especially those at Nag Hammadi in Upper Egypt, have made it even clearer that Bauer was essentially right, and that a thorough and extensive reevaluation of early Christian history is called for.

The task is not limited to a fresh reading of the known sources and a close scrutiny of the new texts in order to redefine their appropriate place within the conventional picture of early Christian history. Rather, it is the conventional picture itself that is

This essay appeared originally in the *Harvard Theological Review* 58 (1965): 279–318. The title is based on the term γνῶμαι διάφοροι used by Hegesippus with reference to the seven doctrinal divisions among the Jews: Essenes, Galilaeans, Hemerobaptists, Masbothei, Samaritans, Sadducees, and Pharisees (Eusebius *Hist. eccl.* 4. 22. 7). From these Hegesippus seems to derive the seven Christian heresies (ibid., 4. 22. 5). The word γνώμη, though not used as a technical term, elsewhere designates doctrines of Christian heretics; cf. Ignatius *Phld.* 3. 3; Justin *Dial.* 35. 4–6.
1. Walter Bauer, *Rechtgläubigkeit und Ketzerei im ältesten Christentum.* A second edition with appendices was published in 1964 by Georg Strecker; see also Georg Strecker, "A Report on the New Edition of Walter Bauer's *Rechtgläubigkeit und Ketzerei im ältesten Christentum*," *JBR* 31 (1965); 53–56. A critical evaluation of Strecker's republication is given by Hans Dieter Betz, "Orthodoxy and Heresy in Primitive Christianity," *Interpretation* 19 (1965); 299–311. *Orthodoxy and Heresy in Earliest Christianity*, an English translation of the Strecker edition of Bauer, is to be published in 1971 by Fortress Press.

called into question. At the same time, the convenient and time-honored labels for the distinction of heretical and orthodox prove to be very dangerous tools, since they threaten to distort the historian's vision and the theologian's judgment. The term *canonical* loses its normative relevance when the New Testament books themselves emerge as a deliberate collection of writings representing various divergent convictions which are not easily reconciled with each other. The criterion "apostolic" is useless when Christian movements that were later condemned as heretical can claim genuine apostolic origin. It is certainly untenable that the orthodox church and only this orthodox church was the direct offspring of the teachings, doctrines and institutions of the apostles' times and that only this church was able to preserve the apostolic heritage uncontaminated by foreign influences.

On the other hand, the criteria used for designating heresies such as "Jewish-Christian" and "gnostic" are questionable. The assumption implied in such criteria, that heresies always derive from undue foreign influences, is misleading, since Christianity as a whole, whether labeled heretical or orthodox, has assimilated and absorbed a staggering quantity of outside influences. Christianity in all its diversified appearances, including its so-called orthodox developments, is a thoroughly syncretistic religion. Furthermore, a label such as *Jewish-Christian* [2] is misleading, since everyone in the first generation of Christianity was a Jewish-Christian; finally, both Jewish traditions and Jewish thought (not to speak of the Old Testament) continued to exert considerable influence upon almost all developments of early Christian theology for a long time.

No less ambiguous and vague is the use of the term *gnostic* as a convenient tag for early Christian heresies. There may be different opinions about the origins of Gnosticism, whether it antedated Christianity and arose out of Judaism, oriental syncre-

---

2. This term was again freely employed in the *History of the Ancient Church* by Jean Daniélou and Henri I. Marrou, *The First Six Hundred Years*, 1964. Early heretical movements are understood as remnants of, or tendencies toward, Jewish sectarianism; heresies of the second century A.D. are seen as developments on the edges of Christianity. See also Jean Daniélou, *Théologie du Judéo-Christianisme: Histoire des doctrines chrétiennes avant Nicée*, vol. 1, 1958 (ET: *The Theology of Jewish Christianity*, 1964).

tism, or Hellenistic philosophy, or whether it was an inner-Christian development in the second century A.D. Such questions are secondary. More important is the recognition of the indebtedness of Christianity as a whole to a theological development that bears many marks of what is customarily designated as "gnostic." The line between heretical and orthodox cannot be drawn by simply using the term *gnostic* for certain developments customarily designated in such fashion. Rather, this is a question of theological evaluation among such developments as well as elsewhere.

This leads to the question of valid theological criteria. Unless this question is taken seriously, the new texts will only serve further to encourage "the fearsome process of conceiving useless hypotheses," [3] whose pretentious claims to objectivity are usually matched only by their historical irrelevance and theological naïveté. On the other hand, the search for theological criteria cannot be avoided by means of a retreat into dogmatic or religious propositions. Such propositions often attempt to fill the gaps and bridge the inconsistencies in the history of orthodoxy by postulating a primitive orthodox church which concealed its true beliefs in certain practices and institutions, and in the—theologically mute—"lex orandi." [4] Any such construction bars further questioning, since it takes for granted that which is actually the challenging, still unresolved task of the theological quest.

In the quest for criteria, the task of the historian and of the theologian cannot be divided into the free inquiry of the one and the dogmatic security of the other. The theological search for the decisive criterion for distinguishing between true and false belief

3. See the complaint of Ernst Käsemann, "Neutestamentliche Fragen von heute," *EVB*, 2:11.
4. This is the position of H. E. W. Turner, *The Pattern of Christian Truth: A Study in the Relations between Orthodoxy and Heresy in the Early Church*, Bampton Lectures, 1954, p. x; cf. pp. 474–75. Thus, in this, the only systematic treatment of the question of heresy in the early church since Bauer, Turner maintains that heresies always are specific types of deviation from a still underdeveloped core of more original true beliefs; e.g., Gnosticism is a "dilution," Marcion's doctrines are a "truncation," Montanism is a "distortion," and Arianism is an "evacuation," pp. 97–148. For further criticism of Turner's very learned and instructive study, see: Strecker in the appendix to Bauer, *Rechtgläubigkeit und Ketzerei*, 2d ed. 1964, pp. 293–300; Wilhelm Schneemelcher, "Walter Bauer als Kirchenhistoriker," *NTS* 9 (1962/63): 21; see also the positive evaluation of Bauer's work by Arnold Ehrhardt, "Christianity before the Apostles' Creed," *HTR* 55 (1962): 73–119 (repr. in Ehrhardt's collected essays, *The Framework of the New Testament Stories*, 1964, pp. 151–99).

coincides with the historical quest for the essential characteristics of early Christianity as such. We have to do here with a religious movement which is syncretistic in appearance and conspicuously marked by diversification from the very beginning. What its individuality is cannot be taken as established a priori.

The quest for criteria which could serve to identify the essential characteristics of that which is distinctively Christian, inevitably leads to a resumption of the discussion of the problem of the historical Jesus. It is beyond dispute that the historical origin of Christianity lies in Jesus of Nazareth, his life, preaching, and fate. Consequently, the quest for the individuality and singularity of Christianity is inevitably bound up with the problem of the historical Jesus. The so-called "old" quest of the historical Jesus, however, has failed in this respect. The "new" quest,[5] on the other hand, implies exactly the question with which we are concerned. Ernst Käsemann has stated the question thus in discussing the problem of the criteria for the legitimacy of the Christian proclamation or kerygma: "We can now put our problem in a nutshell: Does the New Testament kerygma count the historical Jesus among the criteria of its own validity?" [6] Accordingly, we are confronted, not with the quest for a new image of Jesus to be used as the norm for true belief, but with the question, whether and in which way that which has happened historically, i.e., in the earthly Jesus of Nazareth, is present in each given case as the criterion—not necessarily as the content—of Christian proclamation and theology. Only in this way can our inquiry arrive at an evaluation of the orthodox and heretical tendencies of each new historical situation [7]—certainly not in order to open a new heresy trial over the early Christian literature, but in order to recognize in which way the criterion for true Christian faith, consciously or unconsciously, structured the reinterpretation of the religious

5. For this see James M. Robinson, *A New Quest of the Historical Jesus*, SBT, 25, 1959, and esp. the 2d enl. German ed., *Kerygma und historischer Jesus*, 1967.
6. Ernst Käsemann, "Sackgassen im Streit um den historischen Jesus," *EVB* 2 (1964), 53.
7. For the question of the interrelation of the problem of the historical Jesus and the question of heresy, see also pp. 70–73 of my article "Häretiker im Urchristentum als theologisches Problem," in *Zeit und Geschichte*, Bultmann festschrift, 1964, pp. 61–76.

traditions and presuppositions upon which Christianity was dependent, irrespective of whether such religious inheritance was of Jewish, pagan, or (as becomes more and more important in the course of history) of Christian origin.

The complexity of this task cannot be overestimated, although the structure of our question is identical with the problem of systematic theology today. Since no generation of Christian theologians has direct access to the criterion of its own legitimacy, the result of historical research should never be presented as an abstract and timeless norm. It is impossible to isolate this kind of criterion, be it a priori, be it in retrospect. The historical criterion Jesus of Nazareth remains embedded in the historical witness that surrounds him, and cannot be separated from it. For historical inquiry, the New Testament itself has no special claim to have made the correct and orthodox use of the criterion of true faith. The canonical writings of the New Testament must be part and parcel of the historical questioning. Fortunately, we can rely here on a number of detailed studies, to a large extent influenced by Walter Bauer's book, which are concerned with the question of the heretical front in various writings of the New Testament.[8] At the same time, it is by no means necessary that these canonical writings emerge as the direct predecessors of later orthodoxy, and their opponents always as the fathers of the later heretics. But,

8. For bibliographical references until 1958 see my article, "Häretiker im Urchristentum," *RGG*, 3d ed., vol. 3 (1959), pp. 17–21. Publications since 1958 include the following on the Corinthian correspondence: Günther Bornkamm, "Herrenmahl und Kirche bei Paulus," in *Ges. Aufs.*, 2:138–76 (ET: "The Lord's Supper and Church in Paul," in *Early Christian Experience*, 1970) Ulrich Wilckens, *Weisheit und Torheit*, 1959; Dieter Georgi, *Die Gegner des Paulus im 2. Korintherbrief: Studien zur religiösen Propaganda in der Spätantike,* WMANT, 11, 1964. On other letters from the Pauline corpus: Helmut Koester, "The Purpose of the Polemic of a Pauline Fragment (Phil. 3)," *NTS* 8 (1961/ 62): 317–32; Walter Schmithals, "Die Irrlehrer von Rm. 16, 17–20," *Studia Theologica* 13 (1959): 51–69 (repr. in the collection of his essays, *Paulus und die Gnostiker*, 1965, pp. 159–73). On Polycarp of Smyrna and the pastoral letters: Hans von Campenhausen, *Polykarp von Smyrna und die Pastoralbriefe*, SHA, phil.-hist. Klasse, 1951, pp. 5–51 (repr. in the collection of his essays, *Aus der Frühzeit des Christentums*, 1963, pp. 197–252). On the whole question see: Georg Strecker, appendix to Walter Bauer's *Rechtgläubigkeit und Ketzerei im ältesten Christentum*, 2d ed., 1964, pp. 243–306; Walter Schmithals, "Zur Abfassung und ältesten Sammlung der paulinischen Hauptbriefe," *ZNW* 51 (1960): 225–45 (repr. in *Paulus und die Gnostiker*, pp. 175–200); see also my article in *Zeit und Geschichte*, pp. 61–76. Complete collections of all older materials and sources about heretics in early Christianity will be found in Adolf Hilgenfeld, *Die Ketzergeschichte des Urchristentums*, 1884 (repr. 1963).

certainly, the early controversies reflected in the New Testament are related to the great battle over heresy in the subsequent centuries. New sources from recent discoveries, first of all the *Gospel of Thomas,* must be considered as historically of equal value with the canonical writings; they cannot be depreciated by reason of their noncanonical nature.

The following sketch must remain both hypothetical and fragmentary. It is limited to the areas of Syria (both west and east, i.e., Antioch and Edessa) and Asia Minor, including the area of the Pauline mission in Greece across the Aegean Sea. One of its primary aims is to trace the lines from the developments of the "apostolic age" and the first century A.D. into the subsequent history of the ancient church.

The structure of the theological question will be explicated only at a few points in the following historical sketch. This article does not claim to present a final solution with complete documentation. It is, as my friend and colleague Krister Stendahl aptly remarked, a blueprint for further work in the history of early Christian theology. The *Gospel of Thomas* will receive more detailed attention, since solving some of the problems of this recently discovered text will doubtless have far-reaching consequences for the study of early Christianity as a whole. I am primarily concerned with those developments which begin in the earliest period, as the apostolic age is seldom considered in Walter Bauer's study.[9]

Palestine and Western Syria

Our evidence for the Christian beginnings in Palestine and in Syria is very fragmentary. There are, however, clear indications of a rather rapid dissemination of Christian proclamation in this area. From the beginning, there was no uniformity in beliefs and institutions; disagreements must have led to debates and controversies very early. Since, on the whole, these early Christian congregations understood themselves as part of the religious community of Judaism, such controversies were not exclusively internal Christian affairs. Rather they were discussions in which

9. I am, of course, heavily indebted to Bauer's work throughout, and the reader will have no difficulty in finding the respective sections in his book.

non-Christian Judaism participated as a silent or rather loquacious partner. This aspect is a conspicuous element throughout the early controversies, especially in the Syro-Palestinian region.[10]

In the first two decades there are three events which reveal the existence of such conflicts: (1) the circumstances of Stephen's martyrdom; (2) the apostles' council in Jerusalem; (3) the incident in Antioch. With regard to Stephen's martyrdom, the original account in the source used by Luke in Acts 6:1—8:5 is still clear enough to disclose that only the group of the "Hellenists" (Greek-speaking Jews from the Diaspora) was persecuted and forced to leave Jerusalem, whereas the circle around Peter and James remained there unmolested. The reason for this difference in the Jewish attitude toward the two Christian groups seems to have been that the circle around Peter and James remained within the realm of law observance and temple cult, whereas the Hellenists did not. Stephen was martyred, not because he was a Christian, but because as a Christian he rejected the law and ritual of his Jewish past.[11]

The apostles' council presupposes that the mission of the Christian Hellenists had not only grown in number but had created churches that included in their membership numbers of uncircumcised Gentiles. This created a difficulty, because the observance of the law was deemed essential by the Christians in Jerusalem, and probably also by other Christian groups. Yet membership of uncircumcised Gentiles implied that observance of the law could no longer be considered a characteristic mark of *all* Christians. The Jerusalem council did not solve the problem, but only reached a compromise in practice, namely the division of the areas of missionary activity, and the commitment that Paul's churches would collect money for the church in Jerusalem. This collection was designed to demonstrate the unity of all Christian churches (Gal. 2:7–10).

It is apparent from our sources that this compromise between

10. A large portion of the synoptic controversy paradigms have been formulated in this environment; see also below on the Gospel of Matthew, p. 123.
11. For literature and further discussion of the Stephen problem see the commentaries of Ernst Haenchen, *Die Apostelgeschichte*, 15th ed., 1965, ad loc., and Hans Conzelmann, *Die Apostelgeschichte*, 1963, pp. 43 ff., 52–53.

the two leading exponents of the Christian missionary enterprise could not eliminate all conflicts, either in practice or in theory. A third group also present at the council in Jerusalem (Gal. 2:4) had not signed the agreement, apparently because they were convinced that especially the ritual law of the Old Testament should be binding also for Gentile Christians. Paul, very shortly thereafter, encountered grave difficulties which were caused by opponents who insisted that the ritual law was indispensable for salvation.

But problems arose in practice also, precisely among those who had participated in the Jerusalem agreement and who were genuinely sympathetic to the cause of the Gentile mission. This was certainly the case with respect to Peter. While visiting at Antioch, in a display of a truly liberal attitude, he ate with the Gentiles (Gal. 2:12).[12] After the arrival in Antioch of some "people from James" (from Jerusalem), who were not willing to forego the demands of the dietary laws, Peter, and with him Barnabas and most other Jews, withdrew from table fellowship with Gentile Christians. For Peter and his friends this must have been a consistent display of open-minded concern, in this case directed toward the Jewish guests from Jerusalem. Quite the contrary for Paul! To him, this was hypocrisy, motivated by fear (Gal. 2:12–13).

On the surface, this is a conflict over practice. Paul's argument in Gal. 2:15 ff., however, illuminates the underlying theological problem which is based upon his concept of the law: the road from law-observance to life "in Christ" permits only one-way traffic. His concern is not that such withdrawal as Peter's disrupts the documentation of the unity of the one church of Jews and Gentiles. In this case he should have urged also the "people from James" to join the common (sacramental?) meals. But he did not do so. On the contrary, it was Peter and his friends who were interested in such a show of unity, in which even the Gentiles, in a truly liberal gesture, accepted Jewish dietary laws as long

12. For the understanding of Gal. 2:1 ff., I am greatly indebted to my colleague Dieter Georgi, who spent a year at Harvard as visiting professor at the time this article was written; see also Dieter Georgi, *Die Geschichte der Kollekte des Paulus für Jerusalem*, ThF, 38, 1965, pp. 13–30.

as James' people were present.[13] Paul grants that Jews who become Christians may continue faithfully in their law observance, but he protests against the understanding of the relation of Christian life to law that is documented by Peter's and Barnabas' behavior. Their enlightened (Jewish-Hellenistic) attitude makes the demands of the law theologically irrelevant, since it gives sufficient grounds for a liberal return into the observance of the law whenever this seems to be opportune in order to serve higher aims, such as the unity of the church.

The basis of Paul's argument is his interpretation of the death of Jesus and the Christian's participation in it (Gal. 2:18 ff.). The precise structure of this argument will be discussed below. Paul is using a traditional Jewish concept of law and covenant which enables him to understand Jesus' death on the cross as the end of the time of the law (Gal. 3). Therefore, a return into law obedience reverses the direction of God's act of salvation and invalidates the justification which this act has established. He who does so "stands condemned" (Gal. 2:11). This remarkable theological rigidity, bare of all liberality, forced Paul to depart from Antioch, since he obviously lost in the showdown with Peter and Barnabas. For the time being, this ended the controversy without involving a radical break. But his independent missionary work in Asia Minor and Greece did not protect Paul from further confrontations with a hostile Christian propaganda, not even in the churches he had founded. For this, we have ample evidence in Paul's own letters.

Even in Antioch and Syria (i.e., Coelesyria) the controversial issue was by no means eliminated through Paul's departure in A.D. 49. We know that Paul himself returned to Antioch for a brief visit (Acts 18:22–23); but not much can be learned from this brief notice. There is, however, enough evidence that "Pauline" Christianity continued to play a significant role in Antioch: Ignatius, bishop of Antioch around the year 100, represents an Antiochian Gentile Christianity that is emphatically Pauline.[14]

---

13. This is the only possible interpretation of Gal. 2:14; see also Heinrich Schlier, *Der Brief an die Galater,* 12th ed., 1962, ad loc.
14. Rudolf Bultmann, "Ignatius und Paulus," in *Studia Paulina,* de Zwaan festschrift, 1953, pp. 37–51; repr. in *Exegetica,* 1967, pp. 400–11 (ET: "Ignatius and Paul," in *Existence and Faith,* ed. Schubert M. Ogden, 1960, pp. 267–77).

Striking is Ignatius's complete indifference to the values of Old Testament interpretation (*Phld.* 8), and his suspicion of Judaizing heretics, whose Christology is the first gnostic docetism we know. The Pauline center of Ignatius's theology is apparent, but it cannot be defined exclusively as the true continuation of Pauline (and thus "apostolic" and "canonical") doctrine alone. The credal formulae (*Sm.* 1. 1–2; *Trall.* 9. 1–2; etc.), especially in their particular Ignatian interpretation, reveal a new emphasis upon the reality of the earthly Jesus. In a context of increasing speculative mythologization and metaphysical systematization of Christology, Ignatius tried to recapture not only the human reality of Jesus' crucifixion, but also the truly human center of Jesus' person. Whether he succeeded must remain an open question here. In view of the fact that his understanding of martyrdom gives concreteness to this return to the earthly dimension of the revelation in Jesus, his reliance upon essentially nonhistorical language, his sacramentalism, and his lack of interest in the Old Testament pose puzzling problems.

Ignatius's continuation of Paulinism in Antioch has to be seen over against the background of an equally strong development of traditions under the authority of Peter in the same area. The earliest witness, roughly contemporary with Ignatius, is the "Jewish-Christian" Gospel of Matthew.[15] Here Peter is the primary authority of the church (Matt. 16:13 ff.). His "power of the keys" documents a tightly organized church of nonepiscopal character—in striking contrast to Ignatius. The positive role of the results of Old Testament interpretation for the understanding of the gospel and the emphasis upon the renewed law of the Old Testament as the rule of life for the church leave no doubt that the Gospel of Matthew has no intention whatsoever of agreeing with the dangerous development of Paul's (and Ignatius's) radicalism. The conflict which arises in matters of church offices is not only an external one. The most powerful institutional weapon against the heresies was very soon to be the monarchical episcopate. Matthew, however, understands the apostolic authority of Peter as the power of the keys in analogy to the rabbinic authority

---

15. Günther Bornkamm, "Der Auferstandene und der Irdische," in *Zeit und Geschichte*, pp. 171–91, gives a thoughtful evaluation of the differences between Matthew's theology and Paul's.

of teaching and church discipline, represented in the offices of prophets and teachers (scribes; possibly also wise men, as a third category of offices).[16] The *Didache,* also from Syria, gives evidence of the predominance of the same offices (*Did.* 11. 1–2, 7–12; 12; 13), but also speaks of apostles (11. 3–6). At the same time, their authority is only accepted with certain reservations, and the churches are advised to elect bishops and deacons who, as local officers, are expected to replace prophets and teachers (*Did.* 15. 1–2).

It is hard to assess the different theological approaches and traditions which underlie the conflict between what are for the *Didache* the older offices of prophet and teacher (in agreement with Matthew), and the newer offices represented by Ignatius. The wandering of these prophets certainly was connected with the theology of the pilgrim, whose prototype was Jesus in his earthly life. This concept was widespread in Syria through many centuries (cf. the *Gospel* and *Acts of Thomas,* and the pseudo-Clementine letters *De virginitate*). Even if this theology is labeled heretical, its worthy predecessors, such as Abraham in the interpretation of Philo and the Letter to the Hebrews, as well as its powerful heirs, the later monastic movements, should not be forgotten.[17] It is characteristic of the development of antiheretical weapons that the Roman church, which at the time of the Gospel of Matthew did not even dream of the monarchical episcopate (see *1 Clem.*), should later borrow the concept of Peter's power of the keys in order to strengthen the theory of the episcopate, whereas the power of the keys was originally designed to bolster offices which became typical of the major heresies: the prophet in Montanism, and the teacher in Gnosticism.[18]

Although it may be barely possible to reconcile the basic intentions of Matthew's and Paul's theology, further developments of "Jewish-Christian" Petrine tradition in Syria excluded such

16. See Reinhart Hummel, *Die Auseinandersetzung zwischen Kirche und Judentum im Matthäusevangelium,* Beiträge zur evangelischen Theologie, 33, 1963, pp. 27–28, and, for the question of Peter's rule, esp. pp. 59–64.
17. For a discussion of the *Gospel of Thomas* see below, pp. 126 ff.
18. For further detail on the development of these offices, see Hans von Campenhausen, *Kirchliches Amt und geistliche Vollmacht,* 2d ed., BHTh, 14, 1963 (ET: *Ecclesiastical Office and Spiritual Authority,* 1968), passim.

peaceful coexistence. The *Kerygmata of Peter* (the source imbedded in the pseudo-Clementine *Homilies*) [19] combines rigorous insistence upon the continuation of the Old Testament law with gnosticising tendencies (both typical of Ignatius's opponents); Paul (called here Simon Magus) has become the prime scapegoat for all satanic falsifications and aberrations. Pauline Christianity seems nowhere represented. Other Jewish-Christian traditions in Syria, again under the authority of Peter, produced the *Gospel of Peter* and the *Apocalypse of Peter*; [20] however, these writings do not express the same theological concerns as one finds in the *Kerygmata of Peter*.

Only the oldest document of the Syrian Peter traditions, the Gospel of Matthew, has been accepted by the orthodox church (but see also the twenty-first chapter of the Gospel of John); all others were finally rejected. But the high esteem in which these "heretical" traditions were held is expressed, for example, by the reluctant rejection of the *Gospel of Peter* by Bishop Serapion of Antioch ca. A.D. 200. (Eusebius *Hist. eccl.* 4. 12). On the other hand, it should be remembered that the Gospel of Matthew is not rooted in the same soil as the orthodox concept of church and episcopate, represented by Ignatius, even though later orthodox circles found it convenient to use Matthew for their own benefit.

There is still a crying need for a fresh evaluation of the place of the western Syrian writings in the history of early Christian theology.[21] The situation is not yet clear concerning the survival of traditions which are independent of our canonical gospels.

19. For the discussion of this debated subject matter, see Georg Strecker, "The Kerygmata Petrou," in Edgar Hennecke, *New Testament Apocrypha*, vol. 2, 1965, pp. 102–11. The Coelesyrian origin of the *Kerygmata* is widely accepted.
20. Gilles Quispel and Robert M. Grant, "Note on the Petrine Apocrypha," *VigChr* 6 (1952): 31–32, give convincing evidence for the use of the *Apocalypse of Peter* in Theophilus of Antioch *Ad Autolyc*. 1. 14; in my own judgment, however, the evidence for Theophilus's use of the *Kerygma of Peter* (quoted first by Clement of Alexandria) is much less striking, although this does not exclude the possibility of the Syrian origin of the *Kerygma of Peter;* but Syrian origin of the *Apocalypse of Peter* is certainly very probable.
21. Strecker, *Das Judenchristentum in den Pseudo-Clementinen*, TU, 70, 1958, is only a beginning. The presentation of Hans-Joachim Schoeps, *Theologie und Geschichte des Judenchristentums*, 1949 is, for all its erudition, too programmatic to be of much help. But the studies of Arthur Vööbus (esp. his *History of Asceticism in the Syrian Orient*, Corpus Scriptorum Christianorum Orientalium, 184, 14, 1958) and Alfred Adam are of great value.

(e.g., the *Gospel of Peter* and the gospel traditions of the pseudo-Clementines). Even more complex difficulties arise if one tries to do justice to the theological efforts which have gone into the elaboration and reinterpretation of these traditions as they were further developed in Syria, i.e., in an environment that remains an enigma to the Western world. The frequently used label *Jewish-Christian* is not very helpful for the understanding of the religious beliefs and practices of this region. That the question of the law plays a significant role, especially in the pseudo-Clementines, does not in itself call for this label. It is difficult to see why one should consider the partly allegorical, partly ascetic understanding of the law in the pseudo-Clementines as more "Jewish" than the Western messianic and moralistic interpretation of the Old Testament.[22]

Edessa and the Osrhoëne

What can be said about the Christian beginnings in the Osrhoëne, especially in its capital Edessa? Once Walter Bauer had destroyed the wholly legendary edifice of orthodox wishful thinking,[23] there could be no doubt that for several centuries Chris-

22. The data gathered together in this article are by no means exhaustive. But it remains true that we know all too little about Christianity in Syria and Palestine in this early period. The existence of Christian churches in Galilee is probably presupposed in Mark 16:7 (cf. John 21). Acts 8:5 ff. uses a tradition about the beginnings of a church in Samaria that was independent of the Twelve (see also John 4 in comparison with the opposite view in Luke 9:51-56). Perhaps Luke 6:17 gives evidence of Christian communities in the region of Tyre and Sidon; cf. Hans Conzelmann, *Die Mitte der Zeit*, 3d ed., 1960, p. 48 (ET: *The Theology of Saint Luke*, 1960, p. 55). Acts 10:1 ff. presupposes that the church in Caesarea was Gentile Christian from the beginning. There is not enough material for us to guess the character of the Christian communities in the Jordan valley (baptismal sects? predecessors of the Mandaeans?) and in Damascus prior to Paul. Certainly, Paul had once been active as a missionary in "Arabia" (Gal. 1:17; i.e., Nabataea, South of Damascus), but no traces of this work of Paul are left. The geographical localization of the Gospel of John is notoriously difficult (Syria? Asia Minor? Egypt?). Thus I have foregone the opportunity to utilize this gospel as well as the Johannine letters in this geographical sketch. See, however, below, "The Johannine Trajectory," pp. 232 ff. Of course, the *Odes of Solomon* should also be considered here; however, it is not certain whether they originated in western or in eastern Syria.

23. See Bauer, *Rechtgläubigkeit*, pp. 6-48; see also recently A. F. J. Kliin, *The Acts of Thomas*, 1962, pp. 30-33. Turner's critique (*The Pattern of Christian Truth*. pp. 40-46) of Bauer's arguments is not convincing, as Ehrhardt has shown (*HTR* 55 [1962]: 94-95). In the light of new findings, Bauer's reconstruction of course has to be revised; see below. For the history of Christianity in the Osrhoëne in general see esp. Vööbus, *History of Asceticism*.

tianity in Edessa was dominated by the controversies between several major heresies; Bauer envisaged the Marcionites, the Bardesanites, and, last but not least, the Manichaeans. Compared with these, orthodoxy, in any case a latecomer (probably not much before A.D. 200), was in the third and fourth centuries still only a small and insignificant group.

Bauer was, however, probably mistaken in his assumption that the Marcionites were the first Christians to come to Edessa, soon after the middle of the second century A.D.[24] The only substantial piece of Thomas tradition known to Bauer in 1934 was the third century *Acts of Thomas*. Since the discovery of the gnostic library near Nag Hammadi, more important Thomas material has come to light: a *Gospel of Thomas* and a book of *Thomas the Contender*. It seems that this Coptic Thomas material also originates in Edessa or its surroundings.[25] The reasons for this thesis are:

a) The author of the (Coptic) *Gospel of Thomas* [26] is named "The Twin (*Didymos*) Judas Thomas," and in the book of *Thomas the Contender* [27] Jesus' words (written down by Matthew or Matthias) are spoken to "Judas Thomas." This unique appellation of the apostle Thomas has parallels only in the tradition of the Osrhoëne.[28] In the *Acts of Thomas* he is introduced

24. Bauer, *Rechtgläubigkeit,* pp. 27–29. His primary evidence, the mention of Marcion in the Edessene Chronicle and the stereotyped attacks against Marcion (and Mani and Bar Daisan) by Aphraates and Ephrem—whereas other heretics are seldom mentioned—only proves that the Marcionites played a role in Edessa at least in the late third and in the fourth centuries.
25. Arguments for Edessene origin of the *Gospel of Thomas* were first set forth by Henri-Charles Puech in his studies of this document; see the articles quoted in Puech, "Gnostic Gospels and Related Documents," in Hennecke, *NT Apocrypha,* 3d ed., vol. 1, 1963, p. 282; see also W. C. van Unnik, *Newly Discovered Gnostic Writings,* 1960, pp. 49–50.
26. Coptic text of the *Gospel of Thomas* with English translation by A. Guillaumont, H.-C. Puech, G. Quispel, W. Till, and Yassah 'Abd al Masīh, 1959. A good translation into Latin, German, and English is easily accessible in Kurt Aland, *Synopsis Quattuor Evangeliorum,* 1964, pp. 517–30.
27. *CG,* II, 7 (138. 1—145. 19); cf. Puech, "Gnostic Gospels," in Hennecke, *NT Apocrypha,* 1:307; James M. Robinson, "The Coptic Gnostic Library Today," *NTS* 14 (1967/68): 392.
28. It would be misleading to speak of "Syria" in general, since Matthew, from western Syria, knows only the simple name *Thomas* for this apostle (Matt. 10:3; following Mark). Some of these and the following observations regarding the significance of this particular form of the name of the apostle Thomas were first made by Puech, "Gnostic Gospels," in Hennecke, *NT Apocrypha,* 1:286–87, and the literature quoted on p. 282.

as Ἰούδας Θωμᾶς ὃ καὶ Δίδυμος.[29] Also, in the catholic Abgar legend from Edessa, Thomas is called Ἰούδας ὃ καὶ Θωμᾶς.[30] Nowhere in the New Testament is there any connection of the names of Judas and Thomas; but in John 14:22, instead of "Judas, not Iscariot," sy[c] reads "Judas Thomas" (sy[s] reads "Thomas"). For control we can refer to the non-Edessene *Infancy Gospel of Thomas,* in which the writer is called "Thomas, the Israelite (Philosopher)." [31] Thus it is obvious that this tradition of "Judas Thomas (the Twin)" [32] is peculiar to early Christianity in the Osrhoëne.[33]

b) The *Acts of Thomas* shows several pre-Manichaean elements, i.e., it stands halfway between Christian and Manichaean Gnosis. Together with other Acts of Apostles, it was then used by the Manichaeans. It can be affirmed now with respect to the *Gospel of Thomas* found at Nag Hammadi "that it is identical with the document of the same title which our ancient authorities number among the Manichaean Scriptures." [34] There can be little doubt that the *Gospel of Thomas* came to the Manichaeans from Edessa rather than from Egypt.

c) The *Gospel of Thomas* was used by the author of the *Acts of Thomas,*[35] which certainly was written in the Osrhoëne in the early third century A.D., and which is the direct continuation of the eastern Syrian Thomas tradition as it is represented in the second century by the *Gospel of Thomas.*

29. According to the Greek text. The Syriac reads, "Judas Thomas the Apostle"; see also below.
30. It is interesting to note that "Judas Thomas" only appears when Eusebius quotes the text of the Abgar legend verbatim (1. 13. 11), whereas in his own summaries he uses the simple "Thomas" (1. 13. 4; 2. 1. 6). According to Klijn, *Acts of Thomas,* p. 158, the Syriac translation of Eusebius has "Judas Thomas" in all instances referred to above.
31. The Syriac translation of this infancy gospel has only the title "Infancy of the Lord Jesus"; see Oscar Cullmann, in Hennecke, *NT Apocrypha,* 1:390.
32. The *Acts of Thomas* understands the designation "the Twin" as referring to Thomas as the twin brother of Jesus. This is usually considered as an interpretation of the word *twin* which arose from the peculiar interests of the *Acts of Thomas* (the earthly apostle appears as the "twin" of the heavenly redeemer). But this tradition is older, since, according to Puech, "Gnostic Gospels," in Hennecke, *NT Apocrypha,* 1:308, in the book of *Thomas the Contender* Jesus addresses Thomas as his "twin brother."
33. For further reference to traditions about the apostle Thomas, see Walter Bauer, *Das Leben Jesu im Zeitalter der neutestamentlichen Apokryphen,* 1909, pp. 444–45; Günther Bornkamm, in Hennecke, *NT Apocrypha,* 2:426–27.
34. Puech, "Gnostic Gospels," in Hennecke, *NT Apocrypha,* 1:283; see also 299–300.
35. A good survey of the passages in question is found in ibid., 1:285–87.

If this gospel had its origin in the Osrhoëne, but was already known in Egypt in the second half of the second century, as the *Oxyrhynchus Papyri*, 1. 654 and 655 testify, the time of its writing must have been ca. A.D. 150 or earlier.[36] This proves that the Thomas tradition was the oldest form of Christianity in Edessa, ● antedating the beginning of both Marcionite and orthodox Christianity in that area. The greatest remaining obstacle to an evaluation of the history and theology of Christianity in Edessa is the uncertainity about the character of the *Gospel of Thomas* and the nature and origin of the tradition incorporated in it. In order to attempt a brief description of Edessene Christian history in the first centuries, one cannot avoid discussing critically some of the controversial issues connected with the *Gospel of Thomas*.

The origin of Thomas' gospel tradition. In the year 1908 Emil Wendling had already proved beyond doubt that the saying in *POxy,* 1. 6 ("No prophet is acceptable in his fatherland, and no physician performs healings among those who know him") is more primitive than the present narrative in Mark 6:1–6.[37] This result was confirmed through form-critical analysis by Rudolf Bultmann long before the discovery of the *Gospel of Thomas*.[38] Since the discovery of the complete text of this gospel, to which *POxy,* 1 belongs, an unusual lineup in scholarship has occurred.[39] Gilles Quispel had the right intuition from the very beginning. He argued that the sayings of the *Gospel of Thomas* must have "come from a different and independent Aramaic tradition." [40]

---

36. Van Unnik, *Newly Discovered Gnostic Writings,* pp. 49–50 and 53–54, dates the *Gospel of Thomas* not earlier than A.D. 170, since he follows Quispel's improbable suggestion that it made use of the *Gospel according to the Hebrews*; on this question see below, p. 130 n. 42.
37. Emil Wendling, *Die Entstehung des Marcus-Evangeliums,* 1908, pp. 53–56.
38. Rudolf Bultmann, *Die Geschichte der synoptischen Tradition,* 1st ed., 1921; for the discussion of Mark 6:1-6, see ET: *History of the Synoptic Tradition,* 1963, pp. 31 f.
39. For the discussion of this question up to 1960, see Ernst Haenchen, "Literatur zum Thomasevangelium," *ThR* 27 (1961): 147–78, 306–38, esp. pp. 162–78. It is not my intention here to bring Haenchen's bibliography up to date, nor to present a complete survey of my own. I merely want to indicate some trends and preoccupations in the treatment of the problem.
40. Gilles Quispel, "The Gospel of Thomas and the New Testament," *VigChr* 11 (1957): 189–207; cf. also his article, "Some Remarks on the Gospel of Thomas," *NTS* 5 (1958/59): 276–90; and more recently "The Gospel of Thomas and the Gospel of the Hebrews," *NTS* 12 (1965/66), 371–82. I am grateful

His arguments receive convincing support from his acute awareness of the problems of noncanonical tradition in other early
Christian literature (pseudo-Clementines, Makarios, Diatessaron).[41] Unfortunately, Quispel's assumption is that the source
for these primitive and independent sayings of the *Gospel of
Thomas* was the so-called *Gospel according to the Hebrews*.[42]
His disdain for form-critical methodology[43] and his contention
that the *Gospel of Thomas* is not gnostic in character[44] have
failed to enhance the persuasive power of his otherwise valid
hypothesis.

On the other hand, scholars who sought to prove the gnostic
character of the *Gospel of Thomas* have usually tried to strengthen
their arguments for the secondary and heretical character of this
gospel by the hypothesis of its dependence upon the canonical
gospels. The list of authors who have thrown their weight on
this side of the controversy is impressive.[45] However, the evi-

---

for Quispel's presentation of our agreements and disagreements, because his
arguments for and against are both friendly and amusing. I cannot, however, in
this article, engage in a lengthy discussion of the hypothesis of Thomas's dependence upon the Gospel of the Hebrews; I hope to do that in the near future.
41. See also Gilles Quispel, "L'Evangile selon Thomas et les Clementines,"
VigChr 12 (1958): 181–96; idem, "L'Evangile selon Thomas et le Diatessaron,"
VigChr 13 (1959): 87–117; idem, "L'Evangile selon Thomas et le 'text oriental'
du Nouveau Testament," *VigChr* 14 (1960): 204–15; idem, "Der Heliand und
das Thomasevangelium," *VigChr* 16 (1962): 121–53; idem, "The Syrian Thomas
and the Syrian Macarius," *VigChr* 18 (1964): 226–35.
42. Cf. Quispel's articles quoted in n. 40; also Haenchen's critique "Literatur
zum Thomasevangelium," pp. 162 ff.) of this hypothesis. To conceive of this
gospel as a very primitive synoptic-type writing is impossible, as Philipp Vielhauer has shown recently in his treatment of the "Jewish-Christian Gospels" in
Hennecke, *NT Apocrypha*, 1:117–65. Relations, of course, cannot be denied;
but since the *Gospel of Thomas* migrated from Syria to Egypt, the Egyptian
Gospel according to the Hebrews is more likely to depend upon the *Gospel of
Thomas*, unless free tradition explains the similarities.
43. See, e.g., Quispel's glowing remarks, in "Gospel of Thomas and the New
Testament," pp. 206–7. I am pleased, however, to learn from "Gospel of Thomas
and the Gospel of the Hebrews," p. 372, that Quispel has a much more positive
view of form criticism. I appreciate this agreement, since it furnishes us with a
better basis for discussion in future controversies.
44. This thesis was most vigorously argued by Gilles Quispel in his article
"Gnosticism and the New Testament," in *The Bible in Modern Scholarship*, ed.
J. Philip Hyatt, 1966, pp. 252–71, and *VigChr* 19 (1965): 65–85.
45. E.g., Robert M. Grant, David N. Freedman, *The Secret Sayings of Jesus*, 1960;
Haenchen, "Literatur zum Thomasevangelium" and *Die Botschaft des Thomas-
Evangeliums*, 1961; Bertil Gärtner, *The Theology of the Gospel of Thomas*, 1961;
H. E. W. Turner, "The Theology of the Gospel of Thomas," in *Thomas and the
Evangelists*, ed. Hugh Montefiore and H. E. W. Turner, SBT, 35, 1962. See
also Harvey K. McArthur, "The Gospel according to Thomas," in *New Testa-*

dence of Wendling and Bultmann for the primitive character
of the saying *POxy,* 1. 6 (*Gospel of Thomas* 31) has never been
refuted, nor even been seriously debated.[46] Furthermore, the em-
ployment of rigorous form-critical analysis is strikingly nonexistent in a great number of the studies referred to above,[47] with
but one exception, the evaluation of the parables of the *Gospel
of Thomas.*[48] It is evident that the form-critical work of Joachim
Jeremias on the parables has had a much greater impact, especially
on the English-speaking world, than Bultmann's form-critical
publications. Hugh Montefiore's detailed and careful study is especially important in proving clearly "that Thomas's divergences
from Synoptic parallels can be most satisfactorily explained on the
assumption that he was using a source distinct from the Synoptic

---

ment Sidelights: Essays in Honor of Alexander C. Purdy, 1960, pp. 43–77; idem,
"The Dependence of the Gospel of Thomas on the Synoptics," *ExpT* 71 (1960):
286–87. The wisdom of the methodological procedure of the latest and most
extensive publication on this question is beyond my comprehension: Wolfgang
Schrage, *Das Verhältnis des Thomas-Evangeliums zur synoptischen Tradition
und zu den koptischen Evangelienübersetzungen,* suppl. 29 to *ZNW,* 1964.
Schrage tries to prove the secondary character of the tradition contained in the
Gospel of Thomas by a comparison with the Sahidic translation of the synoptic
gospels (and John). However, the Sahidic translation of the New Testament
was not made until the third century at the earliest; cf. Bruce M. Metzger, *The
Text of the New Testament,* 1964, pp. 79–81. Thus, any agreements could only
prove that the Sahidic version was influenced by the *Gospel of Thomas,* which
was certainly known in Egypt by the end of the second century, as is evidenced
by the Oxyrhynchus Logia. Moreover, Schrage's understanding of form-critical
method is glaringly evident in comments such as the following (on Saying 31,
i.e., *POxy* 1. 6): ". . . Thomas has detached the saying from the historical situation to which it was assigned by the synoptic gospels, and has again made it a
'free logion' " (p. 76).
46. I thought that Quispel did not quite expect to receive support from these
quarters. But I am willing to learn from the mysterious author who has written
in the *Weltwoche* (cf. Quispel, "Gospel of Thomas and the Gospel of the
Hebrews," p. 372) that I was mistaken in this regard.
47. A rare exception is the article by Hans-Werner Bartsch, "Das Thomas-
Evangelium und die synoptischen Evangelien," *NTS* 6 (1959/60): 249–61; also
Oscar Cullmann, "Das Thomasevangelium und die Frage nach dem Alter der in
ihm enthaltenen Tradition," *ThLZ* 85 (1960): 321–34 (ET: *Interpretation* 16
[1962]: 418–38). Both of these authors, consequently, ascribe a much higher
probability to the existence of independent tradition.
48. In addition to authors quoted above, who base their judgment largely upon
the parables (like Quispel and Cullmann), see Claus-Hunno Hunzinger, "Ausser-
synoptisches Traditionsgut im Thomas-Evangelium," *ThLZ* 85 (1960): 843–46;
idem, "Unbekannte Gleichnisse Jesu aus dem Thomas-Evangelium," in *Judentum,
Urchristentum, Kirche,* Joachim Jeremias festschrift, suppl. 26 to *ZNW,* 1960,
209–20; Hugh Montefiore, "A Comparison of the Parables of the Gospel according to Thomas and of the Synoptic Gospels," in Montefiore and Turner,
Thomas and the Evangelists, pp. 40–78; first published in *NTS* 7 (1960/61):
220–48.

Gospels. Occasionally this source seems to be superior. . . ." [49] Meanwhile, some scholars have assigned a higher possibility to the derivation of the entire (or almost entire) tradition contained in the *Gospel of Thomas* from an independent early stage of the sayings tradition,[50] thus returning to a confirmation of Quispel's original suggestion. It is my opinion that this view is correct.

Further studies should involve a fresh analysis of the parallel sections in the synoptic gospels: the collection of parables and sayings underlying Mark 4 and Matt. 13; the basis for the Marcan sayings used in Mark 2 and 3; Q sections underlying Matt. 5–7 and Luke 6 as well as other Q material now occurring in Matt. 11:7 ff. // Luke 7:42 ff., Matt. 21–22 par., etc.; and, finally, the sources for the special Lucan material in Luke 12 (Luke 11:27— 12:56 is paralleled by no fewer than thirteen sayings in the *Gospel of Thomas,* seven of which have parallels only in Luke).[51] In such a comparison the synoptic gospels are not only to be used as reference material, i.e., as a convenient referent for stating agreements and deviations, and for discussing priorities in order to determine the relatively greater or smaller value of the *Gospel of Thomas* as a source for the historical Jesus. Rather, form-critical analysis should enable us to assess the parallel development of the same tradition of sayings which is preserved in both the *Gospel of Thomas* and the synoptic gospels. It is not improbable that each contains about as much primary and as much secondary material as the other. *Gemeindetheologie,* not to be confused with Hellenistic mythology,[52] was indeed the power behind the formation of the tradition in both cases.[53]

49. Montefiore, "A Comparison," in *Thomas and the Evangelists,* p. 78.

50. Cf. R. McL. Wilson, "Thomas and the Growth of the Gospels," *HTR* 53 (1960): 231–50; idem, "Thomas and the Synoptic Gospels," *ExpT* 72 (1960/ 61): 36–39; idem, *Studies in the Gospel of Thomas,* 1960; R. A. Spivey, *The Origin and Milieu of the Gospel according to Thomas* (Diss., Yale University, 1962); see also Ernest W. Saunders, "A Trio of Thomas Logia," *Biblical Research* 8 (1963): 43–59; Robert North, "Chenoboskion and Q," *CBQ* 24 (1962): 154–70.

51. An analysis of these materials is given in my article "One Jesus and Four Primitive Gospels," chap. 5 below.

52. See Quispel's remarks to such an effect, in "Gospel of Thomas and the New Testament," p. 206.

53. The Gospel of John is not very likely to have served as a source for the *Gospel of Thomas.* However, parallels are remarkable, as Raymond E. Brown has

The nature of the tradition under the authority of Thomas.
The pattern of "apostolic" tradition which appears under the name
of the apostle Judas Thomas in eastern Syria may be compared
to the Peter tradition in Coelesyria discussed above and the Paul
tradition in Asia Minor to be discussed below. It is important
to distinguish such traditions from later catholic-orthodox claims
to the names and authority of certain apostles. The purpose of
such claims was to establish the legitimate apostolic doctrine and
succession in the antignostic controversy. The successful Roman
attempt to establish the authority of Peter in Rome belongs to
this type of apostolic "tradition." Similar is the later attempt of
orthodox Christians in Edessa, who tried to establish the authority
of Thaddaeus as the apostolic authority of true Christianity in
eastern Syria. However, the Pauline tradition in Asia Minor and
the Petrine tradition in western Syria belong to a different pattern.
There is no doubt that these traditions had their ultimate origin
in the actual, historical missionary activity of these apostles in the
areas in which their names survived; i.e., they were already in
existence before the weapons of the antiheretic controversy had
been forged.

The eastern Syrian Thomas tradition must in my view be
understood as one of these primitive local traditions, and not as
the product of the later antiheretic controversy. Thomas was the
authority for an indigenous Syrian Christianity even before the
formation of noticeable orthodox influence in this area. To be
sure, we know from reliable sources that Peter had in fact been
in Antioch, and that Paul was in fact a missionary in Asia Minor.
In the case of Thomas, unfortunately, we do not have any direct
historical evidence comparable to that for Peter in Antioch and
Paul in Asia Minor, to confirm the assumption that Judas, the
twin (brother of Jesus), actually was the apostle of Edessa. This
must remain a mere conjecture. It is, however, a legitimate historical question to seek a reason for the early existence of Thomas's
authority in that area.

---

shown in his article "The Gospel of Thomas and St. John's Gospel," *NTS* 9
(1962/63): 155–77. In my opinion, this points to some connections in the
tradition and environment of both writings.

In this connection it is necessary to consider again the name "Judas Thomas." The simple name Thomas, the only form that occurs in the canonical tradition, is the transliteration of a Semitic surname,[54] meaning the "twin," into the widely used Greek proper name Θωμᾶς. That the surname "twin" was the original meaning of the underlying Aramaic tradition is still evident in the Greek expression "called twin" (ὁ λεγόμενος Δίδυμος, John 11:16, etc.). What is lost in the canonical tradition is the actual, original name of this apostle: Judas. That this was his given name is as likely as the fact that Peter's given name was Simeon. Yet this Judas is also called the (twin) brother of the Lord. This raises the question whether the canonical tradition did not after all preserve the original name of this apostle elsewhere: in the name of the author of the Letter of "Judas [Jude], the brother of James." For this James is certainly the brother of the Lord. The identity of Judas, the brother of the Lord, with Thomas, is more likely a primitive tradition than a later confusion. Such a primitive tradition was, to be sure, suppressed by later orthodox developments. The first step in this process is visible in the incipit of the Letter of Jude itself: "brother of the Lord" is avoided in favor of "brother of James." Subsequently, 2 Peter incorporated the whole Letter of Jude, and thus the name of the Lord's brother "Jude the brother of James" disappeared completely from the canonical tradition, except for the accidental preservation of the original Letter of Jude. On the other hand, if the designation "Judas Thomas, the twin [brother of the Lord]" is more primitive, it is by no means impossible that its appearance in the *Gospel of Thomas* is derived from the actual historical activity of this apostle in Edessa, or in another area of Palestine-Syria from which Edessene Christianity derived its beginnings. The alternative would be that an early Christian group appropriated the name of one of the brothers of Jesus. But since this group would have preserved an original form of this name that has been lost otherwise in the canonical tradition, even such an adoption would have

---

54. תאמא is not recorded as a Jewish name anywhere in the Mishna and Tosephta, nor in the Jewish papyri, and there is only very slight evidence that it might have been in use as a Phoenician name, as my colleague, Frank M. Cross, Jr., confirms.

taken place before the composition of the canonical gospels or in an independent tradition that developed in an area aside from the regions related to the canonical literature.

In order to determine its nature it is also necessary to consider the genre (gattung) of the material preserved in this Thomas tradition. We are here not advocating the specific synoptic source Q as the literary source for the *Gospel of Thomas*,[55] since the basis of *Thomas* is certainly not identical with any possible form of the second source common to Matthew and Luke. The *Gospel of Thomas* reflects smaller collections [56] which were partly incorporated in Q, but which were otherwise directly available to Luke and Mark (whereas the special traditions of Matthew seem to have no parallels in the *Gospel of Thomas*). Further light can be expected from more detailed studies of the *Sitz im Leben* and theological function of the sayings, the *logoi,* in the early church. An important step in this direction has been taken by James M. Robinson.[57] A direct consequence of his study can be formulated in this way: the *Gospel of Thomas* continues, even if in a modified way, the most original gattung of the Jesus tradition—the *logoi sophon*—which, in the canonical gospels, became acceptable to the orthodox church only by radical critical alteration, not only of the form, but also of the theological intention of this primitive gattung. Such critical evaluation of the gattung, *logoi,* was achieved by Matthew and Luke through imposing the Marcan narrative-kerygma frame upon the sayings tradition represented by Q.[58]

---

55. Cf. the warning of Bartsch, "Thomas-Evangelium und die synoptischen Evangelien," p. 258, although his extreme scepticism regarding Q is certainly unfounded.

56. Possibly more like the collections of sayings used in *1 Clem.* 13 and *Did.* 1. These two examples, of course, emphasize the difficulty of the problem, since the sayings in *1 Clem.* 13. 2 are more primitive than Matthew and Luke, whereas the collection inserted into *Did.* 1. 3–5 may have been composed on the basis of Matthew and Luke. My study *Synoptische Überlieferung bei den Apostolischen Vätern,* TU, 65, 1957, pp. 12–16, 220–37, has been recently carried forward by Bentley Layton, "The Sources, Date, and Transmission of *Didache* 1, 3b—2, 1," *HTR* 61 (1968): 343–83.

57. James M. Robinson, *"LOGOI SOPHON,"* chap. 3 above.

58. Cf. Robinson, above, esp. pp. 112–13; further, idem, "The Problem of History in Mark, Reconsidered," *USQR* 20 (1965): 135, where he says about his study of *logoi* and Q: "I have tried to trace this *Gattung,* whose gnosticizing proclivity is blocked by Matthew and Luke by embedding Q in the Markan gospel form."

Thus, Thomas does not use Q, but he does represent the eastern branch of the gattung, *logoi*, the western branch being represented by the synoptic *logoi* of Q, which was used in western Syria by Matthew and later by Luke. If this parallelism of Thomas's tradition of the *logoi* with Q is seen correctly, Papias's reference to the *logia* which Matthew composed in "Hebrew" should not be overlooked.[59] It may not be a coincidence that Thomas and Matthew appear as a pair in the list of apostles (Matt. 10:3; cf. Mark 3:18; Luke 6:15), and the book of *Thomas the Contender* has an explicit, "The book of Thomas the Contender writing to the perfect," which conflicts with the incipit, "These are the secret words which the Savior spoke to Judas Thomas, which I have written down, I myself, Mathaias" (*sic.* = Matthew?).[60]

The theological character of the Thomas tradition. The present battle over the question whether the *Gospel of Thomas* is gnostic or Jewish-Christian is of little avail. If there is any possibility that this gospel has preserved traditions from the first and second Christian generations, it is very likely that such traditions were as Jewish-Christian as the synoptic sayings source Q, or Paul, or the Gospel of Matthew. The reference to James the Righteous (Saying 12) is certainly interesting, but by no means typically Jewish-Christian; after all, James's commanding position is also recognized by Paul (Gal. 2; 1 Cor. 15:7), Acts 15, and the Letter of James (1:1–2), i.e., it is historical. Furthermore, in the *Gospel of Thomas* the weight and authority of James is surpassed by Thomas (Saying 13), as in the later orthodox church (beginning with Luke-Acts) James's authority is surpassed by Peter. Finally, it would be a mistake to link the *Gospel of Thomas* with the "Jewish-Christian" circles of western Syria from which one may derive the Ebionites who used a modified Gospel of Matthew, assigned a high value to the Old Testament law, and rejected the authority of Paul, since none of these traits was

---

59. James M. Robinson, *"LOGOI SOPHON,"* above, pp. 74 ff., emphasizes this connection rather strongly.
60. Puech, "Gnostic Gospels," in Hennecke, *NT Apocrypha*, 1:307; cf. Robinson, above, pp. 80 f.

typical of Edessa.[61] The designation "Jewish-Christian" is probably not wrong, but it is indeterminate; it says very little.

The same, however, seems to be true of the use of the term *gnostic*. Yet this would be true to a somewhat lesser degree, since Ernst Haenchen [62] probably has been able to present a gnostic reading of the *Gospel of Thomas* as it was current, say, in Egypt in ca. A.D. 175, or in Syria even somewhat earlier.

The crucial problem of Gnosticism, however, is not how to relate second century gnostic writings to subsequent developments —as important as this task may be—but how to interpret early forms of Gnosticism with respect to their roots in early Christian and Jewish theology. Here the *Gospel of Thomas* occupies a uniquely decisive position, since we can see in it a distinctive reinterpretation of originally eschatological sayings and their terminology. The question is not only that of various stages in the growth of the tradition, so as to distinguish between an older "synoptic Palestinian" core and later gnosticizing accretion. We are rather confronted also with the "gnosticizing proclivity" [63] of the gattung *Logoi* itself, i.e., in its oldest and most primitive states. It is to be remembered that a gattung is not just a deliberate choice of an external form, but the manifestation of a distinctive subject matter.

The predecessor of the Christian collection and transmission of one particular aspect of Jesus' sayings was the gattung *logoi sophon*, primarily developed in the Jewish wisdom movement.[64]

61. A collection of Pauline letters was in use in Edessa before the arrival of representatives of the orthodox church. This is shown indirectly through the special introduction of the antignostic third letter to the Corinthians into Edessa, probably in order to fight against the existing concept of Paul; cf. Walter Bauer, *Rechtgläubigkeit,* pp. 45 ff. It is also interesting to note that the sectarian heirs of the Thomas tradition in Syria, the Manichaeans, reflect a positive evaluation of Paul; see *Kephalaia,* ed. Carl Schmidt, Hugo Ibschner, H. J. Polotsky, and A. Böhlig, Manichäische Handschriften der staatlichen Museen Berlin, 1, 1, 1940, p. 13, ll. 19–26.
62. Haenchen, *Botschaft des Thomas-Evangeliums.* One may note that Grant, *Secret Sayings of Jesus,* interprets this noncanonical gospel by appeal to later gnostic writings—a method that he has criticized vociferously whenever it was employed to interpret canonical New Testament writings.
63. James M. Robinson; see n. 58 above.
64. See the excellent analysis by Robinson, *"LOGOI SOPHON,"* chap. 3 above, esp. pp. 85–103. It is known that Bultmann in *The History of the Synoptic Tradition* drew his categories for the analysis of the *logia* of Jesus from the Jewish wisdom literature; see Robinson, above, pp. 71–74.

This existing form served as a focus of crystallization for the preservation of one particular aspect of Jesus' historical appearance and work: his teachings.[65] It is not possible to discuss here the complex questions regarding historical and primitive sayings or groups of sayings in these early pre-Q and pregospel collections. It is highly probable, however, that such collections were dominated by wisdom sayings, legal statements (critique of old conduct and pronouncements regarding new conduct), prophetic sayings (including some I-words, beatitudes, and woes), and parables, just as in Jesus' own teaching. As is partly evident from Q, sayings predicting Jesus' suffering, death, and resurrection, and the material reflecting the development of a christological evaluation of the person of Jesus, were still absent; detailed apocalyptic predictions, such as those contained in Mark 13, were not part of such primitive collections; [66] specific regulations for the life of the church (*Gemeinderegeln*) were equally absent.

What was the theological tendency of such collections of *logoi?* The answer to this depends entirely upon the christological post-Easter frame to which they were subjected. Q domesticated the *logoi* through a kind of apocalypticism which identified Jesus with the future Son of man. Mark (and subsequently Matthew and Luke) were able to incorporate the *logoi* in the "gospel" developed on the basis of the early Hellenistic (Pauline) kerygma. Neither of these developments seems to have touched the *logoi* tradition that found its way into the *Gospel of Thomas.* The criterion controlling *Thomas's logoi* is apparently more closely connected with the internal principle of this gattung as it gave focus to the transmission of Jesus' sayings: the authority of the word of wisdom as such, which rests in the assumption that the teacher

---

65. It is not possible here to enter into the controversy with Birger Gerhardsson, *Memory and Manuscript,* Acta Seminarii Neotestamentici Upsaliensis, 22, 2d ed., 1964. Since my disagreements with this book can hardly be exaggerated, a few critical remarks would not do justice to Gerhardsson's work or to the importance of this controversy.
66. Whether any apocalyptic Son of man sayings were existent at this stage is very doubtful. Cf. Philipp Vielhauer, "Gottesreich und Menschensohn in der Verkündigung Jesu," in *Festschrift für Günther Dehn,* 1957, pp. 51–79; idem, "Jesus und der Menschensohn." *ZThK* 60 (1963): 133–77; both articles are reprinted in his *Aufsätze zum Neuen Testament,* Theologische Bücherei, 31, 1965, pp. 55–91, 92–140; cf. also Norman Perrin, *Rediscovering the Teaching of Jesus,* 1967, passim.

is present in the word which he has spoken. If there is any "Easter experience" to provide a Christology congenial to this concept of the *logoi,* it is here the belief in "Jesus, the Living One" (incipit of the *Gospel of Thomas*). The view that the Jesus who spoke these words was and is the Living One, and thus gives life through his words, permeates the entirety of the *Thomas* sayings.[67] On this basis, a direct and almost unbroken continuation of Jesus' own teaching takes place—unparalleled anywhere in the canonical tradition—and, at the same time, a further development ensues, which emphasizes even further the presence of the revelation in the word of Jesus and its consequences for the believer.

Accordingly, the most conspicuous form of sayings [68] in the *Gospel of Thomas* is the wisdom saying (proverb), often in metaphorical forms (*Bildworte,* etc.), and almost completely paralleled in the synoptic gospels.[69] Not all of these sayings necessarily have allegorical functions, but certainly already in the most primitive stage of the tradition they do serve to emphasize various aspects of the revelation as it is present in Jesus' words. The second conspicuous element is the use of parables,[70] the most genuine vessels of Jesus' own proclamation of the kingdom. It is obvious, however, that the eschatological element, only present in a very qualified sense in Jesus' original proclamation, has not been elaborated further in the *Gospel of Thomas;* rather, it has been altered, almost unnoticeably, in such a way that the emphasis upon the secret presence now expresses a gnostic tension (the mysterious presence of the divine soul in the body) instead of an eschatological one (the secret presence of the kingdom in the world).[71] Similarly close to the most primitive form of *logoi* are a number of law sayings, which express clearly the contrast between the traditional morality and the new morality.[72] Finally,

67. This has parallels in the Gospel of John (cf. John 6:63 and passim), but certainly does not imply literary dependence.
68. In the classification I follow Bultmann, *History of the Synoptic Tradition,* passim.
69. *Gospel of Thomas,* 26, 31–35, 39b, 45, 47, 66, 67, 73, 78, 86, 93, 94. Without parallels, but probably primitive traditions, are 21 (last part), 24, 33a, 40 (?), 74; cf. 80 and 111b.
70. *Gospel of Thomas* 8, 9, 20, 57, 63–65, 76, 107; without synoptic parallels, 97, 98.
71. E.g., in the parables of the wise fisherman (8) and of the pearl (76).
72. Esp. 6, 14 (in part), 25, 99, 101a; cf. 39, 102, 95.

some prophetic sayings and I-sayings seem to preserve the original impact of an early proclamation in which the pronouncement of Jesus' word announces the presence of salvation.[73]

Of course, not all these sayings are gnostic by any definition. Nevertheless, the unbroken continuation of such a *logoi* tradition is endowed by nature with the seed of Gnosticism as soon as it falls under the spell of a dualistic anthropology. This all the more so since it presupposes the secret presence of the Living Jesus in his words. The subsequent growth of the tradition, which probably started very early and without direct influence from other christological formations of the gospel tradition, is only a consistent spelling out of the consequences. It is particularly conspicuous in those sayings in which eschatological terminology receives a clearly gnostic meaning; e.g., Saying 3 (the kingdom in heaven— the kingdom is within you and without you) and 16b (five in a house—they will stand as solitary ones).[74] Most clearly, this gnostic reinterpretation of the concept of the kingdom is present in Saying 49: "You shall find the kingdom; because you come from it and you shall go there again," which is parallel to Saying 50: "We have come from the Light. . . ." This is evidently a primitive equivalent to the classical definition of *gnosis* in the *Excerpta ex Theodoto* 78: "The knowledge of who we have been and what we have become; where we have been, where we have been cast; where we are hastening, where we were redeemed; what birth is, what rebirth." The rich evidence for a detailed unfolding of the gnostic language of revelation (though without a given system) cannot be discussed further.[75]

One should not pass judgement too quickly upon Thomas's gnostic understanding of Christian existence. There is one important element, derived from the life of the earthly Jesus, which controls Thomas's understanding of Christian life to a certain extent: the motif of wandering. It is most poignantly formulated in Saying 42: "Become passersby," and it is certainly related to

73. Cf. 54 ("blessed are the poor," in the "Matthean" form, but without the addition "in spirit"), 58 (?), 68 (but see 69!); further, without synoptic parallel, 16a, 17, 55, 82.
74. See further: 5, 6b, 11, 18a, 22, 75, 88, 91, 111, 112.
75. See for this esp. Haenchen, *Botschaft des Thomas-Evangeliums,* pp. 39–74.

the christological implications of Saying 86: "The foxes have their holes . . . but the Son of man has no place to lay his head and rest." Here, a Christology related to the earthly Jesus coincides with the gnostic understanding of man. This created a most powerful image of the true Christian which influenced deeply the further development of Syrian Christianity and which has become its most important contribution to orthodox Christianity.[76]

The indigenous Thomas Christianity of eastern Syria, growing out of such beginnings during the second and third centuries A.D., was not closely defined by any specific doctrinal or institutional limits. Considering its further development, we cannot even call it typically gnostic, but should rather describe it as a typical example of Hellenistic syncretism—wide open to further influences and developments. Characteristic of such syncretistic unfolding are the following phenomena.

The philosopher Bardesanes, from whom these Edessene Christians were later called Bardesanites, was the great theological figurehead of this type of Christian faith, and was sometimes rightly called the "Clement [sc., of Alexandria] of the East." He was open to astrological and cosmological speculative mysticism, a true Hellenist, and at the same time well versed in Semitic poetry.[77]

At about the same time Tatian launched his innovation, the Diatessaron, as the new form of the written gospel. The fourfold gospel canon had not arrived at Edessa at that time, nor had any of the canonical gospels become established and widely used. Compared to the traditional *Gospel of Thomas,* the Diatessaron must have been a tremendous success. Tatian had learned about the composition of gospel harmonies at Rome in the school of

76. The resulting type of Christian morality and behavior may be labeled "encratite," but it should not be confused with such encratite developments elsewhere, which often have completely different theological roots (e.g. the Marcionites; or Jewish-Christian encratites in Asia Minor); see also Ehrhardt, "Christianity before the Apostles' Creed," p. 95 n. 9, who points out that this term in its early usage can refer to a variety of heresies, and that its later technical use "arose from experiences of the post-Constantinian period."

77. It is certainly wrong to see Bardesanes as a founder of a sectarian type of religiosity, or to label him a representative of eastern Valentinianism. Both of these views stem from the armory of the antignostic Fathers. On Bardesanes see the recent monograph of H. J. W. Drijvers, *Bardaisan of Edessa,* Studia Semitica Neerlandica, 6, 1966.

Justin Martyr. He added the Gospel of John (which was perhaps rejected by Justin because the Valentinians used it) and probably also used the *Gospel of Thomas*.[78] Thus he created the richest "gospel" of his time, unparalleled anywhere.[79] It took the Catholic church centuries to eradicate this heretical document in the East; the orthodox Syrian father, Ephrem, still used it in the fourth century. That Tatian, certainly not a "gnostic," was later labeled an encratite, is understandable for a member of the preorthodox church in eastern Syria.

Such encratitic tendencies are also obvious in the document from a third century development of Edessene Thomas Christianity: the *Acts of Thomas*. Its appreciation for gnostic lore and legend,[80] however, and its distinctly pre-Manichaean theology reflect a rapid development toward the establishment of a gnostic church,[81] as it was accomplished through Mani.

Compared with this rather colorful and supple picture of Thomas Christianity as the indigenous Christian group in Edessa, the more rigorously structured churches did not gain wide acceptance there in the beginning. The Marcionites seem to have been more successful for a while. Orthodoxy, however, did not get to Edessa until about A.D. 200. Their first perceptible figure is Palut, after whom the orthodox Christians, to their great distress, were called the Palutians. Whether Palut was consecrated as "bishop" of Edessa by Serapion of Antioch remains doubtful.[82] One can picture in the third century a situation in which the

---

78. This is the best explanation for the appearance of *Gospel of Thomas* readings in the Diatessaron, to which Quispel has pointed in several articles: "L'Evangile selon Thomas et le Diatessaron," pp. 87–117; "Some Remarks on the Gospel of Thomas," pp. 276–90.

79. Whether the original composition was in Syriac or in Greek is of minor concern for our question. I would tend to conjecture a Greek original in view of the Roman influences that are present (where Justin is Tatian's predecessor) and because of the Western attestation for it (cf. the Dutch version).

80. Cf. Günther Bornkamm, *Mythos und Legende in den apokryphen Thomasakten*, FRLANT, 31, 1933.

81. On the developed Gnosticism of the *Acts of Thomas*, in which the earthly Jesus has been completely replaced by the figure of the gnostic redeemer, see Günther Bornkamm, "The Acts of Thomas," in Hennecke, *NT Apocrypha*, 2: 429–37.

82. This tradition only serves the purpose of connecting Palut's succession to Peter in Rome, which is historically improbable for many reasons; cf. Bauer, *Rechtgläubigkeit*, pp. 22, 25 ff.

orthodox group was just starting to gain strength, at a time when most of the local Christians were drawn towards Mani rather than to Palut's brand of Western orthodoxy. It is not unlikely that the political changes in the East which were taking place at the beginning of the Sassanid period played some role in these developments. Some details could be added; but to gain a clear picture of the events in the third century seems impossible. Thus, it is only in the fourth century that the orthodox church began to amount to anything. Here we find the first significant bishop (Kune) and theologian (Ephrem). Only now does this group manage to propagate its own story of apostolic succession: not Thomas, but Thaddaeus is said to have been the real apostle of Edessa, while Thomas (who cannot be suppressed completely) stayed in Jerusalem (Eusebius *Hist. eccl.* 1. 13).[83] The completely unhistorical Abgar legend, which tries to connect Thaddaeus's mission to Edessa with the time and person of the toparch Abgar V (A.D. 13–50), succeeded in supporting the claims of orthodoxy upon Edessa, even for many modern scholars.[84] One century later, when the brutal methods of Bishop Rabbula succeeded in "converting" legions of heretics, orthodoxy was so well established that later versions of the Abgar legend completely dropped Edessa's original apostle, Judas Thomas (cf. the *Acts of Thaddaeus*).

The Countries around the Aegean Sea

Our sources are more plentiful for the earliest history of theological controversy in parts of Asia Minor, Macedonia, and Achaia. A considerable part of the writings which were later

---

83. The conflict between Thomas and Thaddaeus is usually overlooked, but is clearly present in our sources. The claim of orthodoxy that it derives from Thaddaeus as the original Edessene apostle is perhaps already reflected in the fact that the list of apostles in the heretical *Acts of Thomas* follows Matthew's list (Matt. 10), but drops Thaddaeus. In any case, it is in this area that we have to look for reasons and motives behind the changes in such lists, rather than looking for possible desires to "harmonize" various traditions (against Klijn, *Acts of Thomas*, pp. 158–59; Bauer, *Leben Jesu*, pp. 444–45, is certainly right).
84. To assume that the Abgar legend actually speaks of Abgar IX (A.D. 179–216) is a typical example of saving a "historical" kernel and sacrificing the real intention of a legend. For the orthodox Christians invented the legend for no other purpose than to justify their claim that they had come to Edessa in apostolic times rather than around A.D. 200.

incorporated into the New Testament canon was written in this region, particularly on the western coast of Asia Minor. Most of this literature is more or less the direct result of the battles waged among various groups of Christian missionaries throughout the second half of the first century. To attempt to describe briefly the history of controversies in this area is to put one's hand into a hornet's nest of issues of New Testament studies hotly debated today.

The apostle Paul was undoubtedly the one who started Christian missionary work in the regions around the Aegean Sea. In conformity with the kerygma of the Hellenist church [85] as it was developed in Antioch, Paul's kerygma was the message of Christ's death and resurrection. It implied a strictly eschatological orientation for the understanding of Christian life in this world, together with the insistence that the law had come to an end and had no continuing theological significance for the Christian churches.

The success of Paul's missionary labors was soon to be put to a severe test. Apparently, he had opened the door to a flood of missionary activity. Only a few years later various competing groups of Christian missionaries, Jewish-Christians as was Paul himself, started their propaganda in this area, while Paul was staying (perhaps for some time imprisoned) at Ephesus. The repeated theme of Paul's controversies with these competitors in the missionary enterprise was the question of the continuing validity of several aspects of the religious inheritance of Judaism: the Old Testament, the law, the covenant, and Jewish tradition in general.

The first threat to the success of the missionary work of Paul arose from the propaganda of a group of missionaries who have most legitimately been called Judaizers. They first appear as the opponents of Paul in Galatia. Soon after Paul's death (or departure from this area) a student of Paul tries to refute the same Judaizing antagonists in the Letter to the Colossians.[86] Paul's

85. On "The Kerygma of the Hellenistic Church Aside from Paul," see Rudolf Bultmann, *Theology of the New Testament,* vol. 1, 1951, pp. 63 ff.; see also below, chap. 6, "The Structure and Criteria of Early Christian Beliefs," pp. 223 ff. 86. On the Galatian controversy, see Walter Schmithals, "Die Häretiker in Galatien," *ZNW* 47 (1956): 25–67 (repr. in *Paulus und die Gnostiker,* 1965, pp. 9–46); on Colossians, see the excellent study by Günther Bornkamm, "Die

violent reaction in his Letter to the Galatians shows clearly that something more is at stake than the question of imposing an unnecessary burden like circumcision upon the newly converted Gentiles in Galatia. Nor does Paul consider freedom from the law to be just a welcome source of greater convenience for Gentile Christians. The opponents should not be confused with people teaching an orthodox Jewish observance of the law, and their message is probably understood in a wrong context if it is explained with reference to rabbinic sources. As various references in Paul's letter reveal (e.g., Gal. 4:9–10), these Judaizers must have emphasized the spiritual implications and the cosmic dimensions of the observance of the ritual law of the Old Testament in particular.[87] It is equally obvious that such spiritual renewal of the law was understood as a gospel which must have assigned a particular role to Jesus in the context of this theological endeavor. Such a gospel must have been a call for obedience to the law as the cosmic rule of God (perhaps: revealed through Christ). This obedience, which is a participation in this cosmic order, is primarily accomplished through the observance of certain rituals, of which circumcision is the most conspicuous. Aspects of morality apparently receive only secondary emphasis.

The attempt to reconstruct the opponents' concept of law from Paul's arguments in Gal. 3 reveals a mythologizing of Old Testament covenant[88] theology which has Jewish antecedents. Refuting this view, Paul argues for a historical understanding of the Old Testament covenant and of the law as part of that covenant. The covenant for him has a beginning (the promise to Abraham);

Häresie des Kolosserbriefes," in *Ges. Aufs.*, 1:139–56. It should be added that the heresy of Colossae was perhaps a more limited local phenomenon than is generally assumed. Its roots must lie in the particular form of Jewish syncretism which was prevalent in Lydia and Phrygia at that time; cf. Alf Thomas Kraabel, "Judaism in Asia Minor" (Th.D. diss., Harvard University, 1968).

87. Schmithals, "Häretiker in Galatien," has described very persuasively this theological dimension of the opponents' teaching in Galatia. But he confuses the issues when he denies the central role of the law in the thought of the Galatian opponents.

88. I am indebted for my understanding of the problem of covenant in early Christianity to Klaus Baltzer, *Das Bundesformular*, 2d ed., WMANT, 4, 1964 (*The Covenant Formulary*; Fortress, 1971), which—after preliminary studies of George Mendenhall ("Law and Covenant in Israel and the Ancient Near East," *The Biblical Archeologist*, 17 [1954]: 26–46; 46–72)—for the first time opened up an entirely new perspective for New Testament studies.

and the law, coming only after Abraham and limited in its duration (Gal. 3:17 ff.), the slavemaster until the coming of the Messiah (Gal. 3:24), is not valid beyond the time of its historical termination: the execution of the curse in Christ (Gal. 3:13). Upon it follows the final blessings now realized in the church (Gal. 3:14). Thus, the present time is understood, not as the renewal of the covenant (now in its cosmic dimensions), but as the final fulfillment of its original purpose. It is noteworthy that Paul's reference to the "origin" is not to the creation but to Abraham; it is an appeal to the covenant-constituting act of God at a specific time in the history of his people, rather than to a primordial act of God in the beginning of the world. Paul consciously avoids any appeal to the first chapters of Genesis which played such a vital role in the mythological reinterpretations of the Old Testament tradition in apocalypticism and in wisdom speculations.

The key to Paul's critical refutation of his opponents' law mythology is his understanding of the coming of Christ as a human being at a specific moment of history (Gal. 4:4). Certainly Paul does not try to evaluate the person of Jesus with the categories of a modern historian. Jesus is seen, no doubt, as a figure fulfilling a purpose within a divine plan, i.e., he is understood in theological categories. However, the reason why Jesus fulfills this function is precisely that he was born, lived (Gal. 4:4), and died (Gal. 3:13) as a human being. For Paul, this is epitomized in the crucifixion. Both Paul and his Galatian opponents are concerned with the question of a new understanding of the Old Testament and the Jewish concept of law and covenant. The alternatives are certainly not the word and teaching of Jesus versus the Jewish doctrine of the law; rather Paul sets a specific concept of law and covenant over against the covenant theology represented by his opponents. Both speak the traditional language of Judaism; both have very specific ideas about the place of the coming of Jesus in this traditional schema (though for the opponents this is not clear on the surface). What is the decisive difference? For Paul, what has happened historically with the crucifixion of the man Jesus is not a convenient point of departure for a renewal of covenant theology, but is the criterion for a critical reinterpretation. Paul's insistence upon the most striking *human* aspects of this event, the birth by a woman and the crucifixion, is at the same time his means for evaluating critically the mythical elements of the opponents' covenant theology (as they were inherited from postexilic covenant concepts). For Paul, Jesus did not elevate the religious greatness of the old covenant into new cosmic dimensions; rather he brought it to an end by suffering its consequences, the curse.

Thus, the Christian's task is not to revere powers beyond and above time and history through the observance of their rules (Gal. 4:10),[89] but to be humanly responsible to an existing, visible community: *agape* (Gal. 5:6, 22; cf. 6:22 ff.). In this way, the historicity of the event of revelation becomes the decisive criterion for understanding traditional theologies and mythologies. The failure to demythologize is the failure to apply this criterion and is a fault in line with the "heresy" of the opponents.

In Philippi, a few years later, we find a related, even if somewhat different, controversy.[90] As in Galatia, there is a group of foreign missionaries, Christians to be sure, who proclaim a renewal of the religious tradition of Israel through Jesus Christ. According to Phil. 3, law obedience is their way to otherworldliness and spiritual perfection. Circumcision is part of the requirements (Phil. 3:2). The possession of the traditional qualities distinguishing Israel is an undisputed value (Phil. 3:4 ff.). Paul's argument is by no means that such propaganda places obstacles in the Gentiles' path to the church. This probably was not the case. On the contrary, exactly this kind of religious propaganda must have had considerable appeal in Paul's time. Rather, Paul's accusation is that his opponents have not understood that the coming of the redeemer as a man who died implies a transformation of values for the believer (Phil. 3:7–8), i.e., a giving up of religious prerogatives and a call for the identification with

---

89. Cf. also Col. 2:8, 16 ff.
90. See my article "The Purpose of the Polemic of a Pauline Fragment (Phil. 3)," *NTS* 8 (1961/62): 317–32.

the suffering and crucifixion of Christ (Phil. 3:10–11). This renders impossible the attainment of transhistorical, supernatural, and otherworldly qualities as a part of man's existence.

The further development of a law propaganda with gnosticizing tendencies continued after Paul's death, particularly in Asia Minor. The religious background for these developments is probably to be found in the fact that the (Greek-speaking) Jewish community in the western part of Anatolia was quite strong in pre-Christian and early Christian times. On this, the excavation of the synagogue at Sardis has recently brought valuable information.[91] In the letters to the seven churches in the Apocalypse of John, the adversaries who are labelled "Nicolaitans" (Rev. 2:6, 16) claim to be true Jews (Rev. 2:9; 3:9), engage in daring interpretations of Scripture (cf. Rev. 2:14; also 2:20), and claim to possess mystical insight into the divine (Rev. 2:24).

Ignatius of Antioch, writing to several churches in the province of Asia, gives evidence of perhaps the same Christian group. As with the opponents in the Letter to the Colossians, observance of the ritual law of the Old Testament is found among Ignatius's adversaries (*Mg.* 8–11; *Phld.* 6 ff.). They stress the interpretation of Scripture (*Phld.* 8), but at the same time have developed a clearly docetic Christology (*Trall.* 10; *Smyrn.* 2 ff.). Walter Bauer has set forth an interesting hypothesis based on the observation that Ignatius did not write to Pergamon, Thyatira, Sardes, and Laodicea, i.e., to those of the seven churches of the Apocalypse which seemed to be hardest hit by a hostile Judaizing group. Is it possible, Bauer asks, that by the time of Ignatius these four churches were completely controlled by the opposition?[92] The (Jewish?) Gnostic Cerinthus was teaching at Ephesus at about the same time.[93]

Quite different from the battles with these Judaizers, who were soon to develop a docetic Christology, was the controversy be-

---

91. See esp. Kraabel, "Judaism in Asia Minor"; this "Judaizing Gnosticism" must be distinguished from later groups of encratite Ebionites.
92. Bauer, *Rechtgläubigkeit*, pp. 82–83.
93. The various and often contradictory reports about Cerinthus are collected in Hilgenfeld, *Ketzergeschichte des Urchristentums, op. cit.*, 411–18.

tween Paul and his church in Corinth.[94] The first disturbance among the Corinthians arose from a Jewish Hellenist wisdom teaching which may have been related to their own syncretistic religious background. It led the community to an ambitious boasting in the name of specific religious figures and to demonstrations of individualistic spiritual achievements. There were no theological parties in Corinth.[95] Apollos (Acts 18:24), a Jew from Alexandria, may have contributed to the rise of such boasting in wisdom, when he instructed the church at Corinth after Paul's departure. Paul, however, had no theological or personal quarrel with Apollos, and he was confident that his letter would be successful in settling these internal problems in his church. We can assume that such actually was the result—in spite of fundamental theological implications of the dispute.

The controversy of 1 Corinthians is most illuminating, for it is partly Paul's own eschatological message which must have given rise to the dispute, even though the teaching of the Alexandrian Apollos may have added to the development of the theology and practice of the "strong" in Corinth. The crucial issue is the question of the degree to which the future events of the eschatological timetable of apocalypticism have become present reality through the coming of Jesus. Some people in Corinth would claim that everything had been actualized already, or even that in view

94. For the following description I am indebted to Dieter Georgi and his excellent study *Gegner des Paulus im 2. Korintherbrief.* He shows convincingly that it is necessary to distinguish between the controversies in 1 and 2 Corinthians. With respect to 1 Corinthians, Walter Schmithals, *Die Gnosis in Korinth,* 1956, offers many good observations; see, however, Georgi's review in *VuF,* 1960, pp. 90–96; further, Wilckens, *Weisheit und Torheit,* and my review of Wilckens in *Gnomon* 33 (1961): 590–95. On 1 Corinthians see also Bornkamm, "The Lord's Supper and Church in Paul," in *Early Christian Experience* and James M. Robinson, "Kerygma and History," (see above, pp. 30 ff.). For the history of religions problem of the opponents in 1 Cor. see also Egon Brandenburger, *Fleisch und Geist. Paulus und die dualistische Weisheit* (WMANT 29, 1968); Hans Conzelmann, *Der erste Briefe an die Korinther* (Meyer Kommentar, 5, 11th ed., 1969).
95. To this extent Johannes Munck is quite right; see his chap., "The Church without Factions," in *Paul and the Salvation of Mankind,* 1959, pp. 135–67. I also agree with Munck that the Corinthian Christians regarded their leaders as teachers of wisdom. But I am unable to follow Munck any further in his flat denial of influences from Jewish wisdom theology. On the contrary, Jewish wisdom theology is quite evident. Certain features in Paul's own thought depend on this background, and there is some reason to believe that Apollos was well versed in this wisdom theology.

of the presence of wisdom and knowledge through the teaching of Jesus, as well as of the possession of the Spirit and the sacraments, their ultimate perfection had taken place. Their practices indicate that such radicalization of the fulfillment of mythical expectations made responsibility for the "building up" of an existing Christian community just as unnecessary as was the expectation of future "acts of God in history" (cf. "there is no resurrection of the dead," 1 Cor. 15:12).

In 1 Corinthians in particular, it is evident that Paul's central argument against these developments recalls the cross of Jesus Christ (1 Cor. 1:18 ff.; 2:2). It is seen as an event in past history which corresponds to the future of the final apocalyptic acts of God (1 Cor. 11:26). Thus the present time is still "historical" time; its christological criterion is the crucified Jesus. The Spirit as the eschatological gift derives from the cross (cf. 1 Cor. 2:16; 12:1–3), not from the anticipation of the future. The church as the body of this Jesus is an earthly community in which love rules for its "edification" (1 Cor. 12:4 ff.). Agape is the only phenomenon in which the eschatological future is directly present in the church (1 Cor. 13:8–13). Agape controls the exercise of any other religious qualities and leaves no room for the proud demonstration of eschatological fulfillment which does not "build up" the church.

In this Pauline view, there is a realm of historical time which lasts from the crucifixion to the parousia, and which demands, for the present, a moral responsibility that is willing to face the realities of this world. The Christian must face this responsibility squarely, as Christ has done in his coming and earthly life and death. Contrary to traditional apocalyptic expectation, the events of the future have no direct consequences for the understanding of the present. The apocalyptic events of the future are, however, important elements of a new concept of eschatology, since they limit the course of time. It is precisely for this reason that the present becomes historical time in which there is freedom for existence as a human being. But it is impossible to claim to possess the future in a present religious life which is directly informed by the patterns of the future life.

The real threat to the Pauline mission at Corinth arose on quite different grounds. It resulted from a powerful Jewish-Christian movement which exerted a decisive influence on the further development of the Christian church. Paul had to deal with this disturbance in several letters, by a personal emergency visit to Corinth, and by the sending of Titus (all of this now preserved and attested in the so-called Second Letter to the Corinthians).[96] It was caused by the successful activity of foreign missionaries at Corinth. They represent Jewish-Christian propaganda (2 Cor. 11:22) which understands the Christian message as the renewal of the covenant (2 Cor. 3). Christianity is the true Jewish religion. The methods and means of these missionaries, quite different from those in Galatia, were modeled after and inherited from Hellenized Jewish propaganda and apologetics.[97] The essence of such missionary activity was pneumatic demonstration of the presence of the powerful revival of the true religion of Israel. In the case of 2 Corinthians it is manifested in the performance of miracles, the boasting about mystical experiences, and an artistic spiritual interpretation of Scripture. To this corresponds a Christology that views Jesus as the primary example of such a spiritual revival of true Jewish religion; he is the model of the "divine man" who is not only imitated, but at the same time actually represented, in the performance of his apostle or "minister" ($\delta\iota\acute{\alpha}\kappa\text{ovos}$).[98] The "gospel" which corresponds to such a Christology must have been very similar to the narrative sources and traditions which have been used by our oldest written gospels: the Gospel of Mark and the Gospel of John.

In 2 Corinthians we can see more clearly in which way the new covenant theology of Paul's opponents was shaped by their understanding of the mission of Jesus. For them, Jesus was the basic example of the spiritual and religious person who transcends the limitations of human existence, the divine man ($\theta\epsilon\hat{\iota}\text{os}$

---

96. Cf. Günther Bornkamm, *Die Vorgeschichte des sogenannten Zweiten Korintherbriefes*, SHA, Phil.-hist. Klasse, 1961, p. 2. A short English abstract of this study was published by Bornkamm under the title "The History of the Origin of the So-Called Second Letter to the Corinthians," *NTS* 8 (1961/62): 258–64.
97. Georgi, *Gegner des Paulus im 2. Korintherbrief*, 1964, pp. 83–187.
98. On the Christology of Paul's opponents, see ibid., pp. 282–300; James M. Robinson, "Kerygma and History," see above, pp. 46 ff.

ἀνήρ). Spiritual exegesis of the Old Testament opened up the road for the repetition of the religious experiences of figures like Moses (2 Cor. 3:7 ff.). Paul did not even try to demonstrate his apostolic authority through pneumatic performances; hence, in their view, he had no religious qualities and, therefore, he was not a legitimate apostle. But Paul rejects their "religious" understanding of the Christian values presupposed in their image of the divine man Christ, and calls it "a Christ according to the flesh" (2 Cor. 5:16). He insists that God's real power is only present in human qualities of historical existence, the divine life hidden in the death of Jesus, and that it is revealed only in the word and the work of the apostle for his church (see esp. 2 Cor. 4:7–18). Again the criterion is the humanness and radical historicity of the revelation in Jesus, which makes it impossible even to speak about Jesus' divine qualities.

The Gospel of Mark can be seen as a witness to a remarkable development in the further history of this Corinthian controversy. Mark's basic concept of the "gospel" is Pauline,[99] and it is probably not only a coincidence that we find a "Mark" in Paul's company.[100] However, apart from the narrative of Jesus' passion which corresponds to the Pauline kerygma, the material used by Mark is very much like the Jesus image of Paul's opponents in 2 Corinthians. To be sure, Mark critically interprets the divine man Christology, inherent in the traditional miracle stories, by means of his eschatological view and by means of his theory of the "messianic secret." [101]

The Gospel of Mark, which became the basis of the Gospel of Matthew and that of Luke as well, is only an episode in the light of the subsequent development, even if its (Pauline) escha-

---

99. This Willi Marxsen has shown convincingly: *Der Evangelist Markus*, FRLANT, n.s. 49, 1956, pp. 83–92 (ET: *Mark the Evangelist*, 1969, pp. 126–38).
100. Philem. 24; cf. Col. 4:10; 2 Tim. 4:11; the John Mark of Acts 12:25; 13:5 ff. is a later Lucan construction. In any case, the tradition that connects Mark with Paul is much older than that which finds Mark in Peter's company (1 Pet. 5:13; cf. Papias in Eusebius, 3. 39. 15).
101. This Paulinism of the Gospel of Mark does not, in itself, allow definite conclusions about the place of origin for this gospel. It seems advisable, however, to connect Mark more closely with the area of the Pauline mission. This means that Asia Minor and Achaia, perhaps Antioch, would be more likely than Rome; Galilee is not more than an imaginative error on the part of Marxsen.

tological orientation [102] was understood and adapted as an eschatological theology of the church by Matthew in Antioch. In the area of Paul's missionary work in Asia Minor and Greece, Mark's Gospel was corrected in quite a different way by Luke.[103] Both Luke's Gospel and his Acts of the Apostles manifest in no uncertain terms the victory of Paul's Corinthian (2 Cor.) opponents.

According to Luke, Jesus in his earthly life, driven by the Spirit, "performs" the fulfillment of the true essence of the religion of the Old Testament. This fulfillment is accomplished in Jesus' ministry of powerful teaching and healing, but not through his passion and death. In Luke the passion narrative has become an appendix to the gospel.[104] The powerful and successful activity of the apostles and missionaries carries this new and true religion from Jerusalem to Rome. Nowhere else is the "divine man" motif used so effectively as in Luke, both in his Christology and in his description of the missionary. Luke's missionaries are as proficient as Paul's opponents in 2 Corinthians with respect to the performance of miracles (Acts 3 and passim), the inspired interpretation of the Old Testament (cf. the speeches in Acts), and various spiritual experiences. In Luke-Acts, Paul himself reports his own vision twice to an astounded public (not to speak of us who are aware of 2 Cor. 12:1 ff.). Without doubt, Luke, in all his admiration of the great Apostle to the Gentiles, was a student of Paul's opponents rather than of Paul himself.

A really new factor was introduced into Asia Minor (and perhaps Macedonia) after A.D. 70,[105] again of Jewish, and this time of more distinctly Palestinian Jewish, origin: apocalypticism.[106] The first witness to this new force is the (pseudepi-

---

102. As James M. Robinson, *The Problem of History in Mark*, 1957, has shown. A restatement of this interpretation and further literature on this question can be found in Robinson, "The Problem of History in Mark, Reconsidered."
103. The most satisfactory explanation for the location of the writing of Luke-Acts is Asia Minor. This, of course, does not exclude the availability of "Antiochian" traditions.
104. See Conzelmann, *The Theology of St. Luke*, 1960 (ET of *Mitte der Zeit*); cf. p. 201: ". . . there is no tarce of any Passion mysticism, nor is any direct soteriological significance drawn from Jesus' suffering or death."
105. This view is based upon the observation that apocalypticism as a genuine movement was not an issue in the countries around the Aegean Sea in Paul's lifetime.
106. Cf. Ernst Käsemann, "Zum Thema der urchristlichen Apokalyptik," *EVB*

graphical) Second Letter of Paul to the Thessalonians. The opponents of this Letter use the authority of Paul for the proclamation of an apocalyptic kerygma: "The day of the Lord is at hand" (2 Thess. 2:2). They do this not without some justification, since Paul was in fact a proponent of a certain kind of apocalyptic theology. During the same years (i.e., ca. A.D. 80–90, which is also the time of the composition of such Jewish apocalyptic literature as 4 Ezra), a prophetic conventicle was formed in the neighborhood of Ephesus. Its leader, a prophet by the name of John (not the author of the gospel [107]) produced the Book of Revelation. It is impregnated with apocalyptic traditions from Judaism to a degree unparalleled in early Christianity before A.D. 70. Yet parallel developments had led to the present form of the so-called synoptic apocalypse in Mark and Matthew (cf. *Did.* 16). The Letter to the Ephesians, which belongs to the same period, shows a surprising closeness to the apocalyptic terminology of the Qumran community,[108] as does 2 Cor. 6:14—7:1, a small interpolation into 2 Corinthians when this epistle was edited by the church in Corinth at the close of the first century A.D.[109] It is certainly not impossible that the dispersion of the Qumran community after the Jewish War contributed to these developments; parallels to Qumran in early Christianity seem to be much more conspicuous after A.D. 70 than in the (historical) teaching of Jesus and the genuine letters of Paul.

Even at the risk of oversimplifying complex problems, it is necessary to delineate the picture that Christianity presented at the

2 (1964): 105–31. Käsemann must be given full credit for reopening the question of early Christian apocalyptic. He is certainly right in his emphasis upon the tremendous importance of apocalyptic thought in the early years of Christianity; I would add: upon both Christian heresy and Christian orthodoxy. For the English translation of Käsemann's essay and the continuation of the discussion about apocalypticism see the essays published in JTC, 6 (1969), entitled *Apocalypticism*.

107. I assume that the existence of this historical "Johannine" circle attracted to Ephesus the tradition of John the "apostle" and disciple of the Lord. Of course, it is also not impossible that the Gospel of John was written in Ephesus. The geographical origin of the Gospel of John poses very puzzling problems to the scholar.

108. Cf. Frank Moore Cross, *The Ancient Library of Qumran*, 2d ed., 1961, pp. 216–17.

109. Joseph A. Fitzmyer, "Qumran and the Interpolated Paragraph in 2 Cor. 6, 14—7, 1," *CBQ* 23 (1961): 271–80.

turn of the first century in Ephesus. Several rival Christian groups (whether they were organized as separate institutions is difficult to know) must have existed simultaneously: the originally Pauline church, supported by the Qumran-influenced Paulinist who wrote Ephesians, but also represented by the author of Luke-Acts who in his own way accommodated the tradition of the great apostle to the expediencies of the church; a Jewish-Christian "school" engaging in a daring interpretation of the Old Testament (an early gnostic like Cerinthus would fit this description rather well); a heretical sect, called the Nicolaitans by the Apocalypse of John (Rev. 2:6); and finally, a Jewish-Christian conventicle which was led by the prophet John, and which produced the book of apocalyptic revelations which has been preserved under his name.

In the second century some of these early rival Christian groups grew up to the stature of churches with the claim of universal validity. There is probably a continuous line running from the apocalyptic trend in Paul's church at Thessalonica (2 Thess.) to the rise of Montanism. Apocalyptic traditions and chiliastic hopes are also found in Papias, bishop of Hierapolis around A.D. 135, not far from the Phrygian towns in which Montanism rose in Asia Minor between A.D. 150 and 160 or shortly thereafter. Somewhat as Montanism was a revival and radicalization of a primitive apocalyptic form of Christianity, just so the assumed original intention of Paul's theology found a powerful advocate in Marcion, a Christian merchant and shipowner from Pontus. It would be fair to acknowledge that both Montanus and Marcion were rightful heirs of two forms of primitive Christian beliefs. Both had a justifiable claim to represent the early times of Christianity in Asia Minor. Marcion's suspicion that the Pauline letters had been tampered with was just as correct, in view of the number of pseudo-Pauline writings, as was Montanus's basic contention that the primitive expectation of the parousia, with all its powerful moral implications, had vanished. Both men were shortsighted in their one-sided and biased judgments. But such a sane and sapient modern suggestion should not overshadow the historical relevance of the factual existence of such primitive traditions and their survival power.

One should also consider the price which had to be paid to maintain a more moderate version of the inheritance from the first generations. The "conservative" theology of Asia Minor which emerged around A.D. 100 provides us with typical examples. We have already discussed Luke's sacrifice of the Pauline gospel in order to rescue for the church, as he understood it, the image of Paul as the great and exemplary missionary. What happened to Paul in the pastoral letters is even more telling. The remaining validity of Paul's inheritance is the central issue. The reinterpretation of Paul's theology, even its domestication, has many fascinating aspects. The author of the pastorals understands that the real proof of Paul's apostolic authority is his suffering, rather than any invented glory of his ministry. In agreement with Paul he also knows that the decisive battleground for the authentication of Christian existence is the church in a world of social and political necessities, rather than in the field of theoretical theological verification and speculation.

Yet the pastorals still give the appearance of a sellout of Pauline theology under unfavorable conditions. The eschatological tension of Paul's thought has disappeared. On the other hand, the author of the pastorals is unable to reopen this dimension through the adaptation of categories of space (as, e.g., in Eph. and Col.), since this was the prerogative of Paul's gnostic students. The recommendation of the pastorals is, then, to read Paul for edification (individual and ecclesiastical), rather than as a stimulus to creative reinterpretation in a changed situation. Since theology has become something that can be learned by practice in godliness, the heretic is by definition characterized by certain false theological sentences (if he is not recognized simply by the fact that he engages in theological discourse).

In Polycarp of Smyrna (in his Second Letter to the Philippians) [110] we find, for the first time, a carefully formulated summary of various "heretical" doctrines (*Phil.* 7. 1). The formulation leaves no doubt that, for Polycarp, the true believer

110. Cf. P. N. Harrison, *Polycarp's Two Epistles to the Philippians,* 1936. If Harrison is right, we have to date this second letter (*Phil.* 1–12) in the time of Marcion's beginnings. For the interpretation of Polycarp, *Phil.* 7.1, see James M. Robinson, "Kerygma and History," above, pp. 37 f.

confesses and adheres to a modest minimum of true doctrines composed of Pauline and apocalyptic traditions. The leading criterion has become moderation in the continuation of the inheritance from earlier generations instead of a fresh return to the roots of Christianity, the earthly Jesus. This was to last until the new authority of the New Testament canon finally provided the basis for a new theological departure.

5. One Jesus and Four Primitive Gospels

HELMUT KOESTER

The Problem of the "Historical" Jesus and the Question of Primitive Gospel Forms

To deal with the problem of the "historical" Jesus is to deal with the synoptic gospels (supplemented by occasional appropriations of Johannine material).

The use of apocryphal gospels is beset with a number of notorious difficulties. First, the attempt to recover historically reliable material from the vast sea of noncanonical tradition has proved to be an arduous labor yielding only negligible results. Second, since the canonical gospels are commonly judged to be the most primitive and original literature that could be called "gospel," the often different forms and outlines of the apocryphal gospels appear by comparison as secondary alterations, if not tendentious falsifications. Third, although the search for a single more primitive gospel (*Urevangelium,* "Hebrew Gospel of Matthew," etc.) is by no means dead, it is fortunately not the most prominent topic in New Testament scholarship. It is not easy to see how further progress can be made in resolving any of these problems.

Nearly a century ago, Alfred Resch collected almost three hundred apocryphal sayings of Jesus,[1] but he considered only thirty-six of these to be attributable to Jesus. In a critical appraisal of this work, James Hardy Ropes [2] was able to show that Resch's judgment was too optimistic. Since that time, many more apoc-

This essay appeared originally in the *Harvard Theological Review* 61 (1968): 203-47.
1. Alfred Resch, *Agrapha,* TU, 5, 4, 1889; 2d ed., TU, n.s. 15, 3-4, 1906; repr. 1967).
2. James Hardy Ropes, *Die Sprüche Jesu, die in den kanonischen Evangelien nicht überliefert sind,* TU, 14, 2, 1896. .

ryphal sayings have come to light. In recent years, Joachim Jeremias has tried once more to identify the genuine sayings in this vast material.[3] The result: twenty-one sayings are "historically valuable," but only eleven of these does Jeremias want to claim as "genuine" sayings of Jesus. In a review of Jeremias's book, Werner Georg Kümmel wonders whether even this small number of genuine sayings should not be reduced to no more than half a dozen.[4]

There is even less probability that we will find anything genuine in the vast apocryphal information about Jesus' life, miracles, relatives, etc. Half a century ago, Walter Bauer [5] collected such material in a work of more than five hundred pages. Today it would be easy to add a second volume of equal size.[6] Yet no one would venture to claim that much of this information is historically trustworthy.

The rise of form criticism has undoubtedly made scholars even more cautious. Complete skepticism, it has been said, is the final outcome; and if this be true for the canonical gospels, how much more so for the apocryphal tradition! But whether one is willing to acquiesce in such skepticism or instead prefers to relax the rigorous standards of form criticism in order to obtain more "positive" results, it is often overlooked that the real purpose and aim of the form-critical method is not quite identical with the humble attempt to determine objectively what Jesus said or did in a particular moment of his ministry. To be sure, form criticism has some value in determining authenticity. But its potential is by no means exhausted when one uses this method only as a technique for deciding the question of historicity. Rather, form criticism seeks to identify basic patterns in the history of the tradition and to determine their *Sitz im Leben,* i.e., to determine

---

3. Joachim Jeremias, *Unbekannte Jesusworte,* 3d ed., 1963 (ET: *Unknown Sayings of Jesus,* 2d ed., 1964).
4. Werner Georg Kümmel, in *ThLZ* 78 (1953): 99–101; cf. my article "Die ausserkanonischen Herrenworte als Produkte der christlichen Gemeinde," *ZNW* 48 (1957): 220–37.
5. Walter Bauer, *Das Leben Jesu im Zeitalter der neutestamentlichen Apokryphen,* 1909.
6. Most of the new material is now available in Edgar Hennecke, *Neutestamentliche Apokryphen,* vol. 1, 3d ed. by Wilhelm Schneemelcher, 1959 (ET: *New Testament Apocrypha,* vol. 1, 1963).

the function of traditional material in the life of people and communities. This, however, is a sociological and theological question, and the determination of the *Sitz im Leben* must not be identified with the determination of the place, time, and situation in which Jesus said or did one thing or another.

To be sure, form criticism may very well, as a by-product, demonstrate that only a little of the apocryphal material can qualify as "historical" or "genuine." But this is not its primary function. Its foremost task is to determine the original *Sitz im Leben* of the material which is now available in the apocryphal gospel tradition, however inauthentic it may be with regard to the historical Jesus, and however secondary and derivative may be the use made of it in the contexts in which it is now preserved. The relation of such apocryphal material to comparable canonical traditions has to be assessed. The stage at which both the apocryphal and the canonical traditions can be compared is their original *Sitz im Leben* in the early Christian church.

To what extent and in what way was the tradition in its original *Sitz im Leben* related to the historical Jesus? To be sure, Jesus of Nazareth presumably was the direct originator of at least a small part of the material; and it is, of course, the historian's task to define this portion of the tradition in its most original form as exactly as possible. But this effort is far from exhausting the relation between the tradition and the historical Jesus.

The question to be asked, however, is not, How much of the apocryphal material can be utilized in a search for the "historical" Jesus? Rather, the relevant question is, In which way does the "earthly" Jesus actually determine the *Sitz im Leben* of the tradition in the church? He does this, insofar as he is in substance the content of the church's proclamation and the object of Christian faith. Whether this proclamation and this faith were legitimate, does not depend upon the quantity of genuine Jesus material. Rather, the answer to this question depends upon the degree to which the earthly Jesus was the criterion of the church's proclamation and faith.[7]

7. Cf. the formulation of Ernst Käsemann: "We can now put our problem in a nutshell—does the New Testament kerygma count the historical Jesus among the criteria of its own validity?" "Sackgassen im Streit um den historischen

Thus we are faced with a problem that involves the history of early Christian theology. Insofar as a *Sitz im Leben* includes a theological context, form-critical scholarship has to examine theological questions. In this instance, we have to look for those basic christological insights of the early Christian community which controlled the formation and transmission of the gospel tradition in each of the various sources. Furthermore, we have to ask how the earthly Jesus is reflected not only in the transmitted material but also in the christological presuppositions which governed its formation, composition, and interpretation.

It is generally assumed that such an overriding christological principle found its most powerful expression in the "gospel," i.e., in one particular form of literature which took its pattern from the earliest Christian proclamation, namely the "kerygma" of the passion, death, and resurrection of Jesus.

Julius Schniewind's statement of 1930 has found almost unanimous acceptance: [8]

> There can be no doubt: it is only because there was a kerygma proclaiming that a man who lived "in the flesh" is the "Lord"—only for this reason is it possible to understand the origin of our gospels, including any forms of [sc., Christian] literature that preceded them.[9]

Indeed, the form of the canonical gospels cannot be explained in any other way. It is, in fact, a creation of the kerygma of the early Christian community. The credal formulation which Paul in 1 Cor. 15:1 ff. calls "gospel," and related creeds of the same type, have set the pattern for this literature. This kerygma of the death and resurrection "of the Son of God and Lord, proclaimed in the word, and present in the cult of the church—the Lord who is at the same time the rabbi and prophet Jesus of Nazareth" [10]—

Jesus," *EVB* 2 (1964), p. 53. See also James M. Robinson, *Kerygma und historischer Jesus*, 2d ed., 1967, pp. 50 ff.
8. It is, e.g., quoted again as a key phrase in Günther Bornkamm, "Evangelien; formgeschichtlich," *RGG*, 3d ed., vol. 2 (1958), p. 750.
9. Julius Schniewind, in his important review article, "Zur Synoptikerexegese," *ThR* n.s. 2 (1930): 183.
10. Bornkamm, "Evangelien; formgeschichtlich," p. 750.

has made the written gospel a genuinely Christian type of literature. It can be most clearly seen in the Gospel of Mark,[11] which
is nothing but a passion narrative with a biographical introduction.

For this type of literature, there are no pre- or extra-Christian
parallels. Only the gospels which are developed out of the passion
narrative (Mark and John), and the gospels dependent upon
Mark (Matthew and Luke), have a genuine claim to the title
"gospel." [12] It is also clear that the relation of these gospels to
the earthly Jesus cannot be measured in terms of the quantity of
genuine material transmitted. Nor is Jesus' earthly life directly
reflected in the outlines of these gospels; these outlines, providing
a framework for the incorporation of sayings and narratives, are
actually an extension of the kerygma of Jesus' passion and resurrection. Thus the gospels are pseudobiographical, not truly
biographical.

The relation of the gospels to Jesus must be assessed in terms
of the fact that the gospels themselves wrote of this Jesus as the
one whose suffering, death, and resurrection was proclaimed by
the church. For the canonical gospels, the criterion of their legitimate relation to the earthly Jesus was not historical memory about
what Jesus in fact did or said; it was rather the question whether
traditional material could be understood and interpreted as words
and works of that Jesus who is the Lord, who suffered and was
crucified. The only point of departure from which the earthly Jesus
becomes the criterion of faith is his suffering and death. All other
traditions of Jesus' words and deeds are legitimate, not because
they preserve the exact memory of Jesus' life, but because they
serve as parts of a theological introduction to the proclamation

11. See esp. Willi Marxsen, *Der Evangelist Markus*, FRLANT, n.s. 49, 2d ed.,
1959, pp. 77–101 (ET: *Mark the Evangelist*, 1969, pp. 117–50).
12. Admittedly the use of this term for writings dates from a somewhat later
period. The earliest attestation is found in the middle of the second century
A.D., in *2 Clement* (8. 5) and Justin Martyr (*Apol.* 1. 66. 3; *Dial.* 10. 2; 100. 1).
The term *gospel* in the strict sense belongs only to such writings as Mark and
John, and to those which are dependent upon these earliest "gospels." It is only
here that the kerygma of the cross and resurrection—Paul's "gospel," 1 Cor.
15:1 ff.—has shaped and determined the form of this new literary genre. In
speaking of other written documents as "gospels," however, we are not merely
following long-established usage. Such a use seems legitimate because we are concerned with other writings which contain traditions that have also been incorporated into Mark and other gospels of the kerygma type.

of Jesus' passion and death. In this way, the church in the canonical gospel tradition remains subject to an earthly, human,
"real," and historical revelation which is the criterion of the
tradition.[13]

As for the apocryphal gospels, they are usually understood on
the basis of this fundamental insight into the character of the
genuinely Christian genre of literature called "gospel." Wilhelm
Schneemelcher, in his introduction to the third edition of Edgar
Hennecke's *New Testament Apocrypha*, volume 1,[14] has accepted Schniewind's assessment completely. To be sure, he recognizes in the apocryphal literature the existence of types of gospels
which are quite different in form from the canonical gospels,
and he suggests a probable classification of such types.[15] However, he considers all of these apocryphal gospel forms to be
secondary developments from, and alterations of, the one and only
original form, that of the canonical gospel.

Does this hypothesis explain satisfactorily the phenomenon of
the apocryphal gospels? We know, after all, that many of these
gospels were composed and used by Christian groups which the
orthodox church rejected as heretical. It cannot be presupposed
that all these groups derived their own "kerygma" from that
specific kerygma of the cross and resurrection which is the basis
of the orthodox creed and of the canonical gospels.[16] Is it then
necessary to assume that their gospels had no other source than
the type of gospel which orthodox circles later accepted as
canonical?

There is also another stage in the gospel tradition which is
obviously not covered by Schniewind's hypothesis, i.e., the intermediate stage between that of the free oral transmission and that
of the oldest written gospels known to us. It was first the author

---

13. This does not exclude the possibility that even within the development of
the canonical gospel tradition other elements, related to the earthly Jesus in a
different fashion, could become predominant; see below on the Gospel of Luke,
p. 191.
14. Hennecke, (ET:) *NT Apocrypha*, 1:71–84. This is probably the best treatment of the question now available; see also Arthur D. Nock's penetrating
review in *JTS* n.s. 11 (1960): 63–70.
15. Schneemelcher, introduction to Hennecke, (ET:) *NT Apocrypha*, 1:80–84.
16. See my article "GNOMAI DIAPHOROI," chap. 4, above.

of the Gospel of Mark, through the authority of the creed which
Paul already called "gospel," who made the proclamation of Jesus'
death and resurrection the norm and pattern of the canonical
gospel literature. But Mark himself presumably used written
sources. Matthew and Luke both used Mark and a further written
source, the so-called synoptic sayings source Q. What, we must
ask, can be said about such earlier writings, their theological orientation, and their relation to the earthly Jesus of Nazareth?

It is beyond doubt that earlier written documents were an intermediate stage between free transmission and written gospels. We
can still detect, e.g., a collection of parables used in Mark 4; a
document containing miracle stories called the Johannine *"Semeia
Source"* (but also related to the source of large parts of Mark);
and—above all—the synoptic sayings source common to Matthew
and Luke. Günther Bornkamm speaks of collections "which were
formed according to certain patterns that can be recognized in
other popular literature, both secular and religious, as well." [17]
An inherent theological principle, however, such as is present
in the canonical "gospel," patterned after the kerygma of the cross
and resurrection, does not at first glance seem to exist in these
genres of literature. Furthermore, these genres—collections of sayings or of miracle stories—are in no sense genuinely Christian
creations, but have pagan and Jewish prototypes (wisdom literature, aretalogies, etc.). Does this imply that they are theologically
mute?

This would be very remarkable indeed. For, already in the very
primitive stages of the tradition that preceded any written sources,
theological interests were certainly present, influencing the transmission and alteration of the various individual units handed down
orally. To be sure, this oral stage presents a very heterogeneous
picture. A rich variety of sayings and stories served in various
functions in the preaching, teaching, and worship of the church.
It is not difficult to discover a number of theological, ecclesiological, and sociological principles which conditioned the formation and growth of the tradition at this early stage. Prophetical
injunctions of Jesus were brought into catechisms for purposes

17. Bornkamm, "Evangelien; formgeschichtlich," p. 750.

of instruction, sayings received a setting in brief scenes which could be used in controversies, etc. The motives for the changes and alterations in these and numerous other instances are clear.

Furthermore, the synoptic tradition continued to develop in its free oral form after the composition of written gospels.[18] If, in the history of the oral tradition, practical and theological interests are ever present, it seems inconceivable that theological motivations were absent at the stage in which such oral traditions first crystallized into written sources. Indeed, it is highly probable that from the very beginning major insights into the theological significance of Jesus of Nazareth served as the catalysts in the formation of written sources, and that they continued to influence their development thereafter. As we have seen, this was in fact the way in which the Gospel of Mark came into existence, with the kerygma of cross and resurrection serving as "catalyst."

Schniewind assumed that the principle of the kerygma also applied to the written stages of the tradition which preceded our written gospels.[19] This seems to be a precarious assumption. There are only few traces, if any, of the kerygma (as understood by Paul and Mark) in some of the earlier collections. But this does not imply that they had no particular theological purpose; no doubt, this purpose was somehow related to the earthly Jesus, who was the speaker and/or actor in a large part of this tradition.

Once it is admitted that a variety of christological insights may have been at work in the formation of the tradition into written gospels, there is no necessity to maintain the presupposition that the creeds and canons presupposed in the genres of apocryphal gospels are ultimately distortions of that one kerygma which was basic for the canonical gospels. It is at least an open question, whether the various genres of apocryphal gospels may not have been related to earlier genres of "gospel" literature, such as sayings collections and miracle stories.

In the following sections, I seek to show that there is good reason to make the following assumptions:

18. See my book, *Synoptische Überlieferung bei den Apostolischen Vätern,* TU, 65, 1957.
19. Schniewind, "Zur Synoptikerexegese," p. 183. Bornkamm, "Evangelien; formgeschichtlich," p. 750, does not follow Schniewind at this point.

(1.) Such earlier and primitive gospel sources (collections of sayings and miracle stories) were made for specific theological
purposes.

2. Such collections were made according to principles and patterns
which have no relation to the pattern of the classic passion-
resurrection creed and the "gospel" produced by it.

3. Such primitive sources are very closely related to the forms and
types of the apocryphal gospel literature.

4. These primitive genres of literature also influenced the canonical gospels to a considerable degree, even though the
primary tendencies of these primitive literary genres of gospels
are often better preserved in the apocryphal gospels.

This, of course, raises the question of the basic theological
principles which regulated this preservation and interpretation of
the tradition as a proclamation by or about Jesus of Nazareth.
If the kerygma of the passion and resurrection played no role,
how much do such different (and perhaps more primitive) documents relate to the "historical Jesus" as content or origin of the
tradition? Are different Christian beliefs dominant? Or do non-
Christian factors dominate the forms and types of such a tradition?
Do apocryphal and "heretical" gospels have their origin in very
early layers of the gospel tradition, perhaps even in certain aspects
of the words and works of the historical Jesus himself?

Collections of Sayings

James M. Robinson, in his article *"LOGOI SOPHON,"* [20]
has brought about a basic shift in the investigation of the Coptic
Gospel of Thomas.[21] He neither strains to isolate certain sayings
as possibly genuine, nor does he concentrate on the question
whether or not this newly discovered gospel is dependent on the
canonical gospels.[22] Rather he tries to determine the character and
genre of this "gospel" as a whole, a work which is, in fact, nothing
other than a collection of sayings.

20. Chap. 3 above.
21. For literature on the *Gospel of Thomas*, see Ernst Haenchen, "Literatur
zum Thomas-Evangelium," *ThR* n.s. 27 (1961): 147 ff., 306 ff.; further, in
Hennecke, (ET:) *NT Apocrypha*, 1:278 ff. and 307; also my *"GNOMAI
DIAPHOROI,"* chap. 4 above, pp. 129 ff.
22. On this question, see the literature cited above, pp. 130 ff., nn. 45, 47, 48,
50.

How and why was such a writing composed? What was the theological principle presiding over the formation of this type of "gospel"? How is Christian faith understood, and how does it relate to the earthly Jesus, if the work contains nothing but "words of Jesus"? These are the primary questions which are asked in Robinson's article.

The *Gospel of Thomas* [23] contains a variety of sayings, thematically only loosely connected with each other; "word association," however, as a principle of composition, is frequent. It is not possible to discover any overriding theological concern in the order and arrangement of the sayings, or in the setting of the whole gospel. In spite of the designation of Jesus as the "Living One" in the incipit, and in spite of the designation of the sayings as "secret words," there are no features compelling us to understand the work as a secret revelation after the resurrection. [24] Scenes where Jesus gives instructions privately to his disciples are not uncommon in the canonical gospels, [25] and all the technical nomenclature of the typical "revelation discourse after the resurrection" [26] is missing in the *Gospel of Thomas*. Moreover, the sayings are, at least in part, sayings of Jesus, or modifications of such sayings. Thus, for the *Gospel of Thomas*, "Jesus, the Living One" may well be the earthly Jesus, who at some time in his ministry is assumed to have spoken these words to Judas Thomas. However, this gospel was written and read in a Christian community after Jesus' death. Therefore, these sayings are now understood in terms of a new context and situation, even though no such new "situation" is expressed by the framework of this gospel itself (i.e., a "situation" after Easter, such as is indicated by the passion-resurrection framework of the resurrection appearances of the canonical gospels, or by the situation of a special revelation of Jesus appearing from heaven). What has happened to the

---

23. Quotations are from the edition of A. Guillaumont, H.-C. Puech, G. Quispel, W. Till, and Yassah 'Abd al Masîh, *The Gospel according to Thomas*, 1959. The numbering of the individual sayings in this edition is the same as in Hennecke, (ET:) *NT Apocrypha* 1:511–22.
24. The case is quite different with the closely related *Book of Thomas the Contender*, where Thomas requests Jesus to impart revelations to him before his ascension; cf. H.-C. Puech in Hennecke, (ET:) *NT Apocrypha* 1:308.
25. See Matt. 5:1–2; Mark 4:10–11, 34; 7:17; 13:3; etc.
26. On the revelation discourse, see below, p. 193 ff.

words of the earthly Jesus after his death, when they are repeated without an externally visible break in continuity? For the death of Jesus, his resurrection, and his ascension never explicitly appear. Jesus is always represented as the "Living One," without any concern for the problem of his death, and without any recognition of the fact that his life has become past history.

The sayings themselves, their forms, alterations, and accretions, are our only guides. It is advisable to consider examples from each form-critical category of sayings separately. Any category of sayings has its particular structure and inherent theological tendency. This enables us to discern changes and evaluate them theologically, once such sayings have been detached from their original function in Jesus' proclamation and have been given a new *Sitz im Leben* as words of Jesus "the Living One," in the life of the church after his death. The way in which particular categories of sayings were interpreted, further developed, augmented, and multiplied should reveal the theological tendency which dominated this tradition as a whole.

Generally speaking, the types of sayings represented in the *Gospel of Thomas* correspond to those found in the synoptic gospels (with occasional parallels in John). They reflect, at least partly, the types and forms used by Jesus in his proclamation.[27]

Prophetic and Apocalyptic Sayings

Next to the parables of Jesus, we find the largest number of sayings of Jesus among prophetic and apocalyptic sayings. Furthermore, these sayings, as found in the synoptic gospels, also include a great number of sayings which clearly reflect various stages in the church's eschatology and can readily be distinguished from Jesus' own prophetic proclamation.

Thus, I have chosen to treat this category of sayings in more detail than the others, in order to determine with more precision the *Sitz im Leben* of the sayings in *Thomas* and their relation both to the synoptic tradition and to Jesus' original proclamation.

It may be argued that the category of prophetic and apocalyptic

27. In the classification I follow Rudolf Bultmann, *Geschichte der synoptischen Tradition*, 5th ed., 1961 (ET: *History of the Synoptic Tradition*, 1963), passim.

sayings is least typical of the genre of gospel literature represented by *Thomas,* a genre which James M. Robinson has called "words of the wise." But, first, it is often extremely difficult to assign wisdom sayings and proverbs to a particular person, or time, or stage in the development of the tradition; [28] second, as we will see, the *Gospel of Thomas* lacks such apocalyptic sayings as are characteristic of another type of tradition and gospel literature, namely that of "revelation" or "apocalypse"; third, the designation "words of the wise," if I understand Robinson correctly, should not mislead us to narrow our quest down to the investigation of only sapiential sayings.

On first reading the *Gospel of Thomas,* one gets the impression of its treatment of apocalyptic sayings that they are a secondary spiritualization of canonical apocalyptic material, a view well formulated by Robert M. Grant, who represents the common opinion.

> He has substituted a kind of spiritual understanding for the Gospel of Jesus. . . . Thomas lacks the connection with the past . . . as well as an emphasis upon the importance of the future which was given by Jesus' statements about things to come. He has made the Kingdom almost exclusively present, while in our Gospels it is partly present but will be fully realized only in the future.[29]

I myself once shared this understanding of the apocalyptic sayings of the *Gospel of Thomas.* However, closer consideration of the prophetic and apocalyptic sayings in the *Gospel of Thomas* requires a basic modification of this view.

First of all, among the apocalyptic sayings of *Thomas* which have parallels in the synoptic gospels, there is not a single one which corresponds to the so-called synoptic apocalypse (Mark 13; Matt. 24–25; Luke 21).[30] Most of the apocalyptic sayings of

28. Robinson's assessment of the genre of the *Gospel of Thomas* is quite correct. It is, indeed, the category of the "wisdom saying" which gives the *Gospel of Thomas* its peculiar character. However, the sapiential material would yield but little evidence for the question whether or not *Thomas* is independent of the synoptic gospels.
29. Robert M. Grant, *The Secret Sayings of Jesus,* 1960, p. 113.
30. There are only a few remote contacts with the synoptic apocalypse. One of these is the parable of the thief (Matt. 24:43), which occurs in two variants in the *Gospel of Thomas,* in Sayings 21 and 103. However, this parable (to be distinguished from the parable of the landlord's return, Mark 13:34–36) is

Thomas have their synoptic parallels in the major Q collection of eschatological sayings which is reproduced in Luke 12:35–56; cf. the *Gospel of Thomas* 21c (Luke 12:35),[31] 21b and 103 (Luke 12:39), 16b (Luke 12:52–53), 91 (Luke 12:54–56).[32] Several others are certainly Q sayings: the *Gospel of Thomas* 54, 69, 68 (Matt. 5:3, 6, 11 // Luke 6:20, 21a, 22), 46 (Matt. 11:11 // Luke 7:28), 61a (Luke 17:34; cf. Matt. 24:40). The other sayings of this type have parallels either in the Marcan sayings collection in the parable chapter—the *Gospel of Thomas* 5 and 6 (Mark 4:22), 41 (Mark 4:25)—or in sayings peculiar to Luke: the *Gospel of Thomas* 3 (Luke 17:20–21) and 79 (Luke 11:27–28).

The predominance of Q sayings among these prophetic and apocalyptic sayings of *Thomas* raises the question whether *Thomas* presupposes the particular apocalyptic expectation of Q which is epitomized in the sayings about the coming of the Son of man.[33] But *Thomas* neither reproduces any of the typical Q sayings about the coming of the Son of man or of his "day" (Luke 12:40 par.; 17:24, 26–27, 28 ff.; cf. Luke 12:8–9; Matt. 19:28) nor uses the title "Son of man" for Jesus [34] or for any other figure.[35]

part of the synoptic sayings source Q (Luke 12:39); it was the author of Matthew who introduced this and similar Q material into the synoptic apocalypse (Matt. 24:37–51 // Luke 17:26–27; 34–35; 12:39–40, 42–46). A second instance is the *Gospel of Thomas* 61a ("Two will rest on a bed . . ."); the synoptic parallel is found in Luke 17:34, i.e., again within a Q context (Luke 17:22–37) which was in part incorporated into the synoptic apocalypse first by Matthew (24:26–27, 37–39, 40–41).

31. There is no parallel in Matthew. It is difficult to determine whether it was Luke or Q that added this well-known eschatological admonition (cf. 1 Pet. 1:13; *Did.* 16. 1).

32. Two of the prophetic sayings, formulated as "I-sayings," come from the same context: Sayings 10 (Luke 12:49) and 16 (Luke 12:51). Only the latter can be assigned to Q with certainty (cf. Matt. 10:34), whereas the former has no parallel in Matthew and may come from Luke's special source rather than from Q.

33. On the Christology of the coming Son of man in Q, see: Heinz E. Tödt, *Der Menschensohn in der synoptischen Überlieferung*, 1958, pp. 44 ff.; Ferdinand Hahn, *Christologische Hoheitstitel*, FRLANT, 83, 1963, pp. 32 ff. (ET: *The Titles of Jesus in Christology*, 1969, pp. 28 ff.).

34. Only once does *Thomas* speak of Jesus as Son of man: "The foxes have their holes and the birds have their nest, but the Son of man has no place to lay his head and to rest" (Saying 86; cf. Luke 9:58; Matt. 8:20). Bultmann, (ET:) *History of the Synoptic Tradition*, p. 98 (see also Tödt, *Der Menschensohn*, pp. 44–45) has argued that this saying is a proverb in which *Son of man* is no honorific title, but simply means "man," as contrasted with the animals. Even though this explanation has not been widely accepted (see, against Bultmann; Günther Bornkamm, *Jesus of Nazareth*, 1960, pp. 229–30; Hahn, *Christologische*

This allows for either one of two explanations: (1) Thomas may have carefully avoided this term, and the sayings in which it occurred;[36] but in view of the *Gospel of Thomas* 86,[37] this is not very likely; (2) Thomas presupposes a stage and form of the tradition of eschatological sayings which did not yet contain an apocalyptic expectation of the Son of man. Did such a stage ever exist in the early church's transmission and expansion of Jesus' eschatological sayings?

Rudolf Bultmann was still prepared to ascribe to Jesus those Son of man sayings in which Jesus distinguishes between himself and the future Son of man.[38] But, more recently, Philipp Vielhauer and others have forcefully and persuasively challenged this assumption.[39] Vielhauer argues that the proclamation of the kingdom and the expectation of the Son of man are mutually exclusive concepts with respect to their content and history-of-religions background; and he proves that all sayings about the Son of man

---

Hoheitstitel, pp. 113–14), the *Gospel of Thomas*, which does not use the term as a title, seems to confirm Bultmann's suggestion. The decisive question is whether *Thomas* presupposes a stage of the synoptic tradition in which a titular usage of the term *Son of man* had not yet developed; see below.

35. Saying 106: "When you make the two one, you shall become sons of man." Whatever "sons of man" means here, it is not used as a title for a specific figure. Certainly the suggestion that " 'man' . . . refers to the first immortal man, the Saviour" (Bertil Gärtner, *The Theology of the Gospel of Thomas,* 1961, p. 246) presupposes too much of a gnostic redeemer mythology. A penetrating attempt to distinguish various layers of traditions and redaction within the synoptic sayings source has been published by Dieter Lührmann, *Die Redaktion der Logienquelle* (WMANT, 33, 1969). Lührmann assigns the sayings about the coming Son of man to a comparatively early stage of the tradition of Q, but he questions their historicity. Further elaboration of the stages of tradition which led to the composition of Q must include the *Gospel of Thomas* and its traditions in such a trajectory of the synoptic sayings source. This would also shed more light on the place of the Son of man sayings in this trajectory.

36. Saying 44 presents a variant to the synoptic saying about "the sin that cannot be forgiven." But whereas the Q version of this saying (Luke 12:10 // Matt. 12:32) contrasts the blasphemy against the Holy Spirit with the blasphemy against the Son of man, *Thomas* distinguishes between blasphemies against the Father, the Son, and the Holy Spirit. It is difficult to determine whether this "trinitarian version" of the injunction presupposes Q or rather the more original form of Mark 3:28–29 (Matt. 12:31) and *Did.* 11. 7. It is not unlikely that the *Son of man* was introduced into this saying by the author of Q. The twofold tradition in the synoptic gospels and the reference in *Didache* proves that this saying circulated freely; cf. my *Synoptische Überlieferung,* pp. 215 ff.

37. See above, n. 34.

38. Bultmann, (ET:) *History of the Synoptic Tradition,* pp. 151–52.

39. Philipp Vielhauer, "Gottesreich und Menschensohn in der Verkündigung Jesu," in *Festschrift Günther Dehn,* 1957, pp. 51–79; idem, "Jesus und der Menschensohn," *ZThK* 60 (1963): 133–77. Both articles are now in his *Aufsätze zum Neuen Testament,* 1965, pp. 55 ff. and 92 ff. A similar view is found in Norman Perrin, *Rediscovering the Teaching of Jesus,* 1967, pp. 164 ff.

disclose certain features of a christological development which are absent in the most primitive stage of the synoptic tradition and its eschatology.

For our evaluation of the apocalyptic sayings of Jesus, this implies that there were at least three different concepts of eschatology which occur in gospel literature side by side, often conflated with each other: (1) a developed, and even elaborate, "revelation" about future events, as it occurs in the synoptic apocalypse of Mark 13; (2) the expectation of the Son of man and of "his day," as it is represented in Q, but which is also evident in isolated sayings of Mark (e.g., Mark 8:38) and in the synoptic apocalypse in its present form; [40] (3) the proclamation of the coming of the kingdom, which is older than the two other apocalyptic theories, and ultimately has its roots in the preaching of Jesus.

The *Gospel of Thomas* does not reveal any acquaintance with either the synoptic apocalypse or Q's Son of man expectation. It does contain, however, a number of apocalyptic sayings. The most conspicuous term in these sayings, as well as in the *Gospel of Thomas* as a whole, is *kingdom*,[41] or *kingdom of Heaven*,[42] or *kingdom of the Father*.[43] To be sure, these sayings in the *Gospel of Thomas* almost always show a tendency to emphasize the presence of the kingdom for the believer, rather than its future coming. But it is very questionable, whether such eschatology of the kingdom is a later gnostic spiritualization of early Christian apocalyptic expectation, or rather an interpretation and elaboration of Jesus' most original proclamation.

The *Gospel of Thomas* preserves Jesus' emphasis that the coming of the kingdom cannot be timed or located:

Saying 3: [44] (The Kingdom is not in heaven, nor in the sea. . . .) "the Kingdom is within you and it is without you."

---

40. In the parallels to the synoptic apocalypse in 1 Thess. 4:15 ff. and *Did*. 16, the title used is not *Son of man* but *Lord*, which may be the more original title for this tradition of apocalyptic revelation.
41. Sayings 3, 22, 27, 46, 49, 82, 107, 109, 113.
42. Sayings 20, 54, 114.
43. Sayings 57, 76, 96–99, 113.
44. The translations are usually those of the *editio princeps* of A. Guillaumont et al., 1959.

Cf. Luke 17:20–21: "The kingdom of God does not come with signs to be observed; nor will they say: 'Here it is,' or 'there'; behold, the kingdom of God is among you." [45]

To the saying against those who test the face of the sky and the earth, but do not test the time (Luke 12:56), the *Gospel of Thomas* 91 adds: "and him who is before your face you have not known." This addition to an original saying of Jesus simply makes explicit what is already implied in Jesus' proclamation: men should not look into the future, nor into the past, but believe in the kingdom which is already present in his message.

Thomas condenses this original impact of Jesus' words into the christological title "the Living One," which occurs in sayings formulated in analogy to prophetic sayings of Jesus:

Saying 52: (With respect to the twenty-four prophets in Israel who spoke about Jesus) "You have dismissed the Living One who is before you and you have spoken about the dead." [46]

Saying 111: "The heavens will be rolled up and the earth in your presence, and he who lives on the Living One shall see neither death nor fear."

It is quite obvious that Thomas interprets the kingdom's presence in such a way that he eliminates the tension between present and future which characterizes Jesus' proclamation; past and future can become a unity in the present religious experience:

Saying 18: "Where the beginning is, there shall be the end. Blessed is he who shall stand at the beginning, and he shall know the end and he shall not taste death."

45. Cf. also the *Gospel of Thomas* 113: "(The kingdom . . .) will not come by expectation; they will not say: 'See here,' or 'See there.' But the kingdom of the Father is spread upon the earth and men do not see it."
46. Saying 52 perhaps presupposes Luke 10:23–24 // Matt. 13:16–17, the beatitude of the disciples as eyewitnesses, which is most likely an original saying of Jesus; see also Saying 38.

The kingdom is not only the believer's destiny, it is also his origin:

Saying 49: "Blessed are the solitary and the elect, for they shall find the kingdom; because you come from it, you shall go there again."

This saying is parallel to Saying 50:
   "We have come from the light, where the light has originated through itself."

The metaphor of the "child"—again derived from a genuine saying of Jesus (Mark 10:15 par.)—becomes an important symbol for the true believer in whose religious experience the opposites are reconciled:

Saying 22: "These children who are being suckled are like those who enter the kingdom. . . . When you make the two one, and when you make the inner as the outer . . . and the above as the below . . . the male and the female into a single one . . . then you shall enter the kingdom." [47]

Other prophetic sayings of Jesus in the form of beatitudes, some of them quoted without significant alterations (Sayings 54, 68, 69 = Matt. 5:3, 11, 6), are used to describe this same state of present blessedness; thus, all these designations by which Jesus identified the heirs of the kingdom—the children, the poor, the hungry, those who suffer persecution—ultimately mean in the *Gospel of Thomas* the "Solitary One." In the agonizing eschatological divisions which have been ushered in by Jesus (Luke 12:51–53 // Matt. 10:34–36,[48] quoted in Saying 16), the believers stand as the "Solitaries." [49]

47. On Saying 22 see Howard C. Kee, " 'Becoming a Child' in the Gospel of Thomas," *JBL* 82 (1963): 307–14, and the critical discussion of Kee's article in James M. Robinson, *Kerygma und historischer Jesus*, 2d ed., 1967, pp. 230 ff.
48. This saying does not belong to the context of the synoptic apocalypse; it does not speak about the divisions which will occur before the coming of the Son of man, but about those which Jesus causes through his ministry. Thus it

Jesus radicalized the traditional apocalyptic expectation of the kingdom; his message demands that the mysterious presence of the kingdom in his words be recognized. The Gnosticism of the *Gospel of Thomas* appears to be a direct continuation of the eschatological sayings of Jesus. But the disclosure of the mysterious presence of the kingdom is no longer an eschatological event; it has become a matter of the interpretation of Jesus' words: "The repose of the dead and . . . the new world . . . has come, but you know it not" (Saying 51); thus, "whoever finds the explanation of these words will not taste death" (Saying 1). It is as this discovery of the secret presence of "Life," [50] "Light," [51] and "Repose" [52] in Jesus' words that "everything that is hidden will be revealed" (Sayings 5, 6 = Mark 4:22).[53]

Parables

The *Gospel of Thomas* has preserved a large number of parables.[54] Most of these have direct parallels in the synoptic gospels,[55] and perhaps all are original parables of Jesus.[56] As a rule, these parables are rather brief; exceptions are Sayings 64 and 65 (parables of the great supper, Matt. 22:1 ff., and of the evil husbandmen, Mark 12:1 ff.). Allegorical embellishments and

---

represents an eschatological orientation which is probably more primitive than either Q's expectation of the Son of man or the eschatology of Mark 13.

49. The Solitaries as the possessors of the kingdom also appear in Sayings 4, 23, 49, 75; A. F. J. Klijn, "The 'Single One' in the Gospel of Thomas," *JBL* 81 (1962): 271–78, has argued that this term describes the primordial "One-ness," regained in the eschatological experience of the believer.

50. Saying 4.

51. Sayings 61c, 83.

52. Sayings 50, 51, 60, 90.

53. The "days in which the disciples will seek Jesus and not find him" (Saying 38b) are not the days after Jesus' death, nor the time before his parousia, but the "time" in which men may not be able to understand his words (cf. Sayings 38a, 39).

54. I have not included here the numerous metaphors, since they belong to the wisdom sayings.

55. Sayings 8, 9, 20, 57, 63–65, 76, 107; cf. 21b, 103.

56. This is also not improbable for the parables which lack parallels in the synoptic gospels (Sayings 96, 97, 98, 109); cf. Claus-Hunno Hunzinger, "Unbekannte Gleichnisse Jesu aus dem Thomas-Evangelium," in *Judentum, Urchristentum, Kirche*, Joachim Jeremias festschrift, suppl. to *ZNW*, 26, 1960, 209–20.

interpretations are rare,[57] but indicative of *Thomas*'s gnosticizing tendencies.[58]

I presuppose that the parables of *Thomas* are not taken from the synoptic gospels, but derive from an earlier stage of the tradition of synoptic parables.[59]

In Jesus' proclamation, the parables speak about the kingdom of God and about man's situation in view of its coming. In the *Gospel of Thomas* they speak about the man who has found a great religious treasure:

Saying 8: "The man is like a wise fisherman who cast his net into the sea; he drew it up from the sea full of small fish. Among them he found a large and good fish; that wise fisherman, he threw all the small fish down into the sea; he chose the large fish without regret."

The point is quite different from the judgment parable in Matt. 13:47–48.[60] In *Thomas* we have a wisdom parable which praises the wisdom of the fisherman—the term *wise* occurs twice—as an example of wise discrimination.[61] In the parable of the pearl

57. There is no trace in *Thomas* of the allegorical interpretations which some of the parables he quotes have received in the synoptic gospels; cf. Sayings 9 (the "sower," Mark 4:3 ff., 13 ff.), 57 (parable of the tares, Matt. 13:24 ff., 36 ff.). Perhaps Saying 65 also preserves a version of the parable of the evil husbandman which is more original and less allegorical than Mark 12:1 ff.
58. There are two instances in which the allegorical interpretation makes it difficult to determine whether there was once a more primitive parable and, if so, what it meant: Sayings 21a (the little children in the field who take off their clothes) and 60 (the Samaritan carrying a lamb).
59. For a more detailed treatment, see Hugh Montefiore, "A Comparison of the Parables of the Gospel according to Thomas and of the Synoptic Gospels," in Montefiore and H. E. W. Turner, *Thomas and the Evangelists*, SBT, 35, 1962; first published in *NTS* 7 (1960/61): 220–48.
60. Matt. 13:49–50 is a secondary allegory of judgment which seems not yet tc have become a part of the version which *Thomas* knew.
61. One may wonder whether Thomas refers to the synoptic parable of Matt. 13:47–48 at all. There is an almost exact parallel to Saying 8 in the poetic version of the Aesopic fables by Babrius, who, in the first century A.D., dedicated his work to the son of King Alexander, whose tutor he was. This Alexander seems to have been a petty king in Cilicia, grandson of Herod's son Alexander, mentioned by Josephus (*Ant.* 18, 140). Fable 4 of Babrius (trans. B. E. Perry, *Babrius and Phaedrus*, Loeb Classical Library, 1965) reads:

> A fisherman drew in the net which he had cast a short time before and, as luck would have it, it was full of all kinds of delectable fish. But the little ones fled to the bottom of the net and slipped out through its many meshes, whereas the big ones were caught and lay stretched out in the boat.

(Saying 76 = Matt. 13:45–46) *Thomas* underlines the admonition to seek enduring treasure by adding another wisdom saying from the synoptic tradition: "Do you also seek for the treasure which fails not, which endures, there where no moth comes near . . ." (Matt. 6:20 // Luke 12:33).

The remarkable feature of these parables in *Thomas* is that they are never understood as eschatological parables but rather as admonitions to find the mysterious treasure in Jesus' words and in one's own self.

I-Sayings

I-sayings are more numerous than in the synoptic gospels. Some of them differ only slightly from their synoptic parallels (e.g., Saying 10 = Luke 12:49),[62] but most of them are independent formulations. They do not show Jesus presenting himself in the role of an apocalyptic prophet; nor do we find any trace of the development typical of the synoptic sayings source Q, where the "I" of Jesus corresponds to the future coming of the Son of man;[63] nor is there any sign that Thomas knew the Marcan I-sayings which predict the passion and resurrection of Jesus.[64] Rather, Jesus appears as the divine revealer who makes his disciples "Single Ones" (Saying 23). That is to say, he brings them into an existence that is independent of the historical circumstances of life. Or Jesus, characteristically, is Wisdom, inviting men to bear his yoke (Saying 90 = Matt. 11:28–30).

This is almost an exact parallel from the secular tradition of fables, and at least opens up the possibility that in other instances as well Thomas may have drawn upon the wisdom tradition of his time—even if the application is quite different in Babrius:

> It's one way to be insured and out of trouble, to be small; but you will seldom see a man who enjoys a great reputation and has the luck to evade all risks.

It is, of course, not unlikely that Matt. 13:47–48 used the same fable and turned it into a parable of judgment.

62. Only four of the seventeen I-sayings have synoptic parallels (Sayings 10, 16, 55, and 90 = Luke 12:49; Luke 12:51a // Matt. 10:34a; Luke 14:26, 27 // Matt. 10:37, 38; cf. Mark 8:34; Matt. 11:28–30).

63. See above, pp. 170 ff.

64. Cf. Mark 8:31 parr.; 9:31 parr.; 10:33–34 parr.; also Mark 9:9; 14:21, etc Ever since William Wrede, *Das Messiasgeheimnis in den Evangelien*, 1901, pp. 82–92, many critical scholars have maintained that all of these sayings are secondary formulations (*vaticinia ex eventu*).

Thus, the I-sayings of the *Gospel of Thomas* are primarily revelation sayings which have little basis in the historical teaching of Jesus.[65] Indicative of this type of revelation sayings in the I-style are those sayings in which the revealer presents himself as the divine savior (or Wisdom!) who has come into the world: Saying 28: "I stood in the midst of the world and in flesh I appeared to them. . . ." [66]

The fact that some of these sayings are formulated in the "I am" style suggests a comparison with the "I am" sayings of the Gospel of John. Here, however, one discovers a very remarkable difference. In the *Gospel of Thomas,* these "I am" sayings answer the question "Who are you?"—a question which is even explicitly asked by Salome in Saying 61: "Who are you, man, and whose son?" Jesus answers: "I am he who is from the same; to me was given from the things of my father"; cf. Saying 77: "I am the light that is above, I am the all. . . ." Thus, these sayings are examples of "I am" as an identification formula. This belongs to the category of revelatory language in which the divine qualities of the revealer are emphasized.[67]

By contrast, the "I am" sayings in the Gospel of John are instances of the recognition formula, as Bultmann has shown.[68] The "I" is the predicate of the sentence, answering the question: "Who is (or where is) the one whom we expect?" or: "Where is the salvation, the light, the life that is to come?" In the Gospel of John, the answer ". . . it is I" claims that all this has now come and is present in Jesus of Nazareth. In this way, the stress is upon the appearance among men of the divine revelation (Logos, Father). The identification formula could shift into a recognition formula, because the basic structure of John's Gospel derives from

65. Cf. Bultmann, *Geschichte,* pp. 161 ff. (ET: pp. 150 ff.).
66. Equally significant are I-sayings which speak of the revelation of the divine mysteries; cf. Sayings 62, 108; see also Saying 17: "I shall give you what eye has not seen. . . ." This saying is missing in the canonical gospels, but is quoted, introduced by "it is written," in 1 Cor. 2:9.
67. For examples see Bultmann, *Das Evangelium des Johannes,* 1959, p. 167 n. 2, where the various forms of the "I am" formula are analyzed. In the *Gospel of Thomas,* as elsewhere, there is not a clear-cut distinction between the identification formula on the one hand and the presentation and qualification formulae on the other.
68. Ibid., pp. 167–68. Bultmann considers John 11:25 and 14:6 possible exceptions.

the cross-resurrection kerygma.[69] The narrative context of the gospel, and the fact that the gospel as a whole is directed toward Jesus' glorification on the cross, forced the "I am" sayings into the category of the recognition formula. Whatever was expected as the salvation (the Life, the Light, the Way, the Truth) is present in the story of a particular human being. The *Gospel of Thomas,* on the other hand, does not present a story of Jesus' life, nor is Jesus proclaimed as a man who suffered on the cross "under Pontius Pilate." The concern is exclusively with his words. For these, the historical origin is quite irrelevant. Who Jesus was or that he once lived and died, is without any importance. Thus, the recognition formula is not relevant, since this formula is used to recognize the presence of the revelation in a particular historical man and in his fate. The absence of the recognition formula implies that the sayings collection in itself had no inherent principle by which such sayings could be made to witness to a particular historical event. The sayings collection explains that Jesus and his words—whoever he may have been in his historical appearance—have divine quality. By way of contrast, the gospel of the passion-kerygma witnesses that whatever is divine has become a historical and human reality in the earthly Jesus of Nazareth.

Wisdom Sayings and Proverbs

Wisdom sayings and proverbs are numerous in the *Gospel of Thomas.* Most of these sayings have exact parallels in the synoptic gospels. They are often expressions of general truths which have no relation to any particular historical situation or person:

Saying 31: Prophet in his fatherland (Mark 6:4–5 [70] par.)
     32: The city built on a mountain (Matt. 5:14b)
     33a: What you hear in your ear (Matt. 10:27; Luke 12: 3) [71]

69. Ibid., p. 168, suggests that some of the "I am" sayings of John originally were presentation or identification formulae.
70. On this proverb (*POxy* 1. 6) see *"GNOMAI DIAPHOROI,"* above, pp. 129 ff.
71. See below, n. 78.

33b: Light under a bushel (Mark 4:21; Matt. 5:15 par.)

34: Blind leading the blind (Matt. 15:14; Luke 6:39)

35: House of the strong man (Mark 3:27 par.)

45a: No grapes from thorns (Matt. 7:16; cf. Luke 6:44)

45b: Good heart—good words (Luke 6:45; cf. Matt. 12: 34–35)

47a: Serving two masters (Matt. 6:24; Luke 16:13)

47b: Old and new wine (Luke 5:39)

47c: New wine in old wine skins (Mark 2:22; cf. Matt. 9:17; Luke 5:37) [72]

47d: Old patch on new garment (Mark 2:21; cf. Matt. 9:16; Luke 5:36) [73]

67: Whoever knows the all (cf. Mark 8:36; Matt. 16:26; Luke 9:25)

94: Whoever seeks, will find (Matt. 7:8; cf. Luke 11:10).

There are also some general admonitions:

Saying 26: The beam in your brother's eye (Matt. 7:3, 5; Luke 6:41–42)

39b: Wise as serpents (Matt. 10:16)

92: Seek and you will find (Matt. 7:7; Luke 11:9)

93: On not profaning the holy (Matt. 7:6).

The relationship of these proverbial sayings to their synoptic parallels is most peculiar. To the extent that they represent sayings which Matthew and Luke drew from Q, their synoptic parallels

---

72. The *Gospel of Thomas* adds "and they do not put old wine into a new wineskin, lest it spoil it." This may be a secondary addition in analogy to the first sentence; cf. Hans-Werner Bartsch, "Das Thomas-Evangelium und die synoptischen Evangelien," *NTS* 6 (1959/60): 251–53. But some of these parallelisms in the *Gospel of Thomas* are probably original, as, e.g., in Saying 31 (cf. nn. 70, 80).

73. The reversal of the order "old patch on new garment" instead of "new patch on old garment" (as in the synoptic gospels) is most peculiar. Quispel quite ingeniously reconstructs an old (Aramaic) parallelism which, he says, was the basis of both versions: "They do not put an old patch on a new garment, because it does not match the new, and they do not sew a new patch on an old garment, because there would be a rent." Cf. Gilles Quispel, "Some Remarks on the Gospel of Thomas," *NTS* 5 (1958/59): 281; also idem, "The Gospel of Thomas and the New Testament," *VigChr* 11 (1957): 194–95. Perhaps the reversal is caused simply by the second half of the preceding saying, 47c.

are usually found either in the "Sermon on the Mount" (Matt. 5–7) or the "Sermon on the Plain" (Luke 6). In both of these synoptic contexts we find Sayings 26 and 45a.[74] The parallels of Sayings 33b, 47a, 92, and 94 occur only in the Sermon on the Mount,[75] whereas Luke has the same sayings in different contexts.[76] For Sayings 32 and 93 [77] there are no parallels in Luke at all. On the other hand, Sayings 34 and 45b are paralleled only in Luke's Sermon on the Plain (Luke 6:39, 45), whereas Matthew's parallels are found outside of the Sermon on the Mount (Matt. 15:14; 12:34–35). However, if any of these wisdom sayings of *Thomas* with parallels in the synoptic gospels have no parallels in either Matt. 5–7 or Luke 6, there is always a parallel in the Gospel of Mark; [78] Sayings 31, 35, 47c, 47d, and 67 are found in Mark 6:4–5; 3:27; 2:22; 2:21; and 8:36.[79]

Since no peculiarities of the editorial work of Matthew, Mark, or Luke are recognizable in these proverbial sayings of *Thomas*,[80]

---

74. Matt. 7:3, 5 // Luke 6:41–42; Matt. 7:16 // Luke 6:44.
75. Matt. 5:15; 6:24; 7:7; 7:8.
76. Luke 11:33; 16:13; 11:9; 11:10.
77. Matt. 5:14; 7:6.
78. The only exceptions are Sayings 47b = Luke 5:39, though this saying belongs together with others which Luke drew from Mark: Mark 2:21–22 // Luke 5:36 ff. (= Sayings 47c, d); Saying 33a ("What you shall hear in your ear . . .") = Matt. 10:27 // Luke 12:3, though again this saying is closely connected with the sayings of Mark 4:21 ff.: Mark 4:21 = Saying 33b; Mark 4:22 // Matt. 10:26 // Luke 12:21 = Saying 5.
79. Saying 33b occurs in Mark 4:21 as well as in the Sermon on the Mount (Matt. 5:15). Mark 4:21 is part of the small collection of Q sayings in Mark's Gospel (Mark 4:21–25) which has relations also to other sayings in *Thomas* (cf. Sayings 5, 41). Matt. 5:15 also proves that this saying was an original part of the tradition which has been expanded into the Sermons "on the Mount" and "on the Plain" by Matthew and Luke. It is noteworthy, however, that the form of this saying in *Thomas* corresponds most closely to Luke 11:33 rather than to Matt 5:15 and Mark 4:21 // Luke 8:16.
80. On the contrary, some of these sayings, as they occur in the *Gospel of Thomas*, have a more primitive form than their synoptic parallels. Cf., e.g., Saying 31, which has preserved the original parallelism, whereas Mark 6:4, 5 transformed the second half of the saying ("no physician heals those who know him") into narrative ("and he could not perform any miracles there"). Saying 26 reproduces Matt. 7:3 and 5, but does not have Matt. 7:4 par. "Or how can you say to your brother 'Let me take the speck out of your eye. . . '?" This saying provides, *nota bene*, a good example of the irresponsible way in which some scholars try to prove that Thomas introduced secondary alterations into synoptic sayings: Bartsch, "Das Thomas-Evangelium," p. 255, calls "and then you will see clearly" a secondary addition; but this phrase (in *POxy* 1. 1) is the exact equivalent of the phrase which is found in both Matt. 7:5 and Luke 6:42! Saying 45b = Luke 6:45 preserves the original emphasis upon "good heart—good

there is no reason to assume that they were drawn from the synoptic gospels.[81] Rather, *Thomas*'s source must have been a very primitive collection of proverbs, a collection which was incorporated into Matthew's and Luke's common source Q and thus became the basis of the materials used by Matt. 5–7 and Luke 6 for their "Sermons," and which was also known to Mark.

It is not surprising to find some signs of secondary growth in these wisdom sayings of *Thomas*. They are, in part, natural developments of such proverbial material.[82] Only rarely does Thomas express any secondary and tendentious interpretations in the formulations of the proverbs themselves.[83] His theological bias is explicit in the sayings about seeking and finding:

Saying 92 reproduces the well-known exhortation "Seek and you will find" (Matt. 7:7; Luke 11:9), but adds a tendentious I-saying: "But those things which you asked me in those days, I did not tell you then; now I desire to tell them, but you do not inquire after them."

---

words"; cf. the rabbinic saying, "What was in the heart, was in the mouth" (*Midr. Ps.* 28. 4. 115b; Strack-Billerbeck, 1:639; Bultmann, *Geschichte,* p. 87; *ET,* p. 84.). Cf. also above, nn. 70 and 72.

81. In some instances (e.g., Saying 45), the proverbs of *Thomas* reveal that they were transmitted in the same combinations in which they occur in the synoptic gospels; cf. Bartsch, "Das Thomas-Evangelium," pp. 253–54. This however, is no argument for dependence upon the synoptic gospels, since some of these sayings were certainly combined and confused already in the earliest stages of the tradition.

82. Cf. such additions according to analogy, as Saying 47a: "It is impossible for a man to mount two horses and to stretch two bows"; Saying 33: "What you shall hear in your ear, preach from your housetops" (added to "city on a mountain" and "light not under a bushel"); but this may be an older Q tradition; see above, n. 78.

83. In some instances, scholars have been overly quick to identify Thomas's text as secondary; e.g., Saying 93:

> Give not what is holy to the dogs,
>   lest they cast it on the dung heap.
> Throw not the pearls to the swine,
>   lest they make it [. . . .]"

This is a perfect form of a proverb without any religious or Christian application, whereas Matt. 7:6 shows signs of an application of this proverb to the situation of the church. When Bartsch ("Das Thomas-Evangelium," p. 255) remarks that "Matthew's interpretation, which was determined by the subject matter, i.e., by the situation of the church, has been replaced by an interpretation which is determined by the metaphorical content" of the Logion, he turns all form-critical standards upside down.

Saying 2: "Let him who seeks, not cease seeking until he finds; and when he finds, he will be troubled, and when he has been troubled, he will marvel and he will reign over the All." [84]

Thomas explains what is meant by "finding" in another alteration of a synoptic wisdom saying (Mark 8:36 par.):

Saying 67: "Whoever knows the All but fails himself, fails everything." [85]

Cf. Saying 111b: "Whoever finds himself, of him the world is not worthy." [86]

Speculation about the relation of the self to the origin of being is added to this emphasis upon knowing oneself. This is expressed in several sayings of this type, although they are no longer wisdom sayings of proverbial character. Instead of speaking about the nature of man in general, they contemplate the true nature of the gnostic's self:

Saying 29: "If the flesh has come into existence because of the spirit, it is a marvel; but if the spirit (has come into existence) because of the body, it is a marvel of marvels. But I marvel how this great wealth has made its home in this poverty." [87]

---

84. This is most certainly a secondary and gnosticising version of the exhortation to seek and to find. In the Greek version of *Thomas* (*POxy* 654. 2), as well as in the parallel of this saying which Clement of Alexandria quotes from the *Gospel of the Hebrews* (*Stromateis* 2. 9, 45, 5 and 5. 14, 96, 3), the chain is better preserved, and another line is added: "and on reigning he will rest." Thereby, the saying reveals even more clearly its connection with the theological expectation of the wisdom tradition, namely to find rest; cf. *Sir.* 6. 28; Matt. 11:28–30, which is quoted in the *Gospel of Thomas* 90.
85. Literally: "fails the whole [or: every] place." The translation of Guillaumont et al. reads: ". . . but fails (*to know*) himself, *lacks* everything." Following Ernst Haenchen, *Die Botschaft des Thomas-Evangeliums,* 1961, p. 27, I prefer to repeat the word *fail,* since the Coptic text also has the same verb in both instances.
86. Cf. also the gnostic sayings on finding, Sayings 56 and 80. They are certainly secondary extensions of the more primitive synoptic proverbs on seeking and finding.
87. Cf. also Sayings 84, 87, and 77b.

It is only here that the tradition of wisdom sayings takes its characteristic turn into gnostic theology. Throughout the tradition of these sayings their truth does not depend upon the authority of Jesus. Whether the wisdom saying envisages man's being in general, or whether it discloses man's spiritual nature and origin, its truth is vindicated whenever he finds this truth in himself.

Rules for the Community

Several rules for the community from the synoptic tradition have parallels in the *Gospel of Thomas.* But most of them have been modified considerably.

In the synoptic gospels, as well as in the epistles of the New Testament, or in the *Didache,* such rules reflect the attempt of the early Christian church to enable the Christians to live in this world and to regulate the life of the community accordingly. On the whole, the parenetic tradition of Judaism was utilized, and became the basis for early Christian pareneses and community regulations. Words of Jesus found only occasional usage in such contexts; for this, Paul's letters, the *Didache,* and *1 Clement* are typical witnesses. Quite a few of these regulations were only subsequently made "sayings of Jesus," and were introduced into the synoptic tradition at a secondary stage.

The rules for the community in the *Gospel of Thomas,* whether based upon original words of Jesus or not, always request that the disciple divorce himself from the traditional religious behavior of Judaism and that he separate himself from any concerns with this world. Sayings against fasting, praying, and almsgiving occur several times:

Saying 14a: "If you fast, you will beget sin for yourselves, and if you pray, you will be condemned, and if you give alms, you will do evil to your spirits." [88]

If fasting and keeping of the Sabbath and circumcision are rejected, they are nevertheless valid symbols for the separation from the world (cf. Sayings 27, 53). Jesus' words on "clean and un-

88. Cf. Matt. 6:1 ff.; *Did.* 8. See, further, Sayings 6a, 104.

clean," preserved in Saying 14c in a form that is probably more original than Mark 7:18–20 par., are perhaps intended to emphasize the importance of the inner man.[89]

But it is not just that Thomas spiritualizes religious observances. Rather he understands the commands of Jesus to break with established family ties as demanding a complete separation from society and an acceptance of only the "family" of the truly redeemed. Compare the sayings on Jesus' true relatives (Saying 99) [90] and on hating one's father and mother (Saying 101).[91] A number of sayings imply the rejection of worldly possessions.[92]

The disciples are wanderers who have no home (Saying 42). They heal the sick and accept what is set before them (Saying 14b).[93] If, in this way, they imitate Jesus' own experience of homelessness (Saying 86)—and indeed, this motif was destined to have a powerful influence upon Syrian Christianity—then Jesus' radical divorce from the accepted Jewish interpretation of the law has become a new set of religious rules. They have become test cases for the separation from this world and time. Otherworldliness is the new ideology.

Because of the relation of this gospel to Jesus' *ipsissima vox,* it is an urgent question, whether or not this tradition maintains its original integrity once its *Sitz im Leben* has been transferred from the eschatological proclamation of Jesus to the theology of the church. It seems that the sayings of Jesus were in this case a vital element in the development of a religious self-understand-

---

89. See the saying about the "outside and inside of the cup," Saying 89 (Luke 11:39, 40); Thomas presents this saying in agreement with Luke 11:40 and with the reversal of "outside" and "inside" found only in P[45] C D T a e c, which is usually considered to be a secondary variant of Luke's text. As long as the meaning of this saying is not quite clear, it is impossible to decide whether Thomas's text represents a more original version which was the original version of Luke too, or whether Thomas's version has subsequently influenced the Lucan manuscript tradition, or whether Thomas is dependent upon a variant of Luke's text. On the meaning of this saying see Haenchen, *Die Botschaft des Thomas-Evangeliums* p. 53; Quispel, "Gospel of Thomas and the New Testament," p. 200.
90. Mark 3:33–35 par.
91. Matt. 10:37 // Luke 14:26.
92. Saying 95 forbids the lending of money at profit or with the hope to receive it back (Luke 6:34–35); cf. Sayings 81 and 110. Also Thomas's conclusion of the parable of the banquet (Matthew 22:1–10; Luke 14:15–24): "Tradesmen and merchants shall not enter the places of my Father" (Saying 64).
93. Luke 10:8, 9 (Matthew's parallel is different and secondary).

ing for which the historical Jesus of Nazareth became ultimately irrelevant as a criterion of true faith.

The basis of the *Gospel of Thomas* is a sayings collection which is more primitive than the canonical gospels, even though its basic principle is not related to the creed of the passion and resurrection. Its principle is nonetheless theological. Faith is understood as belief in Jesus' words, a belief which makes what Jesus proclaimed present and real for the believer. The catalyst which has caused the crystallization of these sayings into a "gospel" is the view that the kingdom is uniquely present in Jesus' eschatological preaching and that eternal wisdom about man's true self is disclosed in his words. The gnostic proclivity of this concept needs no further elaboration.[94]

The relation of this "sayings gospel," from which the *Gospel of Thomas* is derived, to the synoptic sayings source Q, is an open question. Without doubt, most of its materials are Q sayings (including some sayings which appear occasionally in Mark). But it must have been a version of Q in which the apocalyptic expectation of the Son of man was missing, and in which Jesus' radicalized eschatology of the kingdom and his revelation of divine wisdom in his own words were dominant motifs.

Such a version of Q is, however, not secondary, but very primitive. At least Paul's debate with his opponents in 1 Corinthians seems to suggest that the wisdom theology which Paul attacked relied on this understanding of Jesus' message.[95] These opponents propagated a realized eschatology. They claimed that divine wisdom was revealed through Jesus. And at least one saying which Paul quotes in the context of his refutation is indeed found in the *Gospel of Thomas* 17 (1 Cor. 2:9).

This would prove that such sayings collections with explicit theological tendencies were in use quite early, and not only in Aramaic-speaking circles in Syria; that the source "Q," used by Matthew and Luke, was a secondary version of such a "gospel,"

94. Cf. James M. Robinson, *"LOGOI SOPHON,"* chap. 3 above, and "The Problem of History in Mark, Reconsidered," *USQR* 20 (1965): 135.
95. See further James M. Robinson, "Kerygma and History in the New Testament," chap. 2 above, pp. 30–46. For further discussion of this question cf. Heinz-Wolfgang Kuhn, "Der irdische Jesus bei Paulus als traditions-geschichtliches und theologisches Problem," *ZThK* 67 (1970): 295–320.

into which the apocalyptic expectation of the Son of man had been introduced to check the gnosticizing tendencies of this sayings gospel; and that the *Gospel of Thomas,* stemming from a more primitive stage of such a "gospel," attests its further growth into a gnostic theology.

Jesus as the Divine Man (Aretalogies)

The older canonical gospels Mark and John, which do not use many sayings but are primarily based upon the passion narrative and its kerygma,[96] use still another source, from which they drew their stories of Jesus' miracles.

That such a source, or sources, containing primarily miracle stories, existed, is widely recognized and needs no further debate.[97] In the Gospel of John the use of this source, known as the miracles source, is quite obvious. In Mark this source is not as apparent as in John. But there can be no doubt that he too used such a source. However, Mark's and John's sources, even though closely related to each other, certainly were not identical.

Important for the scope of this discussion is the question whether these collections of miracle stories about Jesus had any particular theological principle which served as a catalyst that was responsible for their composition and basic orientation. In such primitive gospel sources Jesus appears as a man endowed with divine power who performs miracles to prove his divine quality and character. This sets the tone for their theological tendency. John 20:30–31, most likely the original ending of the miracles source which John used,[98] formulates this tendency rather well: "Now Jesus did many other signs before his disciples which are not recorded in this book; these, however, were written down in order that you may believe that Jesus is the Christ, the Son of God."[99]

96. See above, p. 161.
97. The question of these sources for the miracle stories was most recently reconsidered by Robinson, "Kerygma and History," chap. 2 above, pp. 46–66, where the important literature is also cited. Cf. also Robinson, "The Johannine Trajectory," below, pp. 235 ff.
98. Cf. Bultmann, *Evangelium des Johannes,* ad loc.
99. The last phrase of John 20:31, "and that believing you may have life in his name," was probably added by the author of the gospel; cf. ibid.

This conclusion of John's source is significant because it is typical. Similar conclusions are customary for books which recount the miraculous and powerful acts of great men or of gods: e.g., *Sir.* 43. 27 after the enumeration of the "admirable (feats)" of God; *1 Macc.* 9. 22 after the report about the wars of Judas the Maccabee.[100] It is the typical ending of an aretalogy.

Aretalogies were normally written for purposes of religious propaganda.[101] The religious convictions which incline to the use of this literary genre for propaganda purposes are very much the same everywhere in the Hellenistic world, whether they be Jewish, pagan, or Christian. Aretalogies are not used only to defend certain religious tenets; they are not simply apologetic.[102] Rather, these stories of extraordinary events and performances represent in themselves the essential creed and belief of a religious movement.

Gospels in the form of aretalogies, such as the miracles sources of Mark and John, proclaim that a particular divine power is present and available in these powerful acts of Jesus. Belief in this "gospel" implies that the benefits of such miraculous acts are accessible, or even that these acts can be repeated in the religious experience of the believer. Jesus is the "divine man" ($\theta\epsilon\tilde{\iota}os$ $\dot{\alpha}\nu\dot{\eta}\rho$);[103] he can be imitated by his apostle, who thereby incorporates and represents the revelation in his missionary activity.

---

100. More examples, also from Greek literature, in ibid., p. 540 n. 3.

101. James M. Robinson, "Kerygma and History in the New Testament," chap. 2 above, p. 55, speaks of "the apologetic, missionary scope or *Sitz im Leben* of the miracles source." I would rather not use the term *apologetic* here, since the primary element is certainly that of religious propaganda. Of course, early Christianity borrowed this genre from what is usually known as "Jewish apologetics"; see further below on 2 Corinthians, pp. 189 f.

102. See n. 101 above.

103. A variant of this designation occurs in Acts 2:22: "a man attested . . . by God with mighty works and wonders and miraculous signs." In Lucan theology "by God" emphasized the subordination of Jesus to God (cf. Hans Conzelmann, *Die Apostelgeschichte*, HNT, 1963; also idem, *The Theology of Saint Luke*, 1960, pp. 173 ff.). But this is not necessarily the original intention of the formula which Luke used in Acts 2:22–24. In the New Testament the titles *Christ* and *Son of God* are sometimes connected with the Christology of Jesus as the divine man; cf. John 20:31. The title *Christ* also occurs in 2 Cor. 5:16, a passage which seems to refer specifically to this christological concept; see below, p. 190. For the question of christological titles see Koester, "The Structure and Criteria of Early Christian Beliefs," below, p. 217.

The author of the Gospel of John did not continue this Christology of the divine man uncritically. He emphasizes that the essential part of Jesus' revelation is his "glorification on the cross." [104]

In the Gospel of Mark, the inherent tendency of the tradition of the miracle stories is criticized in a similar way, by means of the creed of Jesus crucified. The true "mystery of the Messiah" [105] is not visible in his performance of glorious acts and miracles. It is present in his suffering, and the disciples are asked to follow him on his road to calvary (Mark 8:34 ff.). It is also quite characteristic of Mark's critique of the divine man Christology that he illustrates his chapters on discipleship (Mark 8–10) with a miracle story in which the disciples *fail* to accomplish the healing (Mark 9:14–29).

The claims of the disciples, apostles, and missionaries who adhered to the divine man Christology before and after Mark were less modest. The first occurrence of this Christology in our sources is in 2 Corinthians.[106] The various letters of Paul, now com-

104. Cf. Bultmann, *Evangelium des Johannes,* esp. to John 17:1. Robinson, "Kerygma and History," chap. 2 above, p. 55, says that, against the theological tendency of the source, John "maintains that the true form of faith is faith in Jesus' word," and that this seems to bring John close to the heresy of the *Gospel of Thomas.* But, at the same time, John indeed uses the criterion of belief in Jesus' crucifixion and resurrection. The word of Jesus recalled to the disciples by the Paraclete, is always the "word" which became flesh and whose glory is present in his death. For a discussion of Ernst Käsemann, *Jesus letzer Wille nach Johannes* 17, 1966 (ET: *The Testament of Jesus,* 1968), see James M. Robinson, "The Johannine Trajectory," below, pp. 256–260.
105. William Wrede, *Das Messiasgeheimnis in den Evangelien,* (2d ed. 1913), posed, more than half a century ago, this problem of the Marcan "messianic secret." The solution is obvious today: Mark's tradition, the stories of the divine man and Messiah Jesus, were subjected to the principle of the cross. In this way, the "secret" revelation of Jesus in his miracles becomes intelligible. On the history of this problem, cf. Georg Strecker, "William Wrede," *ZThK* 57 (1960): 67–91. To my knowledge, the first to call attention to the fact that Mark's tradition was thoroughly "messianic" and that Mark criticized his tradition by the theory of the "messianic secret" was Conzelmann, "Gegenwart und Zukunft in der synoptischen Tradition," *ZThK* 54 (1957): 293 ff. (ET: *JTC* 5 (1968): 42–43).
106. I am somewhat embarrassed to be credited with having discovered the connection between the sources of Mark and John and the opponents of 2 Corinthians, in my article "Häretiker im Urchristentum," in *RGG,* 3d ed., vol. 3 (1959), pp. 18–19. It was, as a matter of fact, Dieter Georgi who first suggested this relationship in his 1958 Heidelberg dissertation, which was published six years later: *Die Gegner des Paulus im 2. Korintherbrief: Studien zur religiösen Propaganda in der Spätantike,* WMANT, 11, 1964. For the following see also Koester, *"GNOMAI DIAPHOROI,"* above, pp. 150–153, and Robinson, "Kerygma and History," above, pp. 47–66.

bined into this canonical epistle,[107] inform us about foreign apostles who had come to Corinth during Paul's stay in Ephesus. Dieter Georgi [108] had demonstrated convincingly that they were Christian missionaries who had adopted the patterns of Hellenized Jewish propaganda. Through their skills in public speaking they were able to come off successfully in the market of religious competition. By powerful miracles and spiritual performances they demonstrated that *Christus praesens* transcended the limitations of human life.

The letters of recommendation (2 Cor. 3:1) with which these missionaries underscored their authority are of special interest for our question. Apparently these letters were written documents in which particular powerful acts were recorded and certified by other churches.[109] At the same time these foreign apostles tried to secure similar written recommendations from Corinth.[110] Indeed such letters, which were nothing other than aretalogies, would serve as an excellent instrument to further the cause of the Christian mission elsewhere.

This religious propaganda must have been the creative milieu in which the aretalogies of Jesus were composed. The self-understanding of the missionary and the understanding of Jesus' person and life are correlatives.[111] What Paul calls the "Christ according to the flesh" (2 Cor. 5:16) was for his opponents the divine man Jesus, whose glorious deeds were remembered and constituted the central "christological" material of their religious convictions.

Once the collections of Jesus' miracle stories had been incorporated into the Gospels of Mark and John, they did not survive independently. Through Mark and John, however, these stories

---

107. Cf. Bornkamm, "Die Vorgeschichte des sogenannten Zweiten Korintherbriefes," SHA, Phil.-hist. Klasse, 1961, 2; and the English summary, "The History of the Origin of the So-Called Second Letter to the Corinthians," *NTS* 8 (1961/62): 258–64; Georgi, *Gegner des Paulus im 2. Korintherbrief*, pp. 25–30.
108. Georgi, *Die Gegner des Paulus im 2. Korintherbrief*, passim. See also idem, "Formen religiöser Propaganda," in *Kontexte*, 3:105–10; this brief article gives an excellent and vivid picture of this type of religious propaganda.
109. Cf. Georgi, *Die Gegner des Paulus im 2. Korintherbrief*, pp. 241 ff.
110. Cf. Paul's formulation in his reference to such letters 2 Cor. 3:1: "to you or from you."
111. Cf. again Georgi, *Die Gegner des Paulus im 2. Korintherbrief*, pp. 213 ff., and 282 ff.; also Robinson, "Kerygma and History," chap. 2 above, pp. 60–61.

and even their theological orientation continued to be influential elements in subsequent literature. In the Gospel of Luke, which is based upon Mark's Gospel, the theme of the aretalogy emerges again, giving to this gospel its basic theological structure. According to Luke, Jesus is the divine man; he performs God's glorious acts as long as Satan is absent, i.e., in his public ministry, which extends from Satan's departure after the temptation to Satan's return into Judas, the traitor.[112] To be sure, the disciples are requested to follow Jesus also in suffering,[113] but this is merely their fate as it was Jesus' fate. The narrative of Jesus' suffering and death, however, no longer serves as the focal point of the revelation. As the story of the archetypical martyr, the passion narrative is no more than the last chapter of the "aretalogy" of Jesus.

The same theology of the divine man is even more blatantly present in the Lucan Acts of the Apostles. What the apostles do in their mighty works corresponds exactly to the things Jesus did *in his lifetime* (contrast Paul, who sees *Jesus' death* documented in his own apostolic life!). Thus, the apostle has become the successor of his master, is endowed with the same divine power, and is guided by the same divine spirit. Even Paul himself, as Acts sees him, has now become a primary example of the missionary who is a "divine man"—the same Paul who wrote 2 Corinthians against such an understanding of the apostolic ministry. The elements which are constitutive for the image of the missionary in Luke's Acts of the Apostles correspond exactly to those found among Paul's opponents in 2 Corinthians: powerful preaching, spiritual exegesis of Scripture, performance of miracles, visionary experiences.

In the extracanonical literature of early Christianity, the same genre reappears in various apocryphal Acts of the Apostles and some apocryphal gospels.

There is, of course, no doubt that the apocryphal Acts of the Apostles are literary products which combine a number of various

---

112. (Luke 4:13; 22:3); cf. Conzelmann, (ET:) *The Theology of Saint Luke,* 1960, p. 28 and passim.
113. Luke 14:25 ff.

themes and motifs.[114] But these books do not simply seek to edify and to minister to the popular desire to be entertained. However desirous of pious edification the mass of Christian people might have been, the basic theological and christological conviction which made it possible to fulfill these desires was the same religious "divine man" motif that had already contributed to the success of Paul's opponents in 2 Corinthians.

The basic pattern of this concept, as it was appropriated by early Christian theology, implies a close correspondence between the acts of Jesus and the acts of his apostles and followers. Luke is the only author of a canonical gospel who revived this concept for his gospel. He is also the only gospel writer who composed a second closely related work about the acts of Jesus' missionaries. This agrees with the theological intention of the Christology of the divine man. Thus, the apocryphal Acts of the Apostles, rather than new gospels, are the later literary representatives of this primitive genre of "gospel" literature. Inasmuch as the stories of martyrs and Christian saints (also monks and hermits) were the legitimate heirs of the same pattern, further investigation in the pursuit of this question would have to include these traditions and literatures.[115]

There is only one type of apocryphal gospel that continues the genre of the aretalogy: the infancy gospels.[116] They elaborate one particular and important aspect of Greek aretalogies and apply it to Jesus: the miraculous birth and childhood of the "divine man" or hero. As in Greek aretalogies, this is a particularly fruitful point of departure for the development of a legendary tradition. The various versions of the *Infancy Gospel of Thomas* give sufficient evidence of the fecundity of this topic.[117] The in-

---

114. Novelistic, aretalogical, teratological elements are conspicuous. See on this problem Wilhelm Schneemelcher and Kurt Schäferdick, "Second and Third Century Acts of Apostles," in Hennecke-Schneemelcher, (ET:) *NT Apocrypha,* vol. 2 (1965), p. 167 ff.; esp. pp. 174 ff. and the literature, pp. 167–68, 175.
115. Cf. the *Historia Lausiaca* and the *Historia Monachorum,* the *Acta Martyrum,* etc.
116. Cf. Cullmann, "Infancy Gospels," in Hennecke-Schneemelcher, (ET:) *NT Apocrypha,* vol. 1 (1963), pp. 363 ff. None of these gospels is an independent continuation of precanonical tradition.
117. More about this in Bauer, *Das Leben Jesu im Zeitalter der neutestamentlichen Apokryphen,* pp. 29–100.

fluence upon Christian theology, perhaps, has been negligible, but their importance for Christian piety and religious edification was considerable.

Gospels as Revelations

A great number of "gnostic gospels" are revelation discourses. One usually describes this genre of literature as a typical gnostic product in which the form of "dialogues of Jesus with his disciples" is chosen in order to impart gnosis, i.e., "revealed knowledge concerning the beginning, the course, and the destination of the universe." [118] It is difficult to detect traces of presynoptic traditions in these gnostic writings, and the "use of the canonical Gospels in most works of this character can be clearly shown." [119] Thus the judgment seems to be justified that, in a search for primitive forms of gospel literature, these secondary products deserve no further attention.

Recent discoveries of gnostic writings, however, call for a reconsideration of this verdict. The *Apocryphon of John* [120] in particular exhibits some features which are not necessarily derived from the canonical gospels. To be sure, the content of these "revelations" is only remotely related to the history of the various genres of gospel literature.[121] But the framework gives some clues for recognizing the sources of the evolution of the "gnostic

---

118. Schneemelcher, in Hennecke, (ET:) *NT Apocrypha,* 1:82.
119. Ibid., 1:83.
120. The *Apocryphon of John* was discovered in 1896 (*Papyrus Berolinensis* 8502), but was fully published only in 1955: Walter Till, *Die gnostischen Schriften des koptischen Papyrus Berolinensis 8502,* TU, 60, 1955. Three parallel versions in Cod. II, III, IV from Nag Hammadi were made available a few years later: Martin Krause and Pahor Labib, *Die drei Versionen des Apokryphon des Johannes im Koptischen Museum in Alt-Kairo,* ADAIK, Koptische Reihe, 1, 1962. In the following I quote from Cod. II from Nag Hammadi, which contains the most complete text of the passages which are of interest here. In the numbering of the Codices, I follow Krause and Labib, pp. 5 ff.
121. The content of these discourses may also appear independently, without the "gospel" frame. Cf. the "Letter of Eugnostos, The Blessed" (*CG,* III) which appears in the form of a gospel in the "Sophia Jesu Christi" in the same Nag Hammadi Codex and in *Papyrus Berolinensis* 8502; see Krause and Labib, *Die drei Versionen,* pp. 234 ff. These contents normally are disclosures of the secrets of the universe and of mankind, of the original fall and the return to the divine origin, almost always related to the interpretation of Gen. 1–3. In which way these relate to the subject matter of more primitive revelation discourses, as described below, must remain an open question.

gospel" [122] and, at the same time, for the origin of some peculiar features in the canonical gospels.

The typical elements of the framework of the "revelations" are well known and are most clearly visible in the *Apocryphon of John:*

1. The scene is usually on a mountain, preferably the Mount of Olives.

2. Jesus appears from heaven accompanied by all the traits of an epiphany.

3. Jesus introduces himself to the disciples; cf. *Apocryphon of John, CG,* II, *1–2:* [123]

> I, John, went away from the temple to the mountain, and I was very grieved in my heart. . . . When I thought this in my heart, the heavens opened and the whole creation was bright and the lower parts of heavens and the whole universe was shaken. I was afraid and I fell down, when I saw a young man (appearing) in the light. But when I saw the form of an old man . . . I marveled. . . . He said to me: "John, John, why do you doubt? . . . It is I who am with you always. I am the Father, and I am the Mother, I am the Son. . . ."

4. Revelations are given, usually in a pattern of question and answer.

5. In the conclusion of these books one often finds a curse formula urging that these secrets not be revealed to the uninitiated; cf. *Apocryphon of John, CG,* II, *31–32:* [124]

---

122. The following paragraphs do not endeavor to explain the form of *all* so-called gnostic gospels. The classification of this literature is no easy task. Wholly unsatisfactory is the attempt to classify these gospels according to their author: "Under the Name of Jesus," "Under the Name of the Twelve" etc. (Puech, in Hennecke, *NT Apocrypha,* 1:231 ff.). Some gnostic gospels seem more nearly to belong to the genre of sayings collections discussed above (the *Gospel of Thomas, the Gospel of Philip,* and perhaps in part *Thomas the Contender*); probably the *Books of Jeu* also are a further development of the same genre. Mixing of various genres is not uncommon and is to be expected; see also below on the *Epistula Apostolorum,* pp. 201 ff.

123. *BG,* 19 ff. Cf. also the second introduction to the *Pistis Sophia,* chaps. 2 ff. (ed. Till, pp. 3 ff.).

124. *BG,* 76; *CG,* III, *39–40;* IV, *49.* A similar curse formula is given in the introduction of the second *Book of Jeu* (ed. Till, p. 304). See further on these curse formulae Puech, in Hennecke, (ET:) *NT Apocrypha,* 1:263.

Cursed is anyone who exchanges these (mysteries) [125] for a gift or for food or for drink or for clothing or for anything else.

These features cannot be derived from the resurrection appearances of the canonical gospels, even though a number of gnostic revelations admittedly have been influenced by the canonical Easter stories.[126] The juxtaposition of temple and mountain (Mount of Olives) occurs in a different context in the canonical gospels.[127] In Mark 13:1, 3 the eschatological discourse called the synoptic apocalypse is introduced in this way:

And when he came out of the temple one of his disciples said to him. . . . And as he sat on the Mount of Olives opposite the temple, Peter and James and John asked him privately. . . .

Furthermore, the "temple ministry" in the Gospel of Luke employs the same pattern: [128] Jesus does not enter Jerusalem, but moves directly into the temple (Luke 19:45); he teaches in the temple (Luke 19:49; 20:1) and spends the night on the Mount of Olives (Luke 21:37).

The features which accompany Jesus' appearance in the *Apocryphon of John* are traditional requisites of a theophany, whereas the resurrection stories of the canonical gospels are not at all dominated by the patterns of a theophany.[129] However, these features are clearly present in the account of Paul's calling (Acts 9:1 ff.) as well as in the appearance of Jesus to the prophet John in the Book of Revelation (Rev. 1:9 ff).

125. In the sentence following this formula the term *mystery* occurs explicitly.
126. Such influence is obvious, e.g., in the *Sophia Jesu Christi* (cf. Puech, in Hennecke, [ET:] *NT Apocrypha* 1:246) and in the first introduction of the *Pistis Sophia,* chap. 1 (ed. Till, pp. 1–2).
127. Only Acts 1:12 juxtaposes the Mount of Olives with Jerusalem (but not with the temple!).
128. Klaus Baltzer, "The Meaning of the Temple in the Lucan Writings," *HTR* 58 (1965): 263 ff., especially 274–75, has drawn attention to this extraordinary feature of Luke's Gospel and has connected it with the Ezekiel pattern of the divine "glory" moving out of the temple and standing on the Mount of Olives.
129. Only occasionally do we find theophany elements in the resurrection stories of the canonical gospels, e.g., Matt. 28:16; but see the *Gospel of Peter* 35 ff., which is perhaps based on a very primitive resurrection story of a theophany type, and the story of the transfiguration in Mark 9:2 ff., which may be an original resurrection story. Thus, theophany elements belong to the original features of resurrection stories, but they no longer determine the character of these stories as they occur in canonical gospels.

In this context we cannot pursue the origin and history of the particular form of theophany which is evident in these accounts.[130] In any case, it is this theophany form that constitutes the "gnostic gospel." Thus, its basic pattern is not derived from the form of the canonical gospels. Rather these gnostic revelation writings must be assigned to the literary genre "revelations" (or "apocalypses").[131]

In Christian literature, the "revelations" continue the Jewish genre of "apocalypses." There are some indications that this literary genre appeared in Christianity at an early stage. The synoptic apocalypse and the apocalypse of the *Didache* as well as the Revelation of John make this evident. Features of the Jewish literary genre "apocalypse" are clearly present at this stage. The intriguing problem is the relationship of this Christian literature to even earlier traditions, which were current in oral form under the name and authority of the Lord.

Before any gospels were written, Christians knew and transmitted apocalyptic sayings under the authority of the Lord. In 1 Thess. 4:15 Paul quotes such a tradition as a "Word of the Lord." First Corinthians 15:51 ff. refers to the same tradition as a "mystery," i.e., with the same term that is the technical designation of apocalyptic secrets in Daniel and in the Qumran literature.[132] Even a cursory examination of Mark 13 (see also Matt. 24–25) and of *Didache* 16 shows that they contain several pieces of apocalyptic tradition which were originally independent, i.e., oral mystery traditions, comparable to the one quoted by Paul, which probably circulated under the authority of Jesus.

As these traditions developed into written apocalypses, features

---

130. The origin of this form doubtlessly lies in the theophanies of the Old Testament, especially Ezek. 1 ff. Its further development is apparent in Dan. 10 and other Jewish apocalyptic texts.
131. Compare also the curse formula at the conclusion of the *Apocryphon of John* with the curses and warnings of the "canonization formula" of apocalyptic writings (Rev. 22:18–19; 2 *En.* 104:10 ff.). Its purpose, however, is to protect the integrity of the book rather than to prevent its disclosure to the uninitiated.
132. Cf. Raymond E. Brown, "The Semitic Background of the New Testament *MYSTĒRION*," pt. 1, *Biblica* 39 (1959): 426–48; pt. 2, 40 (1959): 70–87; idem, "The pre-Christian Semitic Concept of 'Mystery'," *CBQ* 20 (1958): 417–43. These three articles have been reprinted: *The Semitic Background of the Term "Mystery" in the New Testament*, Facet Books, Biblical Series, 21, 1968. See also Bornkamm, "Μυστήριον," *ThWNT* 4 (1942; ET, 1967), esp. sec. B2.

from the oral tradition of "mysteries" tended to disappear, and the patterns which governed the written Jewish apocalypse became increasingly evident. That these apocalyptic instructions appear in all canonical gospels as the last and final section of Jesus' teaching, may still reflect the special character of the oral mystery tradition. But the setting in Mark 13, a revelation given to a limited circle of disciples only on the Mount of Olives opposite the temple, is already a literary pattern.

The author of the Gospel of John places a special instruction to the disciples in the time between Jesus' public ministry (John 2–12) and his passion (John 18–19): the farewell discourses (John 13–17). These Johannine discourses contain no oral mystery traditions at all, but are interpretations of traditional apocalyptic topics in the form of a discourse of Jesus with his disciples: ascension, parousia, coming of the Spirit, fate of the disciples. These Johannine discourses occupy a crucial place in the development of the genre "revelation," since they already exhibit, in form and content, certain features of the gnostic revelation discourse,[133] although their basis continues to be the treatment of traditional apocalyptic topics.

The further evolution of this genre leads to the writing of full-fledged apocalypses. This step was independent of the development of the canonical gospels. Not Christian gospels, but Jewish apocalypses, set the literary pattern for the production of these "revelations" in early Christianity. This is clearly evident in the oldest Christian "revelations" which are preserved: the Apocalypse of John and the *Shepherd of Hermas*.

In the Apocalypse of John a large mass of Jewish and Christian apocalyptic tradition is written down and interpreted anew by a Christian prophet. This tradition appears in the form of a book and under the authority of the Lord Jesus. It is a book that presents the authoritative revelations of Jesus, his words and instructions

---

133. See, e.g., the casting of the discourses into the pattern of the disciples' questions and Jesus' answers. The corresponding pattern of apocalypses is well known: The seer asks and an *angelus interpres* answers and gives explanations and revelations. In the gnostic revelations there is a definite shift in content. Interpretations of Genesis replace revelations about the future. But even the future-oriented revelations do not disappear completely; they often reappear as disclosures about the heavenly realms. The relationship of apocalyptic and gnostic revelations is still to be clarified in detail.

—i.e., it is a book which could very well be called a "gospel"—but, of course, it does not presuppose the existence of canonical gospels.

It is the same apocalyptic genre of "gospel" which we have before us in the gnostic gospels which are "revelations." In the *Apocryphon of John,* as in the Johannine Apocalypse, the canonical gospel and its form have played no role whatever. These books belong to an altogether different and independent genre of gospel literature. This gnostic genre of gospel, of course, has no inherent criterion by which to bind the revelations contained in it to the earthly Jesus of Nazareth. The Apocalypse of John accomplishes this connection insofar as Jesus is presented as the lamb which was slaughtered, which is the Jesus of the orthodox creed. Furthermore, Jesus as the Lord is not primarily the revealer; the interpreting angel is a figure distinguished from Jesus. Rather, Jesus is the object of worship, as the one who was crucified and in whose blood the martyrs have washed their clothes. On the other hand, in the gnostic revelations Jesus has assumed completely the roles of revealer and interpreting angel. His primary dignity derives from these functions. In this way, the genre of the gnostic revelation became the ideal vehicle for gnostic thought and Christology, and secondary influences from the canonical gospels never disrupted the continuous evolution of this independent genre of gospel literature which has its own and peculiar roots in the earliest developments of gospel traditions.[134]

The Canonical Gospel and the Orthodox Creed

The basic pattern of the genre of gospel which determined the canonical gospels has already been discussed.[135] A quite remarkable feature in the evolution of this genre is its power to digest gospel literature and traditions of a different type and christological orientation, and to make these subservient to its own creed of Jesus' death and resurrection. It was, indeed, this orthodox creed and its further development which provided the basic criterion for the growth of the canonical gospel.

134. For an attempt to domesticate this gnostic genre through the orthodox creed, see below on the *Epistula Apostolorum,* pp. 201 ff.
135. See above, pp. 161 f.; cf. also the references, pp. 188 f., as well as the literature in nn. 8, 9, 11, 14, 95.

At the same time, this expansion of the creed and of the gospel reflects at every stage the explicit or implicit controversy with different christological options. These different options are suggested by Christian factions which adhere to the "other gospels," or simply by the challenge to incorporate such other gospels into the established frame of the canonical gospel. The two most important witnesses for the close relationship of gospel and creed in the subapostolic age are Ignatius of Antioch and Justin Martyr.

Ignatius of Antioch reflects the creed of the early orthodox church as it was accepted at the end of the first century A.D. It is an expanded version of the formula which Paul calls "the gospel" in 1 Cor. 15:1 ff. Ignatius's creed, still called "the gospel," [136] now encompasses the events from the birth of Jesus by the virgin (Mary) to his ascension.[137] This corresponds to the canonical gospels of Matthew and Luke, in which the narratives, not only of Jesus' life, but also of his birth, have been incorporated into the frame which was initially provided by the passion narrative.

The historicizing tendency of the creed is present in Ignatius's formulae, insofar as mythical statements (preexistence, conception by Mary, resurrection, descensus, and ascension) are presented on the same level as, and in a continuous sequence with, historical events (birth, suffering, death). In this way is it possible to subject to the (pseudo)biographical framework of the orthodox creed and canonical gospel not only legendary material but also theological data which utilize mythical language.[138]

Ignatius's understanding of the sacraments reveals the *Sitz im Leben* for the inclusion of cultic legends into the written gospels.[139] But, most important, his concept of martyrdom points to a central element of Christian faith through which the church was best able to relate such faith directly to the constitutive historical event: Jesus' suffering and death. The way in which this

---

136. Ignatius *Phld.* 5. 1; 8. 2; 9. 2; *Sm.* 5. 1; 7. 2. It does not seem that Ignatius used written gospels; cf. Koester, *Synoptische Überlieferung,* pp. 6 ff., 24 ff.
137. The most inclusive credal formula is found in Ignatius *Sm.* 1. 1–2; cf. *Eph.* 18. *Mg.* 11, *Phld.* 9, and various references elsewhere in his writings.
138. See, e.g., the grandiose enumeration of the "mythical events" of Jesus' coming and of Jesus' epiphany after his death in Ign. *Eph.* 19.
139. Ignatius *Eph.* 17. 1; 18. 2.

pattern has influenced the formation and interpretation of the passion narrative is well known. But it is also important to note that only this theological pattern of the passion kerygma was able to serve as the point of crystallization around which many other types of Jesus traditions (sayings, miracle stories, etc.) could be gathered into a pseudobiographical frame.

Justin Martyr presupposes that the combination of various types of gospel literature into the canonical genre of the gospel has been accomplished. Justin can take advantage of the fact that the diverse tendencies of more primitive genres had been domesticated and become part of a historical narrative.

Jesus' sayings are no longer eschatological proclamations which represent the law and the wisdom of another world (i.e., of the kingdom of God); they are ethical instructions, consistent in their moral value and useful for the existing society.[140] Insofar as they are predictions and revelations about the future, they have already found partial historical fulfillment in the past and in the present.[141]

Jesus' miracles are no longer prima facie evidence for his divine powers. Rather they have been embedded in the pattern of prophecy and fulfillment. Thus, they testify to Jesus' divine nature only insofar as they fulfill in history what has been predicted.[142] The story and stories of Jesus are true, because they are part of the consistent pattern of predictions—written in the archaic records of the Old Testament—and are their fulfillment—testified in the written memoirs of the apostles.[143] The gospels were for the first time used and evaluated as written historical records and sources [144]—no doubt a momentous step with tremendous consequences!

Justin's guide and criterion, again, is the creed. It is further expanded, and "historical" facts prevail; cf. *Apol.* 1. 31. 7:

140. Justin *Apol.* 1. 14 ff.
141. Justin *Dial.* 35. 2 ff.
142. See, e.g., Justin *Apol.* 1. 48.
143. This pattern occurs throughout Justin's writings; see esp. *Apol.* 1. 12. 10; 31. 8.
144. It is typical for this view of the gospels that Justin's references to the "Memoirs of the Apostles" are paralleled by the references to such assumed historical documents as the "Census records of Cyrenius" (*Apol.* 1. 34. 2) and the "Acts of Pilate" (*Apol.* 1. 35. 9).

In the books of the prophets we find that it was proclaimed before-
hand that Jesus, our Christ, would appear, to be born by a virgin,
to grow up, to heal all sickness and all disease and to raise the
dead, to be envied and to be rejected and to be crucified, to die
and to be raised up and to ascend to heaven, to be and to be called
the Son of God, and that some would be sent by him to all
people to proclaim these things, and that especially the gentiles
would believe in him.

The creed can be verified on the basis of dependable historical
records. For the orthodox church, this is the end of the literary
development of the gospels, even though many traditions were
not definitely fixed at this time. But the creed of the church had
accomplished its work: to turn the gospel into a book containing
trustworthy historical information.

The *Epistula Apostolorum* is indicative of the state of affairs
in the time of Justin Martyr. This writing, orthodox in its theological orientation, is sometimes classified among "conversations
of Jesus with his disciples after the resurrection." [145] Such a
genre, however, of which the *Epistula Apostolorum* is the primary representative, is only the result of a secondary development.
The *Epistula Apostolorum* applies the orthodox creed, and material from the canonical gospels, to the originally independent
genre of the "revelation." The creed which is used for this purpose
clearly exhibits apologetic tendencies and antignostic polemics.

The revelation discourse of the *Epistula Apostolorum* begins
in chap. 13.[146] The proper setting for the discourse—Jesus' appearance to his disciples—is given in chaps. 10–12. But closer
consideration of those chapters indicates that this setting differs
from the introduction of a revelation gospel.[147] There is no
account of a theophany; instead, we find an artificial patchwork
derived from the resurrection stories of all the canonical gospels,
utilizing Jesus' appearance to the women (John 20:14 ff., etc.),
the appearance of Jesus to the disciples (according to Luke

145. This is the case, again, in H. Duensing in Hennecke, (ET:) *NT Apocrypha*,
1:188 ff. Cf. the title of Carl Schmidt's edition of the *Epistula Apostolorum:
Gespräche Jesu mit seinen Jüngern nach der Auferstehung,* TU, 43, 1919.
146. Quotations and references are given to the English translation according to
Duensing, in Hennecke, (ET:) *NT Apocrypha,* 1:191 ff.
147. See above on the *Apocryphon of John,* pp. 193 ff.

24:36 ff., with occasional elements from Matt. 28:10 and John 20:19 ff.), and the story of doubting Thomas (John 20:24 ff.). Not a single feature of the theophany proper occurs (mountain, cosmic signs, appearance in light, etc.). Instead, the *Epistula Apostolorum* tries to emphasize the physical reality of the resurrection of Jesus. No doubt, even though the *Epistula Apostolorum* is modeled after the pattern of a revelation gospel, the original features of its usual introduction have been suppressed.

But also the chapters preceding this setting for the revelation discourse have no parallel in any gnostic revelation. *Epistula Apostolorum* 3 is credal material, interspersed with hymnic elements. It is stated that the universe was created and is preserved through God the Father; then begins the "second article" of the creed:

> And God, the Lord, the Son of God—we believe that the word which became flesh through the holy virgin Mary, was carried in her womb by the Holy Spirit, and was born not by the lust of the flesh but by the will of God (John 1:13), and was wrapped (in swaddling clothes, Luke 2:7) and made known at Bethlehem; and he was reared and grew up [148] as we saw.

Already here it is evident that the *Epistula Apostolorum* uses material and information from the canonical gospels in order to expand the creed, very much in the same way as it is frequently done in Justin Martyr. This is even more conspicuous in chaps. 4–9. The credal statements referring to Jesus' life and death are interspersed with references to the marriage feast in Cana (John 2:1 ff.), several healing miracles,[149] the walking on the sea and the stilling of the tempest (Mark 4:34 ff. and 6:47 ff.), the temple tax (Matt. 17:24 ff.), and the feeding of the five thousand (Mark 6:38 ff. parr.). Such weaving together of credal sentences, summary accounts, and references to details of narratives, proves that these chapters are a secondary composition based, in part, on all canonical gospels.[150]

---

148. This is one of many instances where *Epistula Apostolorum* parallels Justin Martyr's creed; cf. *Apol.* 1. 31. 7.
149. Mark 3:1–6; 5:25–43; 5:1–20; as well as a number of other stories.
150. A reference to Jesus' childhood in *Epistula Apostolorum* 4 shows that also an infancy gospel has been used.

Finally, the revelation discourse itself which begins in chap. 13 resembles the gnostic revelation only very superficially. To be sure, there is the formal pattern of questions and answers. But one looks in vain for the disclosure of the divine mysteries or an eschatological drama. Instead, the outline of the discourse follows the topics of the "third article" of the creed, even though these are not unrelated to the topics of an apocalypse or a revelation.

Thus we find in the *Epistula Apostolorum:* chap. 16, the parousia; chaps. 21–26, an apologetic treatise *De resurrectione;* chap. 27, *Descensus ad inferos;* chaps. 28 ff., last judgment; chap. 30, preaching to all people (which is part of the creed also in Justin Martyr [151]) followed by a long digression about Paul, obviously for polemical purposes; chaps. 41–42 and 46–47 even introduce church-order material. Throughout, the specifically apologetic structuring of the various topics of the creed can be observed. Apocalyptic revelation has been replaced by doctrinal discourse.

The *Epistula Apostolorum* tries to use the creed and the gospel of the church as the criteria of faith, and to refute what must now appear as a dangerous aberration from the original gospel: the gnostic revelation. But the criterion of the earthly Jesus has taken the form of the well-established orthodox creed, and support is readily available in accepted *gospels* which serve as a repository for information about the "historical Jesus."

These gospels of the church have become the true criteria of faith, because they are understood as the legitimate expressions of the creed, to which they correspond in form and structure—not, however, because they are found to record the works and words of Jesus accurately. The honor of having continued and developed the tradition about Jesus' original works and words must go to the more primitive gospel sources and to the apocryphal gospels. The continuation of Jesus' teaching is present in the gospels which preserve and expand his sayings (Q and *Thomas*). The aretalogy of Jesus and of his apostle revives Jesus' powerful works done in his earthly life. The revelation recaptures the appearances

151. Justin *Apol.* 1. 31. 7, quoted above.

of the heavenly Lord who had revealed himself to Paul and to other apostles, and who had disclosed his mysteries to Christian prophets.

The church decided against the heretical tendencies that characterized these direct expansions of Jesus' works and words. But the gospels of the church cannot claim and should not be understood to reflect the preaching and the works of the earthly Jesus in a straight line of tradition. They are primarily gospels *about* Jesus—his suffering, death, and resurrection. Nevertheless, it was only this latter (and, indeed, typically "Christian") genre of a "gospel" which enabled Christian theology to demonstrate the Christian point: faith remains bound to the criterion of the earthly Jesus—whether successfully so or not is to be evaluated in each individual instance.

6. The Structure and Criteria of Early Christian Beliefs

HELMUT KOESTER

Historic Event and Cultural Conditioning

Christianity did not begin with a particular belief, dogma or creed; nor can one understand the heretical diversifications of early Christianity as aberrations from one original true and orthodox formulation of faith. Rather, Christianity started with a particular historical person, his works and words, his life and death: Jesus of Nazareth. Creed and faith, symbol and dogma are merely the expressions of response to this Jesus of history.

The diversifications of this response were caused, and still today are caused, by two factors: first, by the several different religious and cultural conditions and traditions of the people who became Christians; and, second, by the bewildering though challenging impact of Jesus' own life, works, words, and death.[1]

As the history of Christian theology continued to develop, these relationships of cultural conditioning and historical point of reference became more and more complex. Answers of faith from earlier periods, once they had become established traditions, could become substitutes for rather than expressions of the substance of the historical revelation in and through Jesus. Whenever that happens, the cultural conditions and religious symbols of earlier times tend to obscure their true object and grow to become the object of faith themselves—as today the Christian culture of the Western world is frequently, and, even more disturbing, innocently identified with the one and only Christian faith and its real content.

1. Walter Bauer, "Jesus der Galiläer," *Festgabe für Adolf Jülicher*, 1927, pp. 16–34, had already suggested that Jesus was not an unambiguous point of departure.

For a long period, people in America, simple believers and sophisticated theologians alike, have been involved in the controversy over truly American rather than inherited European expressions of Christian beliefs. In recent years the problem has been further confounded by the conviction that even the most progressive expressions of "American" Christianity are outdated, and that a cultural and social revolution calls for a radical departure from all established symbols towards the utopian shores of a new age, in which the cultural and religious symbols will be nothing less than the trees of paradise itself.

But what about the criteria for whatever we have been saying and believing, and will be saying and believing? Or is faith completely subject to the terms dictated by the cultural environment?

Simple answers like "God is dead" seem to suggest that this is the case. The affirmation of cultural change for the sake of change, or the call for a black culture to replace the culture of white Christian man, are concerned only with the external means of expressing religious contents. Thus they cannot be elevated to the status of criteria and canons of faith. The apologetic defense of old religious symbols as well as the desperate search for new ones is only a sign of our loss of criteria. New and valid criteria cannot be derived from such religious symbols themselves, be they Christian or not.

Inasmuch as we cannot escape the cultural, social, and religious forces of our own environment, we have the obligation and responsibility to rediscover the historical criteria and canons which would enable us to determine critically who and where we are. For Christian theology, such criteria can only come out of the historical event of Jesus of Nazareth, as long as it continues to maintain that this is the event through which God himself set the stage for something new that would challenge man's traditional understanding of his world, his environment, his task, and his vision of the future.

I am far from understanding this commitment to the historical origin of Christian faith as an evangelistic or revivalist slogan and program. Rather, I am convinced that history is our best as well as our most demanding teacher. If this be so, the structure of faith as it occurred within the earliest history of Christianity must serve as our primary model for understanding the relationship being considered here: the relationship between the historical event on the one hand, providing the criteria of understanding, and the culturally conditioned expression of faith in creed, symbol, dogma on the other hand, which is always a human attempt—inspired or not—to relate human existence to a historical event in order to establish a symbol that transcends man's own limitations and predicaments.

Problems of Pluralism, Continuity, and Distinctiveness

When one tries to analyze early Christian beliefs and to determine the relationship between historical event and formulated expression of faith, one must be aware of several problems.

First, there is the great diversity and proliferation of creeds, symbols, and confessions of faith. This does not only apply to the history of the "creed" in the narrower and more technical sense, i.e., credal formulations which became the accepted *regula fidei* of the orthodox church, represented in the ancient baptismal symbols, the *Symbolum Romanum,* and the so-called Apostles' Creed.[2] The diversity is even more visible in the existence of basic symbols of belief which, both in form and in content, are completely different from the generally known creeds. Christian faith also found pregnant expression in certain hymnic traditions such as Phil. 2:6 ff.; Col. 1:15–20; John 1:1–4, 9 ff., 14 ff.; and Heb. 1:2–4; furthermore in stories of a cosmological drama, be it past (the gnostic myth), present (e.g., Ignatius *Eph.* 19) or future (viz., the repeated renewal of apocalyptic prophecies); and finally in narratives of the deeds of men who possessed divine power. Of course this does not mean that we must deal with each and every document which gives evidence of theological activity on the part of Christian believers. We are concerned with fundamental patterns and concise formulations of faith. But these comprise many more possibilities than the one suggested by the

2. The basic and most comprehensive study is still Ferdinand Kattenbusch, *Das Apostolische Symbol,* 1894–1900. Among the more recent works see Oscar Cullmann, *The Earliest Christian Confessions,* 1949; J. N. D. Kelly, *Early Christian Creeds,* 1950; Vernon H. Neufeld, *The Earliest Christian Confessions,* New Testament Tools and Studies, 5, 1963. A convenient collection of the most important Greek and Latin texts is by Hans Lietzmann, *Symbole der Alten Kirche,* Kleine Texte, 17–18, 4th ed. 1935.

traditional pattern of the early Christian creed and symbol. In fact, early Christianity availed itself of a number of options available in the religious environment and capable of serving as basic models for the primary formulations of faith. Corresponding to the cultural and religious pluralism of the Hellenistic and Roman eras in general, and of contemporary Judaism in particular, the beginnings of the history of early Christian creed and symbol were extremely diversified.

Second, in all these various basic symbols of faith, the relationship of historical event (Jesus) and language of faith is complex and often bewildering. For example, in the classical form of the creed the predominant element seems to be an enumeration of "events"—i.e., from the creation of heaven and earth to Jesus, the Son of God, his birth through the virgin Mary, suffering and death under Pontius Pilate, burial, resurrection on the third day, ascension, and return for judgment. But actually most of these statements do not describe historical events at all. The whole series of statements is rather developed out of an earlier credal formula, namely that of Jesus' death and of his being raised, in which the death of Jesus on the cross was proclaimed as the eschatological act of God who raised Jesus from the dead. The way in which historical event and theological interpretation are tied together in this eschatological formula is predetermined by the particular option of religious language that is used in this instance. To be sure, the actual events of Jesus' life—e.g., his words and works, his suffering and death—in all their historical particularity and contingency, were no less important in determining both the content and the type of the credal formulation. But as the creed or symbol contributes its own structure, it regulates the type and extent of the historical references which it contains. Thus, it is by no means easy, and perhaps it is impossible, to extrapolate from any particular creed an objective historical event, a seemingly stable historical datum, as it were, that could be used as a criterion to evaluate critically the diverse creeds and symbols of faith.

The historical ambiguity can be further observed in the way in which different expressions of faith relate to specific and quite limited aspects of the life and work of Jesus. As we shall see, there is a certain inherent and congenial relationship of each specific creed or symbol to corresponding historical specifics of Jesus' own life and ministry, e.g., the creed of the resurrection only relates to Jesus' suffering and death, or the symbol of Jesus the divine man refers primarily to Jesus' work as an exorcist.

The correspondence between Jesus' death and the Christians' belief in the resurrection, or between the miracles of Jesus and the great deeds of the church, suggests a factual historical continuity, an impression actually created by the symbol of faith. That Jesus indeed died on the cross, or that he, as a matter of fact, performed exorcisms, provided an appropriate point of departure. However, the structure and content of the symbolic expression of faith dictate the terms for the relationship of the community with Jesus, and thus decide the limits within which certain aspects of the "historical Jesus" may function as parts of the creed at the cost of other aspects of Jesus' history. The creed of the cross and resurrection had little use for Jesus' miracles, and the symbol of the divine man was not too well suited to emphasize Jesus' suffering and death. Yet to grasp genuine historical continuity one must also consider those aspects of an historical event which created, or would create, embarrassment for the theological endeavor, and which presented a challenge to the understanding and conduct of a religious life and to the forces of a particular cultural environment. It is only here that one begins to discover critical canons, drawn from historical events—namely, canons which are not easily absorbed into the expressions of faith in symbol and creed.

Moreover, the question of historical continuity between Jesus and the church has a sociological dimension. Jesus did not found a church or start a social or political movement—much less a revolution. He did not envisage the kingdom of God in any institutionalized form. Yet typical responses to Jesus, and the expressions of faith, the Christologies, which they produced, have very distinct ecclesiological as well as sociological and cultural implications. Admittedly, typical forms of Christian communities and distinct attitudes towards the cultural environment cannot claim to be *direct* continuations of Jesus' words and work. Rather they reflect the historical Jesus only through the medium of the creed or symbol which, in turn, is in its very nature conditioned by the culture and by the religious presuppositions which prevail in the cultural environment. Again, the quest for historical criteria cannot be satisfied with the suggestion of continuity provided by the creed, but must inquire into implications of Jesus' words, works, and fate that would contradict this process of cultural assimilation.

Third, since we find credal and symbolic formulations in sources that date largely from the second and third Christian generation or later, only rarely do we detect pure, original, and uncontaminated expressions of such primary symbols, emphasizing only one particular aspect of Jesus' works and fate. Earlier symbols often are reinterpreted and incorporated into later and different ones, which may even belong to what was originally an incompatible type of religious language and environment.

Nonetheless it is still possible to uncover the original points of departure, which were quite distinct and diversified. Such distinct and peculiar types of creeds and symbols are visible in two different phenomena: first, in the petrified traditional formulae and expressions which do not fit the contexts in which they appear; and, second, in later heretical developments which have preserved independent credal origins because of cultural, religious, and often geographical limitations and biases.

In what follows, I will present four different types of expressions of faith. It is no accident that they coincide with my view of the fourfold origin of gospel literature! [3] In each case the following elements of the structure, perspectives, and implications of such symbols of faith will be considered:

a) the *context,* i.e., the religious environment which provided the language of faith for the formulation of this particular symbol;

b) the *event,* i.e., always "Jesus of Nazareth" in a particular tradition of his teaching, work, life, and death to which this symbol is specifically related;

3. See "One Jesus and Four Primitive Gospels," chap. 5 above.

c) the *credal formulation* (or hymn, or narrative, etc.) that is most typical of this belief;

d) the *sociological implications;* for it seems to me that in each instance the impact upon the understanding of church and society is significantly different. Relevant also are the *geographical origin* and *historical development* of each symbol, as well as certain biases in the development of Christian literature that are clearly related to the history of such creeds and symbols.

Jesus as the Lord of the Future

This belief is probably the most primitive. It is, however, extremely difficult to reconstruct the most original forms of the expressions of this creed, because all extant texts have moved beyond this primitive eschatological orientation towards different theological contexts. Equally uncertain is the precise significance of the christological titles applied to Jesus as the bringer of future salvation.[4] But it is important to note that here and elsewhere the christological titles are a very unsatisfactory guide into the questions of creed and Christology.[5]

a) For the *context* of this eschatological creed, messianic titles are equally ambivalent. The eschatological expectations of apocalyptic Jewish sects were not at all uniform. But we do know of several instances in which one or several future agents of salvation were the focus of hope. The Pharisaic *Psalms of Solomon,* e.g., proclaim the coming of a Davidic figure as the leader of Israel during the final eschatological events. Moreover, the Essene texts from Qumran know of three messianic figures, the eschato-

---

4. Ferdinand Hahn, *Christologische Hoheitstitel,* 1963, esp. pp. 179–89 (ET: *The Titles of Jesus in Christology,* 1969, pp. 161–68), has tried to demonstrate that the title Messiah or *Christos* was originally connected with these eschatological beliefs. This view has been challenged by Philipp Vielhauer, "Ein Weg zur neutestamentlichen Christologie?" in *Aufsätze zum Neuen Testament,* Theologische Bücherei, 31, 1965, pp. 175 ff.; see also Hans Conzelmann, *Grundriss der Theologie des Neuen Testaments,* 1967, pp. 91 ff. (ET: *An Outline of the Theology of the New Testament,* 1969, pp. 72 ff.).
5. This limits considerably the usefulness of the two most recently published "Christologies" by Cullmann and Hahn. Concerning the significance of individual titles the reader may be referred to the appropriate sections in Vielhauer, "Ein Weg zur neutestamentlichen Christologie?" pp. 145–95; and Conzelmann, *Grundriss der Theologie des NT* pp. 91–105 (ET: pp. 72–86) and passim; see also Rudolf Bultmann, *Theology of the New Testament* vol. 1, 1951, pp. 26 ff., 121 ff., and passim.

logical prophet (a prophet like Moses),[6] the anointed king, and the anointed priest, who are divinely appointed rulers of the messianic age and the key figures in the final events.[7] The Qumran texts also demonstrate that such eschatological hopes generated a particular type of community life: sectarian seclusion in a monastic-type congregation, which conceived of itself as the true eschatological people and celebrated the community meal in anticipation of the messianic banquet.[8]

b) The *event:* Jesus did not proclaim himself either as Messiah or as Son of God, nor did he refer in any of his preaching to a particular future figure other than God himself.[9] But Jesus did proclaim the coming of the kingdom of God (see esp. the parables); he preached to the elect of the kingdom, the poor, those who weep, those who hunger and thirst (Luke 6:20–21). He called his disciples to be prepared for the events of the future, to enter through the narrow gate (Luke 13:24), to take upon themselves their mark, the eschatological sign of the elect (Luke 14:27),[10] to leave their father and mother, wife and children, brother and sister (Luke 14:26), and to follow after him. Jesus celebrated a final meal with his disciples in which he said that he would not drink from the fruit of the vine until he would drink it again in the kingdom of God (Mark 14:25).

c) The *belief* of the church which utilizes such Jewish eschatological expectations as outlined above and which corresponds to the eschatological preaching of Jesus, is its expectation of Jesus' coming as the decisive figure of the future. It is difficult

---

6. Frank Moore Cross, Jr., *The Ancient Library of Qumran,* 2d ed., 1961, pp. 116, 223–24.
7. See Karl-Georg Kuhn, "The Two Messiahs of Aaron and Israel," in *The Scrolls and the New Testament,* ed. Krister Stendahl, 1958, pp. 54 ff.; Cross, *The Ancient Library of Qumran,* pp. 219 ff.
8. Cross, *The Ancient Library of Qumran,* pp. 85 ff., 234 ff.
9. Norman Perrin, *Rediscovering the Teaching of Jesus,* 1967, pp. 164 ff.; see also Günther Bornkamm, *Jesus of Nazareth,* 1960, pp. 169–78, 226–31, who, however, assumes that Jesus referred to the Son of man as a future messianic figure; but see the literature quoted above in "One Jesus and Four Primitive Gospels," p. 171 n. 39.
10. On this interpretation of Luke 14:27 and parr., see Erich Dinkler, "Jesu Wort vom Kreuztragen," in *Neutestamentliche Studien für Rudolf Bultmann,* suppl. 21 to *ZNW,* 1954, pp. 110–29; reprinted in Dinkler's collected essays, *Signum Crucis,* 1967, pp. 77–98.

to tie such belief to any one of the messianic titles.[11] But two titles are equally prominent and belong to the same history-of-religions context of eschatological expectations. These are *Kyrios*, i.e., "Lord," and *Son of man*.[12]

The title *Maran* (*Kyrios*, "Lord") indicated vividly the form of this particular symbol and its original place in the life of the church. This title occurs in a liturgical formula which was apparently part of the celebration of the Lord's supper, *Marana-tha*, "Our Lord, come!" (1 Cor. 16:22; *Did.* 10. 6; cf. also Rev. 22:20), as well as in a number of prophetic-apocalyptic sayings about the coming of the Lord Jesus. One of these sayings is preserved as a saying of Jesus in 1 Thess. 4:16: "The Lord himself will descend from heaven with a cry of command, with the archangel's call, and with the sound of the trumpet of God. And the dead . . . will rise" (similarly the apocalypse at the end of the *Didache* employs the title *Lord*).[13]

The fact that Paul uses the same saying a further time in a "mystery," i.e., an apocalyptic secret about the future (1 Cor. 15:51–52), demonstrates clearly the character of this belief: Christian faith is identical with possession of the knowledge that this Jesus of Nazareth is the Lord who will come for redemption and judgment. The Christian community assures itself of this knowledge and faith through sayings about the future given through prophets who speak in the name of the Lord Jesus, and by the liturgical anticipation of his coming in the acclamation "Our Lord, come."

The other title, *Son of man*,[14] also refers originally to the

---

11. See n. 4 above.

12. Jesus was occasionally called "the Prophet"; this is evident from John 6:14; 7:40; cf. Gerhard Friedrich, "προφήτης," *ThWNT* 6 (1959): 847–49. But there are no indications that this eschatological title had any particular significance for the eschatological Christology of the primitive church. The more frequent title Messiah (*Christos*), in the oldest extant texts, belongs in the context of the kerygma of cross and resurrection (see below), and was connected with statements about the parousia only at a later date; cf. Vielhauer, "Ein Weg zur neutestamentlichen Christologie?" pp. 175–85 (against Hahn, *Christologische Hoheitstitel*, pp. 179 ff., 226 ff.).

13. Cf. Siegfried Schulz, "Maranatha und Kyrios Jesus," *ZNW*, 53 (1962): 125–44. On the relationship of the titles *Lord* and *Son of man* in these primitive apocalyptic traditions see n. 15 below.

14. For the present state of the discussion of the title Son of man see "One Jesus and Four Primitive Gospels," chap. 5 above, p. 170 n. 33; furthermore Conzel-

future agent of salvation.[15] In this meaning it occurs primarily in the so-called synoptic sayings source Q, in sayings which also have prophetic-apocalyptic character, e.g.: "As lightning lights up the sky from one end to the other, so will be the Son of man in his day" (Luke 17:24). Only at a secondary stage of development did this title become a designation for the Jesus who suffered, died and rose (Mark 8:31; 9:31; 10:33–34). The use of *Son of man* in the Fourth Gospel for the divine figure who humbled himself to be exalted again is equally secondary. Originally, it had nothing to do with either the cross-resurrection schema or with the humiliation-exaltation pattern of Christology (see below).

But neither particular titles, nor credal formulations, are characteristic vehicles of this primitive "symbol" of faith.[16] What is usually called creed or kerygma has to do with a christological orientation which looks back upon Jesus' life, death, and resurrection. The primarily eschatological belief looks toward that which is to come and already exists as a heavenly reality. Such faith finds its genuine expression in prophetic utterances and apocalyptic traditions about the heavenly world and its impending revelation, and in cultic anticipation of that future. The Jesus of history functions only insofar as he is the originator of words about that future. The tradition, cultivation, and interpretation of

mann, *Grundriss der Theologie des NT*, pp. 151–56 (ET, pp. 131–37); on the linguistic problem see the important review of Geza Vermes' appendix to Matthew Black, *An Aramaic Approach to the Gospels and Acts*, 3d ed., 1967, by Joseph A. Fitzmyer, *CBQ* 30 (1968): 424–28.

15. It is worthy of note that Paul and the author of the *Didache*, who both quote the eucharistic acclamation *Marana-tha* (see above), also use the eschatological title *Kyrios* (cf. 1 Thess. 3:13; 4:15 ff.; *Did.* 16. 1, 7, 8), rather than *Son of man*. *Did.* 16 is probably independent of the closely related synoptic apocalypse, Mark 13 parr. (cf. Koester, *Synoptische Überlieferung bei den Apostolischen Vätern*, TU, 65, 1957, 173 ff.). One may suspect that the title *Son of man*, which occurs for the first time in this particular apocalyptic tradition in Mark 13:26 (Dan. 7:13), was made part of this tradition only when the exact quotation of Dan. 7:13 was introduced. This is confirmed by the Apocalypse of John, where "Son of man" is limited to the typical Danielic references in 1:13 and 14:14. The origin of the eschatological *Son of man* title (beside the quotations of Dan. 7:13) must be located in Q and in the tradition used by the Gospel of John.

16. It is significant that the title *Son of man* never occurs in any credal formula. Conzelmann, *Grundriss der Theologie des NT*, pp. 91–105 (ET: pp. 72–86) is quite right when he limits his discussion of "the christological titles in the kerygma" to *Messiah, Son of God*, and *Kyrios*.

apocalyptic revelations (whether words of the earthly Jesus or of the living Lord) is the primary linguistic expression of this "symbol."

This belief stands in continuity with the earthly Jesus insofar as the believers continue Jesus' eschatological proclamation. Jesus announced the coming of God's kingdom; his church prepares for this event. But the traditional expectations of apocalyptic Judaism suggest that a particular "messianic" figure will act as God's agent who ushers in the future. The church adopts this motif (which is missing in Jesus' own preaching) and identifies Jesus with this coming agent of God, designating him as Lord or Son of man. This ends the continuity with the preaching of Jesus. Jesus is transformed into a divine figure of the imminent future. As the heavenly Lord, Jesus now speaks to the church through prophets and reveals to them the mysteries of the future.[17] This shift in the role of Jesus, which came about through the appropriation of elements from Jewish apocalyptic beliefs, had profound consequences for the understanding of the church and for the development of early Christian literature.

d) The *sociological implications* of this eschatological symbol correspond to the social and cultural orientation of apocalyptic sects. Those who believe in Jesus' words and expect his coming tend to live in separation from the rest of society. They anticipate the blessings of the future in enthusiast experiences (gift of the Spirit, speaking in tongues) and communal meals which emphasize the expected eschatological gifts [18] (viz., "messianic" banquet).

It is likely that a Christian community of this type existed in Jerusalem.[19] The choice of Jerusalem as the place where one

17. The technical term for the secret plan of God, *mystery,* is missing in Jesus' proclamation, but appears very early in the apocalyptic tradition of the church; cf. Mark 4:11 parrs.; 1 Cor. 15:51. Characteristic is the combination of "prophecy" and "mysteries" in 1 Cor. 13:2. For literature on the term *mystērion,* see "One Jesus and Four Primitive Gospels," chap. 5 above, n. 132.
18. Cf. the eucharistic prayers in *Did.* 9–10.
19. The picture painted in Acts 1–6 of the primitive Jerusalem community is certainly an ideal one and cannot be used as direct evidence; cf. Hans Conzelmann, *Die Apostelgeschichte,* HNT, 1963, p. 31; Ernst Haenchen, "The Book of Acts as Source Material for the History of Early Christianity," in *Studies in Luke-Acts,* ed. Leander E. Keck and J. Louis Martyn, 1966, pp. 258–78. But from the little we can learn, it is quite clear that the Jerusalem community, and

would expect the Messiah is significant in itself. To be sure, this early Jerusalem sect was superseded soon by new theological and sociological developments. Yet in later periods of the church this apocalyptic belief produced small sect-like communities, such as the community of the Revelation of John in Asia Minor with its circle of seven churches, or the Montanist movement.

Just as this particular type of creed has produced its own pattern of church life, it also generated its own type of "gospel." It is present in the "Two Ways," i.e., the code of morality and apocalyptic revelation in the so-called *Didache;* in the "Little Apocalypse" which was later incorporated into the synoptic gospels (Mark 13 parr.); in the Revelation of John; and in later apocalyptic writings and revelation gospels—a form of literature which was utilized by gnostic movements of an equally sectarian character.

Jesus as the Divine Man

a) The *context* for this symbol is the Hellenistic belief that divine power can be present in certain charismatic human beings. This belief has found its literary expression in a number of biographies of the Roman period, most of all the *Life of Apollonius of Tyana* by Philostratus, the *Life of Alexander* by Pseudo-Kallisthenes, several lives of Augustus (Suetonius and Nikolaos of Damascus), as well as Lucian's satirical lives of Peregrinus Proteus and the fake prophet Alexander.

However, at the root of these literary productions are actual beliefs in the presence of divine power, as well as actual claims made by prophets, miracle-workers, and wandering philosophers to possess such supernatural abilities.[20] It is documented in

probably other Palestinian communities, had all the makings of eschatological sects which were fairly stationary and had only limited missionary ambitions. On the similarity of the community in Acts 1–6 to the Essene community at Qumran, see Sherman E. Johnson, "The Dead Sea Manual of Discipline and the Jerusalem Church of Acts," in *The Scrolls and the New Testament,* ed. Krister Stendahl, 1958, pp. 129–42; Joseph A. Fitzmyer, "Jewish Christianity in Acts in Light of the Qumran Scrolls," in *Studies in Luke-Acts,* pp. 233–57.
20. The standard work is still Ludwig Bieler, *THEIOS ANĒR: Das Bild des "göttlichen Menschen" in Spätantike und Frühchristentum,* 1935–36, reprinted 1967; but see also Hans Dieter Betz, *Lukian von Samosata und das Neue Testament, religionsgeschichtliche und paränetische Parallelen: Ein Beitrag zum Corpus Hellenisticum Novi Testamenti,* TU, 76, 1961, pp. 100 ff.; Dieter Georgi, *Die Gegner des Paulus im 2 Korintherbrief: Studien zur religiösen Propaganda in*

skilled and persuasive oratory, miraculous healings and exorcisms, ecstatic and visionary experiences, and the like—and legend was only too quick to add wonderful stories about miraculous events at the birth and the death of a divine man.

Apparently Jewish apologetics and propaganda also made use of this appealing device for its missionary enterprise. Philo of Alexandria presents Joseph and Moses as such divine men in his writings, and Jewish missionaries performed miracles and demonstrated their skills in spiritual interpretations of Sacred Scripture.

b) The *events* of Jesus' life and ministry were easily cast into this pattern. To be sure, Jesus himself worked miracles and exorcisms as signs of the coming kingdom (cf. his answer to John the Baptist's disciples, Matthew 11:5, and his response in the Beelzebul controversy, Mark 3:24 ff.; also Luke 11:20). However, especially the latter passages make it clear that Jesus did not understand his miracles as proofs for his own possession of power, but rather as evidence of an eschatological event. They were clearly an integral part of his eschatological proclamation; men were called to the kingdom as they confronted Jesus' works.

c) As soon as these great works of Jesus became the objects of Christian faith, they became part of a divine man Christology.[21] This does not mean primarily certain formulated credal statements about Jesus and his great works, nor is any particular christological title a typical expression of this belief.[22] A formula like "Jesus of Nazareth, a man approved by God through wonders, miracles, and signs, which God performed through him among us" (Acts 2:22) may be primitive, and certainly characterizes the divine man very well. The primary and basic expression of such belief in Jesus, however, is the repetition of performances which demonstrate the presence of such divine power in the person of the apostle or missionary.

Paul's controversy with his opponents of 2 Corinthians gives

---

der Spätantike WMANT, 11, 1964, passim; Gerhard Petzke, *Die Traditionen über Apollonius von Tyana*, (Studia ad Corpus Hellenisticum Novi Testamenti, 1, 1970).

21. On this topic see the excellent article by Hans Dieter Betz, "Jesus as Divine Man," in *Jesus and the Historian: Essays Written in Honor of Ernest Cadman Colwell*, ed. F. Thomas Trotter, 1968, pp. 114–33.

22. It is not possible to prove that *Son of God* was a common designation for the miracle worker in the Hellenistic and Roman world; cf. Arthur Darby Nock, *Early Gentile Christianity and Its Hellenistic Background*, 1964, p. 45.

persuasive evidence for this. These successful missionaries, boasting of impressive records of their great works ("letters of recommendation"; see 2 Cor. 3:1; 5:12) and of outdoing Paul by impressive preaching and inspired interpretation of Scripture, did not preach "another gospel." Rather, they were preaching themselves, as it were (2 Cor. 4:5), for only in this fashion were they able to document the power of God which had begun to appear in Jesus and which was now working mightily in his messengers.

Historical continuity with Jesus is claimed by means of an analogous experience of divine presence and by the repetition of specific actions which demonstrate the possession of a power which is identical with that of Jesus. The appeal of such beliefs derives from, and depends upon, the supernatural and miraculous character of the religious experience and of its powerful demonstration. But this emphasis upon the supernatural elements denigrates the normal human experiences, because divine presence is not found in the common, everyday occurrences, events, actions, and tribulations of men. Thus, there is no continuity of faith and life with the earthly, human Jesus.[23]

d) The *sociological consequences* of the symbol of the divine man are very ambiguous. In general, the Hellenistic parallels show that it does not lend itself easily to the development of communal concepts, even though Lucian's *Peregrinus* talks about an attempt to institutionalize the divine power. In the development of Christianity we have evidence of the way in which superapostles of the divine man type abused existing communities for their own purposes (cf. Paul's battle with his opponents in 2 Cor.).

On the other hand, it is very significant that the symbol of Jesus as the divine man has molded individual Christian piety very decisively, and has created literature that nourishes the desire for religious edification. Mark and John used collections of Jesus' miracle stories, which were obviously produced in order to enhance the belief in Jesus' possession of divine power. Luke,

23. This particular shortcoming of the divine man Christology was seen clearly by Paul, who confronts the aretalogies of his opponents in 2 Cor. by catalogues of his own tribulations (2 Cor. 4:7 ff.; 6:4 ff.; 11:23 ff.).

in his rewriting of Mark's Gospel, revived this particular symbol of Jesus, who accomplishes great deeds in the power of the divine spirit. In Luke's Acts of the Apostles, the miracles of the apostles set the stage for a whole host of apocryphal "Acts of the Apostles." The following centuries witnessed a great increase in the production of hagiographical literature, first in the production of "Acts of Martyrs," later in the composition of *Lives* of famous monks and bishops.[24] There is an obvious tendency in these writings to invent miraculous features at the cost of biographical accuracy. Only a few of the "Acts of Martyrs" have been preserved in their original form; most of them are full of legendary embellishments. As literature of edification, these hagiographic writings often replace the canonical gospels. The famous monk or saint may also become an object of worship that is more "real" and more highly valued than Jesus and his story—in actual practice, if not in theory. This is a quite natural development of the symbol of the divine man. The power of the miracle and the documentation of divine presence in the miraculous events is indeed a symbol that tends to separate Christian faith completely from the criterion of a historical revelation in Jesus and that replaces historical and communal responsibility of Christian faith with personal piety and religious edification.

Jesus as Wisdom's Envoy and as Wisdom

a) The *context* of this belief is to be seen in specific developments of Jewish theology which are generally referred to under the name of wisdom. The contours of this Jewish wisdom theology have only begun to become clearer in recent scholarly debate.[25] Of special interest is the dualistic concept of wisdom which is most clearly visible in the *Wisdom of Solomon* and in Philo of Alexandria. Here divine Wisdom is seen as more than

24. See the *Historia Lausiaca* and the *Historia Monachorum*.
25. The most complete list of publications (up to 1962) is to be found in (Georg Fohrer and) Ulrich Wilckens, "σοφία." ThWNT, 7, 1964, pp. 465–67. Significant publications in recent years include: Hans Conzelmann, "Die Mutter der Weisheit," in *Zeit und Geschichte*, Bultmann festschrift, ed. Erich Dinkler, 1964, pp. 225–34; idem, "Paulus und die Weisheit," NTS, 12 (1965/66): 231–44; Dieter Georgi, "Der vorpaulinische Hymnus Phil. 2,6–11," in *Zeit und Geschichte*, pp. 263–93; Egon Brandenburger, *Fleisch und Geist: Paulus und die dualistische Weisheit*, 1968.

the agent of creation, the figure through which Yahweh is revealed to the righteous man,[26] and the source of knowledge about the world. Wisdom also becomes a mythical figure symbolizing the true divine identity of suffering righteous men. This true identity differs radically from the earthly and human fate of the righteous; it is nonhistorical or ahistorical, and cannot be defined in terms of worldly experience or worldly wisdom; by it the truly wise men differ ontologically from the rest of mankind.[27]

Different, though not unrelated, is the apocalyptic concept, where wisdom is the knowledge of the secret plans of God, i.e., of the mystery of the future.[28] Yet the concept of Wisdom appearing as a stranger in this world and, not finding a place, returning to her heavenly abode, does appear in the context of apocalyptic literature (2 Enoch 42).

Already in pre-Christian Judaism these mythical wisdom speculations were combined with philosophical (especially so-called Middle Platonic) concepts of the *Logos*. This is clearly the case in Philo. Evidence for this can also be found in the prologue of the Gospel of John, which uses the term *Logos* in its presentation of the Jewish myth of Wisdom.

b) It is not easy to see how wisdom mythologies could find a point of connection or reference in the *earthly Jesus*. To be sure, there are a number of wisdom sayings among the traditional sayings of Jesus, e.g., Matt. 11:25–30. It also can hardly be doubted that Jesus himself used forms of wisdom tradition in his preaching, such as proverbs, metaphors, etc.[29] Thus, it is quite legitimate to consider Jesus as a typical wisdom teacher. But this can only be considered as one point of departure for the application of Jewish wisdom speculations to Jesus. The other derives from the fact of Jesus' humanity as such, his birth ("in-

---

26. Already in *Sirach*, Wisdom is thus identified with the Torah.
27. See esp. Georgi, "Der vorpaulinische Hymnus," in *Zeit und Geschichte*, pp. 266 ff., 276 ff.
28. It is this latter concept that dominates the Qumran literature and is utilized by Paul in 1 Cor. 2:6 ff. (though not by his opponents!). On the term *mystery*, see also above, pp. 196 f.
29. Rudolf Bultmann, *History of the Synoptic Tradition*, passim, demonstrated this clearly. Cf. also James M. Robinson, "LOGOI SOPHON," chap. 3 above. See also William A. Beardslee, *Literary Criticism of the New Testament*, 1970, pp. 33–36.

carnation"), and his suffering and death. Therefore the history of the symbol of Wisdom as applied to Jesus implies at least two major components: his sayings, and his earthly, human existence.

c) First, the sayings tradition is expanded to include more and more sayings in which Jesus functions as *Wisdom's envoy*,[30] e.g., Wisdom's pronouncement of judgment over this generation (Luke 11:49–51). Revelatory sayings also belong here, e.g., "I thank thee, Father . . . , that thou hast hidden these things from the wise. . . , and revealed them to babes" (Matt. 11:27). Such sayings already appear at an early stage in the synoptic sayings source Q, and they almost completely determine the character of its later development as we find it in Matthew, who identifies Jesus completely with Wisdom, as well as in the *Gospel of Thomas.* In *Thomas,* Jesus even introduces himself as *Wisdom having come into the world* and having been rejected: "I stood in the midst of the world, and I appeared to them in the flesh; I found all of them drunken; I found none of them athirst. And my soul was afflicted for the sons of man" (Saying 28).

Second, outside of the tradition of the sayings of Jesus, the myth of Wisdom is applied to Jesus in hymnic formulations which present as a cosmic drama in poetic form the incarnation, humiliation, and exaltation of Wisdom. The oldest of these hymns is quoted by Paul in Phil. 2:6 ff: "He who was in the form of God . . . emptied himself to take the form of man . . . , humbled himself to death. Therefore God exalted him." [31] Even more obvious is the Wisdom myth in the prologue of the Gospel of John.[32] The Logos is with God in the beginning, as the agent of creation, the true light of the world. He comes into the world, reveals himself, but is rejected, yet glorified in those who believe.

---

30. Jack Suggs, *Wisdom, Christology, and Law in Matthew's Gospel,* 1970, has been able to demonstrate convincingly that the older tradition of sayings (as represented in Q) sees Jesus as Wisdom's envoy, but never identifies Jesus with Wisdom. Only the author of Matthew moved to such an identification.
31. Georgi, "Der vorpaulinische Hymnus," in *Zeit und Geschichte,* has shown that in Phil. 2 this myth of preexistent Wisdom is interpreted critically.
32. Rudolf Bultmann, *Das Evangelium des Johannes,* is still the best treatment of the background of the Johannine prologue, even though the use of a pre-Christian hymn cannot be maintained; cf. Ernst Käsemann, "Aufbau und Anliegen des johanneischen Prologs," in *Libertas Christiana,* Friedrich Delekat festschrift, 1957, pp. 75–99; reprinted *EVB,* 2, 155–82.

The same humiliation-glorification schema also appears in the Christology of the Letter to the Hebrews. In a hymn quoted in the prologue, the letter speaks of the Son of God in terms closely resembling the description of the Logos in Philo of Alexandria. The presence of wisdom predicates is very obvious in the hymn which is quoted in Col. 1:15–20. Christ is praised in terms which Hellenistic Judaism had produced for the praise of Wisdom, who was the firstborn of all things, through whom all things were made, and by whom all things exist.[33]

In this way the full-fledged application of the wisdom myth to Jesus supersedes the more limited view of Jesus as Wisdom's envoy. This results in a Christology that fully utilizes the mythological and cosmological dimensions of pre-Christian wisdom speculation. The earthly reality of Jesus tends to disappear in favor of a universalistic concept of the humiliation and exaltation of a preexistent divine figure. The death of Jesus may function as the lowest point of the humiliation, but it has lost its significance as a historical event in the life of a human being. Rather it results in a view according to which the earthly reality of Jesus' existence is only the external garment for the presence of the divine reality. The hymn or narrative of a mythical drama of humiliation and exaltation, descent and ascent, is the primary mode in which this symbol is expressed. In gnostic Christology, this mythical narrative merged with the development of the sayings tradition, in which Jesus introduces himself as the divine Wisdom who came in the flesh (*Gospel of Thomas*). But this symbol of Jesus as the earthly counterpart of ultimate divine reality became equally significant to the universalistic Logos Christology of Origen.

d) Representatives of this belief in Jesus as Wisdom's envoy or as Wisdom incarnate appear very early in various areas. Early developments of the source Q attest the presence of this belief in Western Syria or Palestine, and Paul has to cope with this belief

---

33. Wisdom parallels to Col. 1:15–20 are collected in James M. Robinson, "A Formal Analysis of Colossians 1:15–20," *JBL* 76 (1957): 270–87. For a detailed exegesis of Col. 1:15–20 and a complete listing of all important literature see Eduard Lohse, *Die Briefe an die Kolosser und an Philemon*, 1968, pp. 77 ff. For Heb. 1:2–4 cf. H. Koester, ὑπόστασις, *ThWNT*, 8, (1969): 584.

in Corinth (1 Cor. 1–4),[34] where it may have been introduced by Paul's fellow worker, the Alexandrian Jew Apollos. The schisms which occurred in Corinth as a consequence of this, as well as the beginnings of Christianity in Eastern Syria and Egypt, demonstrate clearly the *sociological consequences* of this christological concept.

The Corinthian "parties" referred to in 1 Corinthians are really schools, as it were, in which the teacher (Peter, Paul, Apollos, Christ) is considered as the leader into divine wisdom. Similarly, in Eastern Syria we find Thomas possessing special mysterious knowledge (*Gospel of Thomas,* Saying 13) as the leader of a group of disciples. This corresponds to the function of Moses, who is introduced as the mystagogue in Philo of Alexandria.[35] The typical outcome of this pattern can be seen in the great gnostic schools of Egypt in the second century (Basilides, Valentinus, etc.). Marcion, however, is not typically gnostic, if one considers the sociological consequences of his activities. His work resulted in the organization of a worldwide church. Wisdom theology, on the other hand, is primarily concerned with the cultivation of a tradition of words of wisdom and with the repetition, in mythological stories, of the revelation of wisdom. The place for such activities is the theological school, whereas organized Christian churches became quite irrelevant.

Jesus Raised from the Dead

a) The *background* and *context* of this belief are most complex and cannot be discussed here in any detail. The Christian belief that Jesus was raised from the dead is closely related to the expectation in certain quarters of Judaism that God would finally conquer the powers of unrighteousness, suffering, and death by his eschatological act of raising the dead. Resurrection is thus a mythological metaphor for God's victory over the powers of unrighteousness.

34. See James M. Robinson, "Kerygma and History in the New Testament," chap. 2 above, pp. 42 f.
35. E.g., *De gig.* 54; cf. my review of Ulrich Wilckens, *Weisheit und Torheit,* in *Gnomon* 33 (1961): 594.

The origin of this expectation is most likely the prophetic vision of Deutero-Isaiah, who describes a scene in the divine court in which the suffering righteous, i.e., Israel, is vindicated before its enemies and pronounced righteous by God (Isa. 53). This vision of the vindication of the righteous subsequently underwent various modifications in postexilic Jewish literature. It appeared in the form of a vision of Israel's enthronement over the world, as in Dan. 7 and 10; and it took the form of the belief in immortality, as in *4 Maccabees*. In each instance, however, it represented the eschatological hope that God would act to vindicate his faithful people—whether this be Israel or a select group of certain individuals—who had suffered and died for righteousness' sake. Such divine vindication was always understood as God's eschatological act ushering in a new age for those who had been steadfast and faithful. In the time of Jesus, the hope of resurrection was primarily held by the Pharisees, who were distinguished by this belief from the Sadducees and from the Essenes.[36]

b) Jesus was *crucified* in Jerusalem around the year A.D. 30. It is impossible to determine whether or not he had spoken about his suffering and impending death.[37] After his death several of his disciples had visions of Jesus which convinced them that he was alive. In the framework of the expectation, outlined above, these appearances of Jesus revealed that God had vindicated him by raising him from the dead, i.e., that the first eschatological action of God had occurred; God had begun to vindicate his people Israel. The preaching of Jesus' resurrection was thus the proclamation that the new age had been ushered in. In this way the kerygma of the resurrection of Jesus came into existence, and with it the creed that spoke of Jesus who died, was buried, and was raised.

36. The pioneering treatment of this theology of suffering and vindication is Eduard Schweizer, *Lordship and Discipleship*, SBT, 28, 1960. Cf. George Nickelsburg, *Resurrection, Immortality, and Eternal Life in Judaism* (Diss., Harvard University, 1968); see also my brief treatment, " The Role of Myth in the New Testament," *Andover Newton Quarterly* 8 (1968): 189 ff.
37. All extant traditions in the gospels speaking about Jesus' suffering, death, and resurrection are *vaticinia ex eventu*, formulated according to the pattern of the kerygma of the church; cf. esp. Mark 8:31 ff. parr.; 9:30 ff. parr.; 10:32 ff. parr.

c) Since this *creed* became the central criterion of faith for *
the "canonical" writers and thus is preserved in great variety
and elaborate amplifications, it is difficult to determine its origin
and traditions with precision. Apart from the passion narrative,
pre-Pauline sources and traditions of the canonical gospels reveal
a quite different orientation.[38] But several traditional formulations in Paul's letters and other sources preserve some primitive
elements of this creed: first, the understanding of Jesus' death as
an expiatory sacrifice for sins and transgressions, which occurs
most frequently in these formulae,[39] and which is almost always
implied in the brief and pregnant formulation "for us." Closely
related are the interpretations of Jesus' death as a Passover
(1 Cor. 5:7) and covenant sacrifice (Hebr. 13:20).[40] These *
concepts are traditional parts of the contemporary Jewish understanding of the suffering righteous.[41] Second, several of these
sacrifice interpretations received a firm and lasting place in the
liturgical tradition of the Eucharist. The words of institution as
quoted by Paul (1 Cor. 11:23 ff.) presuppose at least the understanding of Jesus' death as covenant sacrifice ("the new covenant
in my blood," 1 Cor. 11:25), perhaps also the concept of expiatory
sacrifice ("my body for you," 1 Cor. 11:24).[42] Third, these
interpretations of Jesus' death have been combined with the
concept of vindication at a very early stage. "Vindication" always
implies both resurrection and ascension/exaltation.[43] The early

38. They are dominated by the tradition of Jesus as a wisdom teacher, or a
divine man, or an apocalyptic prophet; see pp. 211–223. Formulae interpreting
Jesus' death have been incorporated into the synoptic tradition in rare instances;
cf. Mark 10:45 and the words of institution in the story of the last meal.
39. See Rom. 3:25 ("expiation in his blood . . . passing over former sins");
1 Tim. 2:6 ("ransom").
40. See Conzelmann, *Grundriss der Theologie des NT*, p. 89 (ET: p. 70). For
the Christological formulae in Paul's writings cf. also Werner Kramer, *Christos
Kyrios Gottessohn: Untersuchungen zu Gebrauch und Bedeutung der christologischen Bezeichnungen bei Paulus und den vorpaulinischen Gemeinden*,
AThANT, 44, 1963 (ET, *Christ, Lord, Son of God*, SBT, 50, 1966).
41. Cf. the literature cited in Bultmann, *Theology of the New Testament*, 1:47.
Isa. 53 has, no doubt, influenced not only the Jewish concepts of this period in
a more or less indirect fashion (see Nickelsburg, *Resurrection, Immortality, and
Eternal Life*) but is also clearly reflected in some of the early Christian formulae,
e.g., Rom. 4:25). But the more elaborate use of Isa. 53 for the development
of this christological tradition belongs to a later period; cf. 1 Pet. 2:21 ff.
42. This is quite clearly expressed in the idea of expiatory sacrifice in Matt. 26:28.
43. See Vielhauer, "Ein Weg zur neutestamentlichen Christologie?" pp. 171 ff.;
and Conzelmann, *Grundriss der Theologie des NT*, pp. 86–87 (ET, pp. 67–68),

combination of both concepts is attested in the formulae which Paul quotes in Rom. 4:25 and 1 Cor. 15:3 ff. However, it cannot be demonstrated with certainty that these traditions go back to the Aramaic-speaking church.[44] Fourth, the title for Jesus which is most conspicuous in these traditions is *Christos*. Some of the sacrificial interpretations do not seem to preserve any particular christological title at all (e.g., Rom. 3:25), and it is doubtful whether *Christ* without article in 1 Cor. 15:3 represents a titular usage.[45] But even the occurrence of the simple *Christ* as a proper name in several of these formulae points to a stage in this tradition at which a bilingual (Aramaic and Greek) Christian community employed the title *Messiah* (*Christ*) to express specifically the significance of Jesus' suffering, death, and resurrection. The closely related title *Son of David* also belongs to the same credal tradition. This is most clearly evident in two rather primitive christological formulations: Rom. 1:3–4 and 2 Tim. 2:8.[46]

It is probably no accident that the first theologian of this creed was a Pharisee, Paul. In 1 Cor. 15, Paul demonstrates the close connection of Christ's resurrection with the resurrection of all believers. These are but two stages in God's eschatological act of vindication, which will end with the victory of God over all his enemies. Christ in his resurrection is the first fruits (1 Cor. 15:20); it is meaningless to speak about this resurrection without expecting at the same time the resurrection of all others who belong to him. It is also obvious why the witnesses of Jesus' appearances are so important for this type of Christian creed (1 Cor. 15:5 ff.). They are an essential part of the "gospel" formula which Paul quotes in the beginning of the chapter, 1 Cor. 15:3 ff.

against Hahn, *Christologische Hoheitstitel,* pp. 126 ff., who seeks to demonstrate that ascension and exaltation were introduced only at a later stage, under the impact of the delay of the parousia and with the help of Ps. 110.

44. Literature in Conzelmann, *Grundriss der Theologie des NT,* p. 84 (ET, p. 65); cf. also Vielhauer, "Ein Weg zur neutestamentlichen Christologie?" pp. 179–80.

45. Vielhauer, Ein Weg zur neutestamentlichen Christologie?" pp. 180 ff. For the discussion of this question see especially the contributions of Joachim Jeremias, most recently "Nochmals: Artikelloses Χριστός in 1 Cor. 15:3," *ZNW* 60 (1969): 214–219.

46. See also Ignatius *Sm.* 1. 1; *Trall.* 9. 1; see Vielhauer, "Ein Weg zur neutestamentlichen Christologie?" pp. 185 ff.; Conzelmann, *Grundriss der Theologie des NT,* p. 93 (ET: p. 74).

The point is not to introduce witnesses in order to make a miraculous occurrence credible, but rather to attest the Christians' claim that God had commenced his work of eschatological vindication.

It should be noted that this creed required no recourse to the words of wisdom Jesus spoke, nor to any of his predictions about the future, nor to any miracles he performed.[47] At the same time it ties Christian faith very intimately to a particular historical occurrence, Jesus' suffering and death. It is essential for this creed to stress the reality and humanity of Jesus' coming and suffering.[48] The assurance that Jesus was "born of a woman, born under the law" (Gal. 4:4), characterizes Jesus as a true human being in biological and sociological terms. To speak of Jesus as a semidivine being who raised himself from the tomb [49] by virtue of his divine nature would destroy the whole point. The greatest threat to the creed that Jesus died and was raised sprang from the gnostic belief in Jesus' divine nature, expressed in a mythical story, which tended to eradicate the humanity of Jesus.

47. It is characteristic that there are no references to Jesus' miracles in Paul's writings. Only once does Paul quote a wisdom saying that belongs to the tradition of wisdom sayings of Jesus: 1 Cor. 2:9 (*Gospel of Thomas*, Saying 17); here Paul introduces this saying with the quotation formula γέγραπται. Other sayings of Jesus are occasionally used as legal (1 Cor. 7:10), liturgical (1 Cor. 11:23 ff.), or eschatological tradition (1 Thess. 4:15 ff.), but never as part of "the gospel," i.e., of the message about Jesus that saves those who believe. The fact that such sayings come from Jesus has no primary significance. The same eschatological tradition can appear either as a "*Logos* of the Lord" (1 Thess. 4:15) or as a "mystery" (1 Cor. 15:51); or Paul can present the legal authority of the Lord and his own opinion as quite commensurate (cf. 1 Cor. 7:10 with 7:12, 25, 40); cf. Heinz-Wolfgang Kuhn, "Der irdische Jesus bei Paulus als traditionsgeschichtliches und theologisches Problem," *ZThK*, 67 (1970): 186 n. 95.
48. The typical gospel literature of this creed is thus the passion narrative which became the matrix for the canonical gospels; see "One Jesus and Four Primitive Gospels," chap. 5 above, p. 198 ff.
49. In the traditional formulae of this creed in the New Testament, it is almost always "God who raised Jesus from the dead"; see Rom. 4:25; 8:34; 1 Cor. 15:4; Gal. 1:1; 1 Thess. 1:10; 1 Pet. 1:21; Acts 2:24; Ignatius *Trall.* 9. 2. The intransitive ἀνίστημι "rise," "arise," is comparatively rare in the New Testament; see 1 Thess. 4:14 (certainly influenced by the context in which the eschatological stereotype "the dead will rise" occurs, 1 Thess. 4:16); Mark 8:31; 9:31; 10:34 parr.; John 20:9; Acts 17:3. In the second century A.D. this latter usage is more common; see *Barn.* 15. 9; Ignatius *Sm.* 2. 1. The credal formulation "and risen from the dead" is fixed from Justin Martyr on; see *Dial.* 85. 2; 132. 1; (cf. *tertia die resurrexit a mortuis* in the so-called Roman symbol). But for some time, the earlier formulation "he was raised" still survives; cf. Justin Martyr *Apol.* 1. 31. 7; Irenaeus *Adv. haer.* 1. 10. 1; Tertullian *Adv. Prax.* 2.

The history of this creed in the following centuries reflects a theological impasse. The impasse was created by two fundamental convictions which seem to have excluded each other: on the one hand, the attempt to confess Jesus' divine nature, expressed by the belief in his preexistence and by the shift in the formulation of the creed from "God raised [i.e., vindicated] him" to "He rose from the dead"; [50] and, on the other hand, the insistence upon Jesus' truly human nature, the reality of his suffering and death. As Christianity emerged from the matrix of Jewish religion into the Roman world, the Jewish pattern of suffering and vindication lost its persuasive power. It was thus replaced by various Hellenistic-Roman cultural presuppositions which forced those who believed in Jesus' cross and resurrection to use a new religious language. The man whom God had vindicated became a divine being who rose from the dead. Yet in this creed Jesus' humanity remained the criterion of a gospel that called all those who suffer and die, who are poor and deprived, who neither have social or political identity nor possess accepted moral and religious virtues. It calls them regardless of class, creed, or sex: "Neither Jew nor Greek, neither slave nor free, neither male nor female."

d) The creed of death and resurrection, in spite of its original aloofness to Jesus' works and words, proved to be the only early Christian creed which took the reality of human life and suffering seriously. This creed also created the literary genre, that is, the canonical gospel, which would preserve the record of Jesus' works and words more adequately than other genres of gospel literature. But its strength and power are not recognized, if it is only seen as a congenial combination of a religious concept that has deep roots in Judaism, with a great theological insight into the meaning of Jesus' suffering and death, so as to give expression to the significance of his suffering by means of the language of Jewish expectations and hopes. One gets closer to the central force of this creed when one considers its *sociological implications*, which were seen most clearly by Paul.

The term *ecclesia*, "church," was used for the first time in the Pauline writings and in the circle of early Christian com-

50. See n. 49, above.

munities which had accepted the creed of Jesus' death and resurrection.[51] Two other closely related concepts appear in the Pauline literature: the ecclesiological formulae "in Christ" and "body of Christ." [52] Especially these two latter concepts try to understand the Christian community as a new society that exists solely on the basis of God's work as it is expressed in the cross-resurrection creed.[53] Christological and ecclesiological statements tend to become interchangeable; cf., e.g., the identity of the understanding of the church as "body of Christ" with love and mutual responsibility in 1 Cor. 12–13. This passage, and many others in the Pauline correspondence, demonstrate the attempt to understand the church and its structures as no longer dominated by any traditional religious, moral, or social patterns and ideologies. Rather, the law of Christ (Gal. 6:2) is seen as an eschatological consequence emanating directly from the belief in Christ's suffering and vindication.

Conclusion

The expectation of the future Messiah created an eschatological sect of those willing to prepare for his coming. Belief in Jesus as Wisdom resulted in schools of the wise and of initiates into divine wisdom. Realization of divine power in one's own life generated religious supermen, but not community. The proclamation of God's act in history by which he began to vindicate his people resulted in the birth of the church.

A history of early Christian beliefs, creeds, and symbols from the perspective of these diversified beginnings of heresy and orthodoxy has yet to be written. It is obvious that the pattern of the cross-resurrection creed became the nucleus of the orthodox creed

51. On this term and the whole problem of the concepts of the church in early Christianity, including discussion of important literature, see the excellent concise article of Krister Stendahl's, "Kirche II. Im Urchristentum," *RGG*, 3d ed., vol. 3, 1959, cols. 1297–1304.

52. It is impossible here to discuss the complex problems of these concepts in this article. For a brief treatment and literature see Bultmann, *Theology of the New Testament*, 1:306 ff.; Conzelmann, *Grundriss der Theologie des NT*, pp. 280 ff. (ET: pp. 254 ff.).

53. As in the fixed formulations of this creed, the term *Christ* (whether as a title or as a proper name) seems to be very prominent in the ecclesiological statements related to this creed; see, e.g., 1 Cor. 12:12; Gal. 6:2; and the formula "in Christ."

of the Christian church. Before it came to be what we know as the Apostles' or the Nicene Creed, various motifs from other creeds and symbols were partially incorporated. On the whole, its intention and direction was drastically modified to respond to new religious challenges.

Parallel to this development, the emerging gospel literature of the orthodox church did not restrict itself to a passion and resurrection narrative, but tried to incorporate materials which actually had heretical tendencies, according to the standards of that creed: the divine man type of miracle stories, and the future-oriented apocalyptic predications which Mark appropriated for his gospel, collections of sayings of the wise which Luke and Matthew incorporated, and the myth of Wisdom humiliated and glorified, which is a main theme of the Fourth Gospel.

The merits and failures of this development in gospel and creed are not for us to judge here. To be sure, some are only compromises, and some are outright failures which have had far-reaching theological consequences. The basic insights, however, which can be gained from these developments could very well give some direction to the solution of our own religious problems.

Let me try to summarize them in the following theses:

1. The religious hopes, expectations, and ideologies of Judaism, as they existed in the period of the birth of Christianity, are not our own religious presuppositions. It is our task to clarify the various presuppositions of our own time in order to be relevant to our contemporaries, as well as for the sake of our own identity and integrity.

2. If the Christian message and tradition have anything to say to us, the message is not the religious presuppositions of another period, but the one and only fact that with Jesus of Nazareth God has come into the life and history of mankind in a unique way; i.e., it is the Jesus of history—and by no means an inaccessible object of speculation—which must be the center of our concern.

3. The question of heresy and orthodoxy today is extremely important. But it is not decided upon the basis of any established creed as such. Rather it depends upon the humanity of Jesus. It

is decisive whether or not we are able to affirm for ourselves the basic facts of his humanity: that he was born as an ordinary man, that he preached to the poor, that he ate with the despised; and that he became a victim of the normal mechanics of the established society.

4. It is a question of our *critical* imagination, whether we are able to bring our encounter with this Jesus to bear upon the ideologies and religions of our time. The Pharisees expected the righteous to be justified. Paul knew that it was the righteous man whom God had justified, because Jesus, whom God vindicated, died on the cross as a sinner.

5. The test of orthodoxy is whether it is able to build a *church* rather than a club or a school or a sect, or merely a series of concerned religious individuals. Church is not defined by the arrogance of any inherited or boldly assumed convictions, but by the willingness of persons to accept the mutual responsibility of love as their work for Jesus' sake.

7. The Johannine Trajectory

JAMES M. ROBINSON

I was asked by Dean Krister Stendahl, then chairman of the Research Committee of the Society of Biblical Literature, to present a report on recent research which identified an important growing edge of scholarship on which a cluster of SBL members had been publishing research, for the purpose of suggesting a point of departure for the SBL Gospels Seminar. The presentation focuses upon the Fourth Gospel, but has implications relevant to the synoptic gospels as well. It will seek to outline the growing edge of Johannine research in four areas: (1) literary source theory; (2) theology; (3) history-of-religions trajectory; and (4) the gattung "gospel." Indirectly there will be implications for the reconstruction of the scholarly understanding of primitive Christianity in general and of the role of gospels in particular.

By way of preface, let me sketch a few generalizations about Johannine research behind the most recent period and behind the specific issues with which the paper will be primarily concerned:

1. The location of John in time (and space) has tended to shift over the past generation or two. The date of the gospel has tended to move from around A.D. 125 to around A.D. 90.[1]

This paper was presented at the organizational meeting of the Society of Biblical Literature's Gospels Seminar at Berkeley, California, December 19, 1968.

1. Walter Bauer, *Das Johannesevangelium*, HNT, 6, 2d ed., 1925, and 3d ed., 1933, pp. 237 and 245: "100–125." Adolf Jülicher's *Einleitung in das Neue Testament*, 7th ed., revised together with Erich Fascher, 1931, proposed as *terminus a quo* A.D. 100, though an earlier date was thought to have been possible were it not for the assumption of dependence on all three synoptic gospels; and, as *terminus ad quem*, A.D. 100–125 was proposed, a dating based upon the assumption that John was used by Valentinianism (A.D. 130 on), and on the absence of Johannine argumentation with the Gnosticism which flourished from A.D. 125–75. Indicative is the shift in *RGG*, 1st ed., vol. 3, 1912, p. 613, "middle of the second century" (Wilhelm Bousset); 2d ed., vol. 3, 1929, p. 363, "between 115 and 145 A.D." (Martin Dibelius); 3d ed., vol. 3, 1959, p. 849, "end of the first century" (Rudolf Bultmann); Dibelius and Bultmann agree, against earlier treatments, that Ignatius is not dependent on John. Werner Georg Kümmel, Feine-Behm's *Einleitung in das Neue Testament*, 12th ed., 1963, p. 172 (ET: 1965, p. 175) appeals to the assumption of dependence of Ignatius upon the Fourth Gospel, and the early second century date of P 52 and P Egerton 2,

232

Major reasons for this shift are that earlier datings of Gnosticism and then the discovery of early papyri tended to push the date back, a trend facilitated to the extent that the assessment of the Fourth Gospel as independent of the synoptics gained ground. Perhaps the fact that apostolic authorship has lost most of its advocates [2] has also made it easier to consider an earlier date on its own merits without apologetic or antiapologetic overtones.

2. With regard to space, the redefining of Gnosticism not as the radical Hellenizing, but rather as the reorientalizing of Christianity, together with the oriental style of John, tended to move the gospel from Alexandria or Asia Minor to Syria; [3] then the discovery of the Mandaeans, Qumran, and Nag Hammadi, and the resultant dissolution of the concept of normative Judaism as ap-

---

to argue for the beginning of the second century as *terminus ad quem;* and he uses the assumption of dependence upon Luke to argue for A.D. 80–90 as *terminus a quo.* "Hence it is today almost universally assumed that John was written about the last decade of the first century." Willi Marxsen, *Einleitung in das Neue Testament,* 1963, p. 219 (ET: *Introduction to the New Testament,* 1968, p. 259): "toward the end of the first century." Cf. Reginald H. Fuller, *The New Testament in Current Study,* 1962, pp. 110-11.

2. Indicative of the extent to which this trend has gained ground over the past generation is the position of Raymond E. Brown, S.S., *The Gospel according to John (i–xii), The Anchor Bible,* 1966, p. ci: "We would posit *one principal disciple* whose transmission of the historical material received from John was marked with dramatic genius and profound theological insight, and it was the preaching and teaching of this disciple which gave shape to the stories and discourses now found in the Fourth Gospel. In short, this disciple would have been responsible for Stages 2 through 4 of the composition of the Gospel, as we have posited them." According to pp. xxxiv–xxxv, Stage 2 means: "Over a period lasting perhaps several decades, the traditional material was sifted, selected, thought over, and molded into the form and style of the individual stories and discourses that became part of the Fourth Gospel." This oral stage was followed by two written editions; then a final redaction, into its present form, was carried through by a friend of this disciple of John. Thus, although "John son of Zebedee was probably the source of the historical tradition behind the Fourth Gospel" (p. c), "the Book of Revelation is the work that is most directly John's" (p. cii), and the Fourth "Evangelist" is *not* John. Brown attributes authorship to John only "in the ancient sense of 'author'=authority" (p. xcviii).

3. Cf. Bauer, *Das Johannesevangelium,* 2d ed., 1925, p. 237: "If we interrogate our document itself as to its place of origin, it directs us much farther to the East, where the spirit of oriental mysticism and Gnosticism, which permeates our document, is at home. We are led into the proximity of Palestine by the relationship to Judaism of blunt rejection. Antisemitism of this strength must presuppose a region in which it was possible for the Jews not only to make life difficult for the Christians, but to put them in serious danger. Here too disciples of John as well as oriental prophets and Sons of God could compete with the new congregation and its Lord, making it necessary to oppose them. The conditions for the creation of his book would be found perhaps best of all in Syria, a location advocated already by Ephraem. . . , and where we find in Ignatius of Antioch a contemporary and kindred spirit of our author, . . . and where the Semitic echo of his language fits perfectly."

plying to first-century Judaism, have even brought Jordan into the picture.[4]

3. A third general trend in Johannine research has been a growing recognition of the independence of John from the synoptic gospels.[5] This trend is in part due to increased attention to oral over against written traditions, and the resultant shift of the burden of proof to the one who argues that a written synoptic gospel, rather than the living oral tradition, is presupposed.[6] Helmut Koester refined and narrowed the argument for dependence on the synoptics by pointing out that in the period when the oral tradition was still alive only the presence of an evangelist's additions to or alterations of the oral tradition could prove that the written gospel rather than the oral tradition was the source of the synoptic-like material.[7] As in the case of dating, discussion of the independence of John from the synoptics has been freed from the ballast of seeming to move apologetically toward apostolic authorship; thus independence of the synoptics has been given more serious consideration on its own merits.

A complete independence of John from Mark would involve the assumption that John (or his source) made use of the gat-

---

4. It has taken considerable ingenuity on the part of somewhat one-sided Qumran-advocates to affirm that Qumran has disproved Bultmann's viewpoint, and then to give Qumran credit for first having shifted scholarship on the provenance of the Fourth Gospel into the oriental, Semitic region; for this is precisely what Bultmann had affirmed a generation prior to the discovery of Qumran. The absence of the gnostic redeemer myth at Qumran did seem to diverge from what Bultmann had anticipated concerning Jordanian baptismal sects; but this omission would seem to have been filled in by such Nag Hammadi materials as the *Apocalypse of Adam* (CG, V, 5). Cf. my discussion of the question of non-Christian Gnosticism in "The Coptic Gnostic Library Today," *NTS* 12 (1968): 372–80. Ernst Haenchen, whose Johannine research is an exception to the general Qumranian orientation, nonetheless localized in 1959 the writing of the Fourth Gospel in "some small congregation on the frontier between Syria and Palestine" (*Gott und Mensch*, 1965, p. 112).
5. Ernst Haenchen has traced this development in sec. 1, on "John and the Synoptics," of his essay "Johanneische Probleme," *ZThK* 56 (1959): 19–22, reprinted in *Gott und Mensch*, pp. 78–81. Haenchen himself assumes that the redactor (but not the evangelist) was dependent on the synoptics.
6. Already Julius Schniewind, *Die Parallelperikopen bei Lukas und Johannes*, 1914, 2d ed., 1958, attributed most parallels to oral tradition. Although John "presupposed" the synoptics, he was not "literarily dependent" on them (e.g., John 7 and 21 reveal a "slight" contact due to "reminiscences of the Gospel of Luke," not to literary relation "in the strict sense" [p. 95]).
7. Helmut Koester, *Synoptische Überlieferung bei den apostolischen Vätern*, TU, 65, 1957.

tung gospel without benefit of Mark. This would then pose the question as to whether Mark gets all the credit for inventing the gattung, or whether the emergence of this new gattung must not be attributed to a certain configuration in the development of primitive Christianity such that, independently of each other, two authors at the same stage in the development could do much the same thing. Of course the newness—not to say uniqueness— of the gattung may well have been exaggerated by dialectic theology, and the step from the aretalogy, for example, to the gospel form may prove to have been not too great for such an assumption. That is to say, historical explanation that cannot be found in terms of the customary kind of dependence or causal relationship between two entities may be sought in their shared structural position along a trajectory within the early church.

4. A fourth general trend in Johannine scholarship has been toward the unity of Johannine style. This has discouraged the identification of sources imbedded in John.[8] This trend has often become apologetic in nature, directed specifically against Bultmann's source theory, especially in view of the fact that the sublime discourses of the Lord tended to be attributed by Bultmann to a non-Christian gnostic source.

As a matter of fact, few within the Bultmannian school or outside it have followed him with regard to this assumed source consisting of "revelation discourses"; but precisely the rapid demise of this source tends to draw into focus the first current aspect of Johannine research to which I wish to draw more careful attention: the surprisingly strong survival record of the "miracles source" ($\sigma\eta\mu\epsilon\hat{\imath}\alpha$-*Quelle*) made familiar by Bultmann, but actually going back to the pre-Bultmannian period.[9] Indeed the original

---

8. Eduard Schweizer, *Ego eimi: Die religionsgeschichtliche Herkunft und theologische Bedeutung der johanneischen Bildreden, zugleich ein Beitrag zur Quellenfrage des vierten Evangeliums*, FRLANT, 56, 1939, 2d ed., 1965, esp. pt. 3 (pp. 82–112 of the 2d ed.); Eugen Ruckstuhl, *Die literarische Einheit des Johannesevangeliums: Der gegenwärtige Stand der einschlägigen Forschungen*, Studia Friburgensia, n.s., 3, 1951, esp. pt. 2, pp. 180–219; Bent Noack, *Zur johanneischen Tradition: Beiträge zur Kritik an der literarkritischen Analyse des vierten Evangeliums*, 1954.
9. See above, pp. 51–58 for the discussion through 1965. The usual English translation of *Semeia-Quelle* has been "signs source." However, Alexander Faure, upon whom Bultmann was dependent, used the term *Wunderquelle*, "miracles source" ("Die alttestamentlichen Zitate im 4. Evangelium und die

proponent of unity of style, Eduard Schweizer, sees in the material most generally ascribed to this miracles source an exception to the general rule that pervasive style makes source theories unlikely.[10] Similarly, the current trend, represented by Ernst Haenchen [11] and Robert Fortna,[12] is to enlarge the miracles source into a more extensive narrative source or even gospel.

Quellenscheidungshypothese," *ZNW* 21 [1922]: 112). Bultmann himself usually leaves *semeia* untranslated, but can on occasion (*RGG*, 3d ed., vol. 3, 1959, p. 842) refer to it as "a collection of miracle stories." In his commentary, p. 79 n. 1, he indicates that "miracle" was its common meaning, but adds that the evangelist was aware of the original meaning "sign" (John 6:26; cf. p. 161). Haenchen has proposed that the material distinction between the source's understanding of *semeia* and that of the evangelist be brought to expression by translating *semeia* in the first case as "miracles," in the second as "signs." For these reasons the *Semeia-Quelle* is here referred to as the "miracles source." The reasons given by Robert Tomson Fortna, *The Gospel of Signs: A Reconstruction of the Narrative Source Underlying the Fourth Gospel*, Society for New Testament Studies Monograph Series, 11, 1970, do not seem to me of sufficient force to invalidate this terminological distinction. Fortna's elaboration of his position in this regard in "Source and Redaction in the Fourth Gospel's Portrayal of Jesus' Signs," *JBL* 89 (1970): 151–66, does indicate some inadequacies of the terminological distinction, e.g., that for the source as well as for the evangelist, miracle stories point beyond themselves and thus have a sign function; yet he concedes that for the source they have virtually no symbolic meaning, whereas for the evangelist they have relatively little importance as acts in themselves. Raymond E. Brown, in his critique of Fortna's book at the SBL Gospels Seminar in Toronto, November 1969, even criticized Fortna for going too far in describing the source's view in a way that the terminological distinction would suggest. Yet Fortna in turn obscures the distinction he so clearly sees, when he is unwilling to use the distinguishing terms *miracle* and *sign*. His reason may rest in a harmonistic tendency to affirm that the evangelist nowhere contradicts the source. Yet it is this claim that Haenchen finds hard to accept. For Haenchen considers 3:3, 5 to be a Johannine correction of the tradition about miraculous proof in 3:2b (with the redactor subsequently returning to visible proof by inserting water baptism into the evangelist's purely spiritual regeneration, 3:5); and he considers 20:29 a Johannine correction of the tradition's view reflected in 20:25, 27. Fortna for his part omits both the Nicodemus and the doubting Thomas stories from the source.
10. Cf. Eduard Schweizer's retrospect upon a generation of work following upon his initial emphasis on unity of style in *Ego eimi,* 1939, published in the preface to the second edition of 1965, p. vi.: "What I had generally established, has also been confirmed in terms of [Bultmann's commentary]: the unity of style is such that distinction of sources on the basis of these characteristics seems impossible. An exception is found only in the case of the prologue and the miracle stories, where, at least in the first two, a source can still be proven with high probability. Indeed I thought—here I was more cautious than E. Ruckstuhl—that the fact that sources cannot be proven linguistically does not prove that they did not exist at all. Yet sources, apart from the prologue and miracle stories, seem to me very unlikely." On p. 100 Schweizer lists 2:1–10 as containing no Johannine traits, and 2:13–19; 4:46–53; 12:1–8, 12–15 as containing practically none.
11. Haenchen has been working for a generation toward a commentary on John, which has not yet appeared but which in part is available in manuscript. His position on the Fourth Gospel is published in a series of essays, collected in *Gott und Mensch*, pp. 68–156 (see also pp. 14–16), and in *Die Bibel und Wir*, 1968, pp. 182–311 (see also pp. 9–10). See also idem, "Faith and Miracle,"

General acceptance of the miracles source was not only delayed by its association with the total source theory of Bultmann; as proposed in 1922 by Alexander Faure, to whom Bultmann appealed for its definitive formulation, the theory was also burdened with a comprehensive source theory, based on differing formulae for quoting the Old Testament (and Jesus), a theory that did not gain acceptance.[13] Hence Faure's main thesis tended to distract attention from the miracles source. But this was not a logical consequence. For although Faure used the miracles source as a supporting argument for his main thesis, his case for the existence of the miracles source was not itself dependent on his total source theory.[14] Therefore Bultmann carried through the critical function of distinguishing what was tenable in Faure's

---

Studia Evangelica, TU, 73, 1959, 495–98. In his commentary Haenchen appeals to Ernest Cadman Colwell, *The Greek of the Fourth Gospel,* 1931, to overcome "the basic damage of the work begun by Schweizer." Colwell classified Johannine Greek as common Koine Greek and, on comparing it with other instances such as Epictetus, found that what had been regarded as distinctive of John is simply distinctive of Hellenistic Greek. Thus Haenchen weakens the list of distinctively Johannine stylistic traits to such an extent that this approach ceases to be for him a major consideration in regard to Johannine sources. He expressed his skepticism as early as 1960, in an article reprinted in *Die Bibel und Wir,* 1968, pp. 238–42. Fortna, *The Gospel of Signs,* pp. 203–4, tends to concede this point with regard to Johannine style, but maintains that the earlier source should be expected to be nearer "the rest of the New Testament" (as also early?) than to "later" Koine—presumably with the effect that a Johannine source might be distinguished from the evangelist in that the source would have more New Testament traits and fewer late Hellenistic traits—but such an appeal to minor chronological divergences is probably a council of despair.

12. Fortna argues (*The Gospel of Signs,* pp. 203–14) that his source lacks most (64%) of the distinctively Johannine stylistic traits; when they occasionally appear, they are explained as Johannine editing (p. 205). Some of the stylistic traits are distinctive of the source but not of the evangelist; when such stylistic traits of the source occur in material added by the evangelist, they are attributed to his imitating the style of the source (pp. 214–18).

13. Already Friedrich Smend, "Die Behandlung alttestamentlicher Zitate als Ausgangspunkt der Quellenscheidung im 4. Evangelium," *ZNW* 24 (1925): 147–50, showed that the quotation formulae do not provide a reliable basis for distinguishing sources.

14. According to Faure, *ZNW* 21 (1922): 113 n. 3, a given quotation formula is not a distinguishing characteristic of the miracles source, but rather of the secondary source comprising John 1–12, of which the miracles source was only one ingredient. The miracles source itself contained no Old Testament quotations. How independent of the question of the miracles source is from the question of quotation formulae is indicated by the fact that Bultmann (in his commentary, p. 346 n. 4) unquestionably disagrees with Faure by including 12:38, containing a quotation formula, in the *semeia* source, and yet does not infer that all instances of that formula belong to that source; he expressly points out that verses containing that formula (13:18; 15:25; 17:12) are to be attributed to the evangelist. Fortna, *The Gospel of Signs,* p. 218, attributes both quotation formulae to the source.

essay by accepting the miracles source and rejecting the rest. If a similar critical distinction can be made in our day among Bultmann's sources, the miracles source may continue to gain ground until it attains general acceptance.

If such a miracles source can be successfully worked out, so as to reach a stage of relatively definable text with a scholarly consensus approaching the situation with regard to Q, for example, then a new access to Johannine theology will have been achieved, based upon tracing the history of the Johannine traditions, from oral stages, e.g., perhaps distinguishing oral transmission of individual stories and oral transmission of a cycle of stories, through the miracles source and the Fourth Evangelist, to the final redactor. By identifying on this Johannine trajectory the position of the Fourth Evangelist, one could, with a precision previously unattainable, put in profile just what theological stance the evangelist maintained in relation to the tradition in which he moved.[14a] The study of Johannine theology could thus attain the precision that redactional history has provided to the study of Matthew and Luke within the synoptic tradition.

After a generation in which interest in source theories has given way to more immediately theological interpretation, a fruitful advance may be sought in the investigation of the miracles source, as a new point of departure for a needed return to the problem of literary sources of the gospels. This kind of a return to source theory seems preferable to what Krister Stendahl in launching the Gospels Seminar critically described as a reworking of the well-plowed field of the two-document hypothesis, whose perennial stability can best be freed from the danger of stagnation or dogmatism by being brought within a new and potentially creative context. The "synoptic problem" needs to be recast in terms of a "gospels problem"!

Literary Source Theory

There are of course basic difficulties confronting any attempt to establish written sources behind the Fourth Gospel. In the case

14a. The good article by Jürgen Becker, "Wunder und Christologie: Zum literarkritischen und christologischen Problem der Wunder im Johannesevangelium," *NTS* 16 (1970): 130–48, came to my attention too late for detailed discussion of it. Part 3, pp. 136–43, treats the theology of the miracles source.

of the synoptic gospels, the survival of Mark made the detection of it as a source in Matthew and Luke relatively easy. Moreover, by revealing the limits of this first source, Mark facilitated the argument for the existence of Q, as a necessary postulate to explain the non-Marcan common material in Matthew and Luke. Furthermore the use of Mark and Q by two surviving gospels, rather than just one, has made still easier the general acceptance of the two-document hypothesis as the basic solution to the synoptic problem. None of these conditions prevails with regard to the Fourth Gospel. No other surviving documents shared its source(s), and no Johannine sources have survived.

The mere fact that a source is no longer extant should not be taken as an argument against its existence. Only a very small percentage of ancient literature, and hence, no doubt, of ancient Christian literature, has survived. Indeed there are traces of such in Luke 1:1–4, in Papias, and in fragments and names of lost apocryphal gospels. Yet, in the case of materials of such value as early traditions about Jesus, one should not appeal simply to mere chance or arbitrary loss to explain their nonsurvival. Rather one should seek, within the period leading up to the emergence of the canon, tendencies making intelligible the preservation of what survived and the nonpreservation of what did not survive. With regard to the synoptic materials, the situation can be hypothetically reconstructed without too great difficulty. The survival of Mark was probably not intended by Matthew and Luke, who would have conceived of their works as improved editions of *the* gospel to replace the earlier edition (Mark). The fact that Mark still survived may in part be due to the fact that both Matthew and Luke gained acceptance during the canonizing period, with the effect that the concept of a plurality of gospels had to be tacitly conceded. Yet the loss of Q indicates that this factor alone does not account for the survival of Mark. Perhaps Q was becoming suspect of heresy at a time when its gattung was being exploited by gnostics, and Mark seemed relatively more orthodox because of associations with Rome, which was succeeding in gaining ascendency for its traditions as orthodox.

These considerations making intelligible the survival of Mark and loss of Q make it somewhat easier to understand the loss of the miracles source. Like Matthew and Luke, the Fourth Evangelist probably would have conceived of his work as an improved edition of *the* gospel, without envisaging a useful survival of his source. If the Fourth Gospel did not make use of the synoptic gospels, and was itself only at a relatively late stage brought into the orthodox canonizing process, initially by being edited in an orthodox direction (perhaps with borrowings from the synoptics at this stage, but not earlier, according to Haenchen), then its milieu may have maintained longer than did that of the synoptics the concept of a single gospel, i.e., at least through the evangelist's time; Tatian's Diatesseron is in its way late second century attestation in Syria for the survival of such a concept. Thus the replacement, disuse, and resultant disappearance of the miracles source in favor of the Fourth Gospel could well have taken place before the acceptance of the orthodox concept of a plurality of gospels in the source's region. If the miracles source was associated with a location on the losing side in the struggle for ascendency and for the claim to orthodoxy, then the ecclesiastical strength displayed by Mark could be contrasted to an equivalent weakness on the part of the miracles source, as was also the case with Q. Of course the possibility that the source originated in rural Syria (so Haenchen), and that the Fourth Gospel was published in orthodox form in Asia Minor, could aid in explaining the loss of the one and the survival of the other. Indeed the slowness with which the Fourth Gospel itself gained acceptance in orthodox circles, and then only in an orthodox edition, indicates how unlikely the survival of the pre-Johannine miracles source would have been; not even a copy of the Fourth Gospel prior to the ecclesiastical redaction survived, much less a copy of its source. Thus, even though in some ways the miracles source reflected a kind of Christianity that was incorporated into orthodox Christianity (e.g., Luke-Acts), whereas the protognostic proclivities of the Fourth Evangelist did not, by the time the source's canonization among other gospels became a live option it was too late for the ancient source to be rescued and incorporated, as Mark had been. Rather, the Fourth Gospel, protected against Gnosticism by the redactor, was the only form in which the Johannine traditions entered the canon and survived.

Source theory with regard to the Fourth Gospel has been further impeded by the assumption of dependence upon the synoptic gospels. Not only did this assumption make rather superfluous the search for further written sources; it also prejudiced scholarship about the degree of success that could be expected from such an undertaking. For when one derives the Johannine material with synoptic parallels from the synoptic gospels, one is compelled, in view of the large extent to which the version of these materials in John diverges from the synoptic versions, to attribute to the Fourth Evangelist an extremely free and creative use of traditions, even written traditions. Since it would be impossible to reconstruct any of the synoptic gospels from the Fourth Gospel, presumably one could not reconstruct nonsynoptic sources of the Fourth Gospel. But if the current trend to assume that the Fourth Gospel did not use the synoptic gospels is correct, it is not necessary to ascribe so much freedom to its use of sources; the Fourth Evangelist's freedom in using the Old Testament is less radical than would be his freedom in using the synoptics, yet also less analogous and hence less relevant. Haenchen reflects the general tendency to reduce the amount of creative originality to be ascribed to the Fourth Evengelist, even though he is considerably more skeptical than is Fortna about the possibility of reconstructing in detail the miracles source. There is also a correlative trend, as the emphasis in the study of the synoptics has moved from form criticism and the oral tradition to redactional criticism and the written gospels, to emphasize that the synoptic evangelists are not mere editors but are to be regarded as authors.[15] Since, in spite of this status of theological authorship ascribed to Matthew and Luke, their sources Mark and Q can still be detected, the possibility of being able to detect Johannine sources is by comparison somewhat heightened.

15. Willi Marxsen, *Der Evangelist Markus: Studien zur Redaktionsgeschichte des Evangeliums*, FRLANT, 67, 1956 (ET: *Mark the Evangelist*, trans. Roy A. Harrisville, 1969), introduced the term *redactional history* as a conscious corrective of form criticism's classification of the evangelists as mere collectors rather than authors. Thus it was actually anachronistic for him to refer to their work as "redaction." Ernst Haenchen, *Der Weg Jesu: Eine Erklärung des Markus-Evangeliums und der kanonischen Parallelen*, 1966, p. 24, draws attention to this inconsistency and suggests the term *compositional history* (*Kompositionsgeschichte*). See my discussion of this terminological problem in sec. 1 of the essay "On the *Gattung* of Mark (and John)," in *Jesus and Man's Hope* 1970, pp. 99–106.

The question of the difficulty of reconstructing a source is not identical with the question of whether the source existed. To be sure, if the source can nowhere be laid hold of with any assurance, then the question of whether the source actually existed becomes acute. But if at some place a written source is visible, then the existence of a source is established, and the question becomes merely how extensive the source was and what character it had.

One may make a comparison, for this methodological observation, with the situation as regards Q: questions as to the existence of a written Greek Q are raised again and again. But even such questioners, when confronted, e.g., with the Q preaching of John the Baptist (Matt. 3:7–10; Luke 3:7–9), tend to concede that here a written Greek source must be assumed. For here one has an identical sequence of sixty-three words with only three very minor alterations ("fruit" vs. "fruits," "presume to say" vs. "begin to say," and the presence in Luke only of a superfluous "and"). Consequently the question becomes merely how extensive Q was (i.e., whether some of the "Q" material comes instead from different, and possibly Aramaic, sources), what it was like (including whether Matthew and Luke used different recensions), and whether one wishes to call it Q. Similarly the miracles source has been most clearly detected in John 2:1–12a (the wedding in Cana) followed directly by John 4:46b–54a (the healing of the son of the official from Capernaum). Perhaps the Fourth Evangelist began by interpolating his interpretation woodenly into the source, whose wording he at first left relatively unaltered, but later came to integrate source and interpretation more successfully, so as to make reconstruction of the source progressively more difficult for us. In any case the existence of the miracles source has been most persuasively argued in the case of these two miracle stories, and therefore this argument needs to be summarized, in order to assess the degree of seriousness with which such an approach to the Johannine trajectory should be considered.

First, one may consider the point at which the two stories are thought to join in the source; for here one has evidence of the evangelist's awkward efforts to restore the connection broken by his interpolation of 2:13—4:45. The evangelist conceived of the setting of the first miracle as Jesus' having come from the area of the Baptist's activity (Bethany beyond the Jordan, 1:28) to "Cana of Galilee," which presumably involved carrying out the intention of going "into Galilee" (1:43). One finds an analogous movement in 4:43: "But after the two days [sc., in Samaria, cf. 4:40] he went out from there into Galilee." This movement is restated in 4:45, "When then he came into Galilee. . . ," and 4:47, "Jesus had come from Judea into Galilee." This analogy to the situation of 2:1 ff. is then made explicit in 4:46a: "So he came again to Cana of Galilee, where he made the water wine." [16]

Although in the text as it now stands in chap. 4 the trip to Galilee is a repetition of an earlier movement (cf. 4:3, "again into Galilee"), one can sense that this repetition is motivated in part by the editor's desire to return to an interrupted narration, and is not unambiguously thought of as a distinct second trip. For if the reference in 4:54 to a "second miracle" "on coming from Judea into Galilee" were really referring to a new trip (to which 4:43, 45, 46 seem on the surface to refer), then 4:54 should not speak of the healing of the official's son as the second miracle performed on a clearly distinct instance of "coming from Judea to Galilee," since it would be a first and only miracle on such a second trip; and the language of 4:54 makes it clear it is "second" in relation to the "beginning" of miracles in 2:11. It is such a second miracle only if the trip to which 4:54 refers includes the changing of water into wine as the first miracle (2:1–11). Thus the evangelist betrays the fact that what he actually presents as two trips is still in his mind in a sense a single trip. John 4:43–46a thus seems to be a redactional seam, functioning to restore a broken

16. It is unclear whether there is a connection between the timing "on the third day" (2:1) and "after two days" (4:43). Perhaps the two-day stay in Samaria (4:40) suggested a fitting place for the editor to return to the context of 2:1, whose time reference "on the third day" is then reformulated in 4:43 with the number of 4:40 as "after the two days," somewhat as the editor could have derived from 4:40 ("and he remained there two days") the idea for his editorial filling at 2:12b ("and there they remained not many days"), if already at 2:12 he anticipated the point at which he would terminate the interpolated material and return to his source. Of course the reason for the three days in 2:1 is difficult to ascertain (cf. "on the next day," 1:29, 35, 43), unless one may with Haenchen assume it was to represent the longer time needed to go to Galilee; and the time reference in 2:1 may be due to the evangelist (so Fortna), rather than to the source. Such difficulties indicate the extent to which a thorough interpretation of the Fourth Gospel itself in terms of the miracles source remains to be done.

context in a rather clumsy way (note also the difficulty of 4:44 in its present position).

When one then turns to the end of the story of the wedding in Cana, one finds an almost equally awkward anticipation of 4:46b–54a, again best understandable as reflecting the severing of an original connection: "After this he went down into Capernaum, he and his mother and his disciples, and there they remained not many days, and immediately there was the Passover of the Jews, and Jesus went up into Jerusalem" (2:12–13). That is to say, a trip to Capernaum is narrated, a sojourn providing a context for a story is provided, and yet a Capernaum story justifying the mention of such a setting is omitted; the subsequent narration, a trip to Jerusalem, begins immediately. Thus one misses at 2:12 such a Capernaum story as is provided at 4:46b–54a, precisely the same story which had been introduced at 4:46a by a flashback to 2:1–11, without this flashback's playing any more useful function in the present text than does 2:12. Both 2:12 and 4:43–46a are primarily "useful" in alerting the critic to the seam in the evangelist's editorial activity.

It would seem to be redactional policy, when splitting up a source in order to interpolate material, that one provide an overlapping or repetitious comment, as if one ought to resume the source with some reference to where one left off.[17] One may compare the way in which the editor of 2 Corinthians interrupted (at 2 Cor. 2:13) one letter in order to interpolate another letter (2:14—7:4), and then at 7:5 rephrases (or was 2:12–13 the rephrasing?) from the original letter the last sentence he had recorded before breaking off, thus producing the doublet 2 Cor.

17. Fortna, *The Gospel of Signs,* p. 78, states this policy, and identifies it at 11:3b and 11:5–6a; at 11:7a and 11:11a; and at 5:9a and 5:14b (p. 53 n. 5). In such cases it is difficult to be precise in distinguishing the original wording of the source from the reworking of that wording by the editor, as he reduplicates it in his seam. Though 4:46a seems clearly to be a redactional flashback, one may be uncertain whether 2:12 is the evangelist's anticipation of the next story of the source, or the actual transition to the next story in the source itself (minus the evangelist's 2:12b), as Fortna assumes. The fact that the second story, from a form-critical point of view, begins satisfactorily at 4:46b, and that 2:12a is hence transitional, would in the latter case merely indicate that the author of the miracles source, like Mark, had already begun to introduce the kind of connectives made familiar by Karl Ludwig Schmidt's book *Der Rahmen der Geschichte Jesu,* 1919.

2:12–13; 7:5. Perhaps 1 Cor. 12:31a and 14:1 present a further instance of such a redactor's habit.[18] In John, one may compare the way in which, when the narration of Peter's denial is interrupted to insert the interrogation of Jesus by the high priest (18:19–24), the story of Peter is resumed with the last words ("Peter standing and warming himself") that had been quoted before the interruption (18:18b, 25a).

Such a technique is simplest when a quotation formula provides the seam: rather than the original quotation following the quotation formula, a new quotation with its consequences is interpolated. Then, by simple repetition of the quotation formula, the original context can be restored. In Mark 2:1–12, the quotation formula ("he said to the paralytic") provides both the point at which the discussion on the forgiveness of sins is interpolated into the healing of the paralytic (2:5) and the point at which the latter story is resumed (2:10). In a quite similar way there is apparently a Johannine interpolation into the first miracle story, the wedding at Cana. In 2:3 one finds the quotation formula "the mother of Jesus said [to him]," and in 2:5 its variegated repetition, "his mother said [to the servants]." The intervening material is recognized by both Haenchen [19] and Fortna [20] as Johannine: the unwillingness of John to have Jesus' work motivated by human rather than divine plan, as well as the Johannine engrossment with Jesus' coming "hour," recur at 7:6 in a similar Johannine rebuff to Jesus' kin (with his brothers here alternating with his mother), followed, as in chap. 2, by Jesus' in fact doing what he refused to do at human instigation. Were one to assume the unity of the story, it would be difficult to understand why Jesus' mother, after the rebuff of v. 4, proceeds (in v. 5) as if the intervening material did not exist. This problem is satisfactorily explained if 2:3b–4 is an interpolation by the evangelist into the

---

18. This is part of an argument I presented for the view that chap. 13 is not in its original position in an unpublished paper at the Western Section of the Society of Biblical Literature meeting at Claremont in April 1962. See Jack T. Sanders, "First Corinthians 13: Its Interpretation since the First World War," *Interpretation* 20 (1966): 182 ff.
19. Haenchen, *Gott und Mensch*, pp. 75 f., 93 n. 1.
20. Fortna, *The Gospel of Signs*, pp. 30–32.

miracles source. Needless to say, further research into such redactional habits as the one suggested here would increase considerably the precision with which distinctions of sources could be made.

When one then looks further for redactional activity within the body of the Capernaum story, one notes a redactional overlapping seam at the end of 4:47 and 49. Verse 47b reports in indirect discourse that the officer asked Jesus to go down and heal his son, since he was about to die; v. 49b quotes in direct discourse the officer: "Sir, go down before my boy dies." It looks as if the intervening material has not advanced the story one bit, but that the evangelist is in v. 49 simply recalling the point where he had interrupted his narration. As a matter of fact, the intervening comment by Jesus is rather gratuitous, seemingly unmotivated by and unrelated to the father's request that his son be healed. And the apparent rebuff seems ignored in what follows, since Jesus does in fact heal the son. The inference is that vv. 48–49 (or 47b–49a, with Fortna [21]) are not from the source but were added by the evangelist. This explanation is also suggested by two traits distinctive of the interpolation: a different word is used for the sick child (*paidion*) than is used in the rest of the story (which uses the term *huios* four times when the father and Jesus speak, and the term *pais* once when the servants speak). Furthermore, whereas in the source Jesus addresses the father in the singular, he addresses him within the interpolation in the plural, a slight inconsistency not only indicating the secondary nature of the interpolation but also suggesting that it is addressed to the church.

Such interpolations as 2:3b–5a and 4:47b–49a into the middle of stories are the way one would handle a written source, which had its own fixity; for in the case of oral transmission one could have been freer with the antecedent layer, and built one's own interpretation more integrally and invisibly into the whole. Thus on purely literary-critical grounds one can disengage a few segments of a written source behind John.[22]

21. Ibid., p. 41.
22. One can trace through the bulk of Johannine research not treated here a recurrent recognition, though often obscured by patently misleading contexts, of the pre-Johannine cohesion of these two miracle stories. From such a survey there

A further question concerning the status of the miracles source has to do with its extent; its existence seems to depend upon such literary-critical considerations as those just described, but its limits are not yet set by the analysis confined to two miracle stories. Fortna's study has sought to combine into a single source both Bultmann's miracles source and his passion-resurrection narrative source. Fortna also includes, as the third miracle story, 21:2–14, which Bultmann attributed to the redactor. The outcome is a relatively large source, comprising about a fifth of the total size of the Fourth Gospel.[23] Fortna attributes Bultmann's separation into two main narrative sources to the influence of Faure's division at the end of chap. 12, a division Fortna [24] regards as refuted by the pervasiveness of stylistic traits assembled by Schweizer and his followers. Fortna for his part argues for the distinctiveness of his source from the Fourth Gospel in terms of such stylistic traits. He then proceeds to argue also for the integrity of his source, on the grounds that all but one of the pericopes he assigns to his source contain at least one instance of the usages characteristic of the source.

Fortna uses this as his basic argument for the inclusion of the passion narrative in his source, which is in fact his most important departure from the main line of previous research on the source.[25] But when one looks in his lists of traits distinctive of the source [26] for traits that would bind the passion sections (chaps. 18–20 preceded by 2:14–19; 12:1–15; etc.) to the rest of his source, such connecting links turn out to be rather meager. From a list of nine words quite common in the New Testament but rare in John (and confined there to his source), five occur only once and hence cannot bind two sections; four occur three times each, with at least one

would emerge a heightened awareness of the degree of objectivity, in the sense of scientific verification by means of experimental repetition, to be attributed to this result.

23. Fortna, *The Gospel of Signs*, p. 215 n. 4.
24. Ibid., pp. 217–18 n. 3.
25. Actually, Fortna was in this regard anticipated by Wilhelm Wilkens, *Die Entstehungsgeschichte des vierten Evangeliums*, 1958; on this unsuccessful attempt see Haenchen, *Gott und Mensch*, p. 80 n. 1, and my review, "Recent Research in the Fourth Gospel," *JBL* 78 (1959): 242–46.
26. Fortna, *The Gospel of Signs*, pp. 214–17.

instance in passion sections and one in signs sections (σύν, ἕκαστος, εὐθέως, πρῶτον adverbially). Of eight terms lacking or rare in the New Testament apart from John (and there present only in the source), only one (κραυγάζειν) occurs in passion sections as well as signs sections, and this one is not lacking from the rest of the New Testament. Of five traits from Ruckstuhl's list of "Johannine" traits attributed by Fortna to the source rather than to the evangelist, one (noun plus ἐκ, "made of") occurs once (19:2) within a passion section (out of three occurrences), and a second also (ἑλκύειν meant literally) once (18:10, out of three occurrences, the other two instances being in chap. 21). The latter trait Fortna considers irrelevant, since it is not strictly speaking stylistic, but rather is dependent on a given subject matter. Of some eleven traits not always peculiar to the synoptics but also occurring elsewhere in the New Testament (though rare elsewhere in John, and hence regarded by Fortna as characteristic of the source), six occur in passion sections as well as elsewhere in the source: introductory or resumptive ἦν (19:41); parenthetical or explanatory ἦν (18:10, 13, 28, 40; 19:14, 19, 23); ὡς with numeral (19:14, [39]); singular verb with double subject (18:1b, 15; etc.); noun plus ἐκ, "from among" (18:3); ὄνομα αὐτῷ (18:10). Fortna includes in this list two further traits, which however seem to carry hardly any weight: numeral plus ἐκ (12:2, [4]; [13:21]; 18:[17, 25], 26). This trait is so common in the synoptics that Schweizer did not include it in his list of distinctive Johannine traits. Furthermore it occurs not only in the source but also twice (7:50; 20:24) in Johannine passages. Fortna handles these by arguing that the evangelist imitated the source, although he had initially conceded [27] that this trait should not be listed as evidence for the source. Fortna also appeals to the use of *Rabboni,* 20:16, to unite the passion sections to the signs sections. But this appeal seems to reverse the obvious inference from the statistics, since everywhere else in John *Rabbi* rather than *Rabboni* occurs. In sum, this total result seems to me (though not to Fortna) rather meager evidence to establish the inclusion within the miracle source of a passion and resurrection narrative.

27. Ibid., p. 210.

Fortna himself seems to recognize the independence of the two bodies of materials at the preliterary stage, for he considers the cleansing of the temple in the source as a connecting link which "appropriately joined a cycle of miracle stories to a traditional passion narrative." [28] It is very difficult, on the basis of the material provided by Fortna thus far, to move beyond this disjointed position, which tends to transpose Bultmann's two main written narrative sources back into oral cycles. There are reasons to think these sources were written, but there is not yet a compelling reason to unite them into one written source prior to the evangelist.

Fortna's assumption that we have to do with a single source is perhaps due ultimately, though not intentionally, to the synoptic pattern. He reasons in given cases from the fact that a phrase or detail is from the tradition or has synoptic parallels to the attribution of such ingredients to his source. Since he finds such synoptic-like materials both in the miracle stories and in the passion sections,[29] he is inclined to identify both types as belonging to *the* source, on some such instinctive logic as that things equal to the same thing are equal to each other.[30]

Since Fortna's work and the anticipated publication of Haenchen's commentary mark the growing edge of Johannine research, a comparison of the general lines of similarity and dissimilarity will suggest the course of the debate to come. Although the two works are basically independent of each other, Fortna is dependent upon Haenchen's numerous articles on the Fourth Gospel, and Haenchen had available Fortna's manuscript as he composed the final draft of his own commentary. The two have corresponded, both directly and through me, and have talked personally about their areas of agreement and disagreement, though without noticeable shift in positions.

Fortna's position is in at least one respect quite like that of

28. Ibid., p. 146.
29. E.g., the reconstructed sequence 18:38c; 19:15a; 18:39–40 within the passion narrative is described as "undoubtedly from the source: it parallels the synoptics with just the degree of dissimilarity we have repeatedly found." Ibid., p. 124; cf. the detailed discussion on pp. 124–25.
30. Cf. e.g., ibid., pp. 144–45: "Because the episode of the temple cleansing has a fundamental connection to the events of the passion (even though now separated from them) in the synoptic gospels, it is possible that this connection is traditional and obtained also in John's source."

Haenchen; both men include in their source more of the narrative material than merely the miracle stories. But whereas Fortna simply classifies the source as a gospel "in the narrower [sc., synoptic] sense," [31] Haenchen refers to the miracles source as "a gospel of nonsynoptic type." [32] For him it is only "a sort of crude version of the Gospel of Mark," since it is "a gospel that no longer showed Jesus' glory in secret epiphanies, but rather as visibly and tangibly as possible." [33] Much that Fortna includes in his source is attributed by Haenchen only vaguely to a narrator or to tradition. For Fortna, an argument that a passage is pre-Johannine tradition is usually tantamount to classifying it as part of his source.

Fortna and Haenchen agree in including in their source more than was previously assumed. Not only are narrative materials other than miracle stories included; both assume a passion (and resurrection) narrative. Both Fortna and Haenchen tend to shift from the term *source* to the term *gospel,* no doubt because the kerygma-type gattung including cross and resurrection is the one among the several gattungen used for Jesus traditions that in the more specific sense is to be called gospel, compared with which a mere collection of miracles might seem only a part, a source, but not itself a gospel. Both Fortna and Haenchen agree that there was only one written source for the Johannine traditions. Fortna tends to attribute most traditions to the source, but Haenchen often leaves this question open. Both assume that the source, like the Fourth Gospel, was not dependent on the synoptic gospels; parallels are due to shared traditions. But Fortna is more inclined than Haenchen to use the existence of a synoptic parallel as a reason for including Johannine material in the source.

Haenchen conceives of the Fourth Evangelist as having lived with the miracles source as the gospel used in the worship services of his own congregation, so that the relationship is more oral and recollective than literary; [34] Fortna proceeds in the scissors-and-paste method, presupposing a comparably detailed literary criti-

31. Ibid., p. 221 n. 2.
32. Haenchen, *Gott und Mensch,* p. 113.
33. Ernst Haenchen, "Aus der Literatur zum Johannesevangelium 1929–1956," *ThR* n.s. 23 (1955): 303.
34. Ibid., pp. 303–4; *Gott und Mensch,* pp. 112–13.

cal activity by the Fourth Evangelist. Hence Fortna is bold enough to publish a word-by-word reconstruction of the source, which even in the case of Q would seem courageous, whereas Haenchen is usually elusive in delimiting the source. Haenchen also emphasizes that redactional activity involves not only accretion, which when removed leaves the *Vorlage* relatively intact; it also involves pruning and compressing, with an irretrievable loss of text, to an extent greater than Fortna.

Although in Haenchen's case it is not only the presence of distinctive theological traits that are responsible for the inclusion of traditions within his source, yet the absence of such considerations in traditions that otherwise have in his view lost their verbal exactitude makes him hesitate to associate them with his source. Conversely, for Fortna material distinctions are hardly thought to be necessary in making rather exact source distinctions. Furthermore, Fortna tends to bring the theological position of the source and that of the evangelist closer to each other than does Haenchen, for which reason he speaks of a gospel of *signs* rather than a *miracles* source. Of course the larger the source becomes, and the less it is restricted to miracle stories, the less profile it retains, and the more heterogeneous and Johannine its theology would tend to become.

To be sure, one need not assume that an aretalogy or collection of miracle stories would be materially inconsistent with the inclusion of a passion narrative. The fact of a passion narrative does not imply necessarily a theology of the cross. A Hellenistic portrayal of a divine man can readily include his death and apotheosis. Luke illustrates well the possibility of transforming Mark's tragic passion narrative into a triumphalism worthy of a miracle worker. And in fact the Johannine passion narrative is in this regard more comparable to Luke than to Mark. Hence the theological nature of the source is not basically challenged by the issue of the presence or absence of a passion narrative.[35] But it would be of considerable interest, in terms of tracing the origins of the various gattungen into which Jesus traditions were cast, to know whether the miracles source is in outline (though not necessarily

35. Fortna, *The Gospel of Signs,* pp. 235–45.

in tendency) more comparable to Mark, or whether this parallel in outline is first the contribution of the Fourth Evangelist.

If Fortna has enlarged his gospel of signs beyond the limits one might conjecture for Haenchen's miracles source, there is another stage on the Johannine trajectory at which it is Haenchen who has enlarged and Fortna who has diminished the amount of new material. For Haenchen, the redactor is responsible, not only for the sacraments, futuristic eschatology, and chap. 21 (as in the case of Bultmann's redactor), but also for the beloved disciple and for the few places where the present text is dependent on the synoptic gospels. Conversely Fortna is methodologically very skeptical about attributing material to a redactor; hence this category plays a negligible role in his presentation.[36]

The similarity in basic trends, with the divergences of method and results, makes the post-Bultmannian development of Johannine source theory a fascinating and very promising enterprise. The outcome could be a sharp profile of the Fourth Evangelist which would bring into focus the other major aspects of Johannine research.

Johannine Theology

The detection of a literary source has an importance going far beyond the mere fact of having established a source theory. It also provides a basis for redactional history as a major means of bringing into sharper focus the evangelist's own theology.[36a] The evange-

---

36. Ibid., pp. 4–8. Negative value judgments about attributing material to a post-Johannine redactor have been largely removed from the published form of this section; yet they must have been at work as a limiting factor in the actual research itself. When Johannine research is understood to be concerned not exclusively with the evangelist but with the whole Johannine trajectory, the invalidity of many such value judgments becomes apparent and research is at one specific and important point freed from limitations imposed by a previous conceptualization. Raymond E. Brown, in his critique of Fortna, points out that the redactor is inescapable in the discourses, since one finds here two levels, and the older is that of the evangelist. By limiting himself to the narrative material, Fortna was able to avoid facing this problem fully. Fortna attributes chap. 21 to the evangelist rather than to the redactor, and thus facilitates his effort to derive from chap. 21 the third "sign" of his source. Brown points out how such a view is difficult to maintain, not only because of the scholarly tradition of assigning chap. 21 to the redactor, but also because of the difficulties in making sense of the evangelist's placing the source's conclusion at 20:30–31 and yet continuing in chap. 21 with material from the source, as well as the difficulty of explaining the fishing story of chap. 21 as not a resurrection story.

36a. Jürgen Becker, "Wunder und Christologie: zum literarkritischen und christ-

list seems to have created all the redactional awkwardness in 4:47–49 for the sake of inserting the brief comment: "Unless you see signs and wonders, you do not believe." This is apparently his own comment, which was sufficiently important for him to have gone to all this trouble to include it. Thus study of his redactional activity and detection of the layers of tradition make it possible to bring into sharp profile the evangelist's own tendency. Were one to read the story without such a distinction between the preceding layer and the evangelist's editing, one would fail to see the point of the story from the evangelist's own view, from inside his workshop, so to speak. By watching him work one can see his intentionality more clearly than when one simply observes the finished product and does not know what lies behind it. This is the importance inherent in defining 4:48 as the evangelist's commentary.

Paul Meyer argues [37] that only "some such theological preconception as Bultmann's" would lead one to look for the point or climax of the story in 4:48 (rather than "in the thrice repeated verb 'lives,' " or in 53b). Although one may well concede that (ignoring the Johannine interpolation) Meyer has correctly reflected the point and climax of the original story, one should recognize that the point the story had at the (oral or written) pre-Johannine stage is not necessarily the point the evangelist particularly desired to score as he retold the story. The purely literary observation that the evangelist has made an interpolation, quite apart from its theological content, is sufficient reason to look here for the particular point associated with the story at the evangelist's stage of the story's trajectory.

Meyer contests the dominant view, represented by Bultmann, that 4:48 conveys "Jesus' displeasure over the demand for a miracle as a guarantee for faith," [38] and prefers a positive interpretation,[39] which he puts as follows: "Faith cannot be self-generating

---

ologischen Problem der Wunder im Johannesevangelium," addresses himself to this problem in Part 4, pp. 143–48.
37. Paul Meyer, in a (to my knowledge unpublished) paper presented at the annual meeting of the American Academy of Religion in Dallas, October 18, 1968, on "Seeing, Signs, and Sources in the Fourth Gospel."
38. Bultmann, commentary, p. 151; *RGG*, 3d ed., 3:151.
39. Published by his pupil, Wayne A. Meeks, *The Prophet-King: Moses Traditions and the Johannine Christology,* 1967, p. 40.

but must have its ground in the recognition of something done by God. . . . What is emphatically denied is not the granting of a sign but the possibility of faith apart from the prior meeting of a certain condition; signs must be seen before there can be any faith in the Johannine sense." In this interpretation Jesus' blessing upon those who do not see and yet believe (20:29) cedes its role as interpreting Johannine theology to the presumptuous assertion of Thomas that unless he sees he will not believe (20:25)—which is precisely what the blessing seems to be intended to relativize. The grammatical similarity of 4:48 to 20:25 is then used by Meyer as the grounds for elevating them together to the normative Johannine concept of true faith. However, the less-than-ideal role played in the final scene by Thomas (as documented by the climax in 20:29) should serve to support the majority interpretation that 4:48 implies a criticism. Nonetheless Meyer wonders "whether this purported discrepancy of outlook [between source and evangelist] is not the result of reading back into the gospel issues and connotations that originate in the modern discussions about miracle and faith, of reading back into the 'signs-source' a crasser supernaturalism and into the evangelist's mind a more idealized understanding, more congenial to the modern mind, than this late first-century document anywhere contains."

This accusation of modernizing is strikingly put in question by the most recent of the Nag Hammadi tractates to be published, the *Apocryphon of James* from the Jung Codex (*CG, I, 1*).[40] This document has been dated in the second century A.D. and, like the Gospel of John, is already a topic of debate as to whether it is or is not to be classified as gnostic. Whether it made use of the Gospel of John has also been questioned, though the editors assume it did. It contains passages that come just about as close to Haenchen's interpretation of John 20:29 in the context of the miracles source as one could hope to find (3:17–34; 12:39—13:1): "Woe to those who have (only) seen the Son of Man. Blessed shall they be who have not seen the man and have not had contact with him and have not spoken with him and have not heard anything from him. Yours is life. Know then that he healed

40. *Epistula Iacobi apocrypha,* ed. by Michel Malinine, Henri-Charles Puech, Gilles Quispel, Walter Till, and Rodolphe Kasser, 1968.

you when you were ill in order that you might become kings. Woe to them who have been relieved of their illness for they will return to the(ir) illness. Blessed are those who did not become ill and have known health before they became ill. Yours is the kingdom of God. . . . Woe to those who heard and did not believe. Blessed shall they be who did not see but believe."

Yet even apart from this bit of new documentation, so analogous to the criticism of fascination in the physically miraculous which Haenchen attributes to the Fourth Evangelist, Meyer's criticism of Haenchen is neither materially nor methodologically an accurate appraisal. Materially, Haenchen presents a clear though finely nuanced distinction between the view of the miracles source and that of the evangelist, which is considerably more tenable that the either/or position against which Meyer's criticism is directed. For the source, "Jesus' miracles prove directly and visibly for everyone Jesus' divine status." [41] The evangelist for his part "of course does not in the least doubt that Jesus performed all these miracles." [42]

The evangelist's criticism of the father's request that his son be healed is presented as follows: "But it is and remains an occurrence confined to the earthly sphere, and if Jesus performs it, he is not yet thereby recognized as what faith holds him to be, the giver of the true life with God. Yet the miracle that Jesus performs in the earthly sphere, visible for everyone, can indeed become the sign, the pointer to the true miracle, that in him we see the Father (14:9) and enter into fellowship with him and the Father (14:23). Admittedly, man should not really need such pointers at all. Jesus' word to Thomas, 'Blessed are those that do not see and yet believe' (20:29), applies here as well. But man (as here the officer) usually comes to this true faith only when a miracle opens his eyes for him. John saw this relationship described in our story. At first the father believes only that Jesus will make the son well. Only later does true faith dawn on him: 'He came to faith together with his whole house' (4:53). On this condition John was able to appropriate our story." [43]

41. Haenchen, *Gott und Mensch,* p. 68.
42. Ibid., p. 69.
43. Ibid., p. 88.

Methodologically, the advocates of a distinction in viewpoint between the miracles source and the evangelist have used the source to provide access to the successive stages of interpretation in the history of the transmission of traditions. They have based their viewpoints of the theology of various stages on this trajectory upon the objective results of their source analysis. But Meyer has tended to base a decision with regard to sources upon the theological issue: "Something more is still needed, another element in the argument, before one can make a very persuasive case not only for the extent and profile of such a source but even for its very existence. In the current discussion, very clearly, this crucial additional ingredient consists of the claim that there exists a clear discrepancy between the understanding of the signs which is imbedded in the tradition and the stories themselves on the one hand, and what we find the evangelist doing with this material on the other." Since Meyer has listed only a very few of the literary grounds usually given in support of the source theory, it is premature for him to ascribe to others a need to resort to theological consideration to prove their case. Fortna's dissertation, not yet available to Meyer, shows how, with a theological assessment much like Meyer's, literary-critical considerations alone can lead to the miracles source.

Meyer himself stands methodologically at the stage prior to redactional criticism, in that he either presupposes no literary-critical position in his view of Johannine theology or minimizes its theological relevance.[44] The lack of profile reflected in Meyer's presentation of Johannine theology can be overcome only by a methodological advance leading to the establishment on literary-critical grounds of the stages in the Johannine tradition. On the basis of this objective criterion one can then trace the stages in the trajectory of Johannine theology.

This same inconclusiveness, due to the absence of objective criteria for defining the precise tendency of the Fourth Evangelist's theology within the Johannine trajectory, is visible in the current debate about the validity of Bultmann's theology, when this debate

44. This is evident from the harmonization with which Meyer concludes: "John 19, 35–37 may have been added by the redactor responsible for chap. 21, but it is not wholly discontinuous with the Evangelist's work in the Thomas pericope."

is carried on in terms of Johannine theology. Much as Heinrich Schlier some two decades ago anticipated his defection from Bultmann and conversion to the Roman Catholic church by associating Bultmann with the gnosticizing opponents of Paul in Corinth,[45] Ernst Käsemann in his Shaffer Lectures of 1966 expressed his defection from Bultmann in the provocative form of a rejection of the Fourth Gospel itself, as having shared too fully the gnosticizing culture in which it emerged.[46] According to Käsemann, Christ, rather than being presented by John in a paradoxical or dialectical way that could be brought into the orbit of a normative theology of the cross or incarnational theology, is presented docetically as "the God striding over the earth." In view of the extent to which Bultmann identified his own theology with Johannine theology, Käsemann's challenge to Bultmannian theology was sufficiently frontal for it to be chosen as the program of the 1967 meeting of "old Marburgers," where Günther Bornkamm provided the rebuttal.[47]

Although Bornkamm conceded that Bultmann had gone too far in describing the Johannine Christ as incognito, Bornkamm does maintain the dialectic nature of Johannine theology by arguing that the glory revealed in the flesh is a retrospective position based on the coming of the Paraclete after the departure of Jesus. The glorification of Christ in being lifted up to heaven on the cross, toward which the gospel repeatedly points, is in fact presupposed by the evangelist, for whom it has been read back into the antecedent narrative as the glory retrospectively visible in the flesh.

45. Heinrich Schlier, "Über das Hauptanliegen des 1. Briefes an die Korinther: Eine Abschlussvorlesung," *EvTh* (1949): 462–73, reprinted in *Die Zeit der Kirche: Exegetische Aufsätze und Vorträge*, 1955, pp. 147–59.
46. Ernst Käsemann, *Jesu letzter Wille nach Johannes 17*, 1966 (ET: *The Testament of Jesus: A Study of the Gospel of John*, 1968). Much the same anti-Bultmannian critical appraisal of John, with appeal to a normative role for apocalypticism reminiscent of Käsemann, had already been worked out by the Pannenberg circle. Cf. Ulrich Wilckens, "Das Offenbarungsverständnis in der Geschichte des Urchristentums," *Offenbarung als Geschichte*, ed. by Wolfhart Pannenberg, *Kerygma und Dogma*, Suppl. 1, 1961, pp. 80–87 (ET: *Revelation as History*, 1969 pp. 101–10).
47. Günther Bornkamm, "Zur Interpretation des Johannes-Evangeliums: Eine Auscinandersetzung mit Käsemanns Schrift 'Jesu letzter Wille nach Johannes 17,'" *EvTh* 28 (1968): 8–25, reprinted in *Geschichte und Glaube*, (Gesammelte Aufsätze, 3, 1968), pp. 104–21.

Haenchen, who agrees with Bornkamm in criticizing Käse-mann's view, summarizes this complex Johannine position as follows:

Yet neither the Jews nor the disciples saw the Father in Jesus during his earthly life. When John speaks of many who come to faith (2:11, 23; 7:31; 8:30 ff.), it promptly becomes clear that it is not true faith (2:24–25; 8:40, 47, 59). But the situation is similar even in the case of the disciples: in spite of their having been together so long, it is precisely not the case that Philip has seen in him the Father, as 14:7–9 makes clear; and in 16:29 ff. Jesus replies to the assurance from the disciples that they now believe him to have come from the Father, to the effect that they would soon be scattered and forsake him. John 9:39b reveals the reason for this faithlessness of the disciples: prior to Jesus' glorification the Spirit had not yet come. The Resurrected first breathed it into his disciples (20:22).

As in Paul and to a certain extent in Mark as well, the earthly life of Jesus is for John not yet the time when Jesus' true being is recognized. This is true even though this earthly activity has, according to John, precisely the goal of making the Father visible in him. Nonetheless the earthly life attains this goal, but only belatedly: the Spirit leads the disciples into all truth. Jesus' earthly life is, so to speak, only in retrospect transparent to its real meaning—through the Spirit. The Spirit is explained in its significance primarily in the gospel's statements about the "Comforter," the "Paraclete" (14:16–17, 26; 15:26; 16:5–15). Already in 8:26 Jesus had indicated that he still had a great deal to say. But only after the exaltation of the Son of man will one know that he is the one whom the Father sent. The role of the Spirit is more clearly described in the parting discourses: the Spirit of truth will teach everything (14:26). Jesus has a great deal more to say to them, but they are not yet able to grasp it.

This means however that the new picture of Jesus that the evangelist constructs is itself inspired by the Spirit that leads the disciples into all truth (16:13). . . . But if the emphasis is to this extent shifted to the Spirit, the Paraclete sent to the post-Easter church, then the "earthly Jesus" is in danger of becoming a mere predecessor of the Spirit. John worked against this by recalling that there is an intimate agreement between Jesus and the Spirit: the Spirit "will not speak from himself, but will say what he hears. . . . He will glorify me, for he will take what is mine and proclaim it to you" (16:13–14). Thus the evangelist, led by the Spirit, through proclaiming the true meaning of the message of Jesus, really brings Jesus into his honor for the first time.[48]

In Bornkamm's presentation this somewhat complicated way of reconciling the various statements, including surface contradictions, within the Gospel of John is then given some objective support by appeal to the profile given to Johannine theology by distinguishing if from the miracles source. "In all probability the picture of Christ in the pre-Johannine tradition corresponded in many respects to the picture of the 'God striding over the earth' that Käsemann has projected for the Gospel of John as a whole." [49] Like Haenchen, Bornkamm seeks to do full justice to the degree of material acceptance of that tradition which must be inferred from the fact that the evangelist did in fact appropriate the source for his purposes.

> Without a doubt he really appropriated [the tradition] and to an amazing degree was himself molded by it. But just as uncontestable is the equally pervasive Johannine criticism of that tradition, the constant tendency to interpret the miracles transparently, as a sign or pointer toward Jesus himself, to oppose the crude faith in miracle, and to chastise the persistent, earthbound lack of understanding characteristic of unbelief. . . . When one interprets as does Käsemann Jesus' history according to John in a straight-line and undialectical way, as the history of the God striding over the earth, characterized by docetism and robbed of the reality of the event of the cross, then one has admittedly lit upon the pre-Johannine tradition, but not upon John.[50]

This exchange between Käsemann and Bornkamm, internal as it may be to the post-Bultmannian debate of the past decade or so, serves to illustrate the extent to which a New Testament document, no matter how much agreement there may be as to the specific history-of-religions context of its author (e.g., gnosticizing environment), cannot be adequately defined when treated in isola-

48. Ernst Haenchen, "Vom Wandel des Jesusbildes in der frühen Gemeinde," in *Verborum Veritas,* Gustav Stählin festschrift, ed. Otto Böcker and Klaus Haacker, 1970, pp. 13–14.
49. Bornkamm, "Zur Interpretation des Johannes-Evangeliums," p. 116.
50. Ibid., pp. 116–17.

tion from the Christian trajectory in which it is moving and the broader context of that whole trajectory. Rather the contours of the New Testament document must be disengaged by identifying where the document came from and the direction in which it moved. That is to say, New Testament theology cannot be carried on apart from a reconstruction of the history of the transmission of traditions, since apart from such a reconstruction the hermeneutical activity carried on within the document itself cannot be identified. This in turn means that progress in understanding Johannine theology depends on progress in defining Johannine sources, such as the resolution of the problem of the miracles source, toward which the efforts of Fortna and in part Haenchen are directed. To be sure, this is not intended to minimize the role of the history of religions for understanding New Testament theology; if anything, one should perhaps say that the Johannine trajectory is itself best understood as a small segment within the history of religions. And this intra-Christian trajectory, as a history-of-religions trajectory, must of course be understood in terms of its "environment," the overarching history-of-religions trajectory of the Hellenistic world.

The History-of-Religions Trajectory

The significant moves in the study of the Fourth Gospel during the twentieth century with regard to its location in the history of religions have followed the shift from Adolf Harnack's definition of Gnosticism as the radical Hellenizing of Christianity to Hans Lietzmann's definition of it as the reorientalizing of Christianity. It is relevant to document this growing edge of Johannine scholarship, since the lethargy of the *opinio communis* has tended to obscure it, and instead to attribute the importance of recent discoveries (such as Qumran) to what was not in fact new on the growing edge of scholarship. In 1903 Hermann Gunkel wrote:

> It is uncontested that Pharisaism was one of the leading forces of that period. Yet the popular view, apparently especially current among Jewish scholars today, that it was the characteristic form of the religion of that epoch, indeed ultimately the only one worth considering, is untenable. Pharisaism attained exclusive leadership

only after the rejection of Christianity and after the great defeats by the Romans under Titus and Hadrian, with which a new epoch begins. In the earlier period Judaism was much more richly structured. Alongside the scribes there were other movements, from which the apocalypses are derived, movements that inflamed the population to attempted insurrections, and from which persons arose claiming to be prophets or even the promised Christ himself. All apocalypses seek to be secret writings and transmit secret traditions. Accordingly we are to imagine that there were at that time certain circles that were edified by means of such secret knowledge and that concealed themselves from public attention. From the same time we hear expressly of a secret band of Essenes. The secret traditions of the apocalypses treat especially eschatology, angelology, cosmology, and primal history. This is the real place where foreign material entered into Judaism in floods.[51]

Gunkel then quotes Wilhelm Bousset: "If that is generally conceded of Alexandrian Judaism, it is almost equally true of Palestinian. Here too the influences in question extend ultimately into the very center of the religion." [52]

One such foreign ingredient of the pre-Christian period Gunkel described as follows:

In a later time of the Orient we see then new formations, whose beginning we may put at about the beginning of the Greek period. We usually become acquainted with these phenomena only when they extend their propaganda over onto Greco-Roman terrain. For the time being we do not know where and when they originated in the Orient. One may designate their advocates with a word that was used by these circles themselves: "gnostics" (Mandaje).[53]

It was, then, not surprising that the first major history-of-religions discovery of our century, the Mandaean texts, seemed to Bultmann to confirm that basic approach and provide it with more precision.

When one notes that of all the cited sources the Mandaean texts display by far the strongest affinity to the Gospel of John, then one

51. Hermann Gunkel, *Zum religionsgeschichtlichen Verständnis des Neuen Testaments*, 1903, 3d ed., 1930, p. 29.
52. Wilhelm Bousset, *Die Religion des Judentums im späthellenistischen Zeitalter*, 1903, p. 492; 3d ed., 1926, p. 523.
53. Gunkel, *Zum religionsgeschichtlichen Verständnis des NT*, p. 18.

wonders whether the Mandaeans are not that religious group being sought as the presupposition for Johannine Christianity. Even though this question cannot for the moment be settled, at least it advances our reflection considerably. . . . If we could get a clearer picture of the Essenes, we would perhaps make progress. In any case the Jewish and Jewish-Christian baptismal sects, thorough investigation of which is urgently needed, show what possibilities there were. . . . We cannot get by, in understanding the history of primitive Christianity, with distinguishing, as do Bousset and Heitmüller, between Palestinian and Hellenistic stages of primitive Christianity; rather we must distinguish two layers within Palestinian primitive Christianity. In order to pose the problem as sharply as possible, I could say that one must reckon with the idea that Johannine Christianity represents an older type than does synoptic Christianity. . . . If this construction is correct, it contains as well a part of the solution of the problem left basically in the dark, namely that of the continuity between Palestinian and Hellenistic primitive Christianity: the original primitive Christian baptismal sect may from the very beginning have had a stronger tendency toward Hellenization than did the primitive church, which had as a constitutive ingredient alongside of faith in the Messiah and eschatology the question of the law. . . . Of course all this is initially construction, and is only intended to suggest further tasks for research. I only add to this that the problem of the Hellenization of primitive Christianity seems to me to be closely connected with that of its Syrification. The role of Syria in Hellenistic and primitive Christian history of religion is in urgent need of investigation. If the Gospel of John arose in Syria, as I believe, then the question about continuity would thereby find a more precise answer.[54]

Needless to say, Mandaean studies were readily eclipsed by the Dead Sea Scrolls, which have provided the new history-of-religions ingredient to Johannine studies over the last generation. The standard pattern has been to find in Qumran the explanation of the origin of Johannine dualism, but, in distinction from the Mandaean approach, not the source of Johannine Christology (which was often tacitly left to be explained in terms of its having happened: since Jesus *did* come from and return to heaven, i.e., since these are not *concepts* but rather *events,* no history-of-religions explanation is felt to be really needed). But in Qumranian studies too a more

---

54. Rudolf Bultmann, "Die Bedeutung der neuerschlossenen mandäischen und manichäischen Quellen für das Verständnis des Johannesevangeliums," *ZNW* 24 (1925): 142–45; reprinted in *Exegetica.* 1968, pp. 100–103.

sober appraisal of actually tenable results has followed upon the initial enthusiasm.[55]

Meanwhile Lady Drower has published Mandaean texts in hitherto unequaled quantities, and research in this field, though less well known than Qumran studies, has progressed steadily, with the result that the position of Lidzbarski presupposed by Bultmann has been steadily strengthened. Kurt Rudolph summarizes this trend as follows:

> The original connections of sectarian heretical Judaism with early Gnosticism are further confirmed by an investigation of the Mandaean writings. Already Lidzbarski had emphasized the important role of Jewish elements in Mandaeism, a view that has only been confirmed by more recent investigations (Schlier, Odeberg, Pedersen, Epstein). In my works on the Mandaeans I have also concentrated on this problem and been able to show that the earliest Mandaean or Nasoraean sect arose from a heretical gnostic Judaism which had established itself in Transjordania in the form of baptismal sects. The Jewish elements on the moral and ethical plane in the oldest layer of Mandaean literature show, e.g., close contacts with late Jewish heretical radicalism, as found in the Qumran literature. To this are to be added motifs and speculations that can only be explained on the basis of an originally Jewish milieu; I have been able to show this in more detail in literary critical investigations. . . .
>
> This view of the origin of the Mandaean sect, already advocated by Lidzbarski, has received the support of the two best authorities on Mandaean literature, Lady Drower and R. Macuch. Lady Drower has now given up her earlier view of the Iranian origin of the Mandaeans. . . . I am hence of the well-grounded conviction that the gnostic redeemer myth is of pre-Christian origin. The circles in which we can conjecture it to have originated have already been suggested in the preceding section: Iranian-Jewish circles. At this point further detailed and exacting research is needed, especially by making use of the new texts. In my opinion Paul and the anonymous author of the Gospel of John presuppose a gnostic-type doctrine of the redeemer; they use its terminology, but also oppose it. For them the mythological redeemer or revealer has been transcended by the historical redeemer Jesus Christ.

---

55. Cf. Herbert Braun, "Qumran und das Neue Testament: Ein Bericht über 10 Jahre Forschung (1950–59)," *ThR* n.s. 28 (1962): 192–234, reprinted in book form, *Qumran und das Neue Testament,* vol. 1, 1966, pp. 96–138.

An irreproachable proof for our view is provided, apart from segments of Hermetic Gnosticism and the "Hymn of the Pearl," by Mandaean literature. It is derived from a non-Christian gnostic sect, which has demonized Christ as redeemer.[56]

This persistent trend in the scholarship of the twentieth century has been carried one step further by the Coptic gnostic codices from near Nag Hammadi, which reflect in some of their tractates, such as the *Apocalypse of Adam* and the *Paraphrase of Shem,* what seems to be non-Christian Gnosticism, a gnostic or semignostic Judaism, in some cases localized in the Jordan region and interacting in some way with baptismal movements. The direction of this total movement has been summarized by Oscar Cullmann:

> The most important change in the recent history of research into earliest Christianity is doubtless that this all too schematic view [sc., of Jewish Christianity vs. gentile Christianity] was shaken by the demonstration that in reality the root of Christianity is to be sought beyond the antithesis of Palestinian Judaism vs. extra-Pales-

56. Kurt Rudolph, "Stand und Aufgaben in der Erforschung des Gnostizismus," in *Tagung für allgemeine Religionsgeschichte 1963, Sonderheft* of the *Wissenschaftliche Zeitschrift der Friedrich-Schiller-Universität Jena,* pp. 93 f., 97. Cf. also the statement in his essay, "Problems of a History of the Development of the Mandaean Religion," *History of Religions* 8 (1969): 210–35, esp. p. 210–11: "A further conspicuous fact, which becomes obvious to one who considers Mandaean studies, is the extremely divergent estimate of the age of the Mandaean literature and religion. While Nöldeke, Brandt, and Lidzbarski—that is, those who were best informed about the material—were firmly convinced of a pre-Christian existence of this sect, other scholars, to be sure almost only those who once turned to the Mandaeans for a short time, prefer a late dating. Now, since scientific research is an area in which no authority except the facts can be acknowledged, the presuppositionless and unprejudiced testing of all facts and opinions is taken for granted. But precisely with regard to the short history of Mandaean studies, one can say that well-established prejudices and an inveterate skepticism have done more harm than good and have in no way carried them forward. 'Then finally,' wrote Macuch recently, 'we ought to stop our continual demand for further proofs from the Mandaean scholars: alleged and imaginary skepticism ought to take a modest step in the direction of conciliation.'" Contrast Morton Smith: "The chief contribution of Mandaean studies to New Testament criticism, therefore, is to have called forth the book of Thomas, *Le Mouvement baptiste en Palestine,* which collects the ancient evidence about baptismal sects." "Aramaic Studies and the Study of the New Testament," *JBR* 26 (1958): 305. With relevance to Johannine studies contrast Brown, *The Gospel according to John (i–xii),* p. lv: "The oldest forms of Mandaean theology known to us are to be dated relatively late in the Christian era, and there is no possibility that John was influenced by this thought as we now know it. . . . Literary criticism points to the gnostic layers of Mandaean thought and writing as being relatively late." It is in the light of this rather personal view of Mandaeism that one is to understand Brown's classification of "the postulated gnostic influence" in John as a "difficulty" in Bultmann's source theory, "personal" to Bultmann (p. xxx).

tinian Hellenism, [and] not only in official Judaism, but in a *Palestinian*-Syrian Judaism of a distinctive kind, which in turn was already influenced by oriental-Hellenistic syncretism. This Judaism, sharply distinct from the official Judaism of the time, and in part standing in opposition to it, has been documented on the one hand in Late Jewish apocalypses, and on the other hand in speculations kin to later Gnosticism and to be found in Jewish baptismal sects.

This view, advocated by R. Bultmann (1925) and others, and by me in my book on the gnostic character of the Jewish Christianity of the Pseudo-Clementines (1930), could base itself upon newly available texts (M. Lidzbarski, 1905 and 1915 ff., and now K. Rudolph, 1960), but is especially confirmed by the already mentioned discovery of the scrolls from Qumran, whose real significance for the study of primitive Christianity lies in the clarification of this distinct current within Judaism, and finally also by a part of the Coptic gnostic texts found also after World War II (1947) in Nag Hammadi, Egypt.

Accordingly there were in the primitive Christianity of Palestine itself from the very beginning two streams. To the two forms of Palestinian Judaism we now know, the official kind and that represented by esoteric sectarian circles, there corresponds within *Palestinian* primitive Christianity at the beginning a side-by-side situation of one more legalistic theology, holding rigidly to the Old Testament law and the temple, and another theology, standing more loosely toward the law and the temple, with trains of thought similar to those in esoteric Judaism. The question as to the extent to which Jesus himself was familiar with these special views of Judaism, for which there are some indications, must for the moment remain an open question.

In any case the perspective in which one previously saw the relation of Jewish Christianity and gentile Christianity is thus changing. Views which one previously considered to be elements that entered Christianity only at a relatively late time and outside Palestine now appear, without this judgment being inspired by any apologetic intent, as much older, indeed present from the beginning. The much-discussed question of the origin of Gnosticism also presents itself quite differently from this point of view. The *Gospel of Thomas* (a collection of Jesus' sayings) belonging to the previously mentioned discovery in Egypt, points, at least in terms of one of the sources it used, in the same direction of a gnostic Jewish Christianity,[57]

57. Oscar Cullmann, "Wandlungen in der neuern Forschungsgeschichte des Urchristentums. Zugleich ein Beitrag zum Problem: Theologie und Geschichtswissenschaft," in *Discordia Concors*, Edgar Bonjour Festschrift, 1968, pp. 58–60.

It is in this context that Cullmann locates the Gospel of John.

Rather than a recent shift in the history-of-religions location of John, one has throughout this century a relatively stable picture on the growing edge of research, with a series of manuscript discoveries that have accumulated evidence for what was initially more intuition than documentation. The new ingredient is perhaps a fuller recognition that the documentation does not conform to an unchanging gnostic position, but rather suggests a development from the pre- or proto-Gnosticism of Qumran through intermediate stages attested both in the New Testament and in part of Nag Hammadi into the full gnostic systems of the second century A.D. Thus a gnosticizing trajectory emerges, on which the Gospel of John has its history-of-religions location. The sharper profile that the new history-of-religion materials provide for locating John on this trajectory, when integrated with the history-of-traditions trajectory traced out by means of literary criticism, can together lead to a quantum advance in the interpretation of the Fourth Gospel in the coming generation.

The Gattung "Gospel" [58]

If the Fourth Gospel is independent of the synoptic gospels, this poses the problem of explaining how the same gattung could emerge independently in two trajectories, the synoptic and the Johannine. Perhaps the concept of a shared *Sitz im Leben* can aid in the understanding of such a situation.

The structure of such a solution could be provided by the analogy of Matthew and Luke, where two gospels are moving

58. One may wonder whether the term "gospel" should be used of all the gattungen containing Jesus traditions (not to speak of gnostic "gospels," such as the *Gospel of Truth* and the *Gospel of the Egyptians* from Nag Hammadi, which are even less related in form to other gospels). The Fourth Gospel does not use either the noun or the verb. John 20:30 (cf. 21:25) refers to it simply as a "book" (*biblion*). Matthew begins "Book (*biblos*) of the *genesis* of Jesus Christ. . . ." Acts 1:1 refers back to Luke as the "first volume (*logos*)"; Luke 1:1 begins by referring to a narration (*diegesis*). Only Mark begins: "Beginning of the gospel of Jesus Christ," and even here "gospel" is not an explicit designation for the book itself. but rather for its contents. Only when the gattung of Mark has been more fully clarified will it be possible to determine the extent to which other canonical gospels are in form still within the same gattung, irrespective of what nomenclature they use in self-designation. In some respects, such as the fact that he begins at John the Baptist rather than at Jesus' birth. John is most similar to Mark. Cf. my paper " On the *Gattung* of Mark (and John)", pp. 99–129.

independently of each other at sufficiently similar positions on a trajectory for them to do similar things. Both Matthew and Luke merge the narrative gospel Mark with the sayings collection Q, in that both have arrived at the point where this is the thing to do, probably to keep Q from seeming increasingly disembodied and Mark from seeming inadequately didactic. If it is conceded that this is the situation with regard to Matthew and Luke (who independently agree on other innovations, such as prefixing an infancy narrative and appending resurrection appearances), then it is not inconceivable that a similarly shared position on the gospels trajectory could explain the similarity in form of Mark and John. To be sure, they do not share two written sources, as do Matthew and Luke. Yet one may wonder, as do Leander E. Keck, Morton Smith, Helmut Koester, Dieter Georgi, and Paul J. Achtemeier,[59] whether there is not behind Mark a written source of the aretalogy type comparable to the miracles source of John. In any case one does have in Mark and John the remarkable parallel of what would seem to have been an oral cycle of which Mark itself preserves two versions, and John a third, namely a brief series of miracles grouped around the miraculous feeding of the multitude. If one can thus sense even in the oral period the beginnings of the stream within the gospels trajectory that led to Mark and John, one can then recognize in the redaction carried out on Mark by Matthew and Luke a final move toward orthodoxy comparable to the ecclesiastical redactor at work upon the Fourth Gospel.

Thus through disengaging by means of literary criticism the Johannine trajectory and correlating it to the synoptic trajectory, the two gospel streams become mutually enlightening and the cleft between the synoptics and John is bridged. The synoptic prob-

59. Leander E. Keck, "Mark 3, 7–12 and Mark's Christology," *JBL* 84 (1965): 341–58, though see the criticism by T. A. Burkill, "Mark 3, 7–12 and the Alleged Dualism in the Evangelist's Miracle Material," *JBL* 87 (1968): 409–17. Paul J. Achtemeier, "Toward the Isolation of Pre-Marcan Miracle Catenae," *JBL* 89 (1970): 265–91. The source theories of the other scholars cited have not been published in any detail, though one may mention Morton Smith's paper advocating such a view, "Aretalogies, Divine Men, the Gospels, and Jesus," as well as that of Howard C. Kee, "Aretalogy and the Gospels," both presented for discussion to the Gospels Seminar of the Society of Biblical Literature in October 1970. The Heidelberg dissertation of Thomas L. Budesheim (unpublished) deals with this topic. Several Marcan source theories were published during the rise of form criticism, which tended to eclipse them; they now need to be reexamined for relevant observations.

lem, namely the question as to why the first three gospels are so much alike, becomes, in view of the independence of the Fourth Gospel from the synoptics, a gospels problem: How is it that the Fourth Gospel (and possibly its source) is a gospel of the Marcan (and to that extent synoptic) type? Or, in Koester's terminology, how is it that both Mark and John, independently of each other, represent the shift from the aretalogy type of gospel to the canonical-credal type? [60] Or, if the aretalogy used by John included a passion narrative, would this modify the derivation of the canonical gospel form from the union of the aretalogy of miracle stories with the kerygma's passion and resurrection narrative? For then one might rather think of Mark's blunting or avoiding, in ways comparable to John's "spiritualizing," certain ingredients of an aretalogy: infancy (Mark omits); mighty deeds (Marcan messianic secret); triumphal exit (Mark's ignominious "theology of the cross"). To be sure, infancy narratives may not yet have been known to Mark; and the extent to which aretalogical ingredients were in writing in the Marcan tradition is not yet clear. Thus much sifting of alternatives needs yet to be done, before a clear picture can emerge. Yet to have posed the problem as such may be as important as to have proposed any given tentative solution.

The suggestion that comparable positions on a trajectory, the movemental equivalent to a common *Sitz im Leben,* could explain the comparable forms of Mark and John is an illustration of the way in which the recasting of New Testament research into trajectory patterns could recast old problems in such a way as to lead to new solutions. The historian's task is not merely to continue to study the history of specific dependencies and influences of one fixed point on another fixed point but, perhaps more basically, to orient attention to the history of the morphological stages in the development of early Christianity, as it was borne along on the conveyer belt upon which the whole Hellenistic world was moving. Such a reorientation of scholarly investigation may be the precondition for the possibility of a more adequate grasp of the history of primitive Christianity in the coming generation.

60. "One Jesus and Four Primitive Gospels," see above, pp. 188–89. Fortna, *The Gospel of Signs,* p. 221 n. 2, holds that the miracles soucre, rather than being an aretalogy, was a gospel of the kerygmatic Marcan type.

8. Conclusion
The Intention and Scope of Trajectories

HELMUT KOESTER

In more than one way our essays seek to signal the current cultural crisis in terms of New Testament scholarship. Our trajectories seek to cut new paths through explored as well as unexplored materials. These attempts are quite deliberate. We hope that these experiments are able to open up new perspectives both for understanding early Christian history and for perceiving the present problems of Christianity. We have tried to avoid the pitfalls of "disinterested" research, for we have sensed the danger of merely playing in the sandbox of irrelevant scholarship. We want to be taught by history, not in order to find our own position reaffirmed, but in order to be exposed to and to learn from the complex and agonizing decisions which man as a historic being has made.

But if retreat into the objectivity of scholarship is dangerous, it would be even more disastrous to expect of the scholar that he return us to those attractive tenets of yesteryear which may seem to supply clear and unambiguous solutions of the world's pressing problems. Fundamentalists have all too long abused the words of Jesus as a primer for individual morality and piety. It is no more convincing when radical moralists of a more recent vintage seek to verify their deeply felt opposition to existing structures and institutions of society by reference to Jesus' preaching of the kingdom. "Relevance" is not necessarily a criterion for the validity of scholarship. In any case, it is not worth the tremendous effort involved in research, if one uses historical materials merely to embellish what one already has at one's disposal as the simple answer to a problem of our time.

One must be aware of the fact that today's questions are multifaceted and perplexing and that they cannot be solved by eclectic recourse either to prescientific tenets and symbols, or to the results of the historical scholarship of a former generation. "Relevance" only emerges where there is the courage to follow new trajectories which take into account the complexity of historical developments.

It is my task, in this conclusion, to assess the prospect toward which these essays seem to point as the next step along the path. Since our essays are experiments, it is impossible to predict the results of future ventures along these lines. But a few directions of concern may be pointed out and a few problems stated.

New Standards for the Classification of Early Christian Literature

The distinctions between canonical and noncanonical, orthodox and heretical are obsolete. The classical "Introduction to the New Testament" has lost its scientific justification. One can only speak of a "History of Early Christian Literature." But the task of redefining the standards for analyzing and evaluating it still lies before us. To be sure, form criticism has engendered a new awareness for the question of different genres of literature; the most obvious progress of late has been made with respect to the history of the gospels as literature. However, even though several essays in this volume contribute directly to this task, our work has also sharpened our own awareness of the difficulties.

The "gospel", which had seemed to be a genuinely Christian genre of literature, has emerged more and more as a complex form to which non-Christian genres have made substantial contributions. Yet these relationships need further exploration. The genre *logoi* is the one that can be seen as most obviously emerging out of its Jewish predecessor, the "words of the wise." But other genres, which have contributed to the form of the "gospel" in a similar way, are as yet less clearly defined.

The divine man literature, the aretalogy genre, has many facets and appears in diverse cultural contexts, encompassing such writings as Philo's *Vita Mosis* and Philostratus's *Apollonius* and the Alexander legends, to mention only a few. If we investigate oral traditions which are at the root of this literature, as well as cultural conditions and religious or political purposes which led to their composition, we will bring to light a much more intricate relationship between Christianity and its surrounding culture than is usually assumed. Such an investigation should include the emerging hagiographic literature of the ancient church, where dependence upon pagan prototypes is particularly obvious.

No less puzzling is the question of the genre of the apocalypse or revelation gospel. It is certainly very closely related to Jewish apocalyptic literature. But further clarification of such Jewish literature and of the patterns which have influenced its composition is required. The relation of this literature to the prophetic books of the Old Testament, to the development of the covenant formula, to the genre of the "testament," and, finally, to the "Interpretation of Scripture," is to be investigated as part of the background of this Christian genre. The greatest difficulties, however, arise when one investigates the contribution of early Christian prophets, their activities, and the preservation and transmission of their utterances. Clearly, this phenomenon, which belongs to the forms of oral tradition, has been a vital factor in the adaptation of the literary genre of the apocalypse. Finally, the variety of gnostic revelation gospels must be analyzed in this context. A trajectory that will open up new perspectives has to encompass the whole range of literary activity from the Old Testament book of Ezekiel to the *Pistis Sophia,* and from the *Genesis Apocryphon* to the pre-Genesis speculations of the *Apocryphon of John.*

In such an investigation, the adaptation of the genre apocalypse in early Christianity will not emerge as the straight-line continuation of an already existing and well-established literary genre of Judaism. The accepted schema of evolution from Jewish to Christian literature, and from Christian to gnostic literature, is not satisfactory. No doubt the older Jewish apocalypses antedate the beginnings of Christianity. But the typical Jewish apocalyptic literature (*4 Ezra, 2 Baruch,* etc.) was produced in the same period in which the first Christian apocalypses (synoptic apocalypse, *Apocalypse of John, Shepherd of Hermas*), and probably also the first gnostic revelations (*Apocryphon of John*), were written, i.e., in the second half of the first century and in the beginning of the second century A.D. Thus, Judaism, Christianity, and Gnosticism seem to have developed writings of the same genre almost simultaneously. Similarities, therefore, arose not only from the sharing of the same literary conventions, but also from the influence of cultural conditions which characterized this particular period. Differences, on the other hand, were apparently caused by particular religious experiences and convictions. They are visible in nonliterary symbols and traditions which represent the basic criteria of belief.

The experiences of the Christian church generated a new and often powerful oral tradition. It was an oral tradition quite different from the oral tradition of rabbinic Judaism, since its primary motivation was not the desire to create legitimate interpretations of Scripture but rather the new experience, which was described in symbols such as Resurrection, Spirit, New Covenant. The formulation of such an experience, usually called creed, preceded the adaptation of existing literary forms and the creation of new literary genres. The systematic description of the development of literary genres requires the simultaneous investigation of the evolution of religious beliefs which are documented in creed and symbol.

It can be shown, e.g., that the genre of the apology was more or less inherited from Hellenistic Judaism. Later, direct influences from the philosophical protrepticus upon the Christian apologetic literature have also been pointed out (cf. Aristotle; also Cicero's *Hortensius*). But the most vital factor in Christian apologies was the developing creed of the orthodox church. As early as Justin Martyr, the creed furnished the general outline for the major portions of Christian apologetic writings. Again, in the Latin transformation of this genre into the defense attorney's plea (Tertullian), the creed continued to be the most obvious formative factor at work upon the apology.

Franz Overbeck's distinction between primitive Christian literature (*Urliteratur*) and patristic literature becomes quite questionable, if one also considers the influence of the creed (or of the diverse credal developments) upon the formation of subsequent polemical writings (*Adversus Judaeos, Adversus haereses, Adversus Marcionem,* etc.) and upon the emergence of treatises on particular topics (*De resurrectione, De principiis, De anima*—in both their orthodox and their gnostic versions). There is no justification for the division between "New Testament Introduction" and "Patrology." The same credal developments that formed the apologetic literature also created the gospels of the New Testatment canon. Conversely, the factors deriving from Jewish and pagan literary productions are no less conspicuous in the earliest gospels than they are in the apologetic writings.

It is tempting to outline similar trajectories for the genres of early Christian letters and for the parenetic writings and church orders, as well as for homilies and commentaries. The same close relationship between Christianity and culture, church and society, theology and other religions, including their literary productions, would emerge. The usual distinctions among canonical, apocryphal, patristic, and heretical literature are equally irrelevant for these writings.

It should become a general rule that the literature of the first three centuries must be treated as one inseparable unit. The genres of this literature and their development cannot be evaluated unless one is willing to work through the trajectory that traces the history of such a genre, both in its Christian form and in its non-Christian background, and regardless of the later more or less arbitrary traditional dogmatic, polemical, and theological classifications.

Regional Christian Churches and the Diverse Cultural Conditions of the Roman Era

Walter Bauer was right when he singled out particular regions for his description of orthodoxy and heresy. Further probing into the question of geographical distinctions within cultural and religious developments is certain to yield significant results.

The world which Rome inherited from the Hellenistic empires was thoroughly Hellenized, but it was not monolithic. The degree of Hellenization was quite different in various regions, and the new conditions which Roman rule had created were by no means the same everywhere. This problem is further complicated by the fact that the differences between cities and rural areas as well as between upper classes and lower classes were apparently very considerable as far as education and religious orientation were concerned.

Even if one takes seriously the well-known fact that Christian propaganda had its greatest success among the lower classes of the city population, one has not achieved a very precise sociological profile for early Christianity. The complex religious, cultural, and ethnic pluralism of the Hellenistic and Roman eras makes necessary a more detailed analysis of the particular social and cultural conditions in those places that played a decisive role in the formation of the Christian mission and the establishment of Christian communities.

The problem of western Asia Minor can serve as an example. It was an area which had an indigenous Greek population that had lived under Persian rule for a long period. There were oriental influences as well as strong continuation of other indigenous cultural and religious traditions (Lydian, Phrygian). At the same time, in the Roman province of Asia there was a considerable Jewish population, which apparently had been there ever since the Persian period and which, as the excavations at Sardis have demonstrated, was still a major factor in the fourth and fifth centuries A.D. It was a Greek-speaking Jewish population, Hellenized, but not necessarily syncretistic, and by no means of the same religious orientation as the famed Alexandrian Jews of the early Christian period. The evidence for Judaism in Asia Minor has been studied in depth in Thomas Kraabel's Harvard dissertation of 1968, and detailed studies of the same type are necessary for other areas. Appeal to the traditional categories of Palestinian and Hellenistic Judaism is not only an oversimplification with regard to Palestine, but it overlooks the regional distinctions within Judaism of the Diaspora.

Such studies must give particular attention to the role and status of Jewish communities, including their social and political aspects. It has become increasingly clear that, whatever so-called "Hellenistic" influences early Christianity accepted were mostly mediated through the Hellenized Jewish culture of the time. The focus, therefore should not be on those phenomena which are typically "Hellenistic," as distinct from those which are typically "Jewish." On the contrary, the simultaneous occurrence of both Jewish and Hellenistic elements in the same early Christian writings is clear evidence for the cultural and religious background of early Christianity, namely Judaism in its varying degrees of Hellenization and cultural adaptation to the Greco-Roman world.

New and different types of Christianity developed in areas in which either the Hellenization of Judaism was superficial or where there was no visible connection between the rise of Christianity and Jewish communities. The former apparently was the case in eastern Syria. Our studies have given some attention to the rise of Christianity in those most eastern regions, which were under Roman domination only for limited periods. On the other hand, the formation of a distinctly Western type of Christianity took place in a part of the Roman Empire that had only a relatively small Jewish Diaspora: the Roman province of Africa.

The beginnings of Christianity in Carthage and North Africa are not known. There is no evidence for the assumption that they must have been similar to the beginnings of Christian churches in Asia Minor and Rome. As North African churches emerge into the light of history toward the end of the second century A.D., they appear as typically "Western" Latin-speaking Christian communities with only a few Hellenistic features, and without any traces of a Jewish-Christian past.

This is quite different from the beginnings of the church in Rome. The earliest evidence for Christianity in Rome (Paul's Letter to the Romans) indicates that there was a Jewish matrix of primitive Christianity in that city. All subsequent evidence from the first two centuries in Rome is strangely lacking in typically "Western" features, but is more indicative of the cosmopolitan culture which characterized Rome at that time. *First Clement* and the *Shepherd of Hermas* abound with only slightly Christianized Jewish traditions, and might have been written by any Hellenized Jew anywhere. Almost all influential "Roman" theologians of the second century came from the East: Justin Martyr from Samaria, Tatian from Assyria, Marcion from Pontus, Valentinus from Egypt, the monarchian Theodotus from Byzantium. The early third century is not much different in this respect: Praxeas was from Asia Minor, Sabellius from Libya. Even Hippolytus, the first great "Roman" theologian, may have come from Asia, and is in all respects a typical Greek writer. Indeed Greek was the literary language for almost all the theologians of Rome in the first centuries A.D.

The birthplace of Latin Christianity is not Rome but Africa. Only two Romans of this time are known to have written in Latin: Minucius Felix, whose dialogue *Octavius* was the first apology written in Latin (unless it was dependent upon Tertullian); and the Roman bishop Victor (A.D. 189–99). But both men were from Africa! Latin was well established as the language of the church in North Africa as early as the second half of the second century. The earliest Latin document, the *Acts of the Scillitan Martyrs* (A.D. 180), shows that Christianity had spread to the more remote areas of the country, for Scilli was probably a small town in Numidia. This document also seems to give evidence for the existence and use of Christian scriptures in Latin: "the books [i.e., the gospels or the Old Testament] and the letters of Paul." The earliest Latin translation of the New Testament (the *Vetus Latina*) is certainly a product of North African Christianity, and it was accompanied by a Latin translation of the Old Testament (clearly visible in the quotations of Cyprian). This indicates that Greek culture, mediated through Hellenistic Judaism and documented in its Scripture, namely the Greek translation of the Old Testament, played a much less significant role in North Africa than in Rome. The fact that Latin-speaking Christianity was well established in the Roman and Phoenician population of North Africa had considerable consequences. It is not necessary to add further comments about the well-known and august succession of Latin theologians from Africa in the following centuries (Tertullian, Cyprian, Lactantius, Arnobius, Augustine).

These suggestions concerning Asia Minor, Eastern Syria, and Africa illustrate the close relationship between distinct Christian developments and the particular cultural conditions in limited geographical areas. We have learned to distinguish between different periods of Christian history in the first centuries. We are also beginning to realize that phenomena from the religion of the Hellenistic and Roman eras must be dated with some precision before they can be utilized to determine the interrelationships within Christian, Jewish, and pagan religions. It is equally necessary to focus on the particular situation in a limited geographical area in order to understand the interplay between Christianity and culture in antiquity. Trajectories must be plotted in grids that reflect shifts in space as well as in time.

Jesus of Nazareth and the Cultural Presuppositions of Late Antiquity

It is a truism that our own cultural presuppositions must be questioned when we interpret texts which are written from a different cultural perspective. There is also no question that the cultural, religious, and ideological biases, inclinations, and prejudices of the Greco-Roman world, when they are shared by early Christian writers, are not thereby made normatively Christian, but must be tested critically.

The hermeneutical problem has to do with translation in terms of these varying "languages." But the hermeneutical problem is not fully posed when it is stated only in terms of language and translation, i.e., as the transposition of a given religious truth or theological insight from one language context into another. As long as one was able to assume a clearly formulated point of departure, like *the* primitive kerygma, or the biblical Christ, it was possible to understand hermeneutic as the analysis of new world views or religious doctrines, which may or may not have altered the more original clear-cut religious truth. The truth of the more primitive kerygma thus served as the criterion. But this hermeneutical policy does not meet fully the problem of the historical Jesus.

The man Jesus of Nazareth was a human being who was fully subject to the contingencies and conditions of history. There is no way to escape this fact, in order to boast in the possession of any original formulation of revealed truth which is somehow less ambiguous and less subject to historical conditioning than the historical life, words, and works of a purely human man, Jesus. Furthermore, historical inquiry leads to the recognition of quite complex and different types of creeds and kerygmas, which provide only limited insights into the nature of Jesus' life and work. Not only the language of the most primitive credal formulation is already historically conditioned, but these primitive creeds themselves are also determined by the ambiguous complexity of the historical phenomenon of the earthly Jesus.

This does not mean that the question of the historical Jesus remains a complete enigma to the historian. On the contrary, recent scholarship has made unquestionable progress in this respect. This is true with regard to a number of relatively firm results and with regard to a greater recognition of the limits of such an endeavor, limits which are set by the nature of the material that is available.

Today's historical questions and insights, however, are parallel to the problems which primitive Christian creeds reflect in their endeavor to solve the enigma of the earthly Jesus of Nazareth. Historical scholarship tends to focus on those undigested blocks of information about Jesus which are relatively reliable precisely because they did not quite fit the perspectives and theological views of those Christian writers who, unwittingly, happened to preserve such traditions. To the modern Christian believer, on the other hand, it is elements from the earlier tradition that do not fit his world view and cultural orientation which become a challenge or a stumbling block for his religious convictions. In the case of Jesus these two kinds of problem areas tend to converge. It is the uncensored information which gives the historian opportunity to assess specific circumstances of Jesus' life and work, and which also presents a challenge to any theological attempt to fit Jesus of Nazareth into a given system. Illustrative of such information is the following: Jesus had normal human parents, Joseph and Mary. He was baptized by John, whom he called the greatest among all men. He ate with prostitutes and tax collectors. He demanded that each man love his enemies. He was crucified under Pontius Pilate. Not some lofty religious ideas, not some great and miraculous accomplishments, and not the proclamation of deep divine truths are the stumbling blocks for the believer. On the contrary! He is offended by the human dimension of Jesus, for this is the dimension for which he, the believer, can be held accountable.

The hermeneutical problem is the problem of a conflict, i.e., the conflict between the historical particularity of Jesus' life, work, and death, on the one hand, and the cultural and religious expectations and ideologies available in a certain culture to express the meaning of that life, on the other. This conflict must appear to the historian as the primary problem of the relationship between Jesus and early Christian history. It is also the central question for the theologian, since he must face the question of heresy and orthodoxy, i.e., the integrity and adequacy of the various solutions of this conflict. And it is of crucial importance to the believer, since the structures of this conflict remain the same now as then, as long as Christian faith continues to be "faith in Jesus."

The historical problem of early Christianity, seen as the history of orthodoxy and heresy, or seen as the story of human attempts to "follow after Jesus," or seen as the controversy between Jesus and culture, is identical with the hermeneutical problem of the tension between Jesus' historical particularity and contingency, and the succession of language worlds in which it is brought to expression. There were paradoxical solutions, such as that of Paul, who insisted that only as a fool could he speak of the possession of divine power in weakness. There were radical solutions, such as the Christian ascetics' identification of true discipleship with complete separation from culture and society. And there were rational solutions, such as the apologists' plea for an alliance between the Christian message and the cultural condition of their environment, but without compromise with political power.

The investigation of this history and the analysis of the structures of these conflicts and of the tendencies of its language is the place where the endeavors of the historian, the theologian, and the interpreter are identical. The tracing of such trajectories is intended to open up the theological horizon of the world of early Christianity and of our own world and existence as well. The task of assessing critically the conflicts of Christian existence today goes beyond the scope of the trajectories sketched in this volume, but is entirely consistent with their intention—indeed, should be their outcome.

Indexes

PASSAGES

AUTHORS

SUBJECTS

Type, 11 on 13 and 10 on 11 Garamond
Display, Garamond